THE CASE OF IRELAND

The late eighteenth and early nineteenth centuries have long been seen as a foundational period for modern Irish political traditions such as nationalism, republicanism and unionism. *The Case of Ireland* offers a fresh account of Ireland's neglected role in European debates about commerce and empire in what was a global era of war and revolution. Drawing on a range of writings from merchants, agrarian improvers, philosophers, politicians and revolutionaries across Europe, this book shows how Ireland became a field of conflict and projection between rival visions of politics in commercial society, associated with the warring empires of Britain and France. It offers a new perspective on the crisis and transformation of the British Empire at the end of the eighteenth century, and restores Ireland to its rightful place at the centre of European intellectual history.

JAMES STAFFORD studied history at Oxford and Cambridge, completing his doctoral research in 2016. After postdoctoral work in Oxford and Bielefeld he is now Assistant Professor of History at Columbia University. He is a frequent commentator on contemporary British and European politics for a range of outlets, and was co-editor of *Renewal: A Journal of Social Democracy* from 2015–20.

IDEAS IN CONTEXT

Edited by DAVID ARMITAGE, RICHARD BOURKE
and JENNIFER PITTS

The books in this series will discuss the emergence of intellectual traditions and of related new disciplines. The procedures, aims and vocabularies that were generated will be set in the context of the alternatives available within the contemporary frameworks of ideas and institutions. Through detailed studies of the evolution of such traditions, and their modification by different audiences, it is hoped that a new picture will form of the development of ideas in their concrete contexts. By this means, artificial distinctions between the history of philosophy, of the various sciences, of society and politics, and of literature may be seen to dissolve.

A full list of titles in the series can be found at: www.cambridge.org/IdeasContext

THE CASE OF IRELAND

Commerce, Empire and the European Order, 1750–1848

JAMES STAFFORD

Columbia University

CAMBRIDGE
UNIVERSITY PRESS

CAMBRIDGE
UNIVERSITY PRESS

University Printing House, Cambridge CB2 8BS, United Kingdom

One Liberty Plaza, 20th Floor, New York, NY 10006, USA

477 Williamstown Road, Port Melbourne, VIC 3207, Australia

314–321, 3rd Floor, Plot 3, Splendor Forum, Jasola District Centre, New Delhi – 110025, India

103 Penang Road, #05-06/07, Visioncrest Commercial, Singapore 238467

Cambridge University Press is part of the University of Cambridge

It furthers the University's mission by disseminating knowledge in the pursuit of education, learning, and research at the highest international levels of excellence.

www.cambridge.org
Information on this title: www.cambridge.org/9781316516126
DOI: 10.1017/9781009031905

First published 2022

A catalogue record for this publication is available from the British Library.

Library of Congress Cataloging-in-Publication Data
NAMES: Stafford, James, 1988- author.
TITLE: The case of Ireland : commerce, empire and the European order, 1750-1848 / James Stafford, Columbia University, New York.
DESCRIPTION: Cambridge, United Kingdom ; New York, NY : Cambridge University Press, 2022. | SERIES: Ideas in context | Includes bibliographical references and index.
IDENTIFIERS: LCCN 2021044712 (print) | LCCN 2021044713 (ebook) | ISBN 9781316516126 (hardback) | ISBN 9781009013741 (paperback) | ISBN 9781009031905 (epub)
SUBJECTS: LCSH: Ireland–Commerce–History–18th century. | Ireland–Commerce–History–19th century. | Ireland–Economic conditions–18th century. | Ireland–Economic conditions–19th century. | Great Britain–Foreign relations–18th century. | Great Britain–Foreign relations–19th century. | BISAC: POLITICAL SCIENCE / History & Theory
CLASSIFICATION: LCC HF3535 .S73 2022 (print) | LCC HF3535 (ebook) | DDC 382.09417/09033–dcundefined
LC record available at https://lccn.loc.gov/2021044712
LC ebook record available at https://lccn.loc.gov/2021044713

ISBN 978-1-316-51612-6 Hardback

For Clara

Contents

Acknowledgements

This book is based on a doctoral thesis written at the University of Cambridge, supported by a Doctoral Award from the UK Arts and Humanities Research Council. I am additionally grateful to Emmanuel College, University of Cambridge; the Kurt Hahn Trust; and the Cambridge University History Faculty Doctoral Language Fund for their support, which allowed me to take language learning courses in Besançon and Munich. The British Association of Irish Studies, the History Faculty at the University of Cambridge, and Emmanuel College offered grants that enabled me to conduct archival research in Belfast and Dublin. I conducted additional research and revised the manuscript for publication as a postdoctoral fellow at the German Federal Research Council (DFG)–funded Research Training Group GRK 2225/1 'World Politics', hosted at Bielefeld University.

I would like to extend my thanks to staff at the Cambridge University Library, the Marshall Economics Library, the British Library, the *Bayerische Staatsbibliothek*, the National Library of Ireland, the Royal Irish Academy, the Public Records Office of Northern Ireland and the Manuscripts Room at the National Library of Ireland for their assistance.

John Robertson first suggested the Free Trade crisis and Pitt's Commercial Propositions to me as a possible subject for doctoral research. He has been a consistently inspiring and reassuring presence throughout the long years this book has taken to complete. Different aspects of the book have also benefitted from conversations over many years with István Hont (who supervised this research from 2011 until his death in 2013), Richard Bourke, Joanna Innes, Richard Whatmore, Ian McBride, Tom Pye, Lucian Robinson, Matthew Ward, Anna Plassart, Clara Maier, Peter Hession and Michael Sonenscher. I am also grateful to the two anonymous readers who produced reports on the manuscript for Cambridge University Press, and to Liz Friend-Smith and Melissa Ward for their patience and support throughout its production, editing and revision.

Different parts of this book have taken shape in one form or another over many years at seminars, conferences and job interviews all over Europe and the USA. I would like to thank Emily Jones, Natasha Wheatley, Nick Mulder, Niall O'Flaherty, Julia Nicholls, Emily Jones, Jon Parkin, David Leopold, Sam Zeitlin, Ben Jackson, Marc Mulholland, David Leopold, Hannah Dawson, Eugenio Biagini, Roy Foster, Wencke Meteling, Renaud Morieux, Susan Pedersen, Christopher Brown, Nicholas Dames, Stephanie McCurry, Niamh Gallagher, Colin Reid, Deborah Valenze, Peter Mandler, Maggie Scull, Naomi Lloyd-Jones, Waseem Yaqoob, Tobias Werron, Mathias Albert, Daniela Russ and Simon Hecke for their invitations, encouragement and insights, either during these occasions or in helping me to prepare for them.

I will always be grateful to Johanna, Gerd, David and Ella Stegmaier for giving me such a warm welcome in Munich while I was learning German and finding out about Friedrich Gentz. In Dublin, Adam Larragy and Cliodhna O'Connor were model hosts. Throughout the writing of this book and the thesis that preceded it I have richly profited, both personally and intellectually, from the friendship of Miles Mantle, Florence Sutcliffe-Braithwaite, Alice Blackhurst, Graham Riach, Emily Rees, Lewis Goodall, Hannah Malone, Elizabeth Gilbert, Portia Roelofs, Matthew Kennedy, George Robinson, Sam Sweeney and Paulina Gimpel.

My mother, Deborah Stafford, and sister, Rosie Stafford, always help me to keep things in perspective. This book would have been much harder to write in the absence of their generous understanding of the strange working patterns and long distances that are regrettably involved in a twenty-first-century academic career. My youngest sister, Lydia Stafford, is always in our thoughts; but this is not the place to mourn.

Lastly and most of all, I would like to thank Clara Maier, who was with me virtually every day as this book was researched and written, enlivening every moment, even the most difficult, with her love, spirit and joy. The birth of our daughter, Ada, has provided me with the best possible reason to finally complete this work.

Introduction

Ireland ... remained a land of no particular interest, until a few years ago, during the time of the American War, the suppressed spirit of the people awoke, felt its power, threw off a part of the English yoke ... From this time forward, Ireland was remarkable also for us, as contemporaries and spectators.

'Introduction by the Editor', in Küttner, *Briefe über Irland*[1]

Ireland is still as clay under the potters' hand: the elements of society in that country are still floating in chaos, and await the hand of power to fix and fashion them ... Improvement and civilisation must there descend from above; they will not arise spontaneously from the inward workings of the community.

Lewis, *On Local Disturbances in Ireland*[2]

In the closing decades of the eighteenth century, Ireland became the object of a vigorous debate concerning the promise and perils of commerce in an era of global war and revolution. This debate concerned not just the identity and future of the Irish polity itself, but of the British Empire of which it was a central part and the relationship of that empire to its European allies and rivals. As such, it had many participants: not only Irish and British, but also French, German, Swiss and Italian. Some, like the unidentified editor of the German Celtophile Karl Gottlob Küttner's Irish travel writings, were concerned with Ireland's potential for political agency – its ability to achieve a 'rank among nations'.[3] Others employed Ireland as a field of projection in broader disputes over the meaning of 'improvement' and 'civilisation'. For British politicians like the Whig MP

---

[1] Karl Gottlob Küttner, *Briefe über Irland, an seinen Freund, den Herausgeber* (Leipzig: Johann Phillip Haugs Wittwe, 1785), vii.

[2] George Cornewall Lewis, *On Local Disturbances in Ireland, and on the Irish Church Question* (London: B. Fellowes, 1836), v–vi.

[3] Küttner, *Briefe über Irland*, vi.

George Cornewall Lewis, Ireland was a place where empire was forced to confront the painful history of its own inadequacies.

As Küttner's editor also noticed, this pan-European upsurge of interest in Ireland was new. Since the defeat of the forces of James Stuart in 1692, the Irish Kingdom had been relatively marginal to the politics of both Europe and the British Empire. From the middle of the eighteenth century, however, it became increasingly impossible to ignore. Ireland's uncertain political allegiance and violent religious dissensions troubled and divided British intellectuals and politicians. Its potential for wealth – and poverty – became the object of fevered speculation. Its claims to an ancient Gaelic civilisation and to a long history of English oppression gave it a prominent position in the pantheons of European romanticism and humanitarianism. Its nascent democratic movements – from the 'Volunteer' militia of the 1770s, to the republican United Irishmen and the Catholic Association of Daniel O'Connell – caught the imaginations of radicals and revolutionaries.

Despite the imperial framework for Irish politics in the late eighteenth and early nineteenth centuries, and the ample interest in Ireland exhibited by British and continental European political thinkers, histories of Irish political thought in this period have adopted an overwhelmingly national focus. While they have frequently engaged with the transnational contexts, whether British, Atlantic or European, that have shaped traditions such as unionism, nationalism and republicanism, their ultimate purpose has been to better understand the principal actors in what remains an Irish story.[4] This focus on Irish national and confessional identities has tended to sideline other questions that we might usefully ask of texts produced in and around Ireland during this turbulent period. Where was Ireland located, by Irish and non-Irish contemporaries alike, within the broader political conjuncture of the later eighteenth and early nineteenth centuries? What can debates concerning Ireland tell us about the evolution of British and European political thinking in the era of the American and French

[4] Joep Leersen, 'Anglo-Irish Patriotism and Its European Context: Notes towards a Reassessment', *Eighteenth-Century Ireland/Iris an dá chultúr*, 3 (1988), 7–24; Stephen Small, *Political Thought in Ireland, 1776–1798: Republicanism, Patriotism, and Radicalism* (Oxford: Oxford University Press, 2002); Ultán Gillen, 'Le directoire et le républicanisme Irlandais', in Pierre Serna (ed.), *Républiques soeurs: Le directoire et la révolution atlantique* (Rennes: Presses Universitaires de Rennes, 2009); John Bew, *The Glory of Being Britons: Civic Unionism in Nineteenth-Century Belfast* (Dublin: Irish Academic Press, 2009); Kevin B. Nowlan and Maurice R. O'Connell (eds.), *Daniel O'Connell, Portrait of a Radical* (New York: Fordham University Press, 1985); David Dwan, *The Great Community: Culture and Nationalism in Ireland* (Dublin: Field Day, 2008).

Revolutions, and of Britain's rise to global commercial and colonial hegemony?

In order to analyse these broader questions, we certainly have to understand how Irish thinkers and politicians thought about the evolving shape of European and global politics, and the opportunities (and dangers) these afforded to the different confessional and ethnic communities that constituted the Irish polity. But we also have to concern ourselves with British and continental European debates *about* Ireland. The late eighteenth and early nineteenth centuries have long been identified as a turning point in the governing structures and ideologies of the British Empire, ultimately marking the emergence of 'free trade imperialism' abroad and 'liberal government' at home.[5] Yet the relationship between Britain's Irish policies and the long-run evolution of British governing ideologies remains curiously understudied.[6] Continental European writing on Ireland, meanwhile, is commonly utilised as a historical source for Irish conditions, with little or no reference to its contemporary meaning or resonance for European readers.[7]

If we link together Irish, British and continental European thinking on Ireland, however, then we can open up an entirely new perspective on the history of Irish political thought, and of Ireland's significance to the history of political thought more broadly. Where historians have traced the evolution of distinctively Irish political ideologies, contemporary thinkers understood the problems of Irish government as part of a broader European debate about the relationship between commerce and empire in an age of war, revolution and rapid social change. Ireland occupied a central position in contemporary European discussions of mercantile empire, agrarian reform, international trade and the balance of power.

---

[5] Bernard Semmel, *The Rise of Free Trade Imperialism: Classical Political Economy, the Empire of Free Trade and Imperialism 1750–1850* (Cambridge: Cambridge University Press, 1970); Jonathan Parry, *The Rise and Fall of Liberal Government in Victorian Britain* (New Haven, CT: Yale University Press, 1993).

[6] One of the few existing works to attempt this is Douglas Kanter, *The Making of British Unionism, 1740–1848: Politics, Government, and the Anglo-Irish Constitutional Relationship* (Dublin: Four Courts Press, 2009).

[7] For instance, James Kelly, 'Introduction: Interpreting Late Early Modern Ireland', in James Kelly (ed.), *The Cambridge History of Ireland: Volume III, 1730–1880* (Cambridge: Cambridge University Press, 2018), 1–20. The work of Manuela Ceretta is a vital exception to this rule: Manuela Ceretta, 'L'Irlande entre histoire et politique française', *The Tocqueville Review/La Revue Tocqueville*, 31 (2010), 139–57; Manuela Ceretta, *Il Momento Irlandese. L'Irlanda nella cultura politica francese tra Restaurazione e Secondo Impero* (Rome: Edizioni di Storia e Letteratura, 2013). See also Seamus Deane, 'A Church Destroyed, the Church Restored: France's Irish Catholicism', *Field Day Review*, 7 (2011), 202–49.

By viewing debates about commerce and empire through an Irish lens, we can discern new connections between these central categories of eighteenth- and nineteenth-century political thought. In so doing, we can also think afresh about Ireland's position within the two orders that have shaped so much of its modern history: the British Empire-state and the European states system. Instead of classing Ireland as a 'periphery' – whether of Britain or of Europe – we will consider it as a point of connection between these overlapping circuits of rivalry and exchange.[8] Successive crises of British authority in Ireland were not viewed as *sui generis*, or of purely local significance. Instead, Ireland's society, economy and history were studied and debated in order to provide insights into Europe's future. As a vulnerable and restive outpost of British power and civilisation, Ireland was a field of conflict between rival conceptions of commerce, empire and international order.

An Age of Crisis

Two sets of events, the United Irish risings of 1796–8 and the British–Irish parliamentary Union of 1801, are usually viewed as natural caesuras in the narration of the Irish past. Conveniently falling at the end of a century, 'the '98' and the Union mark a clear distinction between 'early modern' and 'modern' Irish history: between an eighteenth century dominated by the Anglican settler aristocracy that ruled via the Dublin parliament, and a nineteenth defined by the rise of constitutional and physical force nationalisms, under a more direct form of British rule.[9] The perspective taken here, by contrast, seeks to incorporate Ireland into a broader narrative framework that is widely prevalent in British, European, international and global history. In these fields, the period from the mid-eighteenth to the mid-nineteenth century has long been treated as an integrated whole – an intensified period of transition and flux, marking new departures in political, economic and intellectual life.[10]

---

[8] On Ireland as a periphery, see Micheal Hechter, *Internal Colonialism: The Celtic Fringe in British National Development* (London: Routledge & Kegan Paul, 1975); Richard Butterwick-Pawlikowski, Simon Davies and Gabriel Sánchez Espinosa (eds.), *Peripheries of the Enlightenment* (Oxford: Oxford University Press, 2008).

[9] John Pocock, 'The Union in British History', *Transactions of the Royal Historical Society*, Sixth Series, 10 (2000), 181–9.

[10] Jürgen Osterhammel, *The Transformation of the World: A Global History of the Nineteenth Century*, trans. P. Camiller (Princeton, NJ: Princeton University Press, 2014), 58–63.

The most prevalent version of this idea remains that of a global 'Age of Revolutions', stretching from the British American colonists' Declaration of Independence in 1776 through the French and Haitian Revolutions, the revolutions in Portuguese and Spanish America and the European risings of 1830 and 1848.[11] In a British context, a similar period has been described as an 'Age of Reform', facilitating the transition from a 'fiscal-military' to a 'laissez-faire' state.[12] In the history of European statecraft and diplomacy, the breakdown of the eighteenth-century 'balance of power' and its reorganisation by the European 'Concert', created by the Vienna Congress of 1814, suggests a similar periodisation.[13] In the German tradition of conceptual history (*Begriffsgeschichte*), meanwhile, the century from 1750 to 1850 has been described as the *Sattelzeit*: a period of intensified change and production in the intellectual underpinnings of political life, when many central words and concepts took on meanings broadly similar to those that they bear today.[14]

Synthesising all of these approaches and more, the historian Christopher Bayly has described a 'world crisis' stretching from the mid-eighteenth to the early nineteenth century. The Seven Years' War (1757–63), the War of American Independence (1776–83), and the French Revolutionary and Napoleonic Wars (1792–1815) entangled the political orders of West and South Asia with those of Europe and the Americas. They formed a cycle of fiscal and military escalation, driven by the global rivalry between Britain and France, which fundamentally altered the structure, capacities and governing ideologies of states and empires across all of these regions. The advantages of power and wealth shifted decisively to Western Europe as a whole, and to the British Empire in particular. In Europe and the new United States, commercial and demographic expansion, alongside the first stirrings of 'Industrial Revolution', expanded the demand for labour and goods, while deepening the integration of regional economies into global markets.[15]

---

[11] David Armitage and Sanjay Subrahmanyam (eds.), *The Age of Revolutions in Global Context, c. 1760–1840* (Basingstoke: Palgrave Macmillan, 2009).

[12] Arthur Burns and Joanna Innes, 'Introduction', in *Rethinking the Age of Reform: Britain 1780–1850* (Cambridge: Cambridge University Press, 2003), 1–17; Philip Harling and Peter Mandler, 'From "Fiscal-Military" State to *laissez-faire* State, 1760–1850', *Journal of British Studies*, 32 (2014), 44–70.

[13] Paul W. Schroeder, *The Transformation of European Politics, 1763–1848* (Oxford: Clarendon Press, 1994).

[14] Reinhart Koselleck and Michaela Richter, 'Introduction and Prefaces to the *Geschichtliche Grundbegriffe*', *Contributions to the History of Concepts*, 6 (2011), 1–37.

[15] Christopher A. Bayly, *The Birth of the Modern World, 1780–1914: Global Connections and Comparisons* (Oxford: Blackwell, 2004), 86–121.

The growing scale of military conflict and the gathering pace of economic transformation inspired a ferment of new ideas about the relationship between commerce, empire and war. The importance of trade and colonisation to European politics had been recognised since the rise of the Dutch Republic in the seventeenth century, and had long been the object of a practically oriented literature focused on the utility of commerce as a means to power.[16] Power-political analyses of mercantile empire were never neatly separable, however, from a broader set of cultural and ethical ideas about what it meant to live in societies defined by luxury consumption and market exchange. The moral legitimation of what Adam Smith termed 'commercial society' was always unstable and incomplete.[17] Yet by the end of the eighteenth century, many Europeans nonetheless believed that it represented a superior, and distinctively 'modern', mode of life.[18] The identification of commerce with peace and 'civilisation' – often hard to sustain in an eighteenth century defined by wars for control of colonies and trade routes – was encouraged after 1815 by the failure of French attempts to enforce an anti-British commercial blockade, the Continental System, in Europe.[19] Later in the nineteenth century, it would justify the forcible 'opening' and reorganisation of East and South Asian societies that did not conform to European ideals of 'free' trade and private property.[20]

Eighteenth- and nineteenth-century Ireland experienced a series of radical economic, social and political changes that would place it at the heart of European debates over the political economy of Britain and its empire in this global age of crisis. The rise of the linen weaving industry after 1750 and the expansion of tillage agriculture after 1780 were both encouraged by rapidly growing demand for Irish goods in British, imperial and global markets.[21] The second half of the eighteenth century witnessed a significant expansion and improvement of Ireland's road network and the construction of the modern-day centres of major cities including Cork,

---

[16] Julian Hoppit, 'The Contexts and Contours of British Economic Literature, 1660–1760', *The Historical Journal*, 49 (2006), 79–110.

[17] István Hont, *Politics in Commercial Society: Jean-Jacques Rousseau and Adam Smith* (Cambridge, MA: Harvard University Press, 2015).

[18] Jennifer Pitts, *A Turn to Empire: The Rise of Imperial Liberalism in Britain and France* (Princeton, NJ: Princeton University Press, 2005), 14–19.

[19] Anna Plassart, *The Scottish Enlightenment and the French Revolution* (Cambridge: Cambridge University Press, 2015), 187–220.

[20] David Todd, 'John Bowring and the Global Dissemination of Free Trade', *The Historical Journal*, 51 (2008), 373–97.

[21] Louis Cullen, 'Economic Development, 1750–1800', in T. W. Moody and W. E. Vaughan (eds.), *A New History of Ireland, Volume IV: Eighteenth-Century Ireland, 1691–1800* (Oxford: Oxford University Press, 1986), 159–95.

Dublin and Belfast.[22] This period also witnessed a transformation in the Irish landscape, which increased the quantity of land dedicated to grain production and filled upland and marginal acres with small potato farms.[23] Encouraged by wartime demand and the interruption of British trade with Europe in the Napoleonic era, the turn to potato tillage and grain exports enabled explosive population growth, particularly in the west of the country. It also increased Ireland's vulnerability to economic and environmental shocks, laying the foundations for the catastrophic famines of the 1840s.[24]

Economic volatility and demographic transformation were, meanwhile, paralleled by an upsurge in popular politics. Political movements with parliamentary and elite connections, like the Irish Volunteers of the 1780s, the republican United Irishmen and Daniel O'Connell's Catholic Association, increasingly turned to 'the people' – even, in the case of the United Irish revolutionary Wolfe Tone, the 'men of no property' – for support and legitimation.[25] The expansion of popular politics further complicated Ireland's complex confessional settlement, making possible cross-confessional alliances between the Presbyterians who shaped the politics in the north-eastern region of Ulster and the Anglicans and Catholics who predominated in the rest of the island. They simultaneously, however, reawakened deep memories of the bloody violence of religious warfare in the seventeenth century.[26] Political radicalisation, alongside the social dislocation produced by rapid economic change, encouraged the growth of oath-based secret societies among peasants and artisans, in town and country alike.[27] Here, too, the famines of the 1840s imposed a sharp caesura. While the first appearance of the potato blight

---

[22] David Dickson, 'Town and City', in Eugenio F. Biagini and Mary Daly (eds.), *The Cambridge Social History of Ireland* (Cambridge: Cambridge University Press, 2017), 112–28.

[23] Kevin Whelan, 'The Modern Landscape', in F. H. A. Aalen, Matthew Stout and Kevin Whelan (eds.), *Atlas of the Irish Rural Landscape*, 2nd ed. (Cork: Cork University Press, 2011), 73–115, at 80–5.

[24] Cormac Ó'Gráda, 'Poverty, Population and Agriculture, 1801–45', in W. E. Vaughan (ed.), *A New History of Ireland, Volume V: Ireland under the Union 1801–1870* (Oxford: Oxford University Press, 1989), 108–13.

[25] Padhraig Higgins, *A Nation of Politicians: Gender, Patriotism, and Political Culture in Late Eighteenth-Century Ireland* (Madison: University of Wisconsin Press, 2010); Jim Smyth, *The Men of No Property: Irish Radicals and Popular Politics in the Late Eighteenth Century* (Basingstoke: Macmillan, 1992); K. Theodor Hoppen, 'Riding a Tiger: Daniel O'Connell, Reform, and Popular Politics in Ireland, 1800–1847', *Proceedings of the British Academy*, 100 (1999), 121–43.

[26] Jim Smyth, 'Anti-Catholicism, Conservatism, and Conspiracy: Sir Richard Musgrave's Memoirs of the Different Rebellions in Ireland', *Eighteenth-Century Life*, 22 (1998); Irene Whelan, *The Bible War in Ireland: The 'Second Reformation' and the Polarization of Protestant-Catholic Relations, 1800–1840* (Dublin: Lilliput Press, 2005).

[27] Tom Garvin, 'Defenders, Ribbonmen and Others: Underground Political Networks in Prefamine Ireland', in Charles H. E. Philpin (ed.), *Nationalism and Popular Protest in Ireland*

was attended by widespread popular protest, the scale of death and emigration deeply traumatised Irish society, altering landholding and religious practices in ways that – for a time – would militate against insurgent mass politics in the mould of the Volunteers, the United Irishmen, or O'Connell's Repeal Association.[28]

The British Empire in Europe

This long arc of economic transformation and political mobilisation provides a strong justification for locating Irish history in this period within the broader 'world crisis' described above. It also enables us, however, to identify a distinct phase in the long history of Britain's government of Ireland. Here, the most enduring and significant change was the Union of 1801, which replaced a formally autonomous parliament at Dublin with minority Irish representation at Westminster.[29] Following O'Connell's successful agitation, representation at Westminster was broadened to include MPs from the island's Catholic majority in 1829.[30] Over a period of decades before and after the Union, a carefully regulated commercial system based on tariffs and prohibitions, and complemented by a separate Irish currency Exchequer and national debt, was meanwhile dismantled and replaced by an integrated market with common fiscal and monetary institutions.[31] The offices of the Lord Lieutenant and the Irish Chief Secretary, government officials responsible for an extensive administrative apparatus centred on Dublin Castle, became increasingly important in the British cabinet. After the Union, innovations such as parliamentary inquiries, the Irish Constabulary, the census and the Irish Poor Law increased the capacity of both the Westminster parliament and the

---

(Cambridge: Cambridge University Press, 1987), 219–44; James S. Donnelly, *Captain Rock: The Irish Agrarian Rebellion of 1821–1824* (Cork: Collins Press, 2009).

[28] John Cunningham, "'Tis Hard to Argue Starvation into Quiet": Protest and Resistance, 1846–7', in Enda Delaney and Breandán Mac Suibhne (eds.), *Ireland's Great Famine and Popular Politics* (London: Routledge, 2016), 10–34; Emmet Larkin, 'The Devotional Revolution in Ireland, 1850–75', *The American Historical Review*, 77 (1972), 625–52; K. Theodore Hoppen, 'Landlords, Society and Electoral Politics in Mid-Nineteenth-Century Ireland', *Past & Present*, 75 (1977), 62–93.

[29] Joanna Innes, 'Legislating for Three Kingdoms: How the Westminster Parliament Legislated for England, Scotland and Ireland, 1707–1830', in Julian Hoppit (ed.), *Parliaments, Nations and Identities in Britain and Ireland, 1660–1850* (Manchester: Manchester University Press, 2003), 15–48.

[30] Boyd Hilton, *A Mad, Bad, and Dangerous People? England 1783–1846* (Oxford: Clarendon Press, 2006), 384–91.

[31] Cormac Ó'Gráda, *Ireland: A New Economic History, 1780–1939* (Oxford: Clarendon Press, 1994), 43–6; Kanter, *Making of British Unionism*, 111–29.

Castle administration to monitor and discipline the lives of their Irish subjects.[32]

The late eighteenth and early nineteenth centuries have long been recognised as an era of reform and transition across the British Empire. Where once, however, historians spoke of the 'turn to the East' and the 'rise of free trade' as defining features of this period, they now emphasise a complex renegotiation of authority between the different layers of the imperial polity.[33] In the later eighteenth century, the imperative to control Britain's escalating national debt by extracting additional troops and revenues from its dependencies was a common theme across imperial policy: from Ireland to the American colonies and the East India Company.[34] Concern with debt and revenue, however, was only one part of the story. Particularly following the loss of the American colonies, there was a growing aspiration among parts of the British political nation to employ central and executive authority to defend lesser imperial subjects against the depredations of self-governing colonial elites – from East India Company directors to West India slave planters.[35]

Ireland was widely believed to be ruled by one such extractive elite: the 'Anglo-Irish' colonists who had expropriated and replaced an older, Catholic landowning class, of mixed Gaelic and Anglo-Norman descent, in the course of the seventeenth century.[36] For much of the eighteenth century, British ministers had been largely content to allow this Anglican aristocracy to rule Ireland on its own terms.[37] In the period considered by this book, however, they began to intervene more directly, responding to Irish political mobilisation with an ecumenical vision of British rule that sought actively to win the allegiance of the Catholic majority, and to

---

[32] Peter Jupp, 'Government, Parliament and Politics in Ireland, 1801–41', in Hoppit (ed.), *Parliaments, Nations and Identities*, 146–64.

[33] Christopher A. Bayly, *Imperial Meridian: The British Empire and the World, 1780–1830* (London: Longman, 1989).

[34] Robert Donovan, 'The Military Origins of the Roman Catholic Relief Programme of 1778', *The Historical Journal*, 28 (1985), 79–102; John H. Elliott, *Empires of the Atlantic World: Britain and Spain in America, 1492–1830* (New Haven, CT: Yale University Press, 2006), 294–307; Huw V. Bowen, *The Business of Empire: The East India Company and Imperial Britain, 1756–1833* (Cambridge: Cambridge University Press, 2006), 37–42.

[35] Maya Jasanoff, *Liberty's Exiles: American Loyalists in the Revolutionary World* (New York: Vintage Books, 2012), 5–21; Lauren Benton and Lisa Ford, *Rage for Order: The British Empire and the Origins of International Law, 1800–1850* (Cambridge, MA: Harvard University Press, 2016), 28–56.

[36] Jane Ohlmeyer, 'Conquest, Civilisation, Colonisation: Ireland, 1540–1660', in Ian McBride and Richard Bourke (eds.), *The Princeton History of Modern Ireland* (Princeton, NJ: Princeton University Press, 2016), 21–47.

[37] David Hayton, 'The Beginnings of the "Undertaker System"', in *Penal Era and Golden Age: Essays in Irish History, 1690–1800* (Belfast: Ulster Historical Foundation, 1979), 32–55.

guarantee Ireland's prosperity as an integral part of the United Kingdom. This was the vision of empire that stood behind the Union of 1801.

The vicissitudes of British government in Ireland, however, were frequently viewed by contemporaries in a context that was as much European as it was imperial. One of the first histories of English attempts to govern both Scotland and Ireland, the Genevan exile Jean-Louis de Lolme's *History of the British Empire in Europe* (1787), defined its subject in terms that were at once geographical and geopolitical. De Lolme's title was both a casual collective description for the two Kingdoms of Great Britain and Ireland, and a statement of intent concerning the decisive role played by European warfare in his narrative. The threat of Spain, de Lolme claimed, had made the Elizabethan and Jacobean plantations of Ireland an unavoidable necessity for English reason of state. The English general the Duke of Marlborough's victories against the armies of Louis XIV had, meanwhile, rendered the Anglo-Scottish Union of 1707 irresistible to a Scottish nobility that could no longer hope for French assistance against England. The willingness of the Volunteer movement to challenge the restrictive commercial regulations imposed on Ireland by the Westminster parliament was, by contrast, bolstered by the knowledge that France, a 'great European power', had supported the cause of Britain's North American colonists against the British Empire.[38]

The effects of the American and French Revolutions on Irish politics, and the complex diplomatic relationship between the United Irish revolutionaries and the French Republic, are among the most storied aspects of Irish history in this period.[39] Yet the role played by France in the crises and transformations of 'the British Empire in Europe' endured beyond these moments of direct military crisis and threat. Throughout the eighteenth century, commercial and military rivalry between Britain and the French monarchy spurred British and Irish interest in the reform of Irish government. In the era of the French Revolution, this older form of power-political competition was overlaid with a new set of ideological fault lines. Britain assumed the leading role in organising coalitions of counter-revolutionary European states, and became engaged in a profound

---

[38] Jean-Louis de Lolme, *The British Empire in Europe, Part the First* (Dublin: P. Byrne, 1787), 24–5, 125–6.

[39] Marianne Elliott, *Partners in Revolution: The United Irishmen and France* (New Haven, CA: Yale University Press, 1982); Martyn Powell, *Britain and Ireland in the Eighteenth-Century Crisis of Empire* (Basingstoke: Palgrave Macmillan, 2003); Ultán Gillen, 'Monarchy, Republic and Empire: Irish Public Opinion and France, c.1787–1804', DPhil Thesis, Faculty of History, Oxford University, Oxford (2005).

ideological contest with France over the foundations of political and economic order in Europe.[40]

Thanks to the alliance between United Irish radicals and the French Republic, Ireland was drawn into a European debate concerning the relative abilities of the warring powers to withstand the pressures of the conflict and act in the common interests of European commerce and civilisation. Ireland's entanglement in this larger propaganda struggle between Britain and revolutionary France had broad and lasting consequences. Not only in Britain and France, but across Europe, it created a structure of debate concerning Ireland that employed it as a kind of test case for the civilising claims of British power, in Europe and around the world. Britain's ultimate victory in the Napoleonic Wars, and the developing Franco-British *rapprochement* of the 1820s and 1830s, ultimately did little to alter the underlying stakes in European discussions of Ireland. Indeed, they only heightened the interest of Ireland as a country that was apparently profiting little from its political and commercial integration with Britain's victorious empire.

Conquest, Liberty and Aristocracy

Rivalry between Britain and France supplied the crucial context for an abiding concern of Irish political thought in this era: the search for forms of autonomy, within and beyond the British Empire, that could enable the Kingdom to transcend the conquest and subordination that were the legacies of its seventeenth-century conquest and plantation. Thanks to the example set by the Franco-American alliance, Irish Volunteers and 'Patriots' of the 1780s believed that the British Empire could be remade as a permissive structure of liberty, allowing the Kingdom to fully develop its commercial capacities while remaining under the ambit of British military protection. In the expanding power of revolutionary France, meanwhile, the United Irishmen of the 1790s believed they saw a new kind of empire. Immune from the aristocratic corruption and mercantile 'jealousy' that defined the British system of government and commerce, France could guarantee the place of a sovereign Irish 'sister republic' in a new European system of perpetual peace. For the most passionate proponents – in large part not English, but rather Irish and Scottish – of the Union of 1801, the incorporation of parliaments did not betoken the kind of constitutional

---

[40] Marc Belissa, *Repenser l'ordre européen 1795–1802: de la société des rois aux droits des nations* (Paris: Editions Kimé, 2006).

obliteration that would befall many European states over the brutal half-century that separated the first Polish Partitions (1771–3) and the Vienna Congress (1814–15).[41] The example of Scotland showed that, even for England's smaller neighbours, Union could reconcile the commercial and political privileges afforded by representation in the Westminster parliament with the preservation of many local institutions of law, government, education and religion. By consolidating the empire in the face of French aggression, Union would vindicate the progressive potential of Britain's commercial and political system.

Unlike the Scottish Kingdom that had agreed to the Union of 1707, however, Ireland's entire system of law, government and property was the product of conquest and plantation – both English and Scottish – in the sixteenth and seventeenth centuries. The legacy of conquest was a hybrid constitution, modelled on the English division of 'King, Lords and Commons', the Anglican establishment and the common law; but characterised also by its subordinate relationship to Westminster and the exclusion of the majority Catholic confession from property, officeholding and political representation. The Anglo-Irish 'Ascendancy' who dominated the eighteenth-century Irish Kingdom were an aristocracy of recent and dubious heritage, holding lands whose expropriation lingered in the memories of a largely Catholic tenantry. There was no route to the reform of the Kingdom that did not run through a reappraisal of its position of power within Irish society. The Volunteering movement of the 1780s – which would ultimately split apart over the question of Catholic access to the Irish franchise – trusted in the expansion of Irish commerce to soothe the periodic agrarian discontents that disturbed the peace of the Anglo-Irish landholding class. Proponents of Union, by contrast, argued that the baleful effects of religious and political 'faction' could only be overcome once the political power of the Ascendancy was broken by the removal of its exclusive parliament, and Ireland's different confessional communities blended into the enlarged citizenry of an expanded Britain. It was the United Irishmen, however, who defined the problem of Anglo-Irish Ascendancy in a fashion that dramatically linked it to the stark ideological fault lines created by the French Revolution. For these Irish insurgents, Ascendancy was only a particularly egregious example of the aristocratic

---

[41] Richard Whatmore, '"Neither Masters nor Slaves": Small States and Empire in the Long Eighteenth Century', in Duncan Kelly (ed.), *Lineages of Empire: The Historical Roots of British Imperial Thought* (Oxford: Oxford University Press, 2009), 53–81; Richard Whatmore, *Against War and Empire: Geneva, Britain, and France in the Eighteenth Century* (New Haven, CT: Yale University Press, 2012).

corruption that defined the old monarchies of Europe. Because of an intense and malevolent 'jealousy of trade' and its corrupted system of parliamentary government, Britain was incapable of reforming its Irish dependency. Only the armies of revolutionary France could bring about the downfall of Ireland's Anglican Ascendancy and, with it, the entire crumbling edifice of British mercantile and financial power.

The United Irishmen's frontal challenge to both Anglo-Irish Ascendancy and British Empire was of European significance because it went to the core of what the Franco-British rivalry was ultimately about: a struggle to define the social and political forms appropriate to the commercial societies that both nations were fast becoming in the last quarter of the eighteenth century. Was the expansion of material wealth, and of certain kinds of personal freedom, compatible with – even fostered by – the preservation of the aristocratic *mouers* and privileges that remained pronounced features of European life across the eighteenth century, as argued by thinkers such as Montesquieu, Edmund Burke and (in a different way) Robert Malthus? Or did it require instead a wholesale remodelling of political institutions on new principles of rational equality, as demanded by revolutionaries like Condorcet, Thomas Paine and Emmanuel Joseph Sieyès?

These positions were not simply orientations in French and British domestic or imperial politics. Something like the first was maintained by the architects of the Vienna settlement, who regarded the French Revolutionary Wars as a nihilistic crusade against the achievements of eighteenth-century European civilisation, and envisaged a balance of power newly reconstituted and civilised by ties of commercial self-interest.[42] Something like the second was adopted by revolutionary advocates for French-led schemes for European federation and 'perpetual peace', who attributed the recurrent warfare of eighteenth-century Europe to the obstruction of a cosmopolitan commercial sociability through British financial and naval power and the prideful warmongering of monarchs, merchants and nobles.[43] As should already be apparent, neither stance can be caricatured as either reactionary or progressive, 'moderate' or 'radical'. In the post-revolutionary era, liberals in France, Italy and the German lands would effectively combine them, conceding

---

[42] Bo Stråth, *Europe's Utopias of Peace: 1815, 1919, 1951* (London: Bloomsbury, 2016), 23–42.
[43] Isaac Nakhimovsky, 'The "Ignominious Fall of the European Commonwealth": Gentz, Hauterive, and the Armed Neutrality of 1800', in Koen Stapelbroek (ed.), *Trade and War: The Neutrality of Commerce in the Interstate System* (Helsinki: Helsinki Collegium for Advanced Studies, 2011), 177–90.

the irreversibility of the French Revolution's dethronement of old aristocracies, while decrying both its violent methods and its ultimate descent
into military dictatorship. From this perspective, too, the case of Ireland
was inescapable. For all those seeking to understand what Britain's post-
war hegemony might mean for Restoration Europe, it was obvious that its
government of Ireland would provide valuable insights into the character
and prospects of its empire. Across Europe, O'Connellite agitation, and
the growing scandal of Irish rural poverty, poverty became central to post-
revolutionary discussions of the 'principle of nationality' and the 'social
question'.[44] 'Ireland', wrote the French liberal diplomat, parliamentarian
and social investigator Gustave de Beaumont in 1839, 'is a little country,
through which the greatest questions of politics, morality and humanity
are debated'.[45]

Visions of Commercial Society

European debates about the relative merits of French and British Empire
swirled around Ireland with particular intensity because it cast a peculiar,
sideways light on Britain and the politics of aristocratic reform that it came
to represent in the decades after the American and French Revolutions.
Ireland's frequently cited poverty and instability raised the question of
what kind of political agency, and what account of what was coming to be
known as 'political economy', were required to bring about what contemporaries called 'improvement': the progressive betterment of material
conditions that was the mark of a successful 'commercial society'.

Thanks to a generation of revisionist scholarship, the history of eigh-
teenth- and nineteenth-century political economy is no longer viewed in
disciplinary isolation, confined to practitioners from within the field of
economics itself. It is far more commonly examined as part of the broader
context of war, empire and revolution that has been briefly sketched above.
Thus far, however, this revisionist move in the intellectual history of
political economy has touched Ireland in only limited ways, focusing
above all on the question on Ireland's foreign trade and its regulation by
England in the late seventeenth and eighteenth centuries. Here, the central
issue was what István Hont termed the 'rich country-poor country'

---

[44] Georgios Varouxakis, '1848 and British Political Thought on "The Principle of Nationality"', in
Douglas Moggach and Gareth Stedman Jones (eds.), *The 1848 Revolutions and European Political
Thought* (Cambridge: Cambridge University Press, 2018), 140–61; Holly Case, 'The "Social
Question", 1820–1920', *Modern Intellectual History*, 13(3) (2016), 747–75.
[45] Gustave de Beaumont, *L'Irlande sociale, politique, et religieuse* (Paris: Gosselin, 1839), 2 vols., I:i.

problem: the widespread belief that trade and manufactures would shift from comparatively wealthy England to poorer Ireland unless the trade of the latter was ruthlessly restricted by taxes imposed by the Westminster parliament.[46] The apparent diminution of British anxiety about this Irish threat in the last quarter of the eighteenth century, attributable to the growing influence of the Scottish philosopher David Hume and the Welsh clergyman Josiah Tucker, dovetails neatly (though not in Hont's telling) with an older historiography which emphasises the slow but steady conversion of British opinion to the new economic doctrine of 'free trade', supposedly outlined by Adam Smith in his *Wealth of Nations* (1776).[47]

What this latter narrative cannot explain, however, is how Ireland had become such a potent symbol of the limits of liberal political economy in the 1840s, the very decade when Britain fired the starting gun on an extensive round of European tariff reductions through its repeal of the Corn Laws in 1846.[48] This turnaround is all the more striking when we consider the high hopes that some had invested in Ireland's commercial prospects as recently as the 1780s, when the breakdown of Britain's mercantile empire in the Atlantic inspired expectations (and fears) that the Irish Kingdom might yet become 'the mart in Europe for the trade of America'.[49] In order to understand what happened to contemporary understandings of Ireland between the age of Adam Smith and that of Richard Cobden, the American Declaration of Independence and the repeal of the Corn Laws, we have to largely discard an older historiographical perspective that implicitly identifies the entire revolutionary and Napoleonic period as a mere prelude to the eventual coming of Victorian laissez-faire[50]. As has already been suggested, late eighteenth-century and early nineteenth-century discussions of commercial reform occurred downstream of a larger set of concerns and anxieties about the prospects for peace in Europe. They also placed a strong emphasis on

[46] István Hont, 'The "Rich Country-Poor Country" Debate Revisited: The Irish Origins and French Reception of the Hume Paradox', in Carl Wennerlind and Margaret Schabas (eds.), *David Hume's Political Economy* (London: Routledge, 2008), 243–323.

[47] Bernard Semmel, 'The Hume Tucker Debate and Pitt's Trade Proposals', *Economic Journal*, 75 (1965), 759–70.

[48] Paul Bairoch and Susan Burke, 'European Trade Policy, 1815–1914', in Peter Mathias and Sidney Pollard (eds.), *The Cambridge Economic History of Europe Since the Decline of the Roman Empire, Volume 8: The Industrial Economies: The Development of Economic and Social Policies* (Cambridge: Cambridge University Press, 1989), 1–160, at 23–51.

[49] John Holroyd, 1st Earl Sheffield, *Observations on the Manufactures, Trade, and Present State of Ireland*, 3rd ed. (London: Debrett, 1785), 43.

[50] Most notably, Vincent Todd Harlow, The Founding of the Second British Empire, 2 Vols. (London: Longmans, Green 1952–64); Semmel, Rise of Free Trade Imperialism.

agriculture and land reform, in conscious opposition to the eighteenth-century obsession with foreign and colonial trade as the sole guarantors of national power and security.[51] The path towards Ireland's ultimate alienation from the economic orthodoxies of Victorian Britain must be traced through the complex interaction of interlocking, transnational agendas for commercial, constitutional and agrarian reform.

Understanding the stakes and complexity of eighteenth- and nineteenth-century debates over the 'improvement' of Ireland can help us to identify just what it was that made it an object of such interest to European political thinkers, especially in the early nineteenth century. It can also help us to revise dominant understandings of the role of 'political economy' in the history of British rule in Ireland. Here, there has been a stark divergence of approach between historians on the one side and varieties of critical and postcolonial theory on the other. Historians have tended to focus on the formulation of 'policy', examining political and economic thought only insofar as it can be directly connected to the motivation of specific governmental and legislative actions, such as the Irish Poor Law of 1838.[52] Critical and postcolonial theorists, by contrast, have been interested in political economy as a 'discourse' dedicated to the elimination of distinctive Irish modes of life, and ultimately of those millions of Irish subjects who either starved or emigrated from Ireland during the famines of the 1840s.[53]

The present work builds on both approaches, but considers a much broader range of political and economic thinking, linking the eighteenth century to the nineteenth and continental Europe to Britain and Ireland. Rather than studying either the motivations of politicians or the structure

---

[51] Frederik Albritton Jonsson, *Enlightenment's Frontier: The Scottish Highlands and the Origins of Environmentalism* (New Haven, CT: Yale University Press, 2013); Peter Jones, *Agricultural Enlightenment: Knowledge, Technology and Nature, 1750–1840* (Oxford: Oxford University Press, 2016).

[52] R. D. Collison Black, *Economic Thought and the Irish Question, 1817–1870* (Cambridge: Cambridge University Press, 1960); R. D. Collison Black, 'Theory and Policy in Anglo-Irish Trade Relations, 1775–1800', *Journal of the Statistical and Social Inquiry Society of Ireland*, 28(3) (1950), 312–26; Peter Gray, *The Making of the Irish Poor Law, 1815–43* (Manchester: Manchester University Press, 2009); Peter Gray, *Famine, Land and Politics: British Government and Irish Society, 1843–50* (Dublin: Irish Academic Press, 1999); Kanter, *Making of British Unionism*; K. Theodore Hoppen, *Governing Hibernia: British Politicians and Ireland 1800–1921* (Oxford: Oxford University Press, 2016).

[53] David P. Nally, *Human Encumbrances: Political Violence and the Great Irish Famine* (South Bend, IN: University of Notre Dame Press, 2011); David Lloyd, 'The Political Economy of the Potato', *Nineteenth Century Contexts*, 29 (2007), 311–35; David Lloyd, 'Nomadic Figures: The "Rhetorical Excess" of Irishness in Political Economy', in Maureen O'Connor (ed.), *Back to the Future of Irish Studies: Festschrift for Tadhg Foley* (Bern: Peter Lang, 2010), 41–65.

of discourses, it attempts to identify a succession of discrete arguments about the relationship between the evolving problem of Irish government and the politics of commercial society. It treats a broad variety of texts – from lengthy theoretical treatises to pamphlets, magazine articles and political speeches – as interventions in a field of debate that was at once Irish, British and European. This approach goes beyond that of Irish political and administrative history by revealing more about the intellectual provenance, and discursive resonance, of those ideas that mattered to the transformation and contestation of British government in Ireland. It complicates (without seeking to dilute) the critical force of postcolonial writing on political economy, by showing that Ireland was not simply a place where confident, hegemonic British theories of political economy confronted the perplexities of a colonised society. In contemporary European thought, Ireland offered a space of projection for radically differing ideas about what the politics of commercial society should look like.

The Case of Ireland

This book takes its name from a famous pamphlet written by the Irish Anglican philosopher and parliamentarian William Molyneux, *The Case of Ireland, Being Bound by Acts of Parliament in England, Stated* (1698). Molyneux's work was a vigorous defence of the sovereign rights of Ireland's parliament, then sitting at Dublin, to regulate the Kingdom's foreign trade, and a rejection of English assertions that repeated invasions of seventeenth-century Ireland had confirmed its status as a 'colony'. It is commonly described as the *Urtext* of a modern tradition of Irish constitutional nationalism – a status it came to assume much later, in the final quarter of the eighteenth century.[54] Yet Molyneux's *Case* – occasioned, as it was, by a decision of the English parliament to unilaterally impose prohibitory duties on the export of Irish woollens – was also the first of many Irish attempts to come to terms with the arrival of commerce as a central question for European politics, and to understand what this might mean for a polity that was still profoundly marked by the legacies of conquest and religious warfare. It pointed to the significance of Ireland's 'case' in a different sense: as a potentially instructive example to all those who attempted to understand the ways in which society, politics and

[54] Patrick Kelly, 'William Molyneux and the Spirit of Liberty in Eighteenth-Century Ireland', *Eighteenth-Century Ireland: Iris an dá chultúr*, 3 (1988).

international order were being transformed by commerce and colonialism, and the European ramifications of Britain's rise to a position of global influence.

Chapter 1 takes Molyneux as a starting point for a survey of the terrain of political and economic thinking in and about the eighteenth-century Irish Kingdom, and identifies the emergence of an Enlightenment critique of empire in Ireland. This laid the intellectual foundations for the Union of 1801 by connecting the exclusion of the Irish Kingdom from free participation in imperial and European trade with the exclusion of its Catholic subjects, under the terms of the 'Penal Laws', from the benefits of property and political representation. For thinkers such as Josiah Tucker and David Hume, the suppression of Irish commerce was striking evidence of how British policy carried 'jealousy of trade' to extremes that jeopardised the security of the empire. For Charles O'Conor, Edmund Burke, Arthur Young and Adam Smith, meanwhile, the Penal Laws had ruined Ireland's prospects for 'improvement' by alienating the Irish majority from property and the state. It was Smith who linked these two problematics together, creating a new kind of argument for a parliamentary union between Britain and Ireland. This aimed not simply at the rationalisation of imperial trade and revenue, but at the reform of the Anglo-Irish aristocracy who dominated the eighteenth-century Irish parliament.

Chapter 2 explores the high hopes for Irish commerce that were aroused by the American Revolution and the complex interaction of Irish and British attempts to reform and consolidate the remnants of its mercantile empire following defeat at the hands of France, Spain, the Dutch Republic and the newly independent United States. Irish campaigns for 'free trade' and 'legislative independence' were animated by the hope that the liberation of the Kingdom's foreign trade would enable it to chart its own course in a more peaceful Europe, continuing to enjoy the benefits of British naval protection while reducing its economic dependence on Britain and its empire. This vision clashed fundamentally with a rival, British reform agenda, embodied in William Pitt the Younger's unsuccessful Irish Commercial Propositions of 1785, which balanced an extension of imperial trading privileges to Ireland with its closer integration into the British market. The rejection of Pitt's proposals by the Irish parliament, after their heavy modification by British slaving and manufacturing interests, produced an unstable equilibrium, dominated by patronage and executive power that was ripe for criticism by the more radical forces that would take up the fallen mantle of Irish 'patriotism' in the 1790s.

With the return of war against France following the revolution of 1789, the prospects for Irish reform through the expansion of foreign trade rapidly fell away. Chapter 3 explores the consequences of the revolution and its transformation of European politics through an Irish lens, linking the political thought of key Irish radicals to the emerging patterns of a propaganda war between the rival empires of Britain and France. The United Irishmen, a new popular movement seeking explicitly to combine Anglicans, Presbyterians and Catholics in the pursuit of a sovereign Irish republic, launched a more radical critique of mercantile empire and Irish Anglican 'Ascendancy' than had been hazarded by Adam Smith or Edmund Burke. For Wolfe Tone and Arthur O'Connor, two key United Irish emissaries to France, French intervention in Irish politics presented an opportunity to dismantle the Irish Kingdom's sectarian property order and replace it with the peasant proprietorship being spread by French arms in the Low Countries, the Rhineland and northern Italy. Ireland's poverty and instability was, meanwhile, held by a range of French and German observers to be a clear demonstration of the injustice and weakness of the British Empire, and the superiority of the French alternative. Following their defeat in 1798, key United Irish figures including Arthur O'Connor and William James MacNeven mounted powerful defences of Napoleonic conquest. At least as far as its leaders were concerned, the 1798 rebellion was borne not of a radical repudiation of empire, but of an embrace of a French over a British variant.

Chapter 4 establishes the nature and provenance of the case for parliamentary union advanced by British and Irish pamphleteers and politicians in response to the 1798 rebellion. Union it argues, was more than a matter of counter-revolutionary *Realpolitik*. It drew on the intellectual resources of the Scottish Enlightenment to implement a new system of economic and political regulation, driven by a distinctive account of political authority in commercial society. The proponents of Union – William Pitt and his Scottish War Secretary, Henry Dundas, foremost among them – articulated a renewed belief in the ability of commercial integration with Britain to act as a solvent to the confessional and ethnic tensions laid bare by the United Irish risings and attempted French invasions of 1796–8. The spectre of British trade and manufactures fleeing to Ireland was now re-described as a beneficial 'diffusion of capital': one that would give Ireland's shattered Anglican aristocracy the opportunity to re-establish its political legitimacy, while forcing them to share power with a rising Catholic mercantile and professional class. The case for Union was interpreted in a broad European context of state competition and reform, shaped by the extraordinary successes of French revolutionary arms on the European continent in the period since the Terror of 1792–4. Within Britain and Ireland, Union was criticised as a measure that tragically recreated Jacobin centralisation and despotism in its efforts to resist French encroachment. The leading continental defender of British policy, the Prussian diplomat and publicist Friedrich von Gentz, nonetheless hailed the legislative unification of the British Empire as a model for a necessary consolidation of the European states-system in the wake of French revolutionary violence. Britain was hailed as the guarantor of a civil liberty that was threatened by the fanaticism of the French Republic and its Irish supporters.

Chapter 5 recovers the peculiar significance of the Napoleonic Wars for the formation of nineteenth-century British orthodoxies concerning the government of Ireland's rural interior. Already in the last decades of the eighteenth century, booming Irish grain exports had fulfilled older Anglo-Irish ambitions of agricultural improvement, driving a dramatic switch from pasture to tillage agriculture across the 'fertile crescent' of Leinster and south Munster. It was in the decade after 1801, however, that this agrarian transformation first became central to Irish, British and European debates over Irish government. For Thomas Newenham, a County Cork landowner and 'improving' writer, the indispensability of Irish grain to the British war effort proved the glowing potential of a model of Union that rested on an agricultural Ireland supplying the needs of industrial Britain. The attractiveness of this vision was such that Francis D'Ivernois, a Genevan exile who was central to Britain's continental propaganda and diplomacy, was able to employ it as an argument for the Russian Empire to abandon Napoleon's 'Continental System' and reopen the Baltic grain trade to Britain.

For the editors of the *Irish Magazine,* a largely forgotten periodical that transmitted the spirit of United Irish radicalism through the lean later years of the war to the popular Catholic nationalism of O'Connell and the Catholic Association, Ireland's apparent abandonment of commerce and manufactures had fulfilled the darkest predictions made by Irish opponents of the Union of 1801. Patriotic objections to Ireland's agrarian turn found an unlikely echo in the pages of an influential new Scottish Whig journal of politics and political economy, *The Edinburgh Review.* Reviewing and heavily criticising Thomas Newenham's paeans to Ireland's agrarian transformation, the political economist Robert Malthus pinpointed the Irish peasantry's dependency on the potato as a product of the long suppression of the Irish Kingdom by Penal Laws and commercial restraints. Alongside Edward Wakefield, an English land agent who published an exhaustive survey of Ireland's rural economy in 1812, Malthus advanced the dramatic claim that only a transformation of Irish land tenure and consumption habits, under the auspices of the Westminster parliament, could bring about the diffusion of British civilisation promised by the proponents of the Union.

Chapter 6 traces the intellectual consequences of the unravelling of Ireland's grain export boom at the end of the Napoleonic wars. For British political economists such as Malthus and John Ramsay McCulloch, the path towards Irish recovery could only lie through the assimilation of Ireland to what they took to be an English model of large-scale tenant farming and concentrated land ownership. For European thinkers seeking to evaluate the commercial and political system of Britain, however, the parlous condition of the Irish countryside in the decades after 1815 dramatically illustrated the unsustainability of Britain's own 'aristocratic' social order. Thinkers including G. W. F. Hegel, Sismonde di Sismondi and Gustave de Beaumont used the case of Ireland to argue that British political economy systematically ignored the obligations of the sovereign to its poorest subjects, blindly subordinating questions of distribution and political stability to the relentless accumulation of capital. Their critiques were taken up in Britain by a new generation of liberal economists led by John Stuart Mill, and in Ireland by a group of Francophile nationalist intellectuals, Young Ireland. In parallel, but related ways, these thinkers recast the problem of Irish improvement anew, tying it not to the integration of Ireland into British or imperial markets, but on the creation of a stable class of peasant proprietors to match those that had been created in large parts of continental Europe through French, or French-inspired, land reforms. These were now realising an alternative vision of commercial society – which de Beaumont and his main intellectual collaborator, Alexis de Tocqueville, called 'democracy' – centred on smallholding agriculture and artisanal production in the home. It was in this way that the legacies of the French Revolution came to haunt Irish and British thinking on commerce and empire, into the 1840s and beyond.

As this summary suggests, the narrative presented here does not pretend to offer a complete history of politics or political thought in late eighteenth- and early nineteenth-century Ireland; still less one that can do justice to each and every way in which Irish subjects were involved in European and global politics in the age of the 'world crisis'. Such a history would necessarily include many things that are only glancingly discussed here, or left out entirely. Among these would be the relationship between

Irish Catholicism, the British state, and the Papacy;[55] the fate of the United Irish exiles in the United States;[56] political arguments against Irish reform and in favour of coercion and Anglican privilege; the relationship between Ireland and Quebec;[57] and the complex linkages between the Irish national cause and those of Italy and Poland in the years after 1815.[58] These blind spots arise from a deliberate decision to explore what might happen if we adjusted our focus on Irish history to centre on questions of commerce and empire, rather than those of nationalism and religion. These more common preoccupations of Irish history must, of course, always remain in the picture; but in this book, at least, they are not at the centre of the frame.

The Ireland that emerges is neither the hero nor the victim of the capitalist and colonial modernity that was the ultimate product of the era of the American and French Revolutions. We encounter it instead as one place – albeit one among many – where we can gain a vantage point on the intersection of commerce and empire as central problems of European political thought. As the oldest and closest dependency of Europe's leading mercantile empire, Ireland dramatically illustrated the broader problems of political liberty and economic 'improvement' under conditions of imperial rule. Unlike the United States, France, Haiti or the new republics of South America, Ireland did not witness a successful revolution during this period. Unlike Quebec, Poland, British India or French Algeria, it did not present European thinkers with the challenge of how to justify fresh conquests, or to secure the immediate allegiance of new populations to imperial government. Instead, Ireland posed the recurring, never-answered question of whether the new kind of empires created by the rise of global commerce, and the configurations of property and industry that they sought to impose on their subject populations, could ever be reformed or escaped. It did so under the complex conditions created by the interaction of domestic political faction with inter-imperial rivalry.

[55] Ambrose Macaulay, *The Catholic Church and the Campaign for Emancipation in Ireland and England* (Dublin: Four Courts, 2018).
[56] David Wilson, *United Irishmen, United States: Immigrant Radicals in the Early Republic* (Ithaca, NY: Cornell University Press, 1998).
[57] Mary L. Sanderson, 'Limited Liberties: Catholics and the Policies of the Pitt Ministry in an Early Modern Context', *Journal of British Studies*, 59 (2020), 737–63.
[58] Róisín Healy, *Poland in the Irish Nationalist Imagination, 1772–1922: Anti-Colonialism within Europe* (Basingstoke: Palgrave Macmillan, 2017); Nick Carter (ed.), *Britain, Ireland and the Italian Risorgimento* (Basingstoke: Palgrave Macmillan, 2015).

CHAPTER I

The Enlightenment Critique of Empire in Ireland, c. 1750–1776

The transformation of Britain's empire in Ireland in the decades either side of the Union of 1801 was the product of a series of interlocking crises: the loss of the North American colonies, the French Revolutionary Wars and the breakdown of the Irish agrarian economy after the defeat of Napoleon. Its intellectual origins, however, reach further and deeper into the middle of the eighteenth century. Indeed, despite the extraordinary change and disruption of the revolutionary era, there exists a remarkable continuity between the agenda of imperial reform articulated by Irish and British thinkers in the years following the Seven Years' War (1756–63) and the measures implemented in response to the revolutionary challenges of the 1780s and 1790s. It was during this earlier period that the core commitments of an Enlightened vision of Irish government – founded on a belief in the potential of commerce to bind Ireland to Britain, and Ireland's different confessional communities to one another – were first articulated.

These commitments arose out of a set of forthright criticisms of the pattern of English government that had been established in Ireland in the course of the seventeenth and early eighteenth centuries. The eighteenth-century Irish Kingdom was founded on two forms of exclusion – that of Irish Catholics from landed property and state offices, and of all Irish subjects from key branches of imperial and European trade – that provoked frequent accusations of hypocrisy and bad faith. Irish Catholics held that the 'Penal Laws', a long line of statutes passed by the Dublin parliament between the 1690s and the 1720s, had broken the terms of the peace treaty signed between the forces of William of Orange and those of James Stuart at Limerick in 1691.[1] The Anglican 'Anglo-Irish', for their

---

[1] Cadoc D. Leighton, *Catholicism in a Protestant Kingdom: A Study of the Irish Ancien Régime* (London: Macmillan, 2000), 97, 138–9.

part, frequently complained that the parliamentary government established by the English revolution of 1688 had never been fully extended to Ireland, a kingdom whose rights of legislation, at least when it came to matters of foreign trade and revenue, were frequently checked and limited by the authority of Westminster itself. It was this second charge that lay at the heart of the Irish philosopher William Molyneux's *Case of Ireland ... Stated* (1698). 'Since the late revolution in these kingdoms', he complained,

> when the subjects of England have more strenuously than ever asserted their own rights, and the liberty of parliaments, it has pleased them to bear harder than ever of their poor neighbours, than has ever yet been done in many ages foregoing.[2]

In the early eighteenth century, few among Ireland's Anglican ruling class followed Molyneux in publicly disputing Westminster's right to legislate for Ireland. Instead, Anglican merchants, clerics and agricultural improvers asserted that trade restrictions frustrated the improving mission of 'English' colonists', making the Kingdom less useful to the empire as a whole. A residual Catholic aristocracy, represented by the antiquary Charles O'Conor and the philosophical politician Edmund Burke, began in the middle of the eighteenth century to place additional pressure on this Anglican discourse of 'improvement', challenging the Anglo-Irish and the British alike to recognise that the displaced Catholic elite was indispensable to the Kingdom's long-run stability and prosperity. Burke, in particular, offered a novel and quintessentially Enlightened argument against a system of legislation that sought to detach the Irish majority from the historical and sentimental foundations of both religious belief and political obligation.

If Molyneux's pamphlet failed in its attempt to convince the English parliament of the 1690s to resile from commercial legislation binding Ireland, meanwhile, the controversy it generated was remarkably effective in drawing outside attention to the significance of Ireland as a central example of the potential threat posed to Europe by Britain's mercantile empire. The constitutional subordination of a polity that was not a mere American colony, but a European realm, planted with English and Scottish co-religionists, attracted the notice of the most influential French analyst of the British system of commerce and government in the eighteenth century, the jurist and historian Montesquieu, in his *Spirit of the Laws* (1748). It also

---

[2] William Molyneux, *The Case of Ireland's Being Bound by Acts of Parliament in England Stated*, 2nd ed. (Dublin: Anon., 1706), 102.

formed a central part of the criticisms of Britain's 'mercantile system' levelled by the Scottish philosophers David Hume and Adam Smith. For Hume, Ireland illustrated a truth already asserted in Montesquieu's work: the empires established by 'free states' such as Britain rested ultimately on the systematic exclusion of peripheral territories from the fruits of metropolitan 'liberty'. For Smith, as for another influential critic of British commercial policy, the Welsh Anglican cleric Josiah Tucker, union with Ireland was a vital element of the fiscal and commercial reform necessary to enable Britain to both hold its position in a global rivalry with France and to stave off the dangers of a crisis of public credit.

It was Smith, alongside the English agrarian reformer Arthur Young, who took the crucial further step of joining the Scottish and French critique of Ireland's commercial subordination to Burke and O'Conor's arguments against the Penal Laws. Young's optimistic portrayal of the increasingly 'liberal' views of an improving Anglo-Irish aristocracy chimed with the increasing inclination among a rising faction of Irish 'Patriots' to relax some legal restraints on their Catholic countrymen. It was Smith's vision of an Enlightened union, however, that had the longer career ahead of it as a driver of imperial policy. Drawing on the deep intellectual resources of Scottish moral theory and philosophical history, Smith argued in the closing pages of his *Wealth of Nations* (1776) that Ireland possessed an aberrant form of social hierarchy that was incapable of sustaining a stable or prosperous commercial society. Scotland's experience of union, however, showed that integration within the English system of commerce and government could act as a solvent of such unchecked aristocratic power, offering new prospects to the 'middling and lower' ranks. Union was recast as a project not simply for the rationalisation of imperial trade and revenue but for the broader diffusion of the benefits of British commercial civilisation.

Conquest and Colonisation, 1542–1692

The system of religious and mercantile exclusion that was identified and criticised by would-be Enlightened reformers of the eighteenth-century Irish Kingdom was the product of a distended process of conquest and colonisation. English settlement in Ireland had begun as long ago as the twelfth century, with the incursion of a group of Anglo-Norman adventurers under the leadership of King Henry II in 1172. Serious attempts to place the entire island under the control of the English Crown had begun only with the creation of the Irish Kingdom, and with it the Church of

Ireland, by Henry VIII in 1542.[3] They intensified over nearly two centuries of plantation, rebellion and expropriation, as Ireland became a battleground for British and European wars of religion. By the end of the seventeenth century, a new group of settlers, the Anglican 'New English', had displaced a largely Catholic Gaelic and Anglo-Norman landholding class across much of Ireland, while a large influx of Presbyterian Scottish settlers had transformed the religious and ethnic composition of the northern province of Ulster. Choosing to conceptualise this tangle of wars, rebellions and land expropriations as a singular moment of 'conquest', the English parliament sitting at Westminster had repeatedly asserted its right to legislate on behalf of its Irish counterpart, so as to protect what it took to be the vital commercial and political interests of the imperial metropole.

The newly created Irish Kingdom was subject to a century of English attempts at assimilation from the 1550s, notionally directed against Gaelic customs, laws and culture but partially negotiated with an existing elite.[4] The intensification of plantation efforts in the last quarter of the century was driven by the persistent threat of the Spanish monarchy using Ireland as a springboard for an English invasion. Spanish armadas threatened the English coast in 1588, 1595 and 1596, and landed troops at Kinsale, County Cork, in 1601.[5] Early seventeenth-century settlement in Munster and Ulster followed the defeat of Irish insurgencies which enjoyed Spanish support, engaging significant sections of both English and Scottish society in projects to promote urban construction, English jurisdiction and profitable agriculture on captured Irish land.[6] The gradual extension of this strategy into parts of Clare and Connacht under Thomas Wentworth's viceroyalty (1633–41) was one of the key causes of the bloody Irish rebellion of 1641, which haunted confessional relations for centuries thereafter.[7]

---

[3] Brendan Bradshaw, *The Irish Constitutional Revolution of the Sixteenth Century* (Cambridge: Cambridge University Press, 1979).

[4] Ohlmeyer, 'Conquest, Civilization, Colonization', 21–48, at 34–5.

[5] Enrique García Hernán, *Ireland and Spain in the Reign of Philip II*, trans. Liam Liddy (Dublin: Four Courts Press, 2009), 138–229.

[6] Nicholas Canny, *Making Ireland British, 1580–1650* (Oxford: Oxford University Press, 2001), 121–6; Phil Withington, 'Plantation and Civil Society', in Éamonn Ó Ciardha and Micheál Ó Siochrú (eds.), *The Plantation of Ulster: Ideology and Practice* (Manchester: Manchester University Press, 2012), 55–75.

[7] Ohlmeyer, 'Conquest, Civilization, Colonization', 3; Hugh F. Kearney, *Strafford in Ireland, 1633–41: A Study in Absolutism* (Manchester: Manchester University Press, 1959), 90. On the legacies of the 1641 rebellion, see John Gibney, *The Shadow of a Year: The 1641 Rebellion in Irish History and Memory* (Madison: Wisconsin University Press, 2013).

The 1641 rebellion ushered in a second, more far-reaching phase of settlement, as confessional and ethnic conflict escalated in line with the breakdown in political and religious authority taking place across the Stuart Kingdoms.[8] Anglo-Scottish intervention in the Confederate Wars that followed the rebellion was notoriously brutal, spearheaded by the uncompromising military Puritanism of Cromwell's New Model Army. The defeat of the post-1641 Catholic regime by Cromwell and his general, Henry Ireton, was paid for with promises of rebel land; the Act of Settlement (1652) confirmed the wholesale transfer of both Gaelic and Old English property to the loyal 'New English'. The Act of Settlement stipulated that this dispossessed Catholic aristocracy were to be removed to marginal land in the western province of Connacht.[9] Two thousand Catholic landowners were relocated between 1655 and 1657, resulting in the redistribution of some 700,000 acres of land west of the Shannon.[10] A territorial and heritable notion of property rights had only recently – and tenuously – been established in Ireland, via the Tudor process of 'surrender and regrant', which had been used in the sixteenth century to consolidate royal authority over a Gaelic interior where Ireland's ancient systems of communal and clan property still ruled.[11] Now these new property rights were, in their turn, aggressively upended, in the name of religious uniformity and the punishment of rebellion.

The impact of the Cromwellian settlement on Ireland's Catholic gentry was dramatic. On a recent estimate, between 1641 and 1670 the proportion of Catholic ownership of agriculturally viable, privately held land dropped from 42 per cent to 16 per cent.[12] This shift was paralleled by an increase in estate size and concentration, encouraged by Restoration peerage creations.[13] William of Orange's defeat of the Catholic Jacobite regime (1689–91) terminated recurring Catholic attempts to claim back land held in 1641. It set in train another series of expropriations and

---

[8] Eamon Darcy, *The Irish Rebellion of 1641 and the Wars of the Three Kingdoms* (London: Royal Historical Society, 2013).

[9] Ohlmeyer, 'Conquest, Civilization, Colonization', 40.

[10] John Cunningham, *Conquest and Land in Ireland: The Transplantation to Connacht, 1649–1680* (London: Royal Historical Society, 2011), 98.

[11] Robert A. Houston, 'People, Space and Law in Late Medieval and Early Modern Britain and Ireland', *Past & Present*, 230 (2016), 47–89, at 84.

[12] Trinity College, Dublin, 'The Down Survey of Ireland: Mapping a Century of Change', www.downsurvey.tcd.ie/religion.php. Accessed 13 December 2020.

[13] Jane Ohlmeyer, *Making Ireland English: The Irish Aristocracy in the Seventeenth Century* (New Haven, CT: Yale University Press, 2012), 301–5.

regrants, further consolidating the social and political dominance of an Anglican landed aristocracy.[14]

The second half of the seventeenth century also witnessed the emergence of a distinctive Dissenting minority, the Presbyterian 'Ulster Scots', in the north and east of the island. Scottish settlers had played a central role in the Jacobean plantations of Ulster, and Scottish troops had been instrumental in the suppression of the Confederate rebellion of the 1640s. It was following the restoration of the Stuart dynasty in 1660, however, that mass Scottish settlement in eastern Ulster began in earnest. Emboldened by the military intervention of the William of Orange – a Dutch Calvinist – on behalf of the Protestant cause throughout the British Isles, Ulster Presbyterians had convened their own General Synod, on the model of the Scottish Kirk, in 1690.[15] They also played a significant role in the growing prosperity of late seventeenth-century Ireland, combining smallholding agriculture with the domestic spinning and weaving of linen cloth for export to England and the rest of Europe.[16]

Under Charles II's viceroy, James Butler, 1st Duke of Ormond, this consolidated Protestant aristocracy sought to vindicate their ideology of civilisation and plantation via the expansion of profitable agricultural cultivation, urban settlement and forms of proto-industry.[17] The 1660s also marked the beginnings of Ireland's incorporation into an evolving English system of mercantile regulation. Recurrent wars with the Dutch Republic marked the arrival of commercial rivalry, alongside confessional conflict and the fear of invasion, as the key driver of English policy. The regulation of the economic activities of the New English planters accordingly became an increasingly prominent component of Irish government. Alongside their exclusion of Ireland from the system of maritime regulation created by the Navigation Acts, English parliaments became increasingly vigilant in directly regulating Ireland's external trade, banning the direct import of North American tobacco and the export of live cattle.[18]

---

[14] Ibid., 334–5; John Gerald Simms, *The Williamite Confiscation in Ireland, 1690–1703* (London: Faber and Faber, 1956).

[15] Ian McBride, *Scripture Politics: Ulster Presbyterians and Irish Radicalism in the Late Eighteenth Century* (Oxford: Clarendon Press, 1998), 26–8.

[16] William H. Crawford, 'The Evolution of the Linen Trade in Ulster before Industrialization', *Irish Economic and Social History*, 15 (1988), 32–53.

[17] Ohlmeyer, *Making Ireland English*, 372–85.

[18] Carolyn A. Edie, 'The Irish Cattle Bills: A Study in Restoration Politics', *Transactions of the American Philosophical Society*, 60 (1970), 1–6; David Armitage, 'The Political Economy of Britain and Ireland after the Glorious Revolution', in Jane H. Ohlmeyer (ed.), *Political Thought*

In a 1673 memorandum to Ormond's successor, Arthur Capell, the English ambassador to the Netherlands, Sir William Temple, warned that in pursuing the Irish Kingdom's 'improvement', 'a regard must be had of those points wherein the trade of Ireland comes to interfere with any main branches of the trade of England'.[19]

The Case of Ireland and the Woollen Controversy

William Molyneux's *The Case of Ireland* was a product of the moment when the ambitions of Anglo-Irish 'improvement' decisively collided with those of the English mercantile empire. A founder, alongside the statistician William Petty, of the Dublin Philosophical Society, and a regular correspondent of John Locke, William Molyneux's primary intellectual passions lay in the field of natural philosophy.[20] His legal training, however, left him well equipped to both serve as an MP representing Trinity College Dublin in the Irish parliament and assist the Anglican Archbishop of Dublin, William King, in his attempts to dispute the appellate jurisdiction of the English House of Lords over Ireland.[21] Molyneux's decision to compose and publish *The Case of Ireland* in the spring of 1698 caused significant discomfort for both King and Locke, drawing the former into a bitter political controversy concerning the rights of the Irish parliament, and naming the latter – for the first time – as the author of the *Two Treatises of Government* (1689).[22] Molyneux's pamphlet attracted a number of highly critical responses from English Whigs, and it was ultimately condemned in the English parliament as 'of dangerous Consequence to the Crown and People of England'.[23] Uncomfortable though the controversy occasioned by *The Case of Ireland* may have been for its author and his associates, however, it served ultimately to clarify the status of the Irish

in *Seventeenth Century Ireland: Kingdom or Colony?* (Cambridge: Cambridge University Press, 2000), 221–43, at 227–9.
[19] William Temple, 'An Essay upon the Advancement of Trade in Ireland', in Thomas Courtney (ed.), *The Works of Sir William Temple*, 4 vols. (London: Rivington, 1814), III:1–28, at 9.
[20] Patrick H. Kelly, 'Molyneux (Molyneaux), William', in James McGuire and James Quinn (eds.), *Dictionary of Irish Biography* (Cambridge: Cambridge University Press, 2009), http://dib.cambridge.org/viewReadPage.do?articleId=a5878. Accessed 21 January 2020.
[21] Ian McBride, '*The Case of Ireland* (1698) in Context: William Molyneux and His Critics', *Proceedings of the Royal Irish Academy: Archaeology, Culture, History, Literature*, 118C (2018), 201–30, at 206.
[22] Patrick Kelly, 'Locke and Molyneux: The Anatomy of a Friendship', *Hermathena*, 126 (1979), 38–54.
[23] Kelly, 'Molyneux'.

Kingdom within an English mercantile empire that was locked in European warfare with the French monarchy.

Molyneux's pamphlet was directed against a gathering English campaign for the restriction of Irish exports of both raw and finished wool products.[24] The production of woollen cloth was an indispensable staple industry in early modern England, accounting for some 69 per cent of all exports in 1700. It supported the rental value of lands throughout England by maintaining demand for pasture on which sheep could be grazed, and provided extensive employment in the clothing trades.[25] As a consequence of the Dutch *Stadtholder* William of Orange's successful invasions of Stuart Kingdoms in 1688–92, England was now committed to a European war against the might of Louis XIV's France. A steady flow of gold and silver from exports was perceived to be essential to the preservation of England's currency and credit, as well as the tax revenues necessary to finance the war.[26]

Alarm about the state of England's woollen trades had first been sounded in a pamphlet published by the Bristol merchant John Cary, *An Essay on the State of England* (1695). In Cary's account, Ireland appeared as England's most dangerous commercial competitor. Only Ireland produced woollens of a quality comparable to that of England.[27] A survey of England's export markets by country revealed Ireland underselling England in Portugal, France and Spain across a range of products.[28] Cary, therefore, ranked Ireland with France and Holland as one of the few countries who were 'chiefly' able to 'cope with us in our Manufactures'.[29] The risk was that if the 'tools of trade' were taken by the Irish, England's navy and revenue would sink with them.[30] The best solution to Irish competition was to repeal earlier, Restoration-era laws banning the export of live cattle, restoring Irish agriculture at the expense of its textile industry. If Ireland was to have a textile industry, however, Cary wanted it to be in linen: 'the People of *England*', he observed, 'would delight to see *Ireland* thrive when their Manufactures crost not ours'.[31]

---

[24] Hugh Kearney, 'The Political Background to English Mercantilism, 1695–1700', *The Economic History Review*, 11(3) (1959), 484–96; Patrick Kelly, 'The Irish Woollen Export Prohibition Act of 1699: Kearney Re-visited', *Irish Economic and Social History*, 7 (1980), 22–44.

[25] Julian Hoppit, *Britain's Political Economies: Parliament and Economic Life, 1660–1800* (Cambridge: Cambridge University Press, 2017), 217.

[26] Carl Wennerlind, *Casualties of Credit: The English Financial Revolution 1620–1720* (Cambridge, MA: Harvard University Press), 126–41.

[27] John Cary, *An Essay on the State of England in Relation to Its Trade, Its Poor, and Its Taxes, for Carrying on the Present War against France by John Cary, Merchant in Bristol* (Bristol: W. Bonny, 1695), 10–11, 21–2, 38–40.

[28] Ibid., 117, 121, 129–30.   [29] Ibid., 133.   [30] Ibid., 92.   [31] Ibid., 110.

He demanded legislative intervention by the Westminster parliament to 'reduce it to the terms of a colony', compelled by English power to accept English regulation of its foreign commerce.[32]

Molyneux's argument against the restriction of Irish woollens flatly rejected the assertion that the Irish Kingdom could be compared to the other English colonies of the Atlantic. 'Does it not manifestly appear in the constitution of Ireland, that Ireland is a compleat kingdom within itself?', Molyneux demanded of Cary. 'Do English Kings call themselves Kings of Virginia, New England or Mary Land?'[33] Ireland, he asserted, had never been conquered or colonised: its medieval submission to the English Crown had been founded on consent, while subsequent wars had been fought between loyal Crown subjects and rebels. The continuity of the Irish Lordship and the Irish Kingdom had never, therefore, been fundamentally disrupted, even by warfare and expropriation on the scale experienced in the seventeenth century. The latter-day Anglo-Irish were the legitimate holders of lands that had been forfeited through the rebellion of Catholic and Gaelic subjects.[34]

Ireland was therefore, Molyneux urged, entitled to be treated as a realm equal to England within the British monarchy, in line with the principles of the 'law of nations'. Seeking to repress its trade by force, as a coda to what the English held to be a successful conquest, was akin to declaring war on the Crown's own loyal subjects in Ireland. Drawing on an argument first made in defence of the monopolising commercial treaties made by the Dutch East India Company by its chief publicist, the seventeenth-century natural lawyer Hugo Grotius, Molyneux claimed that simply being the first to secure an advantage in trade could never make a nation a legitimate object of warfare. 'I cannot by the Law of Nations, quarrel with a Man, because he, going before me in the Road, finds a Piece of Gold, which possibly if he had not taken it up, I might have light upon and gotten', Molyneux claimed. ''Tis true, we often see Wars commenced not his Account *under hand*, and on Emulation in Trade and Riches, but then this is never made the *Open Pretence*; some other *Colour* it must receive, or else it would not look *fair*.'[35]

Molyneux's plea that the English parliament observe at least the superficial forms of the 'law of nations' in dealing with Ireland, however, was dismissed out of hand. As Cary observed, the principal difference between

[32] Ibid., 114.   [33] Molyneux, *The Case of Ireland*, 144–5.   [34] Ibid., 39, 139–41.
[35] Ibid., 143–4; cf. Hugo Grotius, *The Rights of War and Peace*, ed. Richard Tuck (Indianapolis, IN: Liberty Fund, 2012), II.2.13.5.

the Irish and England's other commercial rivals was that 'it lies in our Power to give Rules to them'.[36] Defenders of Ireland's parliament and trade who sought to avoid the pitfalls of Molyneux's strategy of constitutional confrontation had little choice but to engage the English on their chosen grounds of political and mercantile interest. In his own contribution to the pamphlet controversy the County Down barrister and MP Francis Annesley accordingly characterised the English ban on woollens as imprudent policy, likely to destabilise the English colony in Ireland. Annesley accepted the English argument that Ireland had been conquered but made an artful distinction between 'Colonies for Trade, and Colonies for Empire'. The former relied on strict commercial control because they existed either to 'plant Commodities which your native Country does not produce, as in the West-Indies' or 'to negotiate a trade with the Natives, and build Forts for their security, as in Africa and the East-Indies'. Ireland, however, had been planted with settlers as a means of territorial subjection, designed to 'prevent the charge and hazard of constant Standing Armies'.[37] Since the goal of English rule in Ireland was territorial security, it was inappropriate to restrict Irish trade. This would weaken the loyalty of Protestant settlers and reduce their ability to govern the Catholic majority.[38]

Writing in 1703, Henry Maxwell, another Irish MP from County Down, took this argument one stage further. In a pamphlet published at Dublin and London to coincide with an Anglo-Irish push for parliamentary union, itself timed to coincide with the beginnings of Union negotiations with Scotland, Maxwell repeated Annesley's point that the purpose of colonisation was to avoid the 'danger and expense' of standing armies in the government of a territory. He wrote as the archetypal 'Commonwealthman', opposed to Queen Anne's Tory ministry, and warned that no free state could afford to keep an imperial possession on its borders in subjection by a standing military force.[39] Maxwell's pamphlet also contained a more innovative economic argument, however, that would be reiterated in subsequent debates over the reform of Anglo-Irish trade. For John Cary, as for other English advocates of Irish trade

---

[36] Cary, *Essay*, 133.
[37] Frances Annesley, *Some Thoughts on the Bill, Depending before the Right Honourable the House of Lords, for Prohibiting the Exportation of the Woollen Manufactures of Ireland to Foreign Parts* (London: J. Darby, 1698), 9.
[38] Ibid., 7–8.
[39] Henry Maxwell, *An Essay upon an Union of Ireland with England* (Dublin: Eliphal Dobson, 1704), 8; see also David Hayton, '"Commonwealthman", Unionist and King's Servant: Henry Maxwell and the Whig Imperative', in *The Anglo-Irish Experience, 1680–1730: Religion, Identity and Patriotism* (Woodbridge: Boydell & Brewer, 2012), 104–23, at 108–10.

restriction, Ireland's low wage costs were the key reason for action against its textile industries.[40] Maxwell's pamphlet turned these English arguments in favour of a case for an Anglo-Irish union. Integrating the markets of England and Ireland would make the smuggling trade in raw wool to Holland and France unprofitable by permitting the manufacture of finished cloth in Ireland.[41] Cheap Irish provisions and migrant labour would flood in to England, lowering the costs of English manufactures and ensuring the union-state's permanent dominance in European markets. Union would allow England to benefit from Ireland's poverty and low wages and triumph in European trade competition against Holland and France.

The Declaratory Act (1720) and the Penal Laws (1695–1728)

At least at the start of the eighteenth century, English opinion took little notice of these Anglo-Irish speculations about the potential benefits of a parliamentary union.[42] The Westminster parliament, instead, moved to give decisive legal weight to English assertions of Ireland's subordinate status within what was now, following the Anglo-Scottish Union of 1707, a British empire. In 1720, it resolved a recurring dispute over whether the Lords of Ireland or those of Great Britain were the location of ultimate appellate jurisdiction by passing a 'Declaratory Act'. Like its famous American analogue of 1765, this proclaimed Westminster's superior authority in all matters over Dublin.[43] For much of the eighteenth century, England continued to claim this right of superiority via a precedent of conquest. The leading legal authority of mid-eighteenth-century England, Sir William Blackstone, laid down in his *Commentaries on the Laws of England* (1767) that 'Ireland ... conquered, planted, and governed, still continues in a state of dependence; it must necessarily conform to, and be obliged by, such laws as the superior state thinks proper to

[40] Hont, '"Rich Country-Poor Country" Debate Revisited', 250–3.

[41] Maxwell, *Essay upon an Union of Ireland*, 19–20.

[42] David Hayton, 'Ideas of Union in Anglo-Irish Political Discourse, 1692–1720: Meaning and Use', in D. George Boyce, Robert Eccleshall, and Vincent Geoghegan (eds.), *Political Discourse in Seventeenth and Eighteenth-Century Ireland* (Basingstoke: Palgrave, 2001), 142–69; Jacqueline Hill, 'Ireland without Union: Molyneux and His Legacy', in John Robertson (ed.), *A Union for Empire: Political Thought and the British Union of 1707* (Cambridge: Cambridge University Press, 1995).

[43] Martin Flaherty, 'The Empire Strikes Back: Annesley v. Sherlock and the Triumph of Imperial Parliamentary Supremacy', *Columbia Law Review*, 87(3) (1987), 593–622.

prescribe'.[44] Down to the highly unpopular imposition of an embargo on Irish provisioning exports to the British Caribbean in 1776, the British parliament continued to regulate Irish trade in accordance with shifting conceptions of the economic interest of the metropole.

The Anglo-Irish themselves, meanwhile, sought to stabilise the seventeenth-century property order via the Penal Laws, a series of statutes passed between the 1695 and 1728 and periodically revisited thereafter.[45] The statutes were not conceived as a single system, but they cumulatively impacted nearly every aspect of Catholic life and religious practice, banning proselytism, intermarriage and continental contacts, and denying access to property, the franchise, arms, the professions and formal education.[46] The measure that acted most transparently to secure the land settlement was the 'Act to Prevent the Further Growth of Popery' (1704), which prevented Catholics from inheriting from Protestants, acquiring land by purchase or leasing land for more than thirty-one years. It also subjected surviving Catholic estates to partitive inheritance, facilitating their breakup and sale into Anglican hands. The first Anglican convert within a Catholic landed family was permitted to claim an estate in its entirety, rendering his siblings and parents his tenants.[47]

The penal legislation grew out of a series of bargains between an Anglican-dominated Irish parliament and English ministries.[48] They reflected a reality obscured by the contest over Irish woollen exports the increasing importance of the Irish parliament in the government of the Kingdom. The law-making powers of the Irish parliament – as its Irish defenders would complain throughout the eighteenth century – were formally compromised by the provisions of Poynings' Law (1494), which limited its formal capacity to initiate legislation, and enabled the review and amendment of Irish bills by the British Privy Council. The granting of a permanent 'hereditary revenue' to Charles II had similarly ensured that the Irish parliament, unlike its English counterpart, was not the exclusive guardian of Irish taxation. The sheer quantity of revenue required during

---

[44] William Blackstone, *Commentaries on the Laws of England*, 12th ed., 4 vols. (London: T. Cadell, 1793), 99.

[45] McBride, *Eighteenth Century Ireland: The Isle of Slaves* (Dublin: Gill & Macmillan, 2009), 195.

[46] Sean J. Connolly, *Religion, Law and Power: The Making of Protestant Ireland, 1660–1760* (Oxford: Oxford University Press, 1992), 263–4.

[47] W. N. Osborough, 'Catholics, Land and the Popery Acts of Anne', in T. P. Power and Kevin Whelan (eds.), *Endurance and Emergence: Catholics in Ireland in the Eighteenth Century* (Dublin: Irish Academic Press, 1990), 21–56.

[48] Ultán Gillen, 'Ascendancy Ireland, 1660–1800', in Bourke and McBride (eds.), *Princeton History of Modern Ireland*, 48–74.

the wars against Louis XIV, however, meant that Irish Lord Lieutenants had found it necessary to regularly seek additional funds from the Dublin parliament. It was no longer possible for them to bypass the parliament entirely, as their Stuart predecessors had done.[49] In 1695, meanwhile, intense English hostility to 'standing armies' had led to a political compromise with William III, under which a permanent force of 15,000 men was maintained on the Irish rather than the English establishment. The arrangement would persist throughout the eighteenth century, ensuring Ireland a significant place in a 'fiscal-military' state that was imperial in scope.[50] Just seven years after its supposed humbling by the passing of the Declaratory Act, the Irish parliament decided to construct for itself Europe's first purpose-built legislature: a grand neoclassical domed chamber on Dublin's College Green. Formal dependence on England could readily be reconciled with a growing political confidence among the members of Ireland's Anglican oligarchy.[51]

'Improvement' and the Catholic Question

The passage of the Declaratory Act drew a line under the Irish constitutional and confessional conflicts that had dominated the Kingdom's politics in the era of William and Anne. The 1720s and 1730s were marked, instead, by a series of famines and currency crises.[52] The 'Wood's halfpence' controversy, set in motion by the Irish administration's decision to grant a license for the private minting of copper coinage, provoked the famous satirist and Dean of Dublin Cathedral, Jonathan Swift, to revive Molyneux's constitutional invective in his incendiary *Drapier's Letters* (1724–5). More typical of contemporary Anglo-Irish attitudes, however, was Arthur Dobbs' *Essay on the Trade and Improvement of Ireland* (1729–32). Dobbs, an Antrim MP and landlord who would later serve as the Governor of North Carolina, echoed Maxwell's argument for a parliamentary union that would strengthen Britain's commercial empire. The Irish aristocracy's preference for residing in London and purchasing the foreign luxuries traded by English merchants would guarantee that the gains from growing Irish trade would be equitably shared with England.

[49] Connolly, *Religion, Law and Power*, 267.
[50] Patrick Walsh, 'The Fiscal State in Ireland, 1691–1769', *The Historical Journal*, 56 (2013), 629–56.
[51] Patrick Walsh, *The Making of the Irish Protestant Ascendancy: The Life of William Conolly, 1662–1729* (Woodbridge: Boydell & Brewer, 2010), 3, 156.
[52] Louis Cullen, 'Economic Development, 1691–1750', in Moody and Vaughan (eds.), *New History of Ireland IV*, 130–59, at 140–5.

'Upon an Union with *England* and Inlargement of the Trade of *Ireland*', Dobbs claimed, 'all the acquired Wealth that *Ireland* would have from a constant and regular Employment of their industrious Poor, would be pour'd into *England* by the Rich'.[53]

In the continuing absence of any British interest in revisiting the constitutional settlement so recently confirmed by the Declaratory Act, however, there was a gradual convergence of Irish political aspirations around a virtuous project of collective self-reform. The shift in tone was heralded by Robert Molesworth's celebrated pamphlet *Considerations for Promoting Agriculture* (1723). Molesworth, an erstwhile Whig politician who staunchly believed in the rights of the Irish parliament, praised his contemporaries for their condemnation of Wood's halfpence but cautioned them that the 'Oeconomy of Agriculture' should not be 'thought below the consideration of the higher Ranks among us'.[54] The vogue for agricultural improvement also promoted a *rapprochement* between Anglicans and Ulster Presbyterians active in Dublin's thriving literary and philosophical scene.[55] The success of the *Dublin Journal,* published under Molesworth's patronage by the reformist 'New Light' Presbyterians James Arbuckle and Frances Hutcheson, was a key indicator of the broader shift in Irish political culture: away from the patriotic invective of Molyneux and Swift, and towards the cultivation of a more personal virtue. 'It is certainly much more laudable to inspire men with noble and generous Sentiments', the journal's editors observed in their first edition, 'than it is to fill their Heads with a set of Notions that are of little other Use, than to be evaporated in a Coffee-house'.[56]

Church of Ireland prelates, including major figures such as William King, Edward Synge and George Berkeley, were themselves major landholders and took the obligations of diocesan residence seriously. This enabled them to combine agricultural innovation with moral instruction and parochial reform for their tenants and clergy.[57] In Swift, these clerical

---

[53] Arthur Dobbs, *An Essay on the Trade and Improvement of Ireland*, 2 vols. (Dublin: J. Smith & W. Bruce, 1729), I:70.

[54] Robert Molesworth, *Some Considerations for the Promoting of Agriculture, and Employing the Poor* (Dublin: George Grierson, 1723), 3.

[55] Ian McBride, 'The School of Virtue: Francis Hutcheson, Irish Presbyterians and the Scottish Enlightenment', in D. George Boyce, Robert Eccleshall and Vincent Geoghegan (eds.), *Political Thought in Ireland since the Seventeenth Century* (London: Routledge, 1993).

[56] David Arbuckle (ed.), *A Collection of Letters and Essays on Several Subjects, Lately Publish'd in The Dublin Journal*, 2 vols. (London: J. Darby and T. Browne, 1729), I:5–6.

[57] Toby C. Barnard, *Irish Protestant Ascents and Descents, 1641–1779* (Dublin: Four Courts, 2004), 318–19.

champions of Irish improvement gained a potent critic of what they took
to be the Kingdom's lazy and exploitative landholders, who sought easy
profits through the pursuit of cattle grazing rather than supporting rural
population and staving off famine through the development of tillage
agriculture.[58] For the clerical and intellectual leaders of the improving
movement and those landholders who followed them, the endowment of
new institutions, including charity schools, workhouses, churches, libraries
and hospitals, in Ireland as in England, became an increasingly important
means of demonstrating both status and piety. The foundation of the
Dublin Society in 1731 complemented and expanded these efforts.
Meeting in Trinity College Dublin and founded by gentleman-farmers
from Laois, Fermanagh and Antrim, this was a broad-based improving
association, dedicated to the diffusion of 'useful knowledge', the sponsor-
ship of new manufactures and the promotion of agricultural competitions.[59] By the 1750s, a gathering Irish economic recovery, driven by
exports of linen and provisions, was attracting attention to the Society's
activities outside the British Isles. The first of many regional economic
societies founded in eighteenth-century France, the Breton *Société d'agriculture, du commerce et des arts*, was founded in 1757 in direct emulation of
the Dublin Society.[60]

The agrarian focus of the new vogue for improvement, alongside its
rhetoric of disinterested patriotism and virtue, created a vital opening for
the residual interests of the displaced Catholic aristocracy to join Anglicans
and Presbyterians in the discussion of Irish political economy. In spite of
the low volume of Catholic landownership and the exclusion of Catholics
from urban corporations, Catholic land agents, alongside a growing merchant class benefiting from continental contacts, continued to enjoy
significant informal influence in the eighteenth-century Irish Kingdom.[61]
According to one famous interpretation, the descendants of many former
Catholic landlords assumed head-tenant and land agent functions on
behalf of their Protestant expropriators, forming 'an underground

[58] Ian McBride, 'The Politics of *A Modest Proposal*: Swift and the Irish Crisis of the Late 1720s', *Past & Present*, 244(1) (2019), 89–122.
[59] James Livesey, 'The Dublin Society in Eighteenth-Century Irish Political Thought', *The Historical Journal*, 47 (2004), 615–40.
[60] John Shovlin, 'The Society of Brittany and the Irish Economic Model: International Competition and the Politics of Provincial Development', in Koen Stapelbroek and Jani Marjanen (eds.), *The Rise of Economic Societies in the Eighteenth Century: Patriotic Reform in Europe and North America* (Basingstoke: Palgrave Macmillan, 2012), 73–96.
[61] McBride, *Eighteenth Century Ireland*, 216–20.

gentry'.[62] The very complexity of the Penal legislation ensured that it was easy to manipulate and difficult to enforce. Prominent figures in national politics and large landowners, such as the influential Speaker of the Irish Commons, William Connolly, and the O'Haras, a powerful Sligo political dynasty, hailed from families of recent Catholic converts to Anglicanism but retained loyalties to the political interests of the majority population.

By the middle of the eighteenth century, this mixed and resilient Catholic social constituency had begun to organise itself politically to petition for the relaxation of a range of anti-Catholic legislation. The most prominent spokesman for the Catholic Committee formed in 1756 was Charles O'Conor of Belanagare, an Irish language scholar, Roscommon landlord and scion of a Connacht family tracing its descent to the medieval Gaelic kings of the province. In his *Case of the Roman-Catholics of Ireland* (1755), O'Conor reconfigured the Anglo-Irish discourse of improvement to highlight the iniquities of the most notorious measure regarding landed property, the 'Act to Prevent the Further growth of Popery' (1704). Pleading the loyalty of Catholic Ireland during the 1745 Jacobite rebellion and the Church's repeated injunctions of obedience to temporal authority, O'Conor urged Protestants to consider that the Penal Laws themselves – particularly as they applied to the ownership of property – were a significant obstacle to the agricultural progress of the Kingdom.[63] O'Conor praised the disinterested and ecumenical character of the Irish movement of improving landlords, which he associated with the accession of the Hanoverians and the 'German Spirit of Toleration'. Under a 'Whiggish administration', it was possible for sectarian animosity to give way in favour of common utility. 'Associations to this Purpose were formed: particularly that noble Source of all, the DUBLIN-SOCIETY; whose Encouragement of every *useful* Art hath been confined to *no Party*, or *Religion*'.[64]

With his improving bona fides thus established, O'Conor moved into a more substantive discussion of Irish political economy. He claimed that the Penal Laws lay at the root of Ireland's recurring currency and subsistence crises, producing a national economy that was excessively skewed towards linen production and pastoral agriculture. Like Swift and Berkeley, O'Conor argued that prosperity that lacked a secure basis in

---

[62] Kevin Whelan, 'An Underground Gentry? Catholic Middlemen in Eighteenth-Century Ireland', *Eighteenth-Century Ireland: Iris an dá chultúr*, 10 (1995).

[63] Charles O'Conor, *The Case of the Roman-Catholics of Ireland, Wherein the Principles and Conduct of That Party Are Fully Explained and Vindicated*, 3rd ed. (Dublin: P. Lord, 1756), 42–5.

[64] Ibid., 47.

tillage was illusory. In good years, it 'furnished us with the Specie to purchase the *Luxuries*, and even the *Corn* of other countries', but could not do so when export markets turned against Ireland. O'Conor blamed Ireland's continuing dependence on corn imports on laws limiting the length of Catholic tenures. 'It is evident to *Demonstration*', he argued, 'that such an Occupation as the Improvement of Land is *no Way suited* to a *transient and insecure* interest, but that the wasteful Method of pasturage *is so*'.[65]

Just as the Penal laws interfered with agricultural production and the stability of food supplies, they also militated against that other great priority of the eighteenth-century state: the cultivation of a healthy and growing population. Partitive inheritance and the conferral of estates on Protestant descendants prevented wealthier Catholics – whether merchants or land agents – from fixing their property in land. The Penal Laws O'Conor warned, 'tempt them, above all other People, to quit a Country with which they have but little *Connexion*, and retire into some other with the Prospect of a more *benign* Climate, and a more *ascertained Property*'. This, too, was inimical to imperial interests: Catholic emigrants were leaving 'to strengthen our Rivals, and natural Enemies with our *Seamen*, our *Manufactures*, and our *Specie*'.[66] Not only the logic of agricultural improvement, therefore, but also that of international competition for population and resources, demanded the revision of Ireland's anti-Catholic legislation.

The Catholic Committee's campaign attracted the support of a rising Irish literary and philosophical talent, Edmund Burke, in the course of the 1760s. As the descendant of a long line of County Cork Catholics, Burke had an acute awareness of the long-run effects of the seventeenth-century confiscations on Irish society.[67] In the 1760s, while working as an advisor to the Irish Chief Secretary, William Hamilton, Burke cultivated a connection with O'Conor and the Catholic Committee through his friend and correspondent Charles O'Hara, an Irish MP and another child of Catholic converts to Anglicanism.[68] In 1764, he drafted an 'Address and Petition' to George III on behalf of the Committee, which was taken up again and presented to the Lord Lieutenant in 1777, as the North

---

[65] Ibid., 56.   [66] Ibid., 56–7.
[67] On Burke's Catholic family in County Cork, see Richard Bourke, *Empire and Revolution: The Political Life of Edmund Burke* (Princeton, NJ: Princeton University Press), 27–44.
[68] Ibid., 33, 213–15.

administration contemplated the repeal of the 1704 Act. Like O'Conor, Burke defined the Catholic community in terms of their potential contribution to 'improvement'.[69] The Penal Laws disrupted the healthy functioning of Irish society at every level, compromising the Kingdom's utility as an imperial territory. 'The stock of materials, by which any nation is rendered flourishing and prosperous', he observed in his unpublished 'Tracts Relating to the Popery Laws' (1765):

> are its industry; its knowledge or skill; its morals; its execution; its courage; and the national union in directing these powers to one point and making them all center in the publick benefit ... If we shew that these Penal Laws of Ireland destroy not one only, but every one of these materials of publick prosperity, it will not be difficult to perceive that Great Britain, whilst they subsist, never can draw from that Country all the advantages, to which the bounty of Nature has entitled it.[70]

Under the terms of the 1704 Act, any son could disinherit their father and alienate their estate at a stroke, 'contrary to the order of nature', if they only converted to Anglicanism. The combination of the preference for converts with the law of gavelkind for Catholic inheritance provided a powerful additional incentive for 'the first conformist' to disinherit their siblings on the death of the parent.[71] By undermining Catholic gentry families and generating constant insecurity of property and tenure alike, the Penal Laws struck at the foundation of social order itself, with effects that could be seen in the 'Whiteboy' agrarian violence that spread across southern Ireland in the early 1760s.[72]

Obedience to legislation, Burke claimed, was owed by the governed as an 'act of homage and just deference to a reason which the necessity of Government mas made superior to their own'. It was not necessary that the purpose of legislation was understood by every subject in every instance; but there was no one in Ireland, Burke observed, who was 'so gross and stupid' to regard the provisions of the Penal Laws as conferring 'benefits' on the population. There could be no consent, even 'implied', to legislation that was so clearly vindictive in its intention.[73]

---

[69] Edmund Burke, 'Address and Petition of the Irish Catholics', in R. B. McDowell (ed.), *The Writings and Speeches of Edmund Burke*, 10 vols. (Oxford: Clarendon Press, 1991), IX:429–34, at 430.

[70] Edmund Burke, 'Tracts Relating to the Popery Laws', in McDowell (ed.), *Writings and Speeches*, IX:434–82, at 476.

[71] Burke, 'Address and Petition', 431.

[72] Ibid., 477–8. On Burke's response to the Whiteboy agitation, Bourke, *Edmund Burke*, 212–14.

[73] Burke, 'Address and Petition', 456.

The fundamental purpose of Penal legislation, Burke meanwhile argued, was the uprooting of an old and established religion that commanded the continuing assent of the vast majority of the Irish population. Here, Burke's position owed obvious debts to both John Locke and David Hume, both of whom had written on what they took to be a general human predisposition towards reverence for established authority and opinions.[74] 'It is proper to recollect', Burke observed, 'that this Religion which is so persecuted in its Members, is the old Religion of the Country, and the once Established Religion of the State; the very same which had for centuries received the countenance and sanction of the Laws'. The earliest conquests of Ireland, Burke ironically observed, had been undertaken under a commission from Pope Adrian IV in order to better subject Ireland to papal authority, which was then 'much lower in Ireland than in other Countries'. After many centuries of warfare and plantation inspired by that initial, incomplete incursion into Ireland, the English had inflicted an about-turn on the Irish, adopting a new and 'oppressive system ... to eradicate opinions, why by the same violent means they had been four hundred years endeavouring by every means to establish'.[75]

This situation produced a strange inversion of commonplace arguments concerning the merits and dangers of religious toleration. It was possible, though 'specious', to consider the repression of new religious sects as a prophylactic against the contagion of dissent and violence. To use the coercive power of law to detach an entire people from an established set of beliefs, however, was quite a different proposition. Established religious opinions, like political authority itself, were the product of inheritance. 'It is in the nature of man rather to defer to the wisdom of times passed, whose weakness is not before his eyes, than to the present, of whose imbecility he has daily experience', Burke observed.

> When therefore an Establishment would persecute an opinion in possession, it sets against it all the powerful prejudices of human nature. It even sets its own authority when it is of most weight, against itself in that very circumstance in which it must necessarily have the least; and it opposes the stable prejudice of time against a new opinion founded on mutability; a consideration that must render compulsion in such a case the more grievous, as there is no security that when the mind is settled in the new opinion, it may not be obliged to give place to one that is still newer, or even to a return of the old.[76]

---

[74] Bourke, *Edmund Burke*, 222.   [75] Burke, 'Address and Petition', 470–1.   [76] Ibid., 467.

To seek 'improvement' through enforced religious uniformity was to undermine the real foundations of 'civil society', in the service of a conception of the public interest that was demonstrably disingenuous. By blending 'general persecution with partial reformation', English government in Ireland had done nothing to change the religious opinions of the Irish majority, while excluding them from the benefits of property and protection. It had, thereby, rendered Protestant belief 'noxious' by association. 'If this be improvement', Burke wryly observed, 'truly I know not what can be called a deprivation of society'.[77] It was mere factional posturing that attributed Irish discontents to an underlying tendency towards violence: 'politicks' and 'science' taught that 'the real danger to every State' lay in the persistent application of laws that were seemingly designed 'to render its subjects justly discontented'.[78]

Burke's allusion to 'politicks' and 'science' as the authority for his judgement on the Penal Laws is suggestive of the power of the new theories of politics generated by the European Enlightenment to inspire demands for the reform of empire. The Anglo-Irish political economy of the mid-eighteenth century had envisaged contained and discrete projects for the advancement of Irish trade, agriculture and finance – projects that did not necessarily impinge on the Kingdom's underlying dispensation of political and landed power. As O'Conor argued, they were 'Enlightened' insofar as they involved the purposeful pursuit of public utility under the auspices of new institutions like the Dublin Society, who sought non-sectarian forms of sociability alongside the international exchange of practical and scientific knowledge necessary for the cultivation of agriculture and manufactures.

While they employed a similar rhetoric of improvement, O'Conor and Burke's writings on the Penal Laws argued on the basis of a different and more far-reaching set of propositions concerning the foundations of political obligation. They argued in the strongest terms for the dependence of material 'improvement' on a more expansive form of social peace – something that could only be ensured via a significantly wider distribution of landed property among the Kingdom's Catholic majority. Burke's perspective on the problem of 'improvement', informed by his wide reading in contemporary philosophy and jurisprudence, connected it to Enlightenment reflections on the role of sentiment and opinion in the reproduction of political authority over time. They suggested a potential for discussions of Irish government to move beyond the problematics of conquest and consent suggested by Molyneux's *Case of Ireland*, and its

---

[77] Ibid., 468.   [78] Ibid., 479.

rejection by his English critics. It was the philosophical analysis of the mutual interactions of property, wealth and authority that held the key to the re-foundation of British authority in eighteenth-century Ireland.

Montesquieu, Hume, Smith and Tucker on Ireland and 'Jealousy of Trade'

While Burke and O'Conor were composing their critical reflections on Ireland's landed settlement, Franco-British conflict once again became the central feature of European politics. During the War of the Austrian Succession (1740–8) and the Seven Years' War (1757–63), inter-imperial rivalry was a spur to intellectual innovation in the comparative economic and political analysis of European societies. Both Ireland's commercial subordination to Westminster, and its sectarian landed settlement, were examined within this broader European framework – not for what they might tell observers about Ireland, but for what they might explain or illuminate regarding the character and likely future of Britain's expanding commercial empire. By the onset of the War of American Independence (1776–83), British thinkers including David Hume, Josiah Tucker and Adam Smith had developed a powerful critique of English 'jealousy of trade', of which the Irish woollen legislation was the axiomatic demonstration. Their reflections were embedded in a broader analysis of the nature of the British constitution and its ability to preserve civil liberty under conditions of mercantile empire and military competition. This centred on a downplaying of its similarities to the Roman republic of old, and an accentuation of its modern character as a vessel for an egalitarian commercial society, and for a centralised form of power centred on the authority of the Crown and its ministers.

The originator of this fresh line of thinking regarding Britain and its empire was Montesquieu. The French jurist's ambivalent analysis of the 'English' constitution of liberty had important implications for contemporary understandings of the government of Ireland. In *The Spirit of the Laws* (1748), Montesquieu gave a short and incisive account of Ireland's constitutional and commercial subordination:

> It could be that it [England] had formerly subjugated a neighbouring nation which, by its situation, the goodness of its ports, and the nature of its wealth, made the first jealous; thus, although it had given that nation its own laws, the laws of a free people, the great dependence in which the nation was held was such that the citizens there would be free and the state itself would be enslaved.

> The conquered state would have a very good civil government, but it would be crushed by the right of nations; the laws imposed upon it from one nation to another would be such that its prosperity would be only precarious and only a deposit for a master.[79]

As a subjugated neighbour, Ireland clearly occupied an exceptional position within Britain's mercantile and maritime empire. Montesquieu claimed that this was fundamentally peaceful. Against contemporary French thinkers such as Jean-Francois Melon and the Vincent de Gournay, Montesquieu did not present Britain's mercantile empire as an object of emulation or threat, but as a product of the polity's unique, underlying commitment to liberty and commerce. Britain had founded colonies in America and the Caribbean 'to extend its commerce more than its domination'. Britain's reliance on maritime over landed power, alongside its relative invulnerability to invasion, ensured that it would remain 'the centre of negotiations in Europe', rather than a conquering hegemon.[80]

Ireland formed an exception to this general pattern: conquered and held subject in the interests of commercial 'jealousy'. In asserting that England had given Ireland 'its own laws', Montesquieu signalled that the conquest was more intensive than the mere acquisition of territory. Most modern conquerors, he had asserted in the tenth book of *The Spirit of the Laws*, were satisfied with the mere 'exercise of the political and civil government'; the English, by contrast, had followed the Romans in imposing 'new civil and political government', analogous to their own, on a conquered territory.[81] Montesquieu regarded England's mixed constitution as the fortuitous, but fragile, result of 'impotent attempts to establish democracy' during the seventeenth century.[82] English liberty was a product of the centre, dependent on the leniency of English criminal procedures and the virtue of the legislature rather than the checks to sovereignty provided by the French *parlements* and seigneurial jurisdictions. The republican experiment of the Interregnum had succeeded in eradicating the intermediary ranks and powers that gave monarchy its social form, while encouraging a commitment to a fusion of civil and military power that was characteristic of republics. England could, therefore, be viewed as a 'republic disguised as a monarchy'.[83] Its treatment of Ireland was a testament to this fact. The

---

[79] Charles de Secondat, Baron de la Brède et de Montesquieu, *The Spirit of the Laws*, trans. Anne M. Cohler, Basia Carolyn Miller and Harold Samuel Stone (Cambridge: Cambridge University Press, 1989), 329.
[80] Ibid., 328–9.   [81] Ibid., 139, 144.   [82] Ibid., 22.   [83] Ibid., 19, 70.

empire exercised by a republic, Montesquieu observed, 'is harsher than monarchy, as the experience of all times and all countries has shown'.[84]

England's fractious political culture explained the commercial jealousy that had led Ireland to be 'crushed by the right of nations'. Its origins lay in the deep structures of English politics: the existence of 'two visible powers', Crown and parliament, in the state; and the political competition around them, which instituted an opposition always ready to exploit fears that the country would lose its liberty, either from the domestic ambition of a king or minister or from the machinations of a foreign power.[85] As William's ministers had experienced during the anti-Irish agitation of the 1690s, all the fevered anxiety of Country Party rhetoric could potentially be applied to the nation's interest in trade. England was able to 'offend and be offended in an infinity of ways ... its laws, otherwise gentle and easy, might be so rigid in regard to the commerce and navigation carried on with it that it would seem to negotiate only with enemies'.[86] In a free state, the endless tussle of interest groups and political factions over the terms of trade naturally produced an intensive regime of mercantile regulation. 'It is in countries of liberty', Montesquieu observed elsewhere, 'that the trader finds innumerable obstacles; the laws never thwart him less than in countries of servitude'.[87]

In mid-century Britain, the two leading critics of this system of commercial jealousy and zealous patriotism were the Scottish philosopher David Hume and the Welsh cleric Josiah Tucker.[88] In his 1741 essay 'That Politics May Be Reduced to a Science,' Hume represented the Irish example as the embodiment of an important truth about the power dynamics of 'free states' such as England. These treated subordinate states far more harshly than monarchies, since in a monarchy all subjects are equally subordinate to the King. 'Compare the *Pais conquis* of France with Ireland', Hume urged, 'and you will be convinced of this truth'.[89] England's treatment of Ireland furnished an important support to Hume's argument that civilised, law-bound monarchies – like that of France – could promote liberty as effectively as the post-1688 English political order.[90]

---

[84] Ibid., 144.   [85] Ibid., 325.   [86] Ibid., 328.   [87] Ibid., 345.

[88] On the growing uncertainty regarding England's commercial system that took hold following the War of the Austrian Succession, see Bob Harris, *Politics and the Nation: Britain in the Mid-Eighteenth Century* (Oxford: Oxford University Press, 2002), 33–77.

[89] David Hume, 'That Politics May Be Reduced to a Science', in Eugene F. Miller (ed.), *Essays Moral, Political and Literary* (Indianapolis, IN: Liberty Fund, 1985), 14–32, at 18–19.

[90] David Hume, 'Of Civil Liberty', in Miller (ed.), *Essays Moral, Political and Literary*, 87–97, at 94.

Unlike Montesquieu, however, Hume saw the Irish case as emblematic of the short-sightedness, rather than the vigour, of English commercial empire. In his essay 'Of the Jealousy of Trade' (1752), Hume argued that the sincere patriot should wish for the prosperity of neighbouring nations, since competitive emulation could drive the improvement of all. The wool industry, protected in England and suppressed in Ireland, should not be favoured: if England could not maintain its staple export in open market competition, then it was time to abandon it and develop alternatives.[91] Hume accepted the validity of the English argument that, under open trading conditions, manufacturing industry would migrate to areas where wage costs were lower. Scotland could hope to benefit from this mechanism via the 1707 Union with England, while Ireland, 'peopled from England, possesses so many rights and privileges as should naturally make it challenge better treatment than that of a conquered province'.[92]

For Hume's contemporary, Josiah Tucker, the simple removal of constraints on Irish trade was not a sufficient answer to the growing challenges facing Britain's mercantile empire. His *Essay on the Advantages and Disadvantages Which Respectively Attend France and Great Britain, with Regard to Trade* (1750) offered a disturbing argument about Britain's inability to compete with a French monarchy that was methodically applying the science of commercial greatness to its own domestic policy. Britain, Tucker argued, was hobbled by a system of monopoly that valued the privileges of merchants above the good of the empire. His work was addressed to the Earl of Halifax, the First Commissioner for Trade and Plantations appointed by the ministry of Henry Pelham. Britain's 'most unaccountable *infatuation*' with the restriction of Irish trade was listed as her eighth disadvantage relative to France.

Ireland's close proximity to Britain that rendered it imprudent to treat her in the same way as extra-European colonies. Tucker's 'Third Proposal' for improving Britain's trade situation relative to France was a parliamentary union with Ireland. In advancing the case, he made an argument similar to that which had been offered by Arthur Dobbs: 'whatever Wealth *Ireland* would draw form other Counties by its Produce, Manufactures, and happy Situation; all that would continually *center* in *England*'. Ireland, Tucker noted, was more easily reached from the British capital than many

---

[91] David Hume, 'Of the Jealousy of Trade', in Miller (ed.), *Essays Moral Political and Literary*, 327–32, at 329–31.
[92] Hume, 'Politics', 19.

parts of England – 'the *Communication* between them is not *so easy* by *Land*, for the *Purposes* of *Commerce*, as the *other* is by *Sea*'. The conviction that the British Isles formed a natural economic unit underpinned his scornful response to fears that 'they would run away with our trade.' 'Who would run away with it?' Tucker asked. 'Where would they run to?'[93]

Union, Tucker claimed, would allow for an equalization of taxes and the creation of a powerfully integrated textile-export region around southern Ireland and the south-west of England. Tucker's focus on comparison with France, however, brought a pungent perspective on why this sort of reform might be unlikely under Britain's tumultuous, partisan political system. He declared Britain's fifteenth, and most crippling, trade disadvantage relative to France to be the 'Discouragements and Oppositions which the most generous Scheme will too often meet with from self-interested and designing Men, who pervert the invaluable Blessing of Liberty and a free Constitution to some of the worst of purposes'. By contrast, there were no *soi-disant* 'patriots' to obstruct a 'Good Design' in an absolute monarchy like France, and no means of gaining patronage from the executive by making oneself 'formidable to the Ministry' through parliamentary agitation in favour of monopoly and private interests.[94]

The emergence of William Pitt the Elder and John Wilkes as tribunes of a more demotic–and warlike–variety of English patriotism in the era of the Seven Years' War served only to heighten fears regarding the future direction of British politics and commercial policy. Vast new conquests in Canada and the Indian subcontinent brought Montesquieu's image of a stable maritime empire of commerce and liberty into question. 'It is easy enough to foresee ... that England, with all her glory, will be ruined within twenty years', wrote Jean-Jacques Rousseau in 1755. 'The English have set their minds on being conquerors; therefore they are hastening to be slaves.'[95] For British contemporaries, this 'ruin' took the form of a hugely inflated national debt. In successive iterations of his essay 'Of Public Credit' (1752–64), David Hume became more and more

---

[93] Josiah Tucker, *A Brief Essay on the Advantages and Disadvantages Which Respectively Attend France and Great Britain, with Regard to Trade, with Some Proposals for Removing the Principal Disadvantages of Great Britain*, 3rd ed. (London: T. Trye, 1753), 60–1.

[94] Ibid., 47–8.

[95] Jean-Jacques Rousseau, 'Abstract and Judgement of Saint-Pierre's Project for Perpetual Peace' [1756], in Stanley Hoffman and David Fidler (eds.), *Rousseau on International Relations* (Oxford: Clarendon Press, 1991), 53–101, at 66.

agitated by the scale of Britain's public debt.[96] The rise of systems of public credit implicated more and more of the property of the nation in the fortunes of war. If bankruptcy proved necessary to free up revenue for new military commitments, the transfer of wealth from private to public hands would be so great that the resulting regime would be defined by 'a degree of despotism, which oriental monarchy has ever yet attained'. The alternative would be conquest by a less indebted power.[97]

Imperial overreach produced fresh attempts to impose taxation on the American colonies, prompting a renewed descent into conflict. The critical condition of Britain's empire provided an urgent context for the radical model of fiscal and parliamentary union proposed by Adam Smith in his *Wealth of Nations* (1776). Smith proposed union as one of a range of fiscal reforms to reduce the risk of a public debt crisis. He regarded the expansion of public credit as a dangerous diversion of capital away from direct employment in productive capacity, towards its indirect management via rentiers.[98] While his language was more measured than Hume's, he shared the latter's verdict that Britain was close to a state bankruptcy.[99] To survive, Britain urgently needed to reform its imperial and commercial system, retaining territories capable of supplying revenues and soldiers and letting go those that could not. 'Under the present system of management', he wrote, 'Great Britain derives nothing but loss from the dominion which she assumes over her colonies'.[100]

Productivity and revenue, rather than the political control of markets and resources, lay at the heart of Smith's strategy for national security. The carefully coordinated system of trade restrictions that divided Britain from her empire in Ireland and America was entirely self-defeating. Rather than seeking to distort trade relationships into unnatural transoceanic configurations, Smith argued, the goal of British policy should be to unleash the productive potential and localised trade networks of its existing possessions. This would maximise the tax revenue they could provide to the centre, which could in turn be applied to the maintenance of skilled professional armed forces. To borrow Francis Annesley's

---

[96] Hont, *Jealousy of Trade: International Competition and the Nation-State in Historical Perspective* (Cambridge, MA: Harvard University Press, 2005), 325–54.
[97] David Hume, 'Of Public Credit', in Miller (ed.) *Essays Moral Political and Literary*, 349–365, at 359.
[98] Adam Smith, *An Inquiry into the Nature and Causes of the Wealth of Nations*, 2 vols. (Oxford: Clarendon Press, 1976), V.iii.54.
[99] Ibid., V.iii.58.   [100] Ibid., IV.vii.c.65.

terminology, Smith concluded that *every* colony was ultimately a 'colony for Empire'.

Smith illustrated his thinking with a thought experiment – 'a new Utopia, less amusing certainly, but not more useless and chimerical than the old one'. He described a pan-imperial parliamentary union with equal taxes paid by 'all the different provinces of the empire inhabited by people of either British or European extraction' and a 'fair and equal representation of all those different provinces, that of each province bearing the same proportion to the produce of its taxes'.[101] Smith was aware that such a wholesale expansion of the citizen body posed a risk to any state with a popular element within its constitution. That the granting of full citizenship to all the Italian tribes conquered by Rome after the Social War of the second century BC had been a disaster, making the popular assemblies of *Comitia* that constituted the democratic element in Rome's mixed constitution unmanageable. When the assemblies grew too large, citizens and non-citizens could no longer be distinguished from one another. The representative character of the British constitution was something else altogether: there would be no problem in verifying the identity of new American MPs.

Through a combination of parliamentary representation and the patronage of a strong monarchical executive backed by a modern fiscal state, Britain could achieve what Rome had not, binding its provinces to its mixed constitution without collapsing into civil war and military dictatorship. Smith archly described how, if representation of the American and Irish 'provinces' was linked directly to tax revenues, the numbers of the people in the Commons to be 'managed' by the King's ministers would be equal to 'the means of managing them'.[102] Here, Smith's analysis clearly recalled both Montesquieu and Hume. It was the element of monarchy in Britain's 'mixed' constitution – its capacity for both unity and patronage – that would enable it to grant to its Irish dependency an equal and integral status within a unified British Empire.

Smith, Young and the Political Economy of Anglo-Irish Ascendancy

Smith's remarks on Ireland summarised and developed arguments for union that had been articulated across the seventy years since the re-establishment of English authority in Ireland at the end of the seventeenth

---

[101] Ibid., V.iii.68. [102] Ibid., IV.vii.c.78.

century. The Scottish philosopher went further than Tucker, Dobbs or Maxwell, however, in linking them to a critique of the operation of the Penal Laws that paralleled that of Charles O'Conor and Edmund Burke. When considering whether it would be 'contrary to justice' to ask Ireland to bear the burdens of British taxation, Smith concluded that the benefits to Ireland's majority population would far outweigh the costs of assuming shared responsibility for Britain's fiscal state. He offered a brief, but suggestive, speculation regarding the possible consequences of union for Ireland:

> By the Union with England, the middling and inferior ranks of people in Scotland gained a compleat deliverance from the power of an aristocracy which had always before oppressed them. By an union with Great Britain the greater part of the people of all ranks in Ireland would gain an equally compleat deliverance from a much more oppressive aristocracy; an aristocracy not founded, like that of Scotland, in the natural and respectable distinctions of birth and fortune; but in the most odious of all distinctions, those of religious and political prejudices[103]

Located, as they were, in the middle of a long series of proposals aimed at the rescue of Britain's overextended fiscal state, Smith's observation presented the Penal Laws as a problem of urgent import for the political economy of the entire British Empire. His confidence in union as a mechanism for the 'deliverance' of the lower orders from aristocratic domination was rooted in a broader Scottish analysis of the course of European history since the Renaissance. In the third, historical, book of his *Wealth of Nations*, Smith followed David Hume in describing the transformational effects of luxury consumption and long-distance trade to the feudal monarchies of northern Europe. This had encouraged the barons who had dominated Europe since the fall of Rome into commuting obligations of land and labour into money payments that they could use to purchase prestige goods – thereby destroying their capacity to employ hospitality as a means of securing the loyalty of vassals, tenants and retinues. A 'revolution in public happiness' was brought about through the unintended consequences of the vanity of proprietors and the self-interest of merchants.[104]

It was axiomatic for Enlightened Scots like Smith and Hume that – whatever the excesses of England's vicious party politics – the Union of 1707 had accelerated Scotland's progress along this path from feudalism

---

[103] Ibid., V.iii.89.   [104] Ibid., III.iv.4–15.

to modern liberty. It had denied the Scottish nobility a parliament in which they could make trouble, helped the development of significant trading and imperial interests and – after the Jacobite rising of 1745 – enabled the destruction of private seigneurial jurisdictions of the Highland nobility. It was not merely England's constitution, but the underlying condition of English society, rooted in the rights enjoyed by farmers and tenants and the success of the Kingdom in foreign trade, that had made it a suitable agent for Scotland's deliverance from aristocratic domination.

Ireland, Smith suggested, presented a contrasting and more difficult challenge. The authority of the Scottish nobility had been rooted in a natural deference towards past or present wealth and power: 'the great sources of personal distinction ... the principal causes which naturally establish authority and subordination among men'.[105] This was sustained, as Smith claimed in his *Theory of Moral Sentiments* (1759), by the sympathetic identification of the poor with the good fortune of the rich.[106] When, as in Ireland, social position was determined not by wealth or lineage, but by punitive laws and confessional allegiance, these natural sources of deference and subordination were weak and unstable. The consequences for public order and prosperity were dire. As Smith wrote to the Earl of Carlisle, the Irish Lord Lieutenant confronted with the Irish Free Trade agitation of 1778–9, it was pointless to speculate about the ability of Irish manufactures to compete with their English counterparts. Aside from Ireland's relative dearth of natural resources, the country lacked

> ...order, police, and a regular administration of justice both to protect and to restrain the inferior ranks of people, articles more essential to the progress of Industry than both coal and wood put together, and which Ireland must continue to want as long as it continues to be divided between two hostile nations, the oppressors and the oppressed, the protestants and the Papists.[107]

Smith's proposal of a union as the solution to this problem was drastic. If it was deprived of its own parliament, Smith argued in the *Wealth of Nations*, Ireland would be less troubled by the 'spirit of party' that had overdetermined its social order. The Irish would become, like the Scots, 'more indifferent and impartial spectators' of the distant political contests

---

[105] Ibid., V.i.b1–11.
[106] Adam Smith, *The Theory of Moral Sentiments* (Indianapolis, IN: Liberty Fund, 1976), I.iii.2.3.
[107] Adam Smith, *The Correspondence of Adam Smith* (Oxford: Oxford University Press, 1977), 202, Smith to Lord Carlisle, 8 November 1779, 202–3.

of a Westminster parliament. The benefits of an imperial union would, therefore, extend beyond mere equality of status with other subjects of the British monarchy: by making Ireland, like America and Scotland, a distant 'province' of a 'great' and 'uniform' state, it would exercise a vital cooling effect on the religious passions that had disfigured and disrupted hierarchy and subordination in Irish society.

Smith's judgement was rooted in a highly specific set of arguments derived from Scottish moral philosophy concerning the effect of distance on the passions. In his *Treatise of Human Nature* (1738), David Hume had argued that 'every thing contiguous to us, either in space or time, should be conceived with a peculiar force and vivacity'.[108] In a penetrating discussion of the nature of conscience in the *Theory of Moral Sentiments* (1759), Smith had made the parallel observation that it was unusually difficult to form sympathetic connections with others at great distances – something made it difficult to exercise a cosmopolitan benevolence that extended to the lives and fortunes of distant peoples.[109] Closer to home, however, the effects of distance could be salutary. It removed the institutional preconditions for 'faction', something that Smith, like Hume, identified as a vice that was at its most intense in small states with representative institutions. Smith's judgement on the Irish Kingdom thereby subsumed it within a general Scottish problematic of party competition and parliamentary government. Ireland's unusual feature was that, through the action of the Penal Laws, aristocracy itself had degraded into faction. Smith's account of Irish politics lent itself to the radical solution of a parliamentary union as the ultimate solvent of the tortured legacies of conquest and Reformation.

For British observers with a closer relationship to Ireland's improving aristocracy, such as the agrarian reformer and travel writer Arthur Young, the condition of Ireland under an Anglican aristocracy at the close of the 1770s seemed to be more mixed, and offered greater cause for optimism. Over the previous two decades, Young claimed in his *Tour of Ireland* (1778–9), the Irish Kingdom had 'made as great advances as could possibly be expected, perhaps greater than any other country in Europe'.[110] Young's study of the living conditions of Ireland's rural 'labouring poor'

---

[108] David Hume, *A Treatise of Human Nature* (Oxford: Oxford University Press, 1978), 427.
[109] Smith, *Moral Sentiments*, III.iii.4.
[110] Arthur Young, *A Tour in Ireland, with General Observations on the Present State of That Kingdom, Made in the Years 1776, 1777 and 1778, and Brought Down to the End of 1779*, 2nd ed., 2 vols. (London: T. Cadell and J. Dodsley, 1780), II:146.

suggested a radically different political economy to the society of commerce and wage labour that was developing in England and lowland Scotland. The circulation of cash was limited, but this was an inevitable consequence of the country's relative poverty: 'when great wealth from immense branches of industry has brought on a rapid circulation, and much of what is commonly called luxury', Young argued, 'the more simple mode of paying labour with land can scarcely hold'. While the clothes and housing of Ireland were of poor quality, he claimed, the labouring poor were well fed by the small potato plots they received from landlords in return for their labour. Young claimed that this system of 'conacre' could have a crucial disciplining effect. Exclusion from the cash economy, 'with its defects as well as its advantages', at least prevented the Irish cottier from spending a whole week's wages on the consumption of alcohol, in the manner of the English workman.[111]

To evaluate the 'happiness' of the Irish poor merely on the basis of the 'payment of their labour, their cloaths, or their food', however, was to obscure the most essential thing about their plight: their 'unlimited submission' to the exploitation and violence of their landlords. The degradation of the manners of the Irish gentry, Young suggested, was far worse than a mere catalogue of Penal Laws would suggest. 'The landlord of an Irish estate, inhabited by Roman Catholicks', he claimed 'is a sort of despot who yields obedience in whatever concerns the poor, to no law but that of his will'. The poor could have no recourse to justice in a society where a gentleman receiving a summons from the justice of peace would rather challenge him to a duel than appear before a court.[112] The picture was complicated further by the practice of permanently letting estates to 'middlemen'. This had its origins, Young speculated, in the need for early planters to induce their tenants to endure the peril and hardship of farming expropriated Irish land. These now formed a petty gentry dedicated to extracting rack rents – sometimes in kind – from their impoverished subtenants: a position that left them 'with a variety of opportunities of oppression, every act of which is profitable to themselves'.[113]

Like Smith and Burke, Young feared that the lawlessness and exploitation of the Irish countryside made regular agrarian outrages inevitable: 'Where manners are in conspiracy against law, to whom are the oppressed people to have recourse?'[114] Discussing the sources of Irish unrest, Young drew a careful distinction between what he regarded as ordinary

---

[111] Ibid., II:22.   [112] Ibid., II:29.   [113] Ibid., II:13–14.   [114] Young, *Tour in Ireland*, II:29.

manufacturing protests by weavers in the Protestant north, driven by commercial fluctuations in the market for linen, and the 'Whiteboys' of Cork and Munster, who were the evident victims of aristocratic oppression. That some of the rioters were hanged without trial was evidence enough that the Irish landed class had never identified 'the real cause of the disease, which in fact lay in themselves, and not in the wretches on the gallows'. Abolishing the Penal Laws and reforming the behaviour of exploitative landlords would produce an 'affectionate poor, instead of oppressed and discontented vassals'.[115]

Young reproached his English readers for their lack of attention to the internal dynamics of the Irish countryside. 'A better treatment of the poor in Ireland is a very material point to the welfare of the whole British Empire', he urged. 'By what policy the government of England can for so many years have permitted such an absurd system to be matured in Ireland, is beyond the power of plain sense to discover.'[116] By excluding Catholics from property, the Penal Laws critically endangered the stability of Irish society, disconnecting the peasantry from a responsible gentry of their own religion, who could be expected to ensure their discipline and loyalty.[117] By preventing Catholic middlemen from taking mortgages, they also ensured the Irish agriculture would remain undercapitalised and unimproved.[118]

Young viewed the Penal Laws as part of a larger ensemble of misguided legislation, both Irish and British, that prevented the Irish Kingdom from fulfilling its economic and military potential as a part of the Empire. Like Montesquieu and Tucker, Young argued that restrictions on Irish woollen production demonstrated the baneful influence of private mercantile interests in the fashioning of British policy. Worse still, however, were the restrictions newly imposed on the export of Irish provisions to the colonies – a measure that did not even have the pretence of encouraging manufacturing in England. 'A whole kingdom', Young claimed, was thereby being 'sacrificed and plundered, not to enrich England, but three or four London contractors'![119] Where Arthur Dobbs had emphasised the importance of absentee expenditures in London for the linking together of the fortunes of Irish and English commerce, Young drew up customs house figures to demonstrate the growing value of Ireland as an export market for British produce – something that was directly linked to the improvement of own trading fortunes since the 1750s. Here was proof of Hume and Tucker's dictums regarding the interdependence of British

[115] Ibid., II:30.   [116] Ibid.   [117] Ibid., II:32.   [118] Ibid., II:34.   [119] Ibid., II:139.

prosperity with that of its neighbours. 'Long experience has told us what the effects of Irish wealth are; we feel those effects flowing like vital warmth through the whole extent of our own territory', Yong claimed. 'Shall we yet hesitate to encourage and extend a prosperity which is the source and foundation of our own?'[120]

Reforming Ireland's trading arrangements required a grand bargain that would see the Kingdom making a fixed contribution to the common expenses of the empire, in return for access to European and imperial markets, on the same terms as Britain. To the granting of free trade and an equitable revenue agreement, however, belonged the retention of Britain's ultimate legislative authority over Ireland, and a strengthening of the Crown's prerogative in matters of imperial defence.[121] Young was ultimately, however, at pains to emphasise that the damage done by the Westminster parliament's commercial legislation paled in comparison to that inflicted by the Penal Laws. 'These evils, great and acknowledged as they are', Young reminded his Irish readers, 'are trifles when compared when compared with the poverty and debility which results from the oppression of the Roman Catholics'.[122]

Young had far more confidence than Adam Smith in the capacity even of Ireland's corrupted aristocracy to effect the reformation of Irish society without the radical expedient of a parliamentary union. He placed his trust in a model of Enlightenment derived from his own travels, and his participation in the agricultural societies of Europe. In the first part of his *Tour*, Young had written approvingly of the improving efforts of Anglo-Irish luminaries such as the Louth landlord and parliamentarian John Foster and the future British Prime Minister William Petty, 2nd Earl Shelburne.[123] His comments on the 'despotism' exercised over the Ireland's 'labouring poor' were accordingly tempered by the observation that 'landlords that have resided much abroad, are usually humane in their ideas'.[124] Among the 'principal people residing in Ireland', Young claimed, 'there are great numbers among them who are as liberal in all their ideas as any people in Europe ... they have seen the errors which have given an ill character to the manners of their country, and done everything that example could effect or produce a change'.[125]

In discussing the prospects for the relaxation of the Penal Laws, Young embraced a posture of gradualism that mirrored the approach to reform taken by the Irish parliament from the 1770s. 'Great sudden changes are

---

[120] Ibid., II:131.   [121] Ibid., II:141.   [122] Ibid., II:35.   [123] Ibid., I:119–20, 61–2.
[124] Ibid., II:29.   [125] Ibid., II:154.

rarely prudent; old habits are not immediately laid aside', he claimed. It would be prudent to conciliate the Protestant interest by encouraging the Dublin parliament to offer relief to Catholics piecemeal, beginning with the power of taking mortgages and purchasing land, and culminating in the granting of the right to vote and to bear arms.[126] Here, however, Young went far beyond the mainstream even of reforming Anglo-Irish opinion, which drew a sharp distinction between the civil and political restrictions placed on Catholics. It was essential, he urged, that Ireland 'transfer her anxiety from the faith to the industry of her subjects' and 'consider all religions as brethren, employed in one great aim, the wealth, power, and happiness of the general community'.[127]

Regenerating Empire

Adam Smith and Arthur Young's Irish writings represented contrasting British perspectives on the prospects for the reform of empire in the era of the American Revolution. They each perceived a need to reconfigure the Irish Kingdom's relationship to the British Crown and parliament, and to induce its governing Anglican aristocracy to abandon its anti-Catholic legislation and improve its management of the Irish interior. Young's preferred variety of Irish reform rested on the agency of the most 'liberal' Irish landholders. The task of British government was to encourage this local elite to exercise its authority in the manner that was commensurate with a broader conception of imperial interests. Smith, by contrast, drew on his particular understanding of Scottish and European history to urge that the problems of Irish trade and Irish aristocracy were necessarily connected. A union of the Dublin and Westminster parliaments provided the solution to both, overcoming the spirit of religious faction while guaranteeing the full participation of Irish subjects in the fiscal and commercial system of a newly consolidated empire.

Despite these marked differences in analysis and prescription, however, Smith and Young shared a set of common assumptions regarding the nature and purposes of British rule. Ireland's seventeenth-century settlers had imagined their task to be the civilisation of a barbaric interior, dominated by the retrograde customs of the 'mere Irish' and the 'degenerate' Anglo-Norman settlers.[128] In the eighteenth century, the purpose of

---

[126] Ibid., II:36.   [127] Ibid., II:37.

[128] John Davies, 'A Discovery of the True Causes why Ireland was never brought under Obedience of the Crown of England, until his late Majesty's Happy Reign', in *Historical Tracts by Sir John Davies*, (London: John Stockdale, 1786), pp. 1–227.

imperial government was slowly redefined as an attempt to repair the damage caused by earlier attempts to enforce subjugation and religious conformity. These were now regarded as obstacles to successful integration of the Irish Kingdom into a British empire of commerce. For Smith and Young, as for Edmund Burke and Charles O'Conor, a durable consolida-tion of British authority and an expansion of Irish prosperity could only rest on a healthy constitution of Irish society: one that distributed the benefits of the British connection throughout the social scale, to Smith's 'middling and inferior ranks' and Young's 'labouring poor'.

This, then, was an Enlightened critique of the British Empire in Ireland: driven by a sophisticated account of politics as dependent on the manage-ment of opinion, faction and sentiment, and a commitment to material improvement as a guarantor of both social peace and moral progress. For Smith, in particular, it was advanced as the culmination of a thorough and radical case for a new understanding of 'political economy' as a 'branch of the science of a statesman and legislator', informed not by fleeting calcu-lations of mercantile interest but by a philosophical account of human dispositions.[129]

Far from being an anti-imperial critique of British rule, however, Smith's and Young's reflections suggested a strong interest in the regener-ation of Irish political allegiance, the better to secure the Kingdom's loyalty to an increasingly indebted and beleaguered metropole. This developing search for new ways of ordering the Irish Kingdom's society and politics was motivated by a concern with the fortunes of the British Empire in the escalating cycle of European warfare that had begun with the War of the Austrian Succession (1741–8). Debating Britain's prospects at mid-century, Montesquieu, David Hume and Josiah Tucker had each identi-fied the government of Ireland as a critical issue for the future of British power. For Montesquieu, Ireland's condition as a dependent Kingdom, denied its external autonomy by the imperatives of England's ruthless commercial reason of state, was an inevitable expression of the country's fissile combination of parliamentary government and mercantile empire. For Hume, Tucker and Smith, it signified the domination of British policy by private mercantile interests with little understanding of the political or commercial benefits of granting Ireland a more privileged position in the imperial trading system. As Anglo-Irish critics of the English woollen legislation of the 1690s had long argued, Ireland's low costs of production could be employed to help Britain best its rivals in international

---

[129] Smith, *Wealth of Nations*, IV.1

competition for export markets. The prosperity of an imperial province could never truly threaten that of the metropole. It was this fundamental conclusion that led Smith and Young to their fulsome endorsements of a 'free trade' for the Irish Kingdom, alongside their criticisms of Anglo-Irish dominance of Irish landed society.

By the end of the 1770s, however, any effort to alter the Irish governing settlement had to reckon with the emergence of powerful parliamentary and popular opposition to the very idea that the Irish Kingdom could be governed – however benevolently – as a dependency of Britain. Nurtured by an expanding press, and increasingly well-represented on College Green, a new form of 'Patriot' politics had emerged to challenge British authority in Ireland. Energised by the example of America, it offered its own visions of imperial reform, centred not on the transformation of Irish society, but the freeing of its commerce from any and all forms of British legislative restraint.

CHAPTER 2

Commerce without Empire?
'Free Trade' and 'Legislative Independence', 1776–1787

Between 1778 and 1782, the central elements of the constitutional, commercial and confessional settlement of the eighteenth-century Irish Kingdom were dismantled. The web of British statutes that had restricted the Irish Kingdom's trade with Britain and its colonies were repealed by the Westminster parliament in 1778–9. The Dublin parliament, committed as never before to the direct contestation of imperial commercial policy, simultaneously overturned many of the restrictions on Catholic property holding that had been decried by Burke and O'Conor in the 1750s. In 1782, the British parliament was compelled to repeal the 1720 Declaratory Act after the Irish parliament passed a resolution rejecting any and all British claims to legislate for Ireland. Poynings' Law, the Tudor statute that had frequently been invoked to give the British Privy Council a decisive role in the passing of Irish legislation, was repealed shortly thereafter.[1]

The source of the Irish parliament's new resolve lay far beyond the doors of College Green, in a new popular movement: the Volunteers. At least partially open to Catholics, and powerfully shaped by the 'democratical' culture of Ulster Presbyterianism, the Volunteers combined the attributes of a traditional armed militia with the more fluid associational world of eighteenth-century friendly societies, Masonic lodges and charitable organisations.[2] The Volunteer movement represented a potent politicisation of the Irish culture of 'improvement' described in the previous chapter, alongside a rejection of its focus on Irish agrarian reform.[3] Popular energy swung instead behind a determined campaign for 'Free Trade' and 'legislative independence' that once again tied Ireland's prospects for prosperity to its access to imperial and European markets. *The Case of Ireland,*

---

[1] Powell, *Britain and Ireland in the Eighteenth-Century Crisis*, 170–221.
[2] Higgins, *Nation of Politicians*, 128–30; McBride, *Scripture Politics*, 123–33.
[3] Michael Brown, *The Irish Enlightenment* (Cambridge, MA: Harvard University Press, 2016), 351–7.

composed as a futile complaint against English power politics, now became a manifesto for a serious attempt to place the Irish Kingdom outside the mercantile system of the British Empire. The reach, power and autonomy of the Volunteers created a new reality for both the Anglican political elite and the succession of British ministries who sought to manage and stabilise the Irish Kingdom in the aftermath of the American Declaration of Independence in 1776. 'A New World of Policy has been opened to us', declared the Anglo-Irish MP, diplomat and writer Charles Francis Sheridan following the Irish parliament's declaration of its 'legislative independence' in 1782. 'A new Arrangement of Things has taken Place; and new Maxims, new Principles must be adopted, suited to the Change in our Circumstances.'[4]

What were those maxims and principles to be? Here, both Irish and British politicians faced formidable conceptual problems. The one definite outcome of the Volunteer agitation was that the Irish parliament – already largely autonomous in all matters bar those of foreign commerce – was also to be 'independent' in this respect as well. Yet there was no obvious model for how this 'legislative independence' could be reconciled with a continuing British right of sole decision over question of imperial trade and revenue – something that no one on the British side, no matter how sympathetic they might have been to the Irish cause, was prepared to concede. With Smith and Tucker's preferred option of a union of the Irish and British parliaments ruled out of consideration by the strength of Irish patriotic feeling, British ministries and their Anglo-Irish supporters searched in vain for a constitutional fix that would tie Ireland to British commercial policy while preserving the forms of 'legislative independence'.

This problem would have been difficult enough to manage in isolation. But it was framed by a much larger context: the crisis of imperial government in North America, its escalation into a global conflict that saw Spain, France and the Dutch Republic unite to defeat Britain, and its long-run consequences for the viability of the slave colonies of the British Caribbean. It had been the struggle for American independence, alongside French entry into the war on the American side, that had first inspired the Volunteer agitation for 'Free Trade' in 1778–9. Yet Irish demands for exclusive control over the Kingdom's trade found little

---

[4] Charles Francis Sheridan, *A Review of the Three Great National Questions, Relative to a Declaration of Right, Poynings' Law, and the Mutiny Bill* (Dublin: M. Mills, 1782), 10.

favour with 'friends of America' in Britain, such as the radical Dissenting minister Richard Price or even Edmund Burke, now active in the British parliament as the chief thinker and strategist of the opposition Rockingham Whigs.

Burke's lukewarm support for Irish legislative independence earned him heavy criticism within Ireland, and in particular from the sharp pen of a leading light in the Dissenting wing of the Volunteering movement, the Glasgow-educated Ulster Presbyterian William Drennan. There was little consensus on the Irish side, however, about what form of constitutional connection with Britain might prove to be acceptable. While Drennan hinted at a federal arrangement based on a treaty between the two Kingdoms of Great Britain and Ireland, Charles Sheridan made the case for an expanded role for the Crown and the Irish Privy Council, ensuring the coordination of policy through an unpopular expansion of executive power.

A third, more radical option was fleshed out in pamphlets written by the prominent Volunteers Joseph Pollock and Frederick Jebb in 1778–9. Dismissing traditional Anglo-Irish fears of French invasion, both speculated that Ireland's status as a prize in European power competition could enable it to prosper as a neutral state, formally attached to the British Crown but free to trade as it chose. The dangers of exclusion from British trading networks, however, were vividly demonstrated by a Portuguese embargo on exports of Irish textiles, justified on the basis that an Irish Kingdom enjoying 'legislative independence' could no longer be regarded as a party to British commercial treaties. By the time a peace was signed between Britain, France and the newly established United States in 1783, there was a lively Irish debate about the scope for exercising the Kingdom's newly won control of its commercial policy. This included two possibilities that were particularly concerning to British ministers and their Anglo-Irish supporters: the adoption of protective duties against British goods and the conversion of the entire Irish Kingdom into a 'free port', able to dominate the newly opened trade between Europe and a United States that was no longer bound to trade with the imperial metropole alone.

The British Prime Minister William Pitt the Younger's unsuccessful attempt to agree to a far-reaching commercial treaty with Ireland, the 'Commercial Propositions' of 1785, was a response to the danger posed to the remnants of the British commercial system by an autonomous Irish Kingdom. Had they been implemented, the Propositions would have granted Ireland access to colonial markets and European commercial treaties on identical terms to Britain, in return for a commitment to follow all current and future British statutes governing foreign trade and make a contribution to the cost of naval defence. Pitt's original proposals, however, were watered down under the decisive influence of the West India planter interest, who feared that the British sugar trade would move to Ireland under the generous terms offered by the Propositions. The revision of the plans enabled their Irish opponents – led, among others, by Charles Sheridan's better-known younger brother, the flamboyant Whig playwright and Westminster MP Richard Brinsley Sheridan – to style them as a betrayal of the potential of Irish 'Free Trade' and to defeat the proposals in the Dublin parliament. It also encouraged British advocates of more radical commercial reform, not least Josiah Tucker, to fervently oppose Pitt's plan. As the first stirrings of European revolution began to be felt in the Netherlands and France, the problem of how to reconcile the freedom of Irish commerce with the preservation of British mercantile empire would continue to go unresolved.

Molyneux's *Case* and the 'Friends of America'

The misunderstandings and hostility that defined the relationship between the Volunteer movement and the British parliamentary opposition can be explained by the radical difference of perspective that existed between Irish Patriots and British 'Friends of America'. Over the decade that separated the Stamp Act Crisis of 1765 and the 1776 Declaration of Independence, the American colonists had only gradually edged towards a position incompatible with parliamentary authority over commerce on the basis of arguments that had initially been constructed in defence of the polycentric, negotiated 'imperial constitution' of the earlier eighteenth century.[5] Irish readers of Molyneux's *Case of Ireland*, by contrast, had taken this uncompromising position from the outset.

The radical incompatibility of this Irish conception of 'legislative independence' with British visions of imperial reform is suggested by the place it occupied in Richard Price's influential 1776 pamphlet *Observations on Civil Liberty*. Here, the Welsh Dissenting minister had elaborated his own vision of a new colonial settlement, developing a general theory of republican federation which, he speculated, might apply to a European regime of

[5] Jack P. Greene, *The Constitutional Origins of the American Revolution* (Cambridge: Cambridge University Press, 2011), 162–7.

perpetual peace as much as to Britain's overseas empire. Echoing arguments made in the North American colonies, Price argued that an 'empire'
was simply 'a collection of states or communities united by some common
bond or tye'. An 'empire of freemen' was formed of states with 'free
constitutions of government' that are 'independent of the other states,
with respect to taxation and internal legislation'.[6] Price was clear, however,
that a distinction had to be maintained between 'internal' and 'external'
legislation in order to uphold the right of the Westminster parliament to
regulate colonial trade in the interests of the whole empire. He clarified
this point in a remark relating to Molyneux. 'In arguing against the
authority of communities, and all people not incorporated, over one
another', Price observed, 'I have confined my views to taxation and
internal legislation'. Mr Molyneux carried his views much farther and
denied the right of *England* to make any laws even to regulate the trade
of *Ireland*'.[7]

Price was not the only 'friend of America' who struggled to comprehend
the distinctive demands of Irish patriots within a general model of imperial
reconciliation. In a series of parliamentary exchanges with Lord North's
ministry in 1778–9, Edmund Burke counselled rapid and extensive concession to Irish demands for the repeal of commercial restrictions.[8] This
would demonstrate a spirit of reciprocity and justice that would reassert the
'moderation, prudence and equity' of British policy following the debacle of
America.[9] Burke's critique of the government's Irish policy focused on the
role of honourable political conduct in maintaining a community of affection and interest between the plural communities of the empire. While
Burke had long been critical of British pretensions to parliamentary sovereignty over Ireland by right of conquest, he was ambivalent on the question
of trade regulation, a matter of common concern that could legitimately be
reserved to the chief legislature of the empire.[10] 'I do not mean to impeach
the right of the Parliament of Great Britain to make laws for the trade of
Ireland', Burke wrote to his constituents in Bristol. 'I only speak of what

---

[6] Richard Price, *Observations on the Nature of Civil Liberty, the Principles of Government, and the Justice and Policy of the War with America*, 8th ed. (Dublin: W. Kidd, 1776), 36.

[7] Ibid., 131fn.

[8] William Cobbett, *The Parliamentary History of England from the Earliest Period to the Year 1803*, 36 vols. (London: T. C. Hansard, 1806–20), XIX:1115–26; XX:635–51; XX:272–85.

[9] Edmund Burke, 'Speech on Address, 25 November 1779', in *Writings and Speeches*, IX:532–5, at 508–9.

[10] Richard Bourke, 'Party, Parliament, and Conquest in Newly Ascribed Burke Manuscripts', *Historical Journal*, 55 (2012), 619–52, at 642–4.

laws it is right for Parliament to make.'[11] It was imperative that the British did not force the question of imperial sovereignty, a 'metaphysical quarrel about mere words' that had already done incalculable damage in America. The administration's error lay in forcing the realisation of the right against the interests of the empire and the just claims of imperial subjects. This incompetence had produced the equally unjustifiable Irish decision to raise what amounted to an unconstitutional militia – to 'arm and embody', as Burke put it in a letter to the Irish MP Thomas Burgh, 'on private authority'.[12] There was a dangerous symbiosis, therefore, between the inflexibility of the ministry and the growing militancy of the Volunteers. Both were inimical to the ultimate goal of imperial conciliation.

Burke's stance alienated him from Irish Patriot opinion in the wake of the Free Trade crisis of 1778–9. His letter to Burgh – intended to be confidential – was spread widely in Irish political circles, and provoked an angry response from the Belfast radical William Drennan. Drennan, an Ulster Presbyterian physician who had studied with Adam Smith and his student John Millar at Glasgow University, offered a sharp critique of what he took to be the Rockingham Whigs' indecisive posturing over Irish affairs.[13] He suggested that Burke's long habituation to English politics had addled his concern for political justice: 'I must own, there are some circumstances which would rather tempt me to believe, that Mr. Burke is ... too much an Englishman, to wish for equality of rights and privileges to every part of the British Empire.' His scepticism was motivated by Burke's past adherence to Lord Rockingham's American Declaratory Act of 1766.[14] Party loyalty, Drennan suggested, now prevented Burke from embracing the new cause that was already energising the Irish Volunteer movement, the repeal of the analogous 1720 legislation that proclaimed the sovereignty of the Westminster parliament over its Irish counterpart.[15]

Burke's insistence on the principle of 'equity' as a criterion for imperial policy was difficult to reconcile with Drennan's more rigid adherence to one of 'equality ... the foundation of union between individuals and small communities of men'. Where Burke, following Montesquieu and David

[11] Edmund Burke, 'Two Letters from Mr. Burke to Gentlemen in the City of Bristol, on the Bills depending in Parliament relative to the Trade of Ireland', in *Writings and Speeches*, IX:506–17.

[12] Edmund Burke, 'A Letter from a Gentleman in the English House of Commons, in Vindication of his Conduct', in *Writings and Speeches* IX: 543–63, at 558.

[13] William Drennan, *A Letter to Edmund Burke, Esq.; by Birth an Irishman, by Adoption an Englishman, Containing Some Reflections on Patriotism, Party-Spirit, and the Union of Free Nations* (Dublin: William Hallhead, 1780).

[14] On Burke's role in the Stamp Act Crisis, see Bourke, *Edmund Burke*, 280–309.

[15] Drennan, *Letter to Edmund Burke*, 3–6.

Hume, looked to the civilised monarchy of France, with its 'many Provinces that are very different from each other in privileges and modes of government', as an example of a balanced, extensive commercial society, Drennan cited the republican confederations of the United Provinces and the Swiss cantons as proof that 'an intimate and permanent union between separate communities' was possible 'without the sacrifice of political liberty'.[16]

Drennan's account of a 'union of free nations' echoed Price's plan of imperial federation and implied a strong hostility to executive power. Irish opposition to Westminster's supremacy in matters of trade, however, ensured that even traditional supporters of the Dubin Castle administration were moved to articulate their own visions of what Price had called a 'free empire'. The beginning of the 1780s saw the emergence of a new category of Irish politician – the 'Ministerial Patriot', who had internalised the principle of Irish legislative autonomy, but determined to re-attach the Irish Kingdom to the British Empire by expanding the authority of the administrative apparatus centred on Dublin Castle.[17] While figures such as John Foster, the Chancellor of the Irish Exchequer, were more influential in Irish administration, it was Charles Sheridan who offered the most coherent public account of how a strengthened executive could restore political coordination to the British–Irish relationship.

Charles Sheridan's writings were significant because they offered a coherent attempt to convert Molyneux's *Case* into a workable model for how Ireland could achieve both 'legislative independence' and effective coordination with the policies of an administration ultimately accountable to Westminster. His *Observations on the Doctrine Laid Down by Sir William Blackstone* (1779) criticised the influential account of Westminster's legislative 'omnipotence' laid down by William Blackstone, the leading English constitutional authority of the day.[18] For Sheridan, the genius of the British constitution was that the division of legislative power between the king and parliament could accommodate an imperial system of liberty that permitted unified external action while preserving the equality of its component states. 'I am convinced', he declared, 'that this constitution is the only one ever

---

[16] Ibid., 7.
[17] A. P. W. Malcomson, *John Foster: The Politics of Improvement and Prosperity* (Dublin: Four Courts Press, 2011), 45–90.
[18] David Lieberman, 'The Mixed Constitution and the Common Law', in Mark Goldie and Robert Wokler (eds.), *The Cambridge History of Eighteenth-Century Political Thought* (Cambridge: Cambridge University Press, 2006), 317–46, at 351–4.

devised by the wit of man, under which separate and distant states, forming one Empire, may each of them enjoy the *same* degree of liberty, yet the unity of the Empire be preserved'.[19]

In contrast to Drennan, Sheridan denied the relevance of republican federation to the restructuring of the British–Irish constitutional connection. Taking the Dutch Republic as his example, he speculated that a federal representative assembly resembling the States General could never be equal to the task of managing the distinct interests of diverse and distant political communities. While a principle of equality and unanimity in the assembly's deliberations would endanger the polity's swiftness and unity of action, attempts to institute majority voting risked the oppression of smaller or more remote territories.[20] By contrast, a 'free empire', given unity by the person of a monarch, enjoyed the benefits of a dual representation, under which separate and equal assemblies managed and asserted the interests of their distinct states, while the Crown defined and defended the interests of the whole. 'In our constitution', Sheridan declared,

> the advantages which result from that power's being placed in the hands of one, *viz* the Sovereign, which in republics composed of distinct and distant states, must be lodged in the States General, as in Holland, or in congress, are infinite. The members of a congress, being deputed by different communities, must have *local* interests and strong *prejudices*; the Sovereign can have but *one* interest and even *partialities* would be unpardonable in him … Placed at the head of a greatly diversified and widely extended empire, as was once the case, his power was universal in its use and extent, accommodated to each individual community, yet comprehending them all. He was to all, the bond of union; to all, the dispenser of justice; and enabled to become the protector of the rights of all, by giving a negative to every act of one community, which tended to encroach upon the liberties of another.[21]

Sheridan's elegant evocation of a mixed and balanced structure of imperial authority employed arguments already familiar from the controversy over British rule in America.[22] Unlike many of his American counterparts, however, Sheridan was willing to countenance a visible and active

---

[19] Charles Sheridan, *Observations on the Doctrine Laid Down by Sir William Blackstone, Respecting the Extent of the Power of the British Parliament, Particularly with Relation to Ireland* (London: J. Almon, 1779), 62.

[20] Ibid., 68.   [21] Ibid., 68–9.

[22] Eric Nelson, 'Patriot Royalism: The Stuart Monarchy in American Political Thought, 1769–75', *The William and Mary Quarterly*, 68(4) (2011), 533–72.

role for the Crown in the regulation of both the Irish and the British parliaments. Writing in 1782, he declared himself opposed to the repeal of Poynings' Law: a demand that had been a mainstay of Ireland's Patriot opposition since the 1750s.[23] Sheridan argued that the law had enabled a prudent set of adaptations to the Irish constitution, which could enable it to enjoy the liberty of self-government while recognising British pre-eminence in the empire. There were many virtues, Sheridan argued, in a legislative procedure that ensured the Crown could modify and reject bills publicly, 'in a constitutional mode', rather than 'smothering' them in private by means of the secret weapons of influence.[24] The Irish Privy Council – filled with competent and patriotic politicians – was better capable of representing the Irish Kingdom's interests to the monarch than a House of Lords filled with idle absentees. It also acted as a buffer between Irish discontents and the British Crown: something that Sheridan believed to be essential to the long-term stability of the British connection that he so prized.[25]

The reform of Poynings' Law was another victory won by the Patriot opposition following the achievement of legislative independence. Henry Flood's preferred solution of full repeal lost out to a rival initiative, tacitly supported by the new Irish Chief Secretary, William Eden, and authored by the Patriot MP Barry Yelverton. 'Yelverton's Act' (1782) amended Poynings' Law in precisely the directions Sheridan had feared, stripping the Irish Privy Council and its British counterpart of their respective legislative roles. The constitutional link between the Kingdoms of Britain and Ireland was preserved only by the continued ability of the British Privy Council to veto problematic Irish legislation.[26] The alignment of Irish policy with British interests now relied more than ever on the ability of an Irish Lord Lieutenant, loyal to the British government of the day, to rebuild stable majorities on College Green.

Commerce and the Balance of Power

Throughout the years of British–Irish conflict over 'Free Trade' and legislative independence, it had been clear that what was at stake was not just the internal organisation of a self-evident polity called the

---

[23] Hill, 'Ireland without Union', 290.
[24] Sheridan, *A Review of the Three Great National Questions*, 61. [25] Ibid., 77.
[26] James Kelly, *Poynings' Law and the Making of Law in Ireland, 1660–1800* (Dublin: Four Courts, 2007), 334–7.

British Empire. The bounds of empire were porous: the European balance of power clearly shaped the bounds of possibility for Irish constitutional and commercial claims. In his preface to the popular 1773 edition of Molyneux's *Case*, the leading figure in the 'Patriot' parliamentary opposition, the Anglo-Irish MP Henry Flood, had reflected on how far the circumstances of the Anglo-Irish had changed since the Williamite war. 'Religious bigotry is losing its force everywhere; commercial, and not religious interests are the objects of almost every nation in Europe', he declared. A foreign invasion would no longer result in a disruption of the Irish property order. 'Ireland, to France or Spain, would be a grand commercial object ... No religious scruples would hinder them from guaranteeing to the present possessors of its lands all their estates, without the odious distinction of new and old rights.'[27]

The purpose of such speculation was not to signal a serious desire for Irish separation from the British Crown. Locating Ireland within the shifting schemas of European politics served, instead, to shake established certainties regarding the ultimate interests and allegiance of Ireland's Anglo-Irish landowning class. Bourbon support for the American colonists had changed Irish estimations of the relative merits of Britain and France. For Joseph Pollock, a Newry barrister who led the town's first Volunteer company, French support for the American cause provided proof of David Hume's argument that monarchies were no more hostile to the principles of civil liberty than 'free' imperial states like Britain.

Pollock cited Hume's remark comparing Ireland to the French *pais conquis* and observed that 'the French are, perhaps, even in religion, as liberal a nation as any in Europe ... I believe it will be owned that they are more liberal to Englishmen, than Englishmen are to them'.[28] Britain's American colonies were themselves proof of popular government's tendency towards exclusion and tyranny. The American colonists, Pollock ironically observed, had 'driven Indians from their own woods, through zeal for civilisation, Christianity, and justice' and 'carried others into captivity, because their complexions darkened under

[27] Henry Flood, 'Introduction', in William Molyneux, *The Case of Ireland's Being bound by Acts of Parliament in England Stated* (Dublin: J. Milliken, 1773), xii.
[28] Joseph Pollock, *The Letters of Owen Roe O'Nial* (Dublin: W. Jackson, 1779), 47.

a fiercer sun'.[29] All 'political bodies', Pollock concluded, were 'incapable of a steady or uniform principle of generosity'. Only the political 'self-sufficiency' guaranteed by Volunteer mobilisation could guarantee Ireland's constitutional rights.[30]

For Pollock, separation from the British commercial system was the *sine qua non* of Ireland's future prosperity. The proximity of Britain and Ireland meant that commerce could not be founded on the conventional basis of a mutually beneficial exchange of differing products. 'England is the last country on earth with whom Ireland can trade to advantage', Pollock observed, 'and Ireland is the last country upon earth whose trade alone can be an object to England'.[31] Like Flood, Pollock argued that Anglo-Irish security did not rest on the protection of the British Empire. The Irish Kingdom's independence, like that of the Dutch Republic or the Swiss cantons, could be guaranteed by the 'mutual jealousies' of the powers surrounding it: Britain, France and Spain. Fredrick Jebb, a prominent Volunteer writer who was Master of Dublin's Rotunda maternity hospital, argued along similar lines in his *Letters of Guatamozin* (1780). 'The balance of Europe would preserve this country free, if it were once set loose', Jebb asserted. 'The influence of each particular state would keep it out of the attraction of any one in particular; and the whole would be highly gratified in the downfall of proud England.'[32]

It is due to sentences like these that Jebb and Pollock have often been described as anticipating the United Irishmen's conception of a sovereign Irish nation.[33] Yet, as we have seen, Henry Flood – a serving member of both the Irish and British parliaments and a member of the Irish ministry for the duration of the Free Trade agitation – had also indulged in similar speculations. This should lead us to inquire more deeply into their meaning and context. In order to understand the nature of this Patriot rhetoric, and the specific challenge it posed to the British Empire, we have to disaggregate simple notions of 'independence', recovering the flexible and gradated notions of autonomy that underpinned Irish political demands. Ireland's advanced opposition insisted that their loyalty to the Crown of Ireland did not have to entail subordination to a system of commercial regulation constructed by the British parliament. They did not advocate insurrection or foreign intervention in order to secure this status, but they did conceive of

---

[29] Ibid., 11.   [30] Ibid., 12.   [31] Ibid., 44.
[32] Frederick Jebb, *The Letters of Guatimozin, on the Affairs of Ireland* (Dublin: R. Marchbank, 1779), 19.
[33] Morley, *Irish Opinion*, 40.

the balance of the Irish constitution and the distribution of commercial
privileges and obligations within the British Empire as something that could
be influenced by the European balance of power. It was still possible to
reconcile Irish liberty with allegiance to the British Crown, if the British
parliament was forced to curtail its ambition to regulate Irish trade by the
threat of intervention from other powers.

Even the most extravagant rhetoric about Irish separation from the
empire, moreover, could not obscure the reality that one of the key goals
of the Free Trade agitation of 1778–9 was to secure access to trading
networks that had been formed by British diplomacy and colonisation. As
one British Prime Minister, Lord North, had argued in the British parliament as early as 1779, a free trade to Europe could be viewed a natural right
owed to Ireland's historic status as a kingdom distinct from Britain. Trade
with the imperial system governed by British mercantile legislation, however,
was a privilege in the gift of the British parliament. 'Such an exclusive right
was of the very essence of colonisation', North declared, 'for what nation
under the sun would spend their blood and treasure in establishing a colony
and protecting and defending it in its infant state, if other nations were to
reap the advantages derivable from their labour, hazard, and expence?'[34]
Reviewing the Irish campaign for 'Free Trade' and parliamentary autonomy
in the autumn of 1784, a key ally of Lord North, the commercial expert John
Holroyd, 1st Earl of Sheffield, offered a frustrated assessment of the Patriot
agenda. 'Some of these pretended friends of Ireland', he complained,

> who ... are likely to prove her greatest enemies, have been driven, by the
> absurdity of their pretension, into the most contradictory mode of reason-
> ing: for, on some occasions, they treat her as a separate kingdom, not only
> independent, but utterly unconnected; on others, they claim her as a part of
> the empire, entitled (according to an inauspicious phrase) to a reciprocity of
> equal rights. For the sake of fairness in argument, it is to be wished they
> would chuse one predicament or the other. The attempt to blend both
> characters, is not calculated to promote either candour or perspicuity.[35]

The question of whether an 'independent' Ireland was entitled to
participate in the benefits of British diplomacy and colonisation was
impossible to avoid by the early 1780s. In Portugal, a key European
market for British and Irish goods, Irish claims to autonomy were viewed
as a potential opportunity for the renegotiation of the famous commercial
treaty signed between England and Portugal in 1703. This treaty,

---

[34] Cobbett, *Parliamentary History*, XX:1279.   [35] Holroyd, *Observations on Ireland*, 16fn.

commonly referred to in Britain by the name of the chief English nego-
tiator, John Methuen, had seen Portugal remove prohibitions on the
import of English textiles in return for an English preference for
Portuguese over French wines. Portuguese opinion regarded the treaty as
damaging to the commerce of the Kingdom and its Brazilian empire, but
ultimately necessary for the maintenance of an indispensable British alliance.[36] In 1780, the Portuguese court, spotting an opportunity to rene-
gotiate the treaty at a moment of British weakness, resolved to subject Irish
woollens to the same prohibitions that it had long applied to all foreign
nations except Britain.[37] The goal, as the Portuguese royal councillor
Miguel Antonio de Mélo explained to the British envoy in Lisbon, was
to use Ireland as a bargaining chip to secure more beneficial conditions for
Portuguese trade. De Mélo requested a Portuguese exemption from the
English Navigation Acts and the East India monopoly, alongside 'a general
naturalisation of Portuguese subjects for all civil purposes' in Britain, in
return for Portuguese recognition of the trading rights of the Irish
Kingdom.[38]

British diplomats were bemused by Portugal's demands and refused to
concede the principle that changes in the 'internal police' of the empire
warranted a revision of what had been treaties between sovereigns. 'I have
observed to de Mello [sic] that there can be no principle of the Law of
Nations so well established as, that a Sovereign in contracting with a Foreign
Power comprehends the whole of his Dominions', the British envoy wrote
to the Irish Lord Lieutenant, the Earl of Hillsborough, from a summit at
Lisbon in 1781. In the course of this discussion, however, it emerged that
the Portuguese argument was more subtle than the British had understood.
The Portuguese claimed that in the absence of clear textual evidence of the
1703 treaty's comprehension of the Irish Kingdom, the contracting parties
should rely on historical context when interpreting its provisions. Of greatest relevance was the notorious English legislation against Irish woollens
passed in 1698 – the occasion of Molyneux's constitutional protest.[39]
The argument was developed to its fullest extent in a pamphlet that the
Portuguese, in a further demonstration of their keenness to exploit the

---

[36] José Luís Cardoso, 'The Anglo-Portuguese Methuen Treaty of 1703: Opportunities and
Constraints of Economic Development', in Antonella Alimento and Koen Stapelbroek (eds.),
The Politics of Commercial Treaties in the Eighteenth Century: Balance of Power, Balance of Trade
(Basingstoke: Palgrave Macmillan, 2017), 105–25.

[37] James Kelly, 'The Irish Trade Dispute with Portugal, 1780–1787', *Studia Hibernica*, 25 (1989).

[38] NLI, Bolton MS, 15,869 (3), Letter from Walpole to Hillsborough, 10 October 1781, f.4.

[39] NLI, Bolton MS, 15,869 (3), Letter from Walpole to Hillsborough, 10 October 1781, f.4–5.

commercial opportunities of Irish political autonomy, had specially translated into English and circulated around Dublin in the tumultuous autumn
of 1783, as popular agitation in favour of parliamentary reform and 'protecting duties' against British impots reached its height. 'It is not the
business of the court of Lisbon to enter into metaphysical distinctions
respecting the indivisibility of the British crown', the work bluntly asserted.
The real question was historical: 'How . . . could Queen Anne have legally
demanded from the court of Lisbon, the grant of a privilege of commerce in
favour of the Irish woollen fabrics, while the existing laws absolutely
prohibited their exportation to foreign parts?' The repeal of the restraining
legislation, the Portuguese argued, left Ireland without any established right
to access Portugal's markets.[40]

Irish commercial interests were appalled by the implications of the
Portuguese case against the Irish application of the Methuen Treaty. The
Irish MP and merchant Sir Lucius O'Brien warned the Irish Lord
Lieutenant, the Earl of Carlisle, that the Portuguese exclusion 'must form
a general Precedent for our Trade with all other States'. The hard-won
gains of the of the Free Trade agitation would be lost if the Portuguese
interpretation of the Methuen Treaty was allowed to determine

> how far those Internal Restrictions from Time to Time Imposed on the
> Trade of Ireland by Great Britain . . . can deprive Ireland of those Benefits
> she Claims as well by many Treaties antecedent to those Restraints as by
> others, the Operation of which she considers as now Restored by the
> abrogation of those Restrictive Laws.[41]

The Portuguese court, however, sought Irish sympathy for what they
saw as an attack on British commercial jealousy. 'The high founding
epithet of mistress of the deep, seems in a great measure to be now an
empty name', the Portuguese pamphlet stated.[42] Ireland was invited to
form a treaty of its own with Portugal, under which 'every severe imposition, copied from the example of the sister country, should totally be
done away'.[43] Writing as one British mercantile vassal to another, the
Portuguese court invited Ireland to participate in the new age of commercial freedom precipitated by the British Empire's defeat in America.
'Commerce must in future flow as unbounded as the winds and waves',
the pamphlet observed.

---

[40] Anon., *A Defence of the Conduct of the Court of Portugal, with a Full Refutation of the Several Charges
Alleged Against that Kingdom, with Respect to Ireland* (London: J. Stockdale, 1783), 9.
[41] NLI, Bolton MS, 15,869 (2), Letter from O'Brien to Carlisle, 8 April 1781, f.1.
[42] Anon., *Defence*, 40.   [43] Ibid., 47.

Does not even Ireland exhibit a striking instance of this, in her long and patiently submitting to the arbitrary decrees of the British legislature, which usurped a power not vested in them by the nature of right; till at length convinced of her mistake, and shaking off the torpor of a century, she asserted that liberty to which her nation was so justly entitled?[44]

As the Portuguese issue demonstrated, Ireland's participation in historic trading networks formed by Britain, whether by colonisation or by treaty, was thrown into question by its assertions of political autonomy. The confusion was heightened still further, however, by an escalating debate within Ireland itself as to the correct orientation of the Kingdom's newly autonomous commercial policy. Freed from the restraints of the Declaratory Act and Poynings' Law, the Dublin parliament was now free to regulate Irish trade as it chose. This new room for manoeuvre, moreover, had been won at a moment defined by the defeat of Britain, the independence of America and the conclusion of a peace treaty with France. Debate within Ireland now shifted from the question of the proper means of asserting the Kingdom's rights to its substantive commercial interests within a transformed international environment.

Free Ports and Protecting Duties

If there was broad support for the constitutional principle of 'legislative independence' within Ireland by 1782, there was far less consensus about how the Irish parliament should use its newly won authority to advance the interests of Irish commerce and manufactures. During the Free Trade crisis of 1778–9, a range of British and Irish thinkers had argued that the removal of British trading restrictions would in fact make little difference to Ireland's prosperity. Following the new theories of thinkers like Hume, Smith and Tucker, supporters of Irish 'Free Trade' had claimed that Britain's superiority in skill, capital and mercantile networks meant that there was little chance of Ireland rivalling the imperial metropole in commerce or manufactures. Paradoxically, however, it was this very pessimism about Ireland's prospects – which, as we shall see, was not shared by representatives of Britain's mercantile and manufacturing interests – that ultimately pushed Irish economic debate in more radical directions. If competition with Britain on British terms was impossible, then the Irish Kingdom would have to use its new powers of legislation to reduce its dependence on the imperial metropole.

[44] Ibid., 40–1.

The leading representative of what we might think of as the pessimistic case for Irish free trade was John Hely-Hutchinson, the Provost of Trinity College. In a lengthy analysis published in 1779, *The Commercial Restraints of Ireland Considered* (1779), Hely-Hutchinson argued that Irish agrarian disturbances demonstrated the continuing indispensability of textile manufactures and foreign trade to the political stability of the Kingdom. The 'Whiteboy' disturbances complained of by Edmund Burke in his critiques of the Penal Laws had been most prevalent in 'those parts of the kingdom where manufactures are not established'. They therefore constituted 'proof of the poverty and want of employment of the lower class of our people'.[45] The way to mitigate the impact of a highly unequal distribution of landed property, overlaid with confessional tension, was to generate additional forms of moveable property through foreign trade and industrial employment, so as to compensate the Catholic majority. This was also the way to generate new tax revenues. Addressing himself to North's ministry, Hely-Hutchinson emphasised the connection between Ireland's lack of free access to international markets and its inability to make additional contributions to the British war effort:

> The present inability of Ireland, arises principally from this circumstance, that her lower and middle classes have little or no property, and are not able, to any considerable amount, either to pay taxes, or to consume those commodities that are the usual subjects of them; and this has been the consequence of laws which prevent trade and discourage manufactures.[46]

Hely-Hutchinson asserted that even if Ireland experienced an export boom in its newly liberated woollen industry, its wages would soon outstrip those of England, since 'it is not in the richest countries, but in those that are growing rich the fastest, that the wages of labour are highest, though the price of provisions is much lower in the latter'. Raw materials were more expensive in Ireland already, and would become more so if manufacturing for export were permitted to expand. If English worries about Scottish competition, widely aired in the Union debates of 1705–7, had come to nothing, then there was surely nothing to be feared from Ireland. Citing Adam Smith, he observed that 'though the Scotch have full liberty to export their woollen manufactures, the English work up their wool, and the Scotch make only some kinds of coarse cloths for the lower classes of their people; and this is said to be for want of a capital to manufacture it at home'.[47]

---

[45] Ibid., 69.   [46] Ibid., 217.
[47] Ibid., 107–9. The reference to Smith is to *Wealth of Nations*, II.v.8.

Hely-Hutchinson's arguments about Ireland's modest prospects were calculated to appeal to British opinion at a time when control of Ireland's foreign trade still rested with the British parliament. But they also raised larger and more difficult questions as to how much commercial benefit Ireland could expect to gain from the granting of parliamentary autonomy. As the Dublin parliament's achievement of legislative independence was swiftly followed by a severe post-war recession in 1783–4, the merchants and artisans of Dublin, Cork and Belfast mobilised to demand 'protecting duties' on goods imported from Britain. For those members of the Irish parliament who took up the cause, such as the former East India trader Richard Griffith, Adam Smith's arguments for the superiority of British skill and capital were decisive. In 1779, Smith's pessimistic account of Scottish economic growth under the Union had been used by Hely-Hutchinson in an effort to assuage English concerns about Irish free trade. Griffith cited the same passage, however, as a warning to Ireland. Crucially, he elided Hely-Hutchinson's distinction between different levels of quality and sophistication in manufactures in different parts of Britain, so as to assert more crudely the persistent backwardness of the Scottish economy in a union with England.

> Have not the people of Scotland been always in the possession of a free trade, and have they thereby arrived at arts and manufactures? No. – And wherefore? – Because their markets have been constantly supplied with English fabricks . . . it is much to be feared, that Ireland, is likely to derive as little benefit from her free trade, unless she takes proper measures to protect her own markets.[48]

For Griffith, Irish 'free trade' was a mirage if it simply meant the freedom to be rendered a passive consumer of British manufactured goods. In practice, this sort of free trade was indistinguishable from the colonial system it had supplanted. 'The consequence of our free trade on its present foundation will be, that we shall have permission, nay encouragement, to export our raw materials to Great-Britain, while our markets will be glutted and our warehouses filled with the manufactures of that country.'[49] The advantage England had gained in large-scale textile manufacturing was such that Ireland was incapable of producing for its home market, let alone for European neighbours. While Griffith proclaimed himself no 'friend to the general principle of monopoly', it was necessary now to make an exception due to 'the relative situation of Great-Britain and Ireland'.

[48] Richard Griffith, *Thoughts on Protecting Duties* (Dublin: Luke White, 1784), 10–11.
[49] Ibid., 6–7.

Duties with Portugal, Spain, France and Italy, where a reciprocal exchange
of luxury goods for manufactured textiles was genuinely possible, should
be lowered; but urgent protection was required 'against England, from
which every danger is to be apprehended'.[50]

Critics of the agitation for protecting duties countered with the argument that seeking to compete with England was short-sighted in the
extreme. 'If we examine into the spirit which dictates this plan', observed
the Irish judge and ministerial supporter Richard Johnson, 'we will find it
to be the pride of equality; not an attention to profit ... it will be an
equality of wrong, not an equality of right'.[51] Johnson counselled the Irish
parliament to adopt a radically different commercial policy to that prac-
ticed by Britain and the other European powers. Ireland, he argued, should
set an example to the continent in establishing itself as a free port. This
would enable it to capitalise on the Kingdom's position on the western
edge of Europe as an *entrepôt* for the liberated trade of the former
American colonies. 'The persons most skilled in the American trade
admit', he claimed, that they can make five voyages between any of the
western ports of Ireland and America, in the same space of time that they
can make three to any of the trading ports of England. Ireland's geographical location, he claimed, would allow it 'to make herself a general market
for the commodities of two worlds'. Yet geography alone could not
determine that Ireland's potential would be realised. 'That general market
will always be established', Johnson warned advocates of protective duties,
'where the laws of the country are most favourable to the persons and
property of individuals; and where the restraints upon export and import
are the fewest and least burdensome'.[52]

Britain's wealth, Johnson argued, was far more precarious than either
Hely-Hutchinson or Griffith perceived. The country's continuing prosperity was owing to the possession of captive imperial markets, rather than
unique advantages in skill and capital.[53] Ireland could not hope to emulate
this imperial path to prosperity – nor was this in her interest. By making
herself an offshore centre for European and Atlantic trade, Ireland could
pursue its own distinctive path as a centre of trade rather than manufactures. The correct approach for a poor kingdom on the edge of Europe,
Johnson concluded, was 'to open our ports as much as possible to every

---

[50] Ibid., 8.
[51] Robert Johnson, *Considerations on the Effects of Protecting Duties, in a Letter to a Newly-Elected Member of Parliament* (Dublin: W. Wilson, 1783), 35.
[52] Ibid., 36.   [53] Ibid., 24–5.

species of foreign intercourse, instead of closing them against any. To encourage by every means in our power, every accession of foreign supply, of foreign wealth, and foreign industry amongst us'.[54]

As Johnson's speculations suggested, widespread acknowledgement of Britain's growing superiority in the production of textiles did not settle the question of Ireland's capacity to disrupt and unsettle the political economy of the empire. Despite widespread pessimism over Ireland's ability to compete with British manufactures, Irish speculation still entertained hopes linked to the country's geographical position and its ability to capitalise on the opening of North American markets to European states beyond Britain. This view was not confined to Ireland alone. One striking statement of the Kingdom's commercial potential came from the Genevan exile Étienne Clavière, the mentor of the French economist Jean-Baptiste Say and a future finance minister of the French Republic. In a 1783 letter to the Chancellor of the Irish Exchequer, John Foster, written from the attempted Genevan colony at Waterford, Clavière warned that Britain could no longer count on continued dominance of the American market. France and the Netherlands were offering free ports and extended lines of credit to American merchants, while expanded textile production in Germany would soon enable further competition with British exports. Those who, like Foster's friend and correspondent Lord Sheffield, trusted to Britain's ability to retain American trade in the absence of imperial control were blinded by their 'very strong national prejudices'.[55] Ireland's best hope lay not in competing for American markets by developing its own manufactures, but in using its legislative independence to unilaterally open a series of free ports that would accommodate expanded European exports to the newly independent colonies. Ireland was 'the natural *entrepôt* of the commerce of Europe with other parts of the world, America especially', Clavière explained.

> You know, *monsieur*, that the real winners at the game are those that furnish the room, the carpet, the cards: *voila* the role of Ireland in the great game of commerce: nature indicates it to her ... her ports are easier, safer, and better dispersed than those of Holland. You must in a word have among you the great market for the exchange of the productions of Europe with those of the Indies ... one conceives that the arm in a country situated like

[54] Ibid., 40.
[55] PRONI, Foster-Massereene MS, D562/8536, Clavière to Foster, 1783, f.1. On Foster and Sheffield's connection, see A. P. W. Malcomson (ed.), *An Anglo-Irish Dialogue: A Calendar of the Correspondence between John Foster and Lord Sheffield, 1774–1821* (Belfast: Public Record Office, 1976).

Ireland can by better employed even than in pushing [loom] shuttles ...
Culture, commerce and navigation on foreign accounts ... here is an
inexhaustible source of riches and employment.[56]

Clavière's position represented an opposite extreme to that presented by
Richard Griffith. Instead of confronting British hegemony through a
policy of protecting Irish manufactures, he urged Ireland to displace
London as the centre of European and Atlantic trade. In the years
immediately following Ireland's achievement of legislative autonomy from
Britain, its commercial and political possibilities appeared to be wide open.
Free trade and protection were each canvassed as means of carving out a
niche for an autonomous Irish Kingdom within a European order that had
been transformed by the opening of trade to the American colonies. Far
from being polar opposites, they represented parallel strategies for employing the Irish Kingdom's legislative autonomy to evade Britain's crushing
advantages in manufacturing skill and capital, and diminish the Irish
Kingdom's dependence on British and imperial markets.

From 'Foederal Union' to Commercial Propositions

By 1784, British and Irish politicians were increasingly concerned about the
risks to imperial cohesion created by the legislative autonomy of an Irish
parliament that was under continuous pressure from popular agitation for
protecting duties and parliamentary reform. Securing a stable commercial
settlement, Charles Sheridan wrote to the Irish Lord Lieutenant, Lord
Northington, in August of that year, was the only way of heading off these
new demands. To enable 'union and cooperation' between Britain and
Ireland, it was necessary to remove any and all Irish grievances that could be
attributed to 'English influence over Irish Councils'. The new *cause celebre*
of advanced sections of the Volunteer movement, a reform of the Irish
parliamentary franchise that would permanently dilute the power of
British-aligned Irish ministers, was itself only a means to the end of
securing protecting duties. A new commercial settlement offered the only
hope of defusing the 'political mania of the day'.[57]

As the example of Arthur Young has already shown, projects for an
'arrangement' or 'compact' between the Kingdoms of Ireland and Britain

---

[56] Clavière to Foster, f.2.
[57] NLI, Bolton Papers, MSS 16350/4, Letter from Charles Sheridan to Lord Northington,
August 1784.

had been in contemplation since the outbreak of the Free Trade crisis in 1778. The fullest set of proposals had been drawn up in 1782 by William Ogilvie, a Scottish Whig who had developed a close relationship with the Duke of Portland, the Lord Lieutenant who presided over Ireland's legislative independence under the Rockingham ministry of 1782.[58] A copy of Ogilvie's 'Plan for a Foederal Union, between Great Britain and Ireland' survives in the papers of the Scottish Lord Advocate Henry Dundas, who consulted it when preparing his own plans for parliamentary union in 1799.[59]

Ogilvie's 'Plan' suggested a clear *quid pro quo*: while the 'direction of the Imperial Concerns of Peace and War, and Foreign Negociation' were confirmed to lie in the British Crown-in-parliament, Ireland was to be guaranteed a 'Full and Free Participation of all New Branches of Trade arising, whether from Conquest, Purchase, Colonisation or Treaty'. The 'Power of Regulating Foreign Trade' therefore remained 'exclusively Reserved to the British Legislature', but its application in Ireland rested on a new mechanism, calculated to assuage Irish anxieties about Westminster's legislative supremacy. Instead of being governed by the British parliament, Irish participation in the trading networks opened by British colonisation and diplomacy was to be made conditional on the Irish parliament passing legislation of its own that ensured conformity with British 'regulations and restrictions'. This, Ogilvie suggested, would be sufficient to 'recognise the Independence of the Irish parliament, and to Declare its sole Competence to Make Laws for every Internal Purpose of Taxation and Regulation'.[60] It would also, however, prevent Ireland from undermining the integrity of the British imperial system by using its legislative autonomy to enable the re-export of British colonial goods to European competitors.

The question of Ireland's access to markets opened by British colonisation and diplomacy, however, was only a preliminary to the main business of Ogilvie's proposals. These concerned Ireland's European trade with the continent, and with Britain itself. 'Public Treaties' and 'New Regulations' governing British trade were to be 'transmitted' to Ireland in a similar manner to colonial law with the added proviso that 'Ships and Mariners of Ireland acting in Contravention' of these would be 'considered as

---

[58] James Kelly, *Prelude to Union: Anglo-Irish politics in the 1780s* (Cork: Cork University Press, 1992), 46–8.
[59] William Ogilvie, 'Plan for a Foederal Union, between Great Britain and Ireland', 20 May 1782. NLI, Melville Papers, MS54/24.
[60] Ibid.

Contraband and Treated accordingly', after the expiry of a warning period. The remaining articles specified a range of provisions concerning duties on import and export, bounties, and drawbacks on British–Irish trade. It was in this respect that Ogilvie's proposals set the clearest precedent for the Propositions eventually placed before the British and Irish parliaments in 1784–5. Ogilvie suggested an equalisation of duties to whichever level was lower between those of Ireland and Britain. This principle of reciprocal equality extended to the use of countervailing duties and drawbacks to compensate traders in either Kingdom for the effects of duties on import or export levied in the other. It was completed by a fixed commitment 'that the manufactures of either Kingdom shall be effectually favoured by the other beyond the same Manufactures of any Foreign Country'.[61]

In the version of the Propositions first presented by Pitt and the Irish Chief Secretary, Thomas Orde, to the Irish parliament in February 1785, however, Ogilvie's sweeping statements regarding the necessity of the Irish parliament's agreement to British treaties and colonial regulations were struck out. The sole gesture to Ireland's dependent position within the British imperial system was a requirement – not present in Ogilvie's 'Plan', but echoing a suggestion in Young's *Tour* – that Ireland contribute a section of its permanent 'hereditary revenue' as a contribution to the support of the British Navy.[62] As Orde told the Irish parliament, whether or not the Irish Kingdom would accede to this payment was not a question of imperial subordination, but of its own 'wisdom' and 'generosity' as an independent 'nation'.[63]

Ensuring that Irish trade continued to centre on Britain and its colonies was an urgent priority for Pitt and his circle. British proponents of the measures pointed out that the Irish trade concessions of 1778–82 had produced a system that made little commercial or political sense. 'Lord North ... avowedly opened to Ireland the trade to our Colonies: Mr. Fox virtually extended the Irish commerce with foreign nations', observed George Chalmers, a Scots-American loyalist and prominent government pamphleteer. 'Yet, both these ministers left the trade and navigation between the Sister Kingdoms, which, considering their relationship and proximity, ought to be the most free, obnoxious to [exposed to] many

[61] Ibid.
[62] John Debrett, *The Parliamentary Register*, 54 vols. (London: John Debrett, 1785), vol. 17, 224.
[63] Thomas Orde, *The Commercial Regulations with Ireland Explained and Considered, in the Speech of the Right Hon. Mr. Orde* (London: J. Debrett, 1785), 17.

disputes and liable to some obstructions.'[64] Defending the Propositions in a pamphlet written for British merchants and manufacturers, the Treasury official George Rose argued that they definitively removed any notional ability Ireland might have hitherto enjoyed to trade in colonial goods with foreign countries. The terms of Irish trade with Britain and her empire were henceforth to be founded on the principle of 'equality in trade, for monopoly of consumption'.[65]

While Ireland was, therefore, to be granted the right to re-export colonial goods to Britain without paying additional duties, domestic manufactures in both countries continued to enjoy a measure of protection. This point was made strongly in the report of the Privy Council Committee appointed by Pitt in January 1785 to consider modifications on duties affecting British–Irish trade. Even before Pitt's proposals were subjected to a firestorm of criticism from British manufacturing and mercantile interests, the administration's hand-picked experts rejected tariff-free trade as the basis of subsequent British–Irish relations. 'As there are certainly articles of commerce', its report concluded, 'in which each country has a decided advantage, it is probable that such a plan would occasion the ruin of many of your Majesty's subjects in Great Britain and Ireland, and introduce an immediate convulsion in the commerce of the two kingdoms'. The committee's preferred option was that

> the two kingdoms agree on certain moderate duties, to be imposed on the importation of goods, the growth and manufacture of the other; such as will secure a due preference in the home market, to the like articles of its own growth and manufacture; and yet leave to the sister kingdom, advantages, though not equal to its own, yet superior to those granted to any foreign country.[66]

Unlike the union agreed by the Westminster and Dublin parliaments fifteen years later, the Commercial Propositions of 1785 did not include a clause gradually phasing out these residual trade barriers, calculated by Rose as a common 10 per cent tariff across the most heavily traded goods and raw materials.[67] Rather, they constituted a fixed basis on which British–Irish trade was to be 'encouraged ... extended ... settled, and

---

[64] George Chalmers, *The Arrangements with Ireland Considered* (London: John Stockdale, 1785), 11.

[65] George Rose, *The Proposed System of Trade Explained* (London, 1785), 7.

[66] Privy Council of Great Britain, *Report of the Lords of the Committee of Council, Appointed for the Consideration of Matters Relating to Trade and Foreign Plantations* (London: John Stockdale, 1785), 78–9.

[67] Rose, *System of Trade*, 32.

regulated on permanent and equitable principles for the mutual benefit of both countries'.[68]

Historians of Pitt's proposals have often described them as a 'customs union' or 'free trade area': terms derived from nineteenth- and twentieth-century institutions of international political economy.[69] Neither of these modern archetypes, however, captures the specificities of the 'system' proposed in 1785. While the Commercial Propositions aimed to lower and stabilise tariffs on British–Irish trade, they did not institute tariff-free trade between Britain and Ireland. The formula of reducing duties to the lowest level present in either Kingdom, Pitt observed to the Irish Lord Lieutenant, the Duke of Rutland, actually enabled the preservation of a measure of Irish protection against British goods. While Ireland's principal export, linen, was already imported into Britain duty-free, many British goods paid a duty on entry in Ireland, which the terms of the Propositions allowed the Irish parliament to retain indefinitely. 'Although upon each article taken separately there is an appearance of impartiality and equality', Pitt observed, 'the result of the whole is manifestly to a great degree more favourable to Ireland than to this country'.[70]

As these reflections suggest, the trading system envisaged by the Propositions rested on a carefully constructed system of preferences: one that sought actively to balance the interests of Britain and Ireland, while ensuring the latter's ultimate loyalty to, and contribution towards, the British imperial system. The Commercial Propositions placed the Irish Kingdom in a uniquely privileged position in what remained a managed and hierarchical set of European and imperial trading relationships, quite distinct in inspiration from Smithian or physiocratic conception of 'natural liberty'. Unlike any other British dependency, Ireland would be able to engage in both the colonial and European trades on terms identical to those of Britain itself. It could export its own products into the British market under the stable terms of a fixed agreement, rather than according to the shifting whims of Westminster legislation. The ninth Proposition,

---

[68] Debrett, *Parliamentary Register*, 223.

[69] Semmel, 'Hume-Tucker Debate'; James Livesey, 'Free Trade and Empire in the Anglo-Irish Commercial Propositions of 1785', *Journal of British Studies*, 52 (2013), 103–27; Peter J. Marshall, *Remaking the British Atlantic: The United States and the British Empire after American Independence* (Oxford: Oxford University Press, 2012), 152.

[70] John Manners, 7th Duke of Rutland (ed.), *Correspondence between the Right Honourable William Pitt, and Charles Duke of Rutland, Lord Lieutenant of Ireland, 1781–1787* (London, 1890), Pitt to Rutland, 14 December 1784, 64.

guaranteeing both Britain and Ireland a reciprocal 'effectual preference' in the market of the other, meanwhile placed an effective floor under the duties either Kingdom could levy on a range of goods that were also imported from other European countries.[71]

Writing to Rutland, Pitt drew a direct comparison between a 'permanent system . . . settled by the authority of two distinct Leiguslatures' and a 'treaty between two separate Crowns'.[72] The key difference between the Irish Propositions and Britain's other commercial agreements was the requirement for an Irish contribution to the upkeep of a common Crown, responsible for an imperial navy that 'cannot be under the control of anything but the parliament of this country [Britain]'. Only this could prevent 'the supreme executive power, and with it the force of the empire, being distracted into different channels, and its energy and effect being consequently lost'.[73] Whatever the 'new system' was called, Pitt claimed, what mattered was that 'both the advantage and the obligation should be reciprocal'.[74]

While Pitt's insistence on an imperial contribution went beyond the terms of European treaties between 'Crowns', his language was populated with the commonplaces of eighteenth-century commercial diplomacy. In the words of the leading contemporary synthesiser of the 'law of nations', the Swiss diplomat Emmerich de Vattel, eighteenth-century commercial treaties established a fixed and limited 'conventional right' of territorial and market access for a given trading partner.[75] Granting this right to one foreign state could mean preferring its goods over those of a third country: limiting, rather than extending, the natural duty of cosmopolitan mutual assistance that underpinned global commerce in the absence of positive law.[76]

The 1785 Propositions conformed closely to Vattel's ideal-type of a commercial treaty based on relationships of reciprocal preference. They did not embody either of the principles of nineteenth-century Britain's 'free trade empire', which unilaterally abolished British duties and monopolies without reference to other powers, and allowed at least the white settler

---

[71] Debrett, *Parliamentary Register*, 225.
[72] John Manners (ed.), *Pitt-Rutland Correspondence*, Pitt to Rutland, 14 December 1784, 71.
[73] Ibid., Pitt to Rutland, 14 December 1784, 73.
[74] Ibid., Pitt to Rutland, 14 December 1784, 72.
[75] Emmerich de Vattel, *The Law of Nations, or, Principles of the Law of Nature, Applied to the Conduct and Affairs of Nations and Sovereigns* (Indianapolis, IN: Liberty Fund, 2008), I.8.§93.
[76] Ibid., II.2.§32.

colonies to largely determine their own trade and revenue policies.[77] Nor did they aim to entirely abolish barriers to trade between the Kingdoms of Ireland and Britain. Instead, they constrained both Kingdoms to prefer one another's goods over those of any other nation, fixing duties at a moderate – but meaningful – level. Rather than employing 'free trade' as an instrument of a broader 'imperial integration', Pitt and his advisers constructed a mixed system of preference and restraint, purpose-built for the Irish Kingdom, and designed to counter the specific threats that Ireland posed to the integrity and boundaries of the British colonial system.[78]

Sugar, Manufactures and the Revision of the Propositions

The unravelling of Pitt's proposals began with their first public airing. In a speech to the Irish parliament delivered in February 1785, Orde made an Irish case for the Commercial Propositions that seemed calculated to inspire British disquiet. He presented them almost exclusively as a superior means of securing the interests of the Irish Kingdom through closer cooperation with a Britain that had 'relaxed the principle of interested jealousy' in favour of 'the real interest and advantage of both countries'.[79] By allowing Ireland to re-export colonial goods to Britain, Orde suggested, the Propositions held out the prospect that 'Ireland, from her happy situation, may become an emporium of trade, and even Britain may supply herself from her market'.[80] Orde also challenged the developing consensus in Britain that the country had gained sufficient advantages in skill and capital to dispense with fears about the consequences of Irish wage competition for British manufacturing. 'These are circumstances which will diminish every year, which may even be transferred to this country', Orde projected.[81] The Commercial Propositions offered the prospect for a major redistribution of economic power within the British Empire, in favour of the Irish Kingdom.

This first iteration of the Propositions unsurprisingly passed the Irish parliament by a wide margin. This early success, however, came at a high

---

[77] Anthony Howe, 'Free Trade and Global Order: The Rise and Fall of a Victorian Vision', in Duncan Bell (ed.), *Victorian Visions of Global Order* (Cambridge: Cambridge University Press, 2007), 26–46.

[78] For 'imperial integration', see Livesey, 'Free Trade and Empire', 107.

[79] Orde, *Commercial Regulations*, 8–10.   [80] Ibid., 13.   [81] Ibid.

price. In Britain, Orde's bold statement of the advantages Ireland would gain from a new imperial settlement outraged merchants and manufacturers alike. It was circulated widely in England and Scotland in pamphlet form, complete with outraged annotations by members of the Committee of Merchants and Traders of the City of London. Orde, Commercial Regulations, 19–31. British alarm was further increased by the publication of John Holroyd's *Observations on the Manufactures, Trade and Present State of Ireland* (1785), a substantial work that began during the agitation for protecting duties but rapidly re-tooled to address the prospective trade agreement.[82]

Sheffield's writings on Ireland formed part of a broader campaign for the defence of Britain's Atlantic empire following the loss of the North American colonies. His reputation as a commercial writer rested on a comprehensive demolition of the British Prime Minister the Earl of Shelburne's plan for a commercial treaty with the United States, published the previous year and criticised by Etienne Clavière in his correspondence with John Foster. Shelburne's proposed treaty had attempted to restore British–American trade by abolishing duties on American imports and opening Britain's Caribbean colonies to American shipping.[83] Sheffield's response set out a tough rationale for evaluating the impact of radical reforms on the power structures of the empire:

> Our great national object is to raise as many sailors and as much shipping as possible, so far acts of parliament may have effect; but neither acts of parliament nor treaties, in matters merely commercial, will have any force, farther than the interests of individuals coincide, and wherever advantage is to be gotten, the individual will pursue it.[84]

Sheffield's remark suggested an approach to matters of policy and regulation that was redolent of Adam Smith. Like Smith, who saw the Navigation Acts as a price worth paying to employ the skilled sailors necessary to sustain the British navy, Sheffield recognised a complex set of trade-offs between commercial and political interest in the construction

---

[82] On the politics surrounding the composition of Sheffield's work, see Kelly, *Prelude to Union*, 112–13.

[83] Charles R. Ritcheson, 'The Earl of Shelburne and Peace with America, 1782–1783: Vision and Reality', *The International History Review*, 5(1983), 322–45.

[84] Lord Sheffield John Holroyd, *Observations on the Commerce of the American States*, 6th ed. (London: J. Debrett, 1784), 247–8.

of imperial policy.[85] Britain's slave colonies in the Caribbean required high levels of expenditure to protect, and demanded that British consumers to accept high monopoly prices for their sugar. Only the 'advantage to our navigation', Sheffield argued, countered this 'enormous expence'.[86] By keeping ships and seamen under British control active in transatlantic trade, commerce in sugar and slaves enabled Britain to maintain its naval superiority over France.

Sheffield's defence of the West India plantation interest was a product of his commitment to the principles of the Navigation Acts. He had argued that Shelburne's American peace proposals would render the Caribbean colonies worthless by allowing British shipping to be driven out of the Caribbean trades by their American counterparts. The colonies would meanwhile supply themselves with food from North America, devastating the Irish provisioning industry and encouraging Irish retaliation against Britain. Ireland would then deliver the coup de grâce to the British Empire in the Atlantic, Sheffield warned, by opening its markets to cheaper sugar from the French and Spanish colonies in the Caribbean and becoming the destination of choice for British colonial goods. All these could then be smuggled into Britain, undermining revenue and ruining what remained of the slave and sugar trades.[87]

Sheffield's fears concerning Ireland's potential to devastate Britain's strategically vital Caribbean empire were carried over into his later work analysing Pitt's Commercial Propositions. Sheffield had little time for fears about Ireland's capacity to undersell British manufacturers in the making of textiles, and supported measures to lower and equalise duties on Anglo-Irish trade. The real danger was that revenue derived from Britain's colonial trades would be diverted away from the political heart of the empire. Sheffield's great concern was with the second of the Commercial Propositions, which abolished duties on the re-export of colonial goods from Ireland to Britain:[88]

> [Ireland's] object is to become the mart in Europe for the trade of America, for which she is so well suited by her western situation, immediately open to the ocean, and accessible almost with every wind ... her ships can be victualled infinitely cheaper; and every necessary of life being low, as well as public taxes, the general charge of conducting trade will be proportionably less.[89]

---

[85] John E. Crowley, 'Neo-Mercantilism and the Wealth of Nations: British Commercial Policy after the American Revolution', *The Historical Journal*, 33 (1990), 339–60.
[86] John Holroyd, *Observations on the American States*, 186–7.   [87] Ibid., 168–9.
[88] Holroyd, *Observations on Ireland*, 19.   [89] Ibid., 43.

It was Ireland's superior geographic location as a 'staple' for European and oceanic trade, rather than its capacity to compete with British goods on price, that provided the foundation for Sheffield's nightmare scenario: a migration of employment and revenues associated with insurance, warehousing and dock labour from Britain to Ireland.[90] 'No man of the least commercial knowledge', he concluded, 'can hesitate in declaring the measure a slow, perhaps, but certain poison, to the commerce, manufactures, and population of Great Britain'.[91]

Sheffield's assertion of the strategic indispensability of Britain's slave colonies rallied one vital parliamentary interest group, the British West India planters, in their opposition to Pitt's proposals. A second front was opened by the leading figure in the Whig parliamentary opposition, Charles Fox, who gathered a broad coalition of manufacturing interests organised by the Birmingham pottery entrepreneur Josiah Wedgwood.[92] By conducting parliamentary hearings with leading manufacturers, particularly from northern England, Fox and his supporters were able to solicit a body of expert opinion that directly contradicted the Privy Council inquiry commissioned by Pitt and Rose. In the course of more sustained investigation of the process of production in the burgeoning mechanised textile industries of Lancashire, manufacturers articulated an uncompromising vision of future competition between Irish and British production.

Robert Peele, a leading Lancashire cotton manufacturer and the father of the future Prime Minister, told parliament that the introduction of machinery into the business made it easier, rather than more difficult, for employment to be transferred from Britain to Ireland. Machines could be exported far more easily than skilled labour, and they could be worked by Ireland's cheap and unskilled hands. The Irish Kingdom's cost advantages would not be obviated by Propositions' 10 per cent average tariff. Peele himself stated that he would move his enterprise to Ireland within a few years of the agreement's ratification. Since there 'was very little of Skill in the Manufacture', he claimed, 'I am so convinced that the Manufacture may be as well done in Ireland'.[93] Fox triumphantly wielded Peele's submission as evidence of the hubris and abstraction of the belief that Britain's advantages over Ireland in manufacturing skill and capital were permanent and immutable. 'I know this to be the fashionable position of the present times, and of the present government: but general positions of

---

[90] Ibid., 49.   [91] Ibid., 48.   [92] Kelly, *Prelude to Union*, 114–17.
[93] House of Commons, *Minutes of the Evidence Taken before a Committee of the House of Commons* (Dublin: P. Byrne, 1785), 15–20.

all kinds ought to be very cautiously admitted', he urged. 'I do not think that great capital will always overbalance cheapness of labour, nor that cheap labour will always overbalance great capital; as general theorems, I dispute both, at the same time that I am clearly of opinion, that under certain circumstances both may be true.'[94]

For defenders of the measures, such as Arthur Young, attending to the needs of particular manufacturing industries was a pointless distraction from the common interest of the empire in expanded British–Irish trade. Echoing Hume and Tucker, Young argued that the vigour of Irish competition would encourage British manufacturers to divert 'ill-employed capitals into more productive channels, in which we enjoyed superior advantages'.[95] As we have seen, however, this argument for 'free' competition was not followed through by the framers of the Propositions, who had staked their credibility on the claim that the tariffs they retained were sufficient to protect domestic producers in both Kingdoms from the disruptive influence of expanded competition.

In pamphlets published in response to Sheffield and the British manufacturers, Rose and Chalmers accordingly backtracked on Orde's original claims about the benefits Ireland was likely to enjoy as a result of the passage of the Commercial Propositions. Ireland's free access to European and colonial markets since the 1780s, they averred, had hardly shaken British trading dominance. The mere ability to re-export colonial goods to Britain was unlikely to bring about a rapid transformation in Ireland's hitherto modest prospects.[96] Chalmers meanwhile argued against Sheffield that the increase in British–Irish trade enabled by the Propositions was precisely calculated to reinforce Britain's naval strength. 'By opening freely the ports of the sister kingdoms to each other for ships navigated by *British* subjects, the *principle* of the Navigation Act will be extended', he declared.[97] Responding to Peele's warnings about a flight of manufacturing to capital to Ireland, he bullishly suggested that the industrialist's competitors in Lancashire would welcome his departure: 'such are the constant competitions of a manufacturing country'. Britain's surplus of available capital was such that expanded British investment in Irish production would not occasion unemployment at home. The success of an uprooted industry,

---

[94] Cobbett, *Parliamentary History*, XXV:613.
[95] Arthur Young, 'Observations on the Commercial Arrangement with Ireland', *Annals of Agriculture*, III (1785), 257–91, at 259.
[96] Rose, *System of Trade*, 15–23.
[97] George Chalmers, *An Answer to the Reply to the Supposed Treasury Pamphlet* (London: John Stockdale, 1785), 29–30.

meanwhile, could not be guaranteed by low labour costs alone. 'Mr Peele may carry his cash to Ireland', noted Chalmers, 'but he cannot easily transport his warehouses, his workmen, his credit, or his customers'.[98]

Even while the ministry's pamphleteers moved to reassure British audiences that the Propositions would not, after all, enable Ireland to usurp Britain's position as the 'emporium' of world trade, Pitt engaged in a round of revisions that further – and critically – undermined their appeal to Irish parliamentarians. The version of the agreement that passed the British House of Lords at the end of May 1785 doubled the number of Propositions from eleven to twenty, and extended existing provisions so as to strengthen Irish obligations under the agreement. Pitt reintroduced Ogilvie's original insistence on the Irish Kingdom's automatic implementation of British regulations applicable to the colonies, and extended it to establish Westminster's primacy over copyright and patents.

To further appease the West India interest, Pitt meanwhile added a range of new Propositions that were designed to ensure that Irish ports handled Caribbean goods on the same terms as their British counterparts, restricting opportunities for smuggling and preventing the Irish parliament from creating fiscal incentives for the landing of West India goods in Irish ports. The original ninth Proposition, which had specified a general reciprocal preference between Britain and Ireland for each other's goods over those from all other countries, was expanded into a new sixteenth Proposition that specifically required the Irish Kingdom to apply duties on American goods at whatever level the Westminster parliament might determine. Two new Propositions also bound the Irish Kingdom to observe the monopoly of the British East India Company, requiring Irish goods to be shipped to India in Company ships, and via British ports.[99]

The pattern of British revisions to the Propositions demonstrates that it was Sheffield's argument concerning the Irish Kingdom's potential as an entrepôt for Atlantic and European trade, rather than manufacturers' fears of Irish competition on wages, that proved politically decisive in London. Pitt saw no need to modify his proposed tariff regime for British–Irish trade. The new provisions sought instead to protect the interests of the East India Company and the West India slave and sugar traders, while closing off any residual possibility that the Irish Kingdom could establish itself as a hub for trade with the independent American states. The Irish

[98] Ibid., 84–5.   [99] Kelly, *Prelude to Union*, 143–51.

Kingdom would not be permitted to force the dissolution of the British colonial system through exertions of its 'legislative independence'.

The Irish Debate on the Revised Propositions

The extent of British demands for modification to the Propositions of February 1785 meant that Pitt was forced to reformulate them as a 'Commercial Bill' and resubmit them at College Green for Irish approval. By the summer of 1785, however, a coordinated publicity campaign by the parliamentary opposition in Britain and Ireland had succeeded in sowing considerable Irish doubt about the proposals. The course of the British debate over the Propositions had aroused extensive press attention in Ireland. Rising popular hostility, combined with the decisive criticism of the leading Patriot MP Henry Grattan, would eventually lead to the defeat of the proposals in the Irish House of Commons and their withdrawal from consideration in August 1785.[100]

Charles Fox's British campaign against the Propositions featured a rapid alternation of roles between a defender of British commercial interests and Irish constitutional rights.[101] The conduct of opposition in both countries, however, was animated by a consistent understanding of Ireland's position within the empire. This was based, as Rutland explained to Pitt in an exasperated letter of 1782, on a rejection of written agreements that sought to fix and secure Ireland's alignment with British legislation. Grattan's view, Rutland reported, was that 'everything should be left to national faith, and nothing covenanted'.[102] Despite his evident frustration, the Irish Lord Lieutenant had grasped something essential about an emergent Whig conception of Ireland's position in the empire. In the writings and speeches of the Anglican priest Thomas Lewis O'Beirne and the playwright and Westminster MP Richard Sheridan, the legislative constraint implied by Pitt's revised resolutions were contrasted with a vision of the British–Irish relationship as an association of trust between 'independent' Kingdoms.

O'Beirne, born an Irish Catholic, converted to Anglicanism and worked as private secretary to the leading Rockingham Whig the Duke of Portland during his time as Irish Lord Lieutenant in 1782.[103] By 1785, he was a key

---

[100] Ibid., 183–96.
[101] Paul Kelly, 'British and Irish Politics in 1785', *The English Historical Review*, 90 (1975), 536–63.
[102] *Pitt-Rutland Correspondence*, Rutland to Pitt, 4 July 1785, 108.
[103] Anon., *The Annual Biography and Dictionary, for the Year 1823* (London: Longman, Hurst, Rees, Orme and Brown, 1823), vol. 7, 455.

contact between the British opposition and their patriot allies in Dublin, writing pamphlets against the Propositions for both British and Irish audiences.[104] Writing anonymously as a British patriot, O'Beirne had made the argument that the ninth Proposition would hamstring any attempt to restructure Britain's commercial relationships with her European neighbours by requiring British ministers to preserve Ireland's favoured status in the scale of British duties.[105] Re-emerging as an Irishman to warn his countrymen about the dangers of the agreement, O'Beirne joined Fox and Richard Sheridan in raising alarm in Ireland about the new provisions Pitt had introduced to his system in an effort to appease the British parliament.

The new fourth Proposition, alongside the older provision demanding a perpetual Irish contribution to the British revenue, provided the focus of the Whig case against Pitt's proposals. Both O'Beirne and Richard Sheridan argued that the concession of legislative independence in 1782, as agreed by their allies in Rockingham's ministry of that year, should be regarded as a durable and final settlement of British–Irish relations. As indicated by their attention to Ogilvie's proposals for a 'foederal union' during Rockingham's premiership, British Whigs had, in fact, been deeply interested in the pursuit of a more comprehensive settlement that was – in its fundamentals – largely identical with that now proposed by Pitt. In 1785, however, Fox's supporters at Westminster and Dublin revived the Patriot demand for 'Free Trade', arguing that the provisions of Pitt's 'system' threatened to limit the Irish Kingdom's legal right to send ships under its own flag to all regions of the world. 'Under the insidious pretence of granting us the *ne plus ultra* of trade', O'Beirne wrote, 'and of compleating what is said to have been left imperfect in our commercial emancipation – we are required to relinquish our constitution; we are to pass once more under the yoke of dependency'.[106]

In a speech at Westminster that became a rallying cry for Irish opponents of Pitt's system, Richard Sheridan styled the Propositions as a betrayal of Ireland's hard-won legislative independence and commercial freedom. By binding the Irish Kingdom to British colonial regulations and preventing her from modifying its duties to favour other European powers ahead of Britain, the Propositions closed off the promising vistas of trade

---

[104] Kelly, *Prelude to Union*, 164.
[105] Thomas Lewis O'Beirne, *A Reply to the Treasury Pamphlet, Entitled the Proposed System of Trade with Ireland Explained* (London: J. Debrett, 1785), 65.
[106] Thomas Lewis O'Beirne, *A Letter from an Irish Gentleman in London, to His Friend in Dublin, on the Proposed System of Commerce* (London: J. Debrett, 1785), 14–15.

that had been opened by the constitutional revolution of 1782. The British compensation for this Irish concession was meanwhile far more limited than Pitt was prepared to admit. The Irish Kingdom already enjoyed access to the British colonial system for all purposes except the re-export of colonial goods to Britain itself. By ministers' own admissions in the British parliament, its domestic manufactures could not expect to benefit from a limited expansion of its access to the British market. This was a poor equivalent for the sacrifice of revenue and autonomy demanded by the Propositions:

> Thus restrained and dependent, her prospects of European commerce were to be proportionably diminished ... From whence was she to receive the boasted compensation? ... Upon what terms was the British market to be opened? If he was to adopt the language and sentiments of those who propose this boon, he should answer, upon terms as shall effectually prevent Ireland from ever profiting, in the smallest degree by the concession. To this point, all their arguments had tended: to this, all their evidence had been pointed.[107]

O'Beirne, meanwhile, raised the issue of the East India Company monopoly, the subject of the new ninth Proposition that required the Irish parliament to observe the East India Company charter as long as Britain did the same. O'Beirne speculated that as and when the Company's charter next came up for renewal in Britain, the Irish Kingdom would have the opportunity to decline to pass the resulting legislation and thereafter trade freely with India. Under the terms of the Commercial Propositions, however, Ireland was to be 'peremptorily excluded' from 'all connection with the countries beyond the Cape of Good Hope, to the Streights of Magellan, whether foreign or British', on the basis of laws made not in Dublin but at Westminster.[108]

The alternative to legislative alignment through Pitt's proposals was a conception of the empire as a free association of independent kingdoms, in which Britain enjoyed a pre-eminence that was largely informal. Here, the opposition were able to draw on the intellectual and rhetorical authority of Edmund Burke. In a brief speech on the Propositions, delivered in the British parliament in May 1785, Burke sought to reconcile his faction's apparently contradictary championing of British mercantile interests and

---

[107] Richard Brinsley Sheridan, *The Legislative Independence of Ireland Vindicated, in a Speech of Mr. Sheridan, on the Irish Propositions in the British House of Commons* (Dublin: P. Cooney, 1785), 13.
[108] O'Beirne, *Letter from an Irish Gentleman*, 27–8.

Irish constitutional liberties. The problem with Pitt's proposals, Burke claimed, was that they fundamentally misconceived the balance of power and responsibility between the Kingdoms of Britain and Ireland. 'Pre-eminence and dignity' within the empire, Burke observed, were 'due to England', since

> it was she alone that must bear the weight and burden of empire; she alone must pour out the ocean of wealth necessary for the defence of it. Ireland and other parts might empty their little urns to swell the tide; they might wield their little puny tridents; but the great trident that was to move the world, must be grasped by England alone; and dearly it cost her to hold it.[109]

Seeking to fix the relationship between the two Kingdoms on the basis of equality and reciprocity, Burke claimed, was to overturn this 'order and decree of nature'. Pitt's proposals violated Ireland's legislative independence by insisting on an unrealistic fixed contribution to the British revenue, while simultaneously undermining Britain's natural political and economic predominance within the empire by conceding too much to Ireland on questions of trade. Burke insisted that the British Empire could only be maintained as a hierarchical structure of authority through bonds of trust and consent, sustained by the generosity and prudence of the metropole. Pitt's determination to bind the Irish Kingdom into a fixed imperial fiscal system suggested that the lessons of the American crisis had not been learned. 'The supremacy of the parliament over Ireland had been renounced', Burke surmised, 'but the idea of contribution followed closely at the heels of the renunciation of dominion'. Instead of pursuing the farce of seeking to fund the British navy with Irish revenues – only four or five frigates could be kitted out, Burke quipped, before the Irish Exchequer would be bankrupted – Burke urged the administration to focus on reforming the Irish revenue, so that it could continue to sustain imperial troops.[110]

As Rutland noticed, the Whig argument against the Propositions was perfectly calibrated to appeal to the sentiments of Irish MPs who, like Grattan, refused to see a contradiction between the defence of Irish constitutional liberties and the cohesion of the imperial polity. Unlike the advanced Patriots of the later 1770s, the opponents of Pitt's

---

[109] Edmund Burke, 'Speech on Irish Commercial Propositions, 19th May 1785', in R. B. McDowell (ed.), *The Writings and Speeches of Edmund Burke*, vol. IX, 10 vols. (Oxford: Clarendon Press, 1981–2016), IX:589–93, at 591.
[110] Ibid., 589.

Propositions did not engage in speculation concerning the Irish Kingdom's ability to call on French assistance to vindicate its claims against Britain. Instead, they defended 'Free Trade' as the freedom for Ireland to autonomously develop its commercial capacities in a way that would enhance its ability to support common needs of both the empire and the Crown. As the author of one anonymous Dublin pamphlet put it,

> Let us rival Great Britain in affection; let us rival her likewise in constitutional adherence to ourselves. Let us not abate our zeal, or narrow our views, in thus apparently narrowing our field of action. Let us on the contrary animate our exertions, not ceasing to feel, that we multiply our powers of availing the empire, and perpetuate our inherent weight, by maintaining our constitutional rights, faculties and function, concentrated and entire.[111]

Supporters of the Irish administration, as represented by John Hely-Hutchinson and Charles Sheridan, had little that could match these flights of Patriot rhetoric. They relied on a meaningful, but ultimately formal, distinction between the old system of legislative restrictions on the Irish parliament and the new treaty that required Ireland to voluntarily observe British mercantile regulation as the price of entry to its colonial markets. Like North and Pitt, Sheridan argued that the regulations governing British trade had never been within the jurisdiction of the Irish legislature. 'This trade forms no part of the inheritance of the Irish legislature', Sheridan observed, 'no part of its commercial dominion'.[112] John Hely-Hutchinson, meanwhile, urged Irish readers to remember that the colonies were 'British property; she has a right to grant them on what conditions she pleases'.[113]

To agree to accept British regulations over the colonies – as Ireland had already been doing since 1782 – was, therefore, in no sense to diminish the Kingdom's legislative autonomy. 'Without such restraints' on legislative decision, Hely-Hutchinson observed, 'no commercial agreement could ever be framed between two independent legislatures'.[114] What mattered was that the commitments the Irish parliament was to make under Pitt's

---

[111] Anon., *An Address to the King and People of Ireland, upon the System of Final Adjustment, Contained in the Twenty Propositions, Which Have Passed the British House of Commons, and Are Now before the British House of Lords* (Dublin: R. Marchbank, 1785), 28.

[112] Charles Sheridan, *Free Thoughts upon the Present Crisis, in Which Are Stated the Fundamental Principles, upon Which Alone Ireland Can, or Ought to Agree to Any Final Settlement With Great Britain* (1785), 49.

[113] John Hely-Hutchinson, *A Letter from the Secretary of State to the Mayor of Cork on the Subject of the Bill Presented by Mr. Orde* (Dublin: P. Byrne, 1785), 5.

[114] Ibid., 37.

system were freely entered into. 'Limitations, which arise out of the power of the legislature, and depend for their duration on the same power', he concluded, 'are not arguments against, but the clearest proofs in support of legislative independence'.[115]

The 'Free Trade' demanded by Pitt's critics, Charles Sheridan meanwhile argued, would prove to be a 'naked' and 'barren' right in the absence of 'friendly intercourse' with the British Empire.[116] Even were this not case, it would still be 'essential to the prosperity of the two kingdoms, that the local interest of either should never be pursued to the injury of the common interests of both'.[117] It was for this reason that a reciprocal guarantee of preferential treatment for British and Irish goods was so important to the cohesion of the empire. The commercial advantages that Ireland might gain from a more favourable treatment of European and American produce were illusory when compared to the political security provided by the British connection.

Josiah Tucker on Ireland and the Slave Trade

As Sheridan's defence suggested, the idea that Pitt's Propositions represented a radical break with the commercial system of the British Empire was disclaimed by all but a few of their supporters, in Ireland as in Britain. Pitt's proposals were designed to consolidate this system by including Ireland within it. It was for this reason that the most ardent proponent of radical reform to the British colonial system, Josiah Tucker, welcomed the failure of Pitt's proposals – at least in the short term.[118] Despite his trenchant criticism of the Lockean doctrines of self-government that underpinned both Irish and American claims to 'independence', Tucker welcomed the prospect of continued Irish legislative autonomy in matters of trade and revenue.[119] Like Sheffield, Tucker dismissed the prospect of Irish competition with Britain in manufactures, arguing that Ireland's real potential was its ability to function as a commercial entrepôt between the

---

[115] Ibid.   [116] Sheridan, *Free Thoughts*, 26–31.   [117] Ibid., 35–6.

[118] Josiah Tucker, *Reflections on the Present Matters in Dispute between Great Britain and Ireland: And on the Means of Converting These Articles into Mutual Benefits to both Kingdoms* (London: T. Cadell, 1785), 4.

[119] J. G. A. Pocock, 'Josiah Tucker on Burke, Locke and Price: A Study in the Varieties of Eighteenth-Century Conservatism', in J. G. A. Pocock (ed.), *Virtue, Commerce and History: Essays on Political Thought and History, Chiefly in the Eighteenth Century* (Cambridge: Cambridge University Press, 1985).

European and Atlantic worlds.[120] Unlike Sheffield, however, he saw the Kingdom's best prospects for realising its disruptive potential as lying in a rejection of Pitt's Propositions.

Tucker believed that the Irish Kingdom now had a unique opportunity to break free of the venal mercantile interest groups that blighted Britain's ability to pursue a policy of commercial liberty. The Tory cleric's predictions for the Kingdom's future were as glowing as those of any Anglo-Irish Patriot. Unlike Charles Sheridan and John Hely-Hutchinson, Tucker did not worry about the Kingdom's relative lack of mercantile capital or native shipping. Ignoring the East India and Levant Company monopolies would draw over English merchants seeking free access to the markets of the East.[121] Dispensing with the Navigation Acts would demonstrate to the British legislature that 'the best and surest means of encouraging the breed of sailors, is to encourage the cheapness of freight, and to promote rivalship and emulation among all ranks and classes in society'.[122] Freeing the trade in Irish corn would enable Ireland to become 'a kind of magazine or granary' for the import and re-export of American grain to the rest of Europe, once again leading Britain by example.[123]

Tucker's most extravagant claim for the promise of Irish Free Trade, however, related to the same question that had animated Sheffield: the fate of the slave and sugar trade in the British Caribbean. Tucker's opposition to the slave trade was longstanding.[124] In his writings on Ireland, he condemned slavery as a violation of the Christian law to 'do unto others as we would have done to us'.[125] Because they enjoyed the privileges of colonial self-government, framing and enforcing laws for their own benefit, British slave-owners were more cruel and exploitative than those of France and Spain, where 'absolute governments' were a 'check on the tyranny of their intermediate subjects'.[126]

Slavery was also, however, a species of 'monopoly': one that – like the Navigation Acts or the East India Company charter – could be destroyed through judicious appeals to the 'self-interest' of traders. Here, too, the 'present state of Ireland' would prove transformative for the empire as a whole. By opening its markets to French and Spanish sugar, the Irish would reveal to British traders that a more lenient labour regime produced a cheaper, superior product. Once English 'adventurers' started to use the

---

[120] Tucker, *Reflections on the Present Matters in Dispute*, v–vi.   [121] Ibid., 5–8.   [122] Ibid., 23–4.
[123] Ibid., 32–3.
[124] Christopher Leslie Brown, *Moral Capital: Foundations of British Abolitionism* (Chapel Hill: University of North Carolina Press, 2006), 159.
[125] Tucker, *Reflections on the Present Matters in Dispute*, 8–9.   [126] Ibid., 10.

Irish flag to trade freely with the East Indies, they would discover that sugar cultivated by 'freemen' was cheaper still. 'The principles of morality, and of national commerce, agree in this respect in perfect harmony', enabling a gradual process of emancipation that remained firmly under the control of the slave-owning planter.[127] Africans themselves could, meanwhile, be brought to abandon the practice of 'trucking for their own flesh and blood' if they were taught to cultivate sugar – alongside other commodities such as 'rice, indigo, cotton, cochineal'. All Europe could then be 'supplied with sugars, and all the products of the warmer climates, without slavery, without colonies, without governments and placemen'.[128]

For Tucker, the undermining of empire through the legislative auton-omy of the Irish Kingdom would, therefore, act as an educative process for those same British mercantile interests who had so violently opposed the first iteration of Pitt's Irish proposals. Once these witnessed the flourishing of Ireland as a free port, 'new interests and connections would be formed' in Britain itself that would break down mercantile support for the colonial system.[129] Only under these circumstances, Tucker predicted, could an incorporating union of the Westminster and Dublin legislatures, which he had advocated since the 1750s, be brought to pass. Union, for Tucker, now stood at the end of a process of commercial Enlightenment that had begun with American independence and would continue through the Dublin parliament's rejection of Pitt's Commercial Propositions.

A Revolution in Retrospect

Tucker's surprisingly critical verdict on Pitt's Commercial Propositions underlines the account offered here of their nature and purposes. The Propositions were defined by the same Vatellian principles of reciprocity and balance that shaped commercial negotiations throughout eighteenth-century Europe. They sought to bind Ireland into a British mercantile empire that, while undergoing a process of piecemeal reform, still rested on a complex structure of positive law and privilege, rather than Smithian 'natural liberty'. As such, it was the Proposition's opponents, rather than their supporters, whose position anticipated the unilateral and permissive system of free trade developed by the British Empire and its self-governing dominions in the nineteenth century.

---

[127] Ibid., 15. [128] Ibid., 16–17. [129] Ibid., 34.

The problem of Ireland's commercial relationship to the British Empire had been raised as a result of the uncompromising vision of 'legislative independence' realised in the constitutional 'revolution' of 1782. Anglo-Irish 'Patriots' had framed their demands in terms that were fundamentally different to those of their North American counterparts. They rejected even the formal distinction between 'external' and 'internal' legislation drawn by the American colonists, instead insisting that Ireland's historic status as a European realm, the full equal of Britain in its sovereign rights, entitled it to the pursuit of an autonomous commercial policy, answerable only to the Crown.

At a few decisive moments – the entry of France into the American war, the Portuguese exclusion of Ireland from the Metheun treaty, the Irish agitations for protecting duties and free ports – Irish 'legislative independence' threatened to break the bounds of empire and establish Ireland as a European commercial power in its own right. Pitt's proposals were designed to close down this space of possibility. They ultimately foundered because they threatened to re-inscribe, in the form of a parliamentary 'treaty', the very legislative subordination that the constitutional 'revolution' of 1782 had sought to overthrow. This allowed the Propositions to be understood as a threat to the promising vistas of global 'Free Trade' opened by the revolution of 1782.

The drama of Ireland's eighteenth-century 'constitutional revolution', however, would ultimately end on a bathetic note. After the failure of the Propositions, Pitt and his Irish supporters abandoned hopes of a comprehensive solution to the problem of Irish autonomy, re-committing themselves to the old arts of parliamentary management through patronage and negotiation. The most accurate analyst of the politics of 'legislative' independence turned out to be Henry Dundas, a master of Scottish patronage whose influence north of the border made him indispensable to successive eighteenth-century British ministries. Corresponding with Adam Smith on Irish policy during the 'Free Trade' crisis, Dundas had observed that, failing a full union, 'the Irish Parliament must be managed by the proper distribution of the loaves and fishes, so that the Legislatures of the two Countrys [sic] may act in union together'.[130] Empire by patronage could only endure, however, in the presence of both popular quiescence and international peace. This was not the prospect that awaited Ireland or Europe in the 1790s. Just one year after the successful passage of the Franco-British Treaty of Commerce through the Irish parliament in 1786,

---

[130] Smith, *Correspondence*, Henry Dundas to Adam Smith, 30 October 1779.

revolution in the Netherlands pitched the European order into a fresh crisis: one that would ultimately result in the downfall of the French monarchy, and the outbreak of a global war that would last for a generation. Property and religion, the central questions of the French Revolution, were forced to the centre of Irish politics, engendering new forms of popular radicalism that looked past the legacies of Molyneux, and placed their faith in the reforming agency of the new republican empire that had arisen in France.

CHAPTER 3

Property, Revolution and Peace, 1789–1803

The French Revolution transformed the terms of Irish debate over the relationship between the Anglican landed elite and the Catholic majority. The storming of the Bastille and the convening of the National Assembly proved conclusively to many Anglican and Presbyterian radicals that a largely Catholic people could be trusted to fight for its liberties.[1] Spreading news of the events in France was crucial for the formation of the United Irishmen, a new movement whose political ambitions went far further than the constitutional 'Patriots' of the 1780s.[2] Doing away with the Patriot ideal of a mixed imperial constitution, the United Irishmen disputed the right of the Westminster parliament to decide questions of war and peace, a position that allowed them to capitalise on popular resentment against the taxation and military recruitment demanded by war with revolutionary France.[3] By 1794 at the latest, they were actively seeking French military assistance for Irish rebellions against the British Empire. This was eventually offered in the form of attempted French landings at Bantry Bay, West Cork, in December 1796, and Killala, County Mayo, in August 1798.[4]

The United Irishmen owe their historical reputation to their efforts to found an Irish Republic on cross-confessional lines.[5] Yet they were also staunch advocates of an Irish national sovereignty that demanded rebellion against the British Crown – a position that required them to offer distinctive arguments about the nature of the British Empire and the European order in the era of the French Revolutionary Wars. Because these arguments centred on the contribution of commerce to British power, they were closely linked to another underrated element of United Irish

---

[1] Nancy J. Curtin, *The United Irishmen: Popular Politics in Ulster and Dublin, 1791–1798* (Oxford: Clarendon Press, 1994), 34–5.
[2] Gillen, 'Monarchy, Republic and Empire', 98–9.
[3] McBride, *Eighteenth Century Ireland*, 351–3.   [4] Elliott, *Partners in Revolution*.
[5] Ian McBride, 'Reclaiming the Rebellion: 1798 in 1998', *Irish Historical Studies*, 31 (1999), 395–410.

ideology: the society's advocacy of social and economic reform in the interests of the Irish majority.[6] The United Irishmen were committed to the transformation of Ireland's sectarian and heavily unequal property order, eventually coming to regard this essential to the popular mobilisation necessary to drive out the forces of the British Empire.[7] 'If a revolution ever takes place', the United Irishman Thomas Addis Emmet told a British investigating committee in 1799, 'a very different system of political economy will be established from what has hitherto prevailed here'.[8]

This new focus on the condition of Irish rural society – on rents, leases, tithes and taxation, as well as the ultimate ownership of the land itself – marked a further area of divergence between United Irish radicalism and the Patriot politics of the 1780s. As we have seen in the previous chapter, the competing visions of Irish commercial autonomy entertained by Irish patriots and Whigs had all centred on the expansion – rather than the distribution – of the gains of foreign trade. The condition of Ireland's rural interior was largely kept out of elite discussion of the Kingdom's constitutional and commercial status. In the years immediately after the failure of Pitt's commercial propositions, however, this exclusion had begun to break down. A wave of 'Rightboy' disturbances, centred on Munster but extending to Cork, Kerry, Limerick, Tipperary, Queen's and Kilkenny, had set off a fresh controversy concerning the tithes levied by the Church of Ireland on a largely Catholic and Presbyterian population.[9] Irish improving literature, undergoing a revival under the auspices of the newly established Royal Irish Academy, was increasingly concerned with the condition of the rural poor in the south and west, as booming grain exports to Britain began to transform the Irish landscape and challenge linen as a source of export earnings.[10]

The French declaration of war against Britain in 1793 placed the Irish agrarian economy at the centre of the geopolitical and ideological confrontation between the British Empire and revolutionary France. In the early years of the revolution, France had abolished residual feudal obligations, introduced a civil code including mandatory partitive inheritance, and

---

[6] James Quinn, 'The United Irishmen and Social Reform', *Irish Historical Studies*, 31 (1998), 188–201.

[7] Nancy Curtin, 'The Transformation of the Society of United Irishmen into a Mass-Based Revolutionary Organisation, 1794–6', *Irish Historical Studies*, 24 (1985), 463–92.

[8] Thomas Addis Emmett, Arthur O'Connor and William J. MacNeven, *Memoire; or, Detailed Statement of the Origin and Progress of the Irish Union* (1800), 36.

[9] James Kelly, 'Inter-Denominational Relations and Religious Toleration in Late Eighteenth-Century Ireland: The "Paper War" 1786–88', *Eighteenth-Century Ireland : Iris an dá chultúr*, 3 (1988), 39–67.

[10] See Chapter 5.

extensively redistributed land confiscated from the Catholic Church and noble émigrés. French armies proclaimed the 'abolition of feudalism' across Europe, attacking the property and privilege of aristocracies and church establishments.[11] Revolutionary advocates of European war regarded the necessary defence of the young republic from foreign inter-ference as part of a broader project to purge European politics of the inequality and corruption that had produced recurrent wars throughout the eighteenth century.

The United Irishmen followed both French revolutionaries and English radicals in declaring themselves enemies to the aristocratic power and commercial monopoly that they held to be characteristic of British rule.[12] They identified the political and religious privileges of Anglo-Irish Ascendancy with the political corruption that had produced poverty and warfare across eighteenth-century Europe. Trusting to popular faith in the French Republic as an agent of peace and prosperity, Irish emissaries to the French Directory promised that Irish 'men of no property' would inevita-bly rise in support of even a small invading force.[13] Emphasising, by turns, the Cromwellian expropriation of the Catholic nobility and the unjust exactions of land agents, tithe collectors, excise men and military recruiting officers, United Irish propaganda claimed that a French-aided revolution was the only route to agrarian justice for the Irish majority.[14]

The popular political economy of the United Irishmen combined disparate, and sometimes contradictory, arguments from a range of Irish, British and French sources. The Paineite radicalism of the Anglican parliamentarian Arthur O'Connor – a relative latecomer to the move-ment – was in an unacknowledged tension with the militant Irish protec-tionism demanded by the mainstream of the United Irishman: from Wolfe Tone, an Anglican barrister, to William James MacNeven, a Catholic physician who had travelled widely in continental Europe.[15] These

---

[11] John Markoff, *The Abolition of Feudalism: Peasants, Lords, and Legislators in the French Revolution* (University Park: Pennsylvania State University Press, 1996).
[12] Amanda Goodrich, *Debating England's Aristocracy in the 1790s: Pamphlets, Polemics, and Political Ideas* (Woodbridge: Boydell Press, 2005).
[13] Gillen, 'Monarchy, Republic and Empire', 185.
[14] Smyth, *Men of No Property*; Kevin Whelan, 'Introduction to "The Poor Man's Catechism" (1798)', *Labour History*, 75 (1998), 22–32.
[15] For biographical studies of these figures, see Frank MacDermot, 'Arthur O'Connor', *Irish Historical Studies*, 57 (1966), 48–69; C. J. Woods, 'MacNeven, William James', in McGuire and Quinn, *Dictionary of Irish Biography*; Marianne Elliott, *Wolfe Tone: Prophet of Irish Independence*, 2nd ed. (Liverpool: Liverpool University Press, 2012); Jorg Lähme, *William Drennan und der Kampf um die irische Unabhängigkeit: Eine politische Biographie* (Göttingen: Wallstein Verlag, 2012).

contrasting visions of political economy were framed by a shared belief in the ability of the French Republic to guarantee Irish autonomy in a transformed European order. Yet here, too, there were important differences of emphasis in the revolutionary rhetoric of different United Irish leaders. Where Tone was preoccupied with the indignity of Ireland's subordinate position within Britain's empire, Belfast radicals such as the Presbyterian minister William Steel Dickson and the radical journalist Thomas Russell connected the case of Ireland to critiques of British colonial conquest and the Atlantic slave trade.[16] O'Connor's and MacNeven's enthusiasm for French power after the failure of the 1798 rising, meanwhile, led them to produce lengthy apologetics for Napoleonic conquest, aimed at readers in Britain and continental Europe as well as in Ireland itself.

An examination of the published writings of a small collection of leading United Irishmen cannot of itself provide the basis for a thoroughgoing reinterpretation of this multi-layered, regionally varied and frequently secretive mass movement. The limited selection of texts examined here, however, encompasses the most sustained engagement by United Irish figures with questions of commerce and international order in the era of the French Revolution. It thereby enables us to better parse some of the United Irishmen's central political demands, and to establish their relationship to broader European controversies over commerce and empire. To further this attempt to locate the political thought of key United Irishmen in this understudied intellectual context, the chapter concludes by considering the place occupied by Ireland in the revolutionary propaganda produced in France and the German lands. Placing these distinct, but related, sets of political arguments alongside one another can show us something important about the position Ireland was coming to occupy in the European imagination in the era of the French Revolution. French attempts at invasion encouraged widespread interest in the idea that Ireland could prove to be the weak link in the British imperial system. They began to establish Ireland in the ideological position it would occupy throughout the early nineteenth century: as a prominent battleground between rival visions of commercial society, represented by the warring empires of France and Britain.

---

[16] James Quinn, *Soul on Fire: A Life of Thomas Russell* (Dublin: Irish Academic Press, 2002); Ian R. McBride, 'Dickson, William Steel', in McGuire and Quinn, *Dictionary of Irish Biography*.

'A Rank among the Primary Nations of the Earth'

Theobald Wolfe Tone has frequently been described as the 'first Irish nationalist'.[17] This claim is commonly explained with reference to this desire – shared with the rest of the United Irish organisation – to integrate Ireland's Catholic majority into the 'nation' proclaimed by Henry Grattan and other Anglo-Irish Patriots in the 1780s.[18] In Tone's writings, however, the integration of Catholics into the political nation frequently appears, like the mission to the French Directory, as only the necessary means to a higher end: the recovery of glory and renown for an Irish nation that had been too long subordinate to Britain.[19] Tone sought not merely an 'independent' Ireland, but one possessed of a flag, a navy and a 'rank among the primary nations of the earth'.[20] By its very nature, this claim entailed a particular imaginary of international order: one that repudiated both Britain's mercantile empire and Ireland's 'mixed constitution' and looked forward to a Europe reconstituted, under French leadership, on the basis of national sovereignty and equality.

Tone made his first public intervention on the question of Irish sovereignty on a topic related not to the French Revolution, but the pursuit of British commercial ambitions in the Pacific and East Asia. Following the publication of James Cook's account of this third Pacific voyage in 1784, there was an explosion of British interest in possibilities for opening a fur trade from what is now western Canada to China. This scheme was of particular interest to the East India Company, whose finances were constantly pressured by the need to purchase Chinese tea with its own supplies of gold bullion; it attracted Pitt's attention for the same reason. The Spanish monarchy, however, still claimed a monopoly on trade in the Pacific Ocean and began in the 1780s to launch a series of its own expeditions to identify the extent of interloping by Britain and the new United States. The inevitable collision occurred at the end of 1789, with the Spanish seizure of four British vessels in the Nootka Sound and two whalers off the coast of Patagonia. When news eventually reached London, Pitt and his cabinet made release of the ships and compensation of the traders affected the precondition of any discussion with the Spanish over

---

[17] McBride, *Eighteenth Century Ireland*, 369.   [18] Elliott, *Wolfe Tone*, 4–5.
[19] McBride, *Eighteenth Century Ireland*, 370.
[20] Theobald Wolfe Tone, *Spanish War! An Enquiry How Far Ireland Is Bound, of Right, to Embark in the Impending Contest on the Side of Great-Britain?* (Dublin: P. Byrne, 1790), 42. The phrase recurs in Tone, *An Argument on Behalf of the Catholics of Ireland* (Dublin: P. Byrne, 1791), 6.

trading rights in the Pacific Ocean: a stance that led many on both sides to suspect that war was imminent by the spring of 1790.[21]

The Nootka Sound crisis was the first time the British–Irish relationship established after 1782 had been tested by the prospect of renewed European war. It came at a volatile moment in Irish politics, as the defeated Irish advocates of a regency led by the Prince of Wales sought to form themselves into a 'Whig' faction capable of active political coordination with the Foxite opposition at Westminster.[22] Tone, a frustrated, impoverished young barrister with a growing interest in oppositional politics, identified an opportunity to make an impression on the political scene with a pamphlet, *Spanish War!* (1790), criticising the Irish parliament's seeming complaisance in a British rush to war.

Tone's case against Irish participation in the war began with the relatively uncontroversial claim that the Irish parliament, like its British counterpart, had a right to withhold supplies from the Crown if it so chose.[23] More striking was his assertion that the British parliament had no right to force the Irish Kingdom into a war without the active consent of its own legislature. It was possible, Tone argued, for two realms to share a monarch but not to share a foreign policy. The 'union of the executive' did not entail 'a union of power or of interest'. The Electorate of Hanover, he observed, was not bound to contribute troops to the British war effort, while the Habsburg dukedom of Tuscany were 'at this hour, neutral, and therefore flourishing in the midst of a bloody and destructive war' with the Ottoman Empire.[24] If legislative independence were to have any meaning, Tone claimed, Ireland would have to be able to exercise an effective 'negative voice' over questions of peace and war.[25] This need not have the effect of preventing Britain from prosecuting its own war aims – but it would enable Ireland to pursue a 'safe and honourable neutrality'.[26]

The extent to which Irish commerce and manufactures was likely to benefit from neutrality, as opposed to participation in a war alongside Britain, was the central focus of Tone's pamphlet. Ireland, argued Tone, could have no interest in British schemes of expansion in the Pacific. Its

[21] Alan Frost, 'Nootka Sound and the Beginnings of Britain's Imperialism of Free Trade', in Robin Fisher and Hugh Johnson (eds.), *From Maps to Metaphors: The Pacific World of George Vancouver* (Vancouver: University of British Columbia Press, 1993), 104–27.

[22] Neil Herman, 'Henry Grattan, the Regency Crisis and the Emergence of a Whig Party in Ireland, 1788–9', *Irish Historical Studies*, 32 (2001), 478–9; Elliott, *Wolfe Tone*, 77–8.

[23] Tone, *Spanish War!*, 8–9.

[24] Ibid., 22; See also Schroeder, *Transformation of European Politics*, 79–80.

[25] Tone, *Spanish War!*, 11.   [26] Ibid., 7.

interest was 'to foster and cherish a growing trade, to cultivate and civilise a
yet unpolished people, to obliterate the impression of ancient religious
feuds, to watch with incessant and anxious care of an infant constitution'.[27] Particularly given the notorious exclusion of Irish ports and
shipping from access to the East India Company's trading monopoly,
there could be little benefit for Ireland even from a British victory in the
conflict.[28] The prospect of commercial loss, alongside the widespread
impressment of Irish subjects to serve in the navy, was meanwhile all but
certain. Tone provided a selection of Customs House figures that showed a
high volume of Irish agricultural and manufacturing exports to Spain. 'The
rising prosperity of Ireland', Tone concluded, was to be 'immolated on the
altar of British pride and avarice'.[29]

Tone's vividly hostile characterisation of British aspirations in the Pacific
was surprising, given his own interest in schemes of colonisation on the
Hawai'ian islands discovered by Cook. Tone had written to Pitt himself to
propose a British colony in 1788, and would address himself to British
cabinet ministers again on the same subject just a few months after the
publication of his pamphlet. Tone – who stressed the need for 'a colony
purely military' able 'to temper the ferocity of the Natives by the arts of
European culture' – could evidently understand the attractions of colonial
conquest.[30] His objection to empire was limited to the observation that the
fruits of British naval power would never be equitably shared with Ireland:

> to Ireland nothing is certain but a heavy loss of trade, men and money [...]
> whereas England may not only support the contest, but be absolutely
> enriched by a Spanish war, even during its continuance. Her powerful
> navy, her infinite number of corsairs bring in wealthy prizes from every
> point of the compass. Where then, is the equality of empire? Or what are
> our temptations to war?[31]

Britain's failure to consult Ireland's interest in its dispute with Spain
proved, Tone concluded, that it was past time for the Kingdom to 'spurn
the idea of moving an humble satellite round any power, however great'.[32]

Spanish War! advanced a diagnosis of Ireland's shameful subordination
to Britain that would remain largely unchanged throughout Tone's mete-
oric career in revolutionary politics. Yet it lacked an account of the kind of

[27] Ibid., 13.   [28] Ibid., 14.   [29] Ibid., 20.
[30] Wolfe Tone, 'Proposals and Memorials Relative to the Establishment of a Military Colony in the
Sandwich Islands, and the Liberation of Spanish America by Theobald Wolfe Tone', in R. B.
McDowell, et al. (eds.), *The Writings of Theobald Wolfe Tone 1763–98*, vol. 1, 3 vols. (Oxford,
1790), 69–89, at 73.
[31] Ibid., 29.   [32] Tone, *Spanish War!*, 42.

political agency that would be able to achieve the political status he demanded for Ireland. In his *Argument on Behalf of the Roman Catholics of Ireland* (1791), provoked by a dispute within the Belfast Society of United Irishmen over the participation of Catholics in celebrations of Bastille Day, Tone identified the Catholic majority as the crucial component of any political coalition capable of establishing a meaningful form of Irish autonomy. Emboldened by the French Revolution and the increasing volume of Catholic and Presbyterian complaint against Protestant 'Ascendancy', Tone linked his earlier argument for Irish national power to a demand for Catholic inclusion in the structure of Irish parliamentary representation. The popular component of the Irish constitution needed to be strengthened in order to shift the direction of policy away from subservience to Britain. In a country whose population was overwhelmingly Catholic, there was an obvious conclusion to be drawn:

> Ireland, as deriving her government from another country, requires a strength in the people which may enable them, if necessary, to counteract the influence of that government, should it ever be, as it indisputably has been, exerted, to thwart her prosperity: ... this strength may be most constitutionally acquired, and safely and peaceably exerted through the medium of a Parliamentary Reform ... no reform is honourable, practicable, efficacious, or just, which does not include as a fundamental principle, the extension of elective franchise to the Roman Catholics.[33]

Ireland was 'without pride, or power, or name, without ambassadors, army, or navy; not of half the consequence in the empire of which she has the honour to make a part, with the single county of York'. Existing in a state of 'shamefull depression' and 'disgrace', Ireland possessed no 'national government, in which we differ from England, and from all Europe'. The purpose of an cross-confessional movement for parliamentary reform was – the phrase recurs from *Spanish War!* – 'to create a rank for our country among the nations of the earth'.[34]

Tone's *Argument* suggested that the French Revolution presented an opportunity for the development of an independent Irish foreign policy, focused on the economic development of the Kingdom. The crucial context was the possibility for Franco-British *rapprochement* that had been identified by British, French and Swiss reformers in the wake of the convening of the Estates General in the summer of 1789.[35] Tone, an early admirer of Thomas Paine, was undoubtedly impressed by the latter's

---

[33] Tone, *Argument*, 15.   [34] Ibid., 5–7.
[35] Whatmore, *Against War and Empire*, 232–3, 246–7.

dedication of Part I of the *Rights of Man* to the cause of Franco-British peace.[36] Viewed from this perspective, Tone's *Argument* contained more than the simple claim that the revolution demonstrated the love Catholic subjects could have for liberty. It had also discredited the fears of Bourbon universal monarchy and Jacobite conquest that had underpinned both the British revolutions of 1688 and the Williamite conquest of Ireland. The geopolitical justification for Protestant Ascendancy and Irish subservience to Britain was rapidly evaporating. 'Where is the dread now of absolute power, or the arbitrary nod of the Monarch in France? Where is the intolerance of Popish bigotry?' demanded Tone.

> Their wise and venerable National Assembly, representatives, not of their constituents merely, but of man, whose nature they have exalted beyond the limits that even Providence seemed to have bounded it by, have with that disinterested attention to the true welfare of their species, which has marked and dignified all their proceedings, renounced the idea of conquest, and engraven that renunciation on the altar, in the temple of their liberty.[37]

Where Anglo-Irish Patriots such as Joseph Pollock and Henry Flood had argued that 'the balance of Europe' was capable of supporting Irish claims within the British Empire, Tone now claimed that the peaceful intentions of revolutionary France were the best guarantor of the Irish Kingdom's independence. By following the moral example of French reform, unencumbered by fears of French intentions, Ireland could mobilise the popular forces necessary to secure its autonomy from Britain.

The French declaration of war in 1793 dramatically heightened the stakes of the developing confrontation between the United Irishmen and British government in Ireland. Between 1793 and 1796, a series of events placed Tone at the centre of an effort to secure French support for an Irish rebellion against British Empire. Despite the concession of an extensive franchise to Catholic voters in 1793, the reconstituted Catholic Committee – with Tone, symbolically replacing Edmund Burke's son Richard as chair – was frustrated in its campaign for a relaxation of restrictions on Catholic officeholding in municipal corporations and army ranks, as well as in the Irish parliament itself.[38] A crescendo of political violence, beginning with riots against militia recruitment in 1793 and

---

[36] Thomas Paine, 'Rights of Man, Part 1', in B. Kuklick (ed.), *Political Writings* (Cambridge: Cambridge University Press, 1989), 60–1; Tone, *Argument*, iii–iv.

[37] Tone, *Argument*, 39–40.

[38] Deirdre Lindsay, 'The Fitzwilliam Episode Revisited', in D. Dickson, et al. (eds.), *The United Irishmen: Republicanism, Radicalism and Rebellion* (Dublin: Lilliput Press, 1993), 197–209.

culminating in a bloody attempt to expel Catholics from Armagh in 1795, demonstrated both the fragility of public authority and the increase of confessional tensions across the island.[39] The trial and suicide of William Jackson, a radical preacher accused of being a spy for France, meanwhile set the stage for the repression of the United Irish societies of Belfast and Dublin. Driven underground, the United Irish movement refashioned itself as an oath-based secret society, centred on Dublin rather than Belfast, dedicated to the revolutionary cause and cooperating closely with the Catholic 'Defender' groups that had originally been established in response to intimidation by Protestant 'Peep O'Day Boys' and the newly founded Orange Order.[40] Tone, forced into exile in the United States following the suppression of the United Irish societies, was appointed as a representative to the French Republic by what was now an avowedly secretive and insurrectionary organisation, comparable to the Jacobin forward parties who had already laid the ground for French expansion into Savoy, Belgium, the Netherlands, Switzerland and the Rhineland.[41]

The progress of the Irish reform movement, and the limited extent of Irish toleration towards Catholics, had been keenly observed in Paris since the beginning of the revolution, while leading Irish radicals had been in contact with the French Republic since 1792. Outrage at British support for the counter-revolutionary insurrection in the Vendée had led the Committee of Public Safety to conduct espionage missions and make preliminary offers of support to the Defenders and the United Irishmen alike. It was the timely coincidence of the renewal of controversies over Catholic political rights with the political and military consolidation of the Thermidorian regime in 1795, however, that placed French intervention in Ireland on the agenda of the new Directory.[42] In February 1796, Tone travelled from the United States to Paris on the strength of an introduction from the French ambassador to Washington.[43]

The commencement of Tone's negotiations with the Directory concerning the likely course of an invasion had revealed that the French

---

[39] Thomas Bartlett, 'An End to Moral Economy: The Irish Militia Disturbances of 1793', *Past and Present*, 99 (1983), 41–6; McBride, *Eighteenth Century Ireland*, 413–22.

[40] Curtin, *The United Irishmen*, 58–66.   [41] Elliott, *Partners in Revolution*, 72–3.

[42] Elliott, *Partners in Revolution*, 71–4.   [43] Elliott, *Wolfe Tone*, 271.

government had only a tentative commitment to the establishment of an Irish 'sister republic'.[44] There was more interest in a strategy of what the French, in imitation of the Vendée 'chouan' rebels supported by Britain, called *chouannerie*.[45] Tone lobbied strongly against French plans to arm the Defenders and turn Ireland into the 'British Vendée'. 'Tho' France has every right and every provocation to retaliate on England the horrors of the war in La Vendée', Tone wrote to the French general Henri Clarke in the summer of 1796, 'it would be scarcely just to make [Ireland] suffer for the crimes of her oppressors'.[46] Instead, a French invasion had to be one based on overwhelming force, capable of supporting the rapid formation of a government led by Catholic and Dissenting elites. Only this could successfully overturn British resistance and establish control over the countryside, prior to the formation of a National Convention capable of framing a constitution for an Irish Republic.[47] From the beginning of his contact with France, Tone had emphasised that only a fully realised Irish revolution was capable of bringing about the precipitous decline in British naval and financial power that would be the primary benefit of a French invasion. If Ireland 'were to join and co-operate with France', Tone had written to Pierre Auguste Adet, the French minister to the United States in 1795, 'it must operate the certain destruction of England, and by consequence to the establishment of the liberty of mankind'.[48]

There could be little hope, Tone warned in his memorials to the French government concerning plans for invasion, that merely defeating British allies on the European continent would be enough to contain its power. The achievement of a global monopoly on commerce controlled by the British navy – enabled, in significant part, by the manpower and provisions it sourced from Ireland – was a real and present danger. It justified an urgent French focus on an Irish invasion strategy:

> England [. . .] will console herself for the disgrace of her arms by land in the acquisition of power and territory and commerce by sea; but these very acquisitions render it, if possible, incumbent not merely on France but on

[44] Elliott, *Partners in Revolution*, 77–133.

[45] Sylvie Kleinman, 'Initiating Insurgencies Abroad: French Plans to "chouannise" Britain and Ireland, 1793–1798', *Small Wars & Insurgencies*, 25 (2014), 784–99.

[46] Wolfe Tone, 'Memorandum to General Henri Jacques Guillaume Clarke on the Encouragement of Chouannerie in Ireland, 4 April 1796', in T. W. Moody, R. B. McDowell and C. J. Woods (eds.), *The Writings of Theobald Wolfe Tone, 1763–1798*, vol. 2, 3 vols. (Oxford, 1998–2007), 145–6.

[47] Wolfe Tone, 'Second Memorial to the French Government on the Present State of Ireland, 29 February 1796', in Moody et al., *The Writings of Theobald Wolfe Tone*, vol. 2, 88–97, at 91.

[48] Wolfe Tone, 'To Pierre Auguste Adet, 10 August 1795', in Moody et al., *The Writings of Theobald Wolfe Tone*, vol. 2, 3–7, at 4.

all Europe to endeavour to reduce within due limits and to prevent that enormous accumulation of wealth which the undisturbed possession of the commerce of the whole world would give her; and this reduction of her power can be alone, as I presume, accomplished with certainty and effect by separating Ireland from Great Britain.[49]

The French project for an invasion of the Irish Kingdom placed its rural interior at the centre of European high politics. Consideration of the mechanics of an Irish revolution led Tone to advance his most ambitious accounts of the social transformation that could be wrought in an independent Ireland in alliance with revolutionary France. The 'Addresses' Tone drafted for distribution after the planned landing of a force of 15,000 French troops at Bantry Bay sought to convert Irish economic grievance into political support for the invasion, while preventing revolution from degenerating into the mere *chouannerie* that Tone had so deplored.

His 'Address to the Peasantry of Ireland', drafted two months before the failed French landing at Bantry Bay, accordingly sought to buttress the authority of the French in determining the course of events following the collapse of British rule. In keeping with the spirit of the new French regime, it emphasised a separation between the bloodshed of the Terror – 'the crimes which unhappily for a short period disgraced the revolution, which exist no longer and of which no trace remains' – and the long-term benefits of the 'removal of . . . feudal rights' claimed by landlords 'brother peasants' in France, 'which are at this moment in full effect, and which will exist from generation to generation'.[50]

This transition, Tone emphasised, was fundamentally one of status: 'the laborious peasantry of France are immense gainers; they are no longer obliged to stand bareheaded like slaves behind their landlords'. The dismantling of feudal and clerical privilege, combined with the dramatic decline in real rents caused by the introduction of the *assignats*, had enabled the 'industrious' peasants to buy up church and émigré land distributed by the government. The results, Tone concluded, were nothing short of miraculous:

> At this hour almost all the lands in France are, as they ought to be, the property of those who cultivate them; those who before the revolution were

---

[49] Wolfe Tone, 'First Memorial to the French Government on the Present State of Ireland, 22 February 1796', in Moody et al., *The Writings of Theobald Wolfe Tone*, vol. 2, 61–70, at 62.

[50] Wolfe Tone, 'An address to the peasantry of Ireland, 14 October 1796', in Moody et al., *The Writings of Wolfe Tone*, vol. 2, 347–53, at 348–50.

no better than slaves, like yourselves, are now become substantial preoprie-
tors; and instead of a race of miserable farmers, oppressed by their landlords
and fleeced by their clergy, they have obtained for themselves and their
children, for ever, every man an estate more or less according to this means
and his industry.[51]

The account of the French land reforms Tone held out to his prospective
audience of Irish peasants was dramatic in its social consequences, but
strikingly devoid of popular agency. Property left vacant by its clerical and
émigré owners, the 'Address' emphasised, had passed through the hands of
the French government before being made available for purchase by an
industrious peasantry. This, of course, was a very partial account of what
had really happened during the early years of the revolution, during which
the situation in the French countryside had rapidly escalated out of the
control of a distant National Convention, and subsequent legislation
securing property to its new owners (by no means all of them erstwhile
peasants) had largely acted to render a *de facto* situation *de jure*.[52] It was
one that conformed closely, however, to the politics of the new French
Directory, which sought to 'terminate the revolution' and establish France
as a stable republic that had abolished aristocratic privilege while protecting its reformed property order.[53]

In Tone's 'Address to the People of Ireland on the Present Important
Crisis', he extolled the virtues of France's republican government, but
focused his argument on the question of Irish autonomy that had
preoccupied him since the start of the decade. 'The object for
[Ireland's] immediate consideration', he urged, 'is not whether she shall
adopt this or that form of government, but whether she shall be inde-
pendant under any'.[54] It was 'base', Tone claimed, 'to exist in depen-
dance on the will of a foreign power ... unnoted and unknown as a
nation in Europe'. The enervating effects of dependence, Tone claimed,
could be seen most especially among the 'wretched peasantry', who were
'half-fed, half-clothed, miserable and despised, defrauded of their just
rights as human beings, and reduced, if the innate spirit of your country
did not support them, as it were by miracle, below the level of the beasts
of the field'.[55] The root of Ireland's debasement – political, social and

---

[51] Tone, 'Letter to Adet', 352.
[52] Markoff, *Abolition of Feudalism*; Peter McPhee, 'The French Revolution, Peasants, and Capitalism',
American Historical Review, 94 (1989), 1265–80.
[53] Biancamaria Fontana, 'The Thermidorian Republic and its Principles', in B. Fontana (ed.), *The
Invention of the Modern Republic* (Cambridge: Cambridge University Press, 1994), 118–38.
[54] Tone, 'Address to the People', 377.   [55] Ibid., 378.

spiritual – was the 'monopoly' of parliamentary representation by Anglo-Irish Ascendancy, an 'aristocracy' who, unjustly terrified of the loss of property gained by conquest, were paid by England to 'destroy and smother your arts, manufactures and commerce in the cradle'. While parliamentary government was irretrievably corrupted in both Britain and Ireland, it was still employed in the former to 'advance their trade and manufactures by all possible means ... upon the same principle that the farmer manures the soil he means to cultivate and feed the beasts he destines for labour'. Ireland, by contrast, was to be kept 'a colony of idlers to consume her manufactures and to recruit her fleets and armies'.[56]

The elimination of aristocratic domination of Ireland's politics, Tone claimed – in a passage that was difficult to reconcile with what he intended to tell the 'peasantry' – did not imply wholesale confiscation of Anglo-Irish property. 'The lapse of time and change of circumstances', he vaguely observed, made 'a resumption of property' taken by Ireland's Cromwellian invaders impossible. Instead, a national and uncorrupted parliament would apply revenue to the development of an army and navy, as well as in projects of economic improvement: 'the making of roads, the cutting of canals, the opening of mines, the deepening of our harbours and calling into activity the native energy of the land'. The alternative to an Ireland debased and ruined by the government of an aristocratic faction, in hock to Britain's rapacious mercantile empire, was a condition of what Tone termed 'independence':

> We shall be a nation, not a province; citizens, not slaves. Every man shall rank in the state according to his merit and his talents. Our commerce shall extend into the four quarters of the globe, our flag shall be seen on the ocean, our name shall be known among the nations, and we shall at length assume that station for which God and Nature have designed us.[57]

As this peroration suggests, a concern with national grandeur, expressed through the realisation of Ireland's potential as a global trading power, still supplied the animating spirit of Tone's revolutionary rhetoric. In this, he remained the Irish Whig, and the enthusiast for colonial and military adventure, that he had been at the start of his tumultuous career in radical politics. What had changed in the course of the 1790s was the extent of his conception of national dignity, and the seriousness with which he pursued the goals of securing popular support, and foreign military intervention, in the hopes of realising it.

---

[56] Tone, 'Address to the Peasantry', 382–3.   [57] Ibid., 386.

Tone's determination to place Ireland at the centre of the developing Franco-British struggle was motivated by a powerful belief in the unique capacity of the French Republic to facilitate a cross-sectarian alliance in favour of Irish sovereignty. This belief led him, in turn, to consider the means by which the 'peasantry' of Ireland could be brought to support a republican politics of 'independence'. His interest in the political capacities of the 'men of no property' was not based on any substantive account of the claims of labour in democratic politics, such as that put forward by his close friend and political associate Thomas Russell.[58] Nor did it seek to locate Ireland in a broader analysis of the progress of 'commercial society' in the manner of his fellow emissary to the French Directory, Arthur O'Connor. Instead, Tone's conceptions of empire and political economy rested on a simple, but effective, argument for the peculiarly shameful character of an Irish poverty that he understood as the consequence of political dependence on Britain. Here, too, national reputation was all.

War, Empire and Slavery

Tone's writings presented the French Revolution and the outbreak of war between Britain and France as strategic opportunities for advancing the cause of Irish 'independence', through an alliance between Presbyterian, Catholic and Anglican Irishmen. For two of his erstwhile contemporaries in the Belfast Society of United Irishmen, however, the stakes of the confrontation were far higher. The Presbyterian minister William Steel Dickson and the former British East India soldier Thomas Russell were vital figures in organising United Irish politics in Ulster, the epicentre of the movement for much of the 1790s. Following the French declaration of war in 1793, they each made arguments against Irish involvement in the conflict that went far beyond Tone's appeal to the nation's interest in the trade of the world. For Dickson and Russell alike, the war between Britain and France had to be interpreted as part of a broader reckoning with the moral consequences of Britain's empire: consequences that ensnared the souls and consciences of every Irish subject whose consumption and military service implicated them in the sins of slavery and military aggression.

The sermons of the New Light Ulster Presbyterian minister William Steel Dickson were crucial to the popular framing of the French Revolutionary Wars within a perspective that was at once Enlightened

---

[58] On the context for Tone's famous remark, see Gillen, 'Monarchy, Republic and Empire', 184–7.

and millenarian.[59] Like his near-contemporary, William Drennan, Dickson had been a student of Smith and John Millar at Glasgow University. In his *Three Sermons on the Subject of Scripture Politics* (1793), Dickson offered a condensed, cyclical history of the rise and decline of commercial society, with recognisable links to Adam Ferguson's *Essay on the History of Civil Society* (1767) and Rousseau's *Discourse on the Origins of Inequality* (1755) and *Social Contract* (1762). He combined this, however, with a striking account of the French Revolution as heralding the redemption of mankind and the coming of universal peace.

The first sermon, delivered to the Volunteer convention at Dungammon in 1793, began by construing the Christian principle of 'loving one's neighbour as oneself' as an injunction to consider 'the happiness of man' in society and history. The laws which regulated 'the general division of men into magistrate and subject', Dickson laid down, 'have received the name of politics, and constitute a most interesting branch of morality, considered as a science'.[60] In small and primitive communities, Dickson explained, political authority was both personal and impermanent, held by elders in times of peace, and chieftains in times of war.[61] Under the pressure of competition between groups and the increase of population, however, private property, territorial expansion and a division of labour are introduced. This threefold development 'lays the foundation of a permanent distinction in ranks ... dependence for bread gives an influence, which is often lasting, and generally increases, as superiority in wealth prevails'.[62]

The combination of this inequality and dependence with the growing territorial extent and populousness of modern states led to Dickson's claim that 'all governments tend to despotism; and by degrees, more or less rapid, terminate in it'. In a passage indebted to the arguments of Rousseau, he described the concentration of political power in fewer and fewer hands made possible by the expansion of modern states. Direct democracy had become impossible and representation necessary, but this had permitted

---

[59] Ian McBride, *Scripture Politics: Ulster Presbyterians and Irish Radicalism in the Late Eighteenth Century* (Oxford: Clarendon Press, 1998), 199.

[60] William Steel Dickson, *Three Sermons on the Subject of Scripture Politics* (Belfast, 1793), 8–9.

[61] Ibid., 9. Cf. Adam Ferguson, *An Essay on the History of Civil Society* (Edinburgh: Edinburgh University Press, 1978), 84–7.

[62] Dickson, *Three Sermons*, 10.

ambitious magistrates to corrupt the legal principles that enabled societies to be governed in a way that was compatible with human freedom.[63]

Dickson stopped short of locating the British or Irish systems of government directly within this cycle of state formation and decline. His primary concern was the criticism of Church establishments, which had been hopelessly enmeshed in the 'policy' of ambitious rulers in the course of the universal history of law and government. The progress of political corruption had destroyed the natural, superintending relationship of rational religion over both morality and politics.[64] This question, Dickson explained in a second sermon, was central to the problem of interstate relations. He reminded his auditors that 'the way of peace [. . .] extends to the ends of the earth, . . . it should not be limited by country, climate, or complexion – by modes of religion, or forms of government'. Universal benevolence, not national pride or jealousy, was the basis of any rational understanding of politics. 'The political fiction of a natural enmity between any nations or societies of men', he warned, 'is blasphemy against nature, and nature's God'.[65]

National rivalry, Dickson argued, stemmed ultimately from the subordination of religion to 'policy': 'The peace of the gospel can never prevail among men, till the passions, the political interests, and the domineering spirit of religious party, be swallowed up in the ocean of universal goodwill', he declared. Dickson claimed that 'in all the religious contests which have distracted nations, and terminated so often in scenes of blood, *the religion of the state*, and not the religion of Jesus, has been the subject, and the love of power, pre-eminence, or riches, the leading principle'.[66] He offered the history of religious warfare and exclusion in the England, Ireland and Scotland, the 'lands of our nativity', as a series of 'melancholy, but undeniable examples' of this tendency in human history. But his strongest opprobrium was reserved for the malicious conduct of the European powers in India and the New World, which had sinfully frustrated the 'extension of the gospel' to all the peoples of the earth:

> The covetousness, rapacity, cruelty, and violence of the professors of Christianity, have universally caused the name of God to be blasphemed among the heathen, and the religion of the Messiah to be rejected. Of this we have many instances in the conquest of America by the Spaniards; and it

---

[63] Ibid., 10–11. Cf. Jean Jacques Rousseau, 'The Social Contract', in V. Gourevitch (ed.), *The Social Contract and Other Later Political Writings* (Cambridge: Cambridge University Press, 1997), 39–153, at 106, 10–12.
[64] Dickson, *Three Sermons*, 14–15.   [65] Ibid., 30–1.   [66] Ibid., 34.

is not improbable, that succeeding generations will be informed of the like barbarities, practised by our own countrymen, in the east; though few of them have yet been published among us. These enormities . . . convince us, that the peace of the gospel can never prevail among men, till the passions, the political interests, and the domineering spirit of religious party, be swallowed up in the ocean of universal goodwill.[67]

The history of Spanish and British Empires was set in sharp contrast to the foreign policy of the new French Republic. 'One great and enlightened nation has burst the chains of prejudice and slavery', declared Dickson. France had 'disclaimed the idea of conquest for dominion, opened the temple of liberty for all religious denominations at home, and sent forth her arms, *not to destroy*, but *restore* the liberty of the world, and extend her blessings to all who dare, and by daring, deserve to be free'. For the British monarch, the lesson was clear. With one eye on the unfolding Terror, Dickson prayed that 'the ear of the Prince may be open to the voice of humanity reciting her grievances, and supplicating redress; and the necessity and horrors of revolution precluded, by seasonable and radical reform!'[68]

Dickson's sermons represented the translation, into the political language of 'New Light' Irish Presbyterianism, of the French Republic's recurring tendency to present its policy as being conducted in the interests of humanity and European society, as opposed to the unprincipled monarchical *raison d'état* of its opponents.[69] This opened a political space where the duty of obedience owed to Irish Crown – and to the British Empire that stood behind it – could conceivably be suspended, if the parliament at Dublin refused to adopt the programme of religious liberty and parliamentary reform demanded by the United Irish movement. It was this implication of Dickson's argument that Thomas Russell advanced in a pamphlet published from the Belfast offices of the United Irish newspaper, the *Northern Star*, in September 1796. Russell's work – which he rashly signed under his own name – appeared just months before Tone's attempted landing at Bantry Bay, and some two weeks before the beginning of its author's own long imprisonment for treason.[70] It made a case against Irish participation in the war that was grounded not in Tone's terms of national interest, but the requirements of individual religious conscience. Support for the British Empire could not be rendered

[67] Ibid., 34–5.   [68] Ibid., 35.   [69] Belissa, *Repenser l'ordre européen*, 47–8.
[70] Thomas Russell, *A Letter to the People of Ireland, on the Present Situation of the Country* (Belfast: Northern Star, 1796), 24; Wolfe Tone, 'Diary, 14 October–13 November 1796', in *Writings*, vol. 2, 360, 29 October 1796.

compatible with the Christian duty of universal benevolence: a duty that was binding on every member of the political community, no matter how lowly in station.

The binds of moral obligation linking ordinary Irish subjects to empire were those of consumption, the fiscal state and military service. Russell emphasised that every peasant and artisan in the country had both the right, and the obligation, to act politically, since they fought in the army and navy and supplied taxes and labour for the maintenance of the empire. He lamented that 'the insolent enslavers of the human race' had prevented

> the mass of mankind from interfering in political pursuits; force, and argument, and wit, and ridicule, and invective, have been used by the governing party, and with such success, that any of the lower, or even middle rank of society who engage in politics, have been, and are, considered not only as ridiculous, but in some degree culpable.[71]

Attacking this fraud against the rights of the majority, Russell offered a radical redefinition of the political community as being one not of property, but of labour: 'the possession of land without cultivators is of no value to a man ... even in a pecuniary view, the mass of the people are entitled to a share in the government as well as the rich'.[72] He told his readers that 'the earth was given to man by he who alone had a right to give it, for his subsistence; let not those then who raise the fruits of it among us be despised'.[73]

This right of political representation, however, implied a parallel duty of political responsibility, which Russell defined in cosmopolitan terms. Every subject, Russell urged, had a duty to 'attend to the government and politics of the state in which he lives. This is his duty to his neighbour in the most extensive sense of the word – embracing the whole family of mankind'.[74] Ireland was currently engaged in a war of aggression against France, and every Irish individual was therefore contributing to this through their taxes, labour and military service. 'Mankind are used to disregard actions which do not immediately fall under their observation', Russell wrote of the 150,000 Irish soldiers he estimated to be in imperial service:

> Let us for a moment consider the miseries which this multitude of men have inflicted on people who never injured them; the number of our fellow creatures whom they have killed or mangled ... Are then these dreadful scenes less real, or are the Irish nation less accountable for them because

---

[71] Russell, *Letter*, 15–16.   [72] Ibid., 17.   [73] Ibid., 18.   [74] Ibid., 19.

they are acted at a distance, because they occur in France, Flanders, in Holland, in the Atlantic, in the East or West Indies?[75]

Russell drew on a deep wellspring of Belfast radicalism by linking the Franco-British war to the fate of the slave trade. In the early 1790s, a powerful Irish movement against the trade had emerged, led by Belfast women such as the radical poet Mary Birkett, who had begun to develop the anti-imperial image of Ireland that was to persist through Daniel O'Connell's antislavery activism and beyond.[76] Russell drew on the providential rhetoric of the anti-slavery movement to remind readers that the trade was a major object of the war between Britain and the French Republic. Under the French constitutions of 1793 and 1795, slavery and the slave trade had been abolished throughout the French dominions. The rebel slave colony of Saint-Domingue – soon to be renamed the Haitian Republic – had become a major battleground in the Franco-British war in the Caribbean.[77]

Accordingly it was the issue of the slave trade, the products of which permeated every level of Irish society, that provided Russell with the clearest example of how closely the British Empire's war of aggression against France was connected to the personal conduct of individual Irish subjects. Russell – who himself refused to consume rum or sugar – asked whether the Irish people were really

> willing to employ their treasure and their blood in support of that system, because England has 70 or 7000 millions engaged in it, the only argument that can be adduced in its favour, *monstrous* as it may appear? Do they know that that horrid traffic spreads its influence over the globe; that it creates and perpetuates barbarism and misery, and prevents the spreading of civilization and religion, in which we profess to believe?[78]

The slave trade provided the ultimate justification for Russell's repeated exhortations to the peasants and artisans of Ireland to cast off the aspersion that they were incapable of political action or decision. 'Every man who contributes to the war', he claimed, was contributing to the support of slavery, and 'every person who drinks whiskey, or anything stronger than water; every person who wears shoes, pays something to the government'.

---

[75] Ibid., 21.
[76] Nini Rodgers, 'Two Quakers and a Utilitarian: The Reaction of Three Irish Women Writers to the Problem of Slavery, 1789–1807', *Proceedings of the Royal Irish Academy, Section C*, 100C (2000), 137–57, at 148–51.
[77] Robin Blackburn, 'Haiti, Slavery, and the Age of the Democratic Revolution', *The William and Mary Quarterly*, 63 (2006), 643–74.
[78] Russell, *Letter*, 21–2.

It was therefore 'not only the right but the *essential duty* of every man to interest himself in the conduct of the government [...] with what indignation should infamous intolerable proposition be rejected, that the mass of the people have no right to meddle in politics'.

This duty, Russell reminded his readers, was ultimately owed not to man, but to God. 'The great object of mankind', he wrote, 'should be to consider themselves as accountable for their actions to God *alone*, and to pay no regard or obedience to any men or institution, which is not comfortable to his view'.[79] The global machinations of Britain's empire of commerce and slavery forced every Irish subject – whether as soldier or taxpayer – to sacrifice 'his abilities, his judgment, his conscience, and his eternal happiness' to its rapacious aggression. The purpose of achieving a 'union' among the 'Irish nation' was not to pursue glory and renown on the terms sought by Tone. It was to advance 'brotherly love to our fellow-creatures', and assure its adherents of their chance of becoming 'acceptable in the sight of the Almighty, all perfect and adorable author of Nature'.[80]

Russell, like Dickson, thereby placed the political aspirations of the United Irish movement in a cosmopolitan perspective that linked the conscience and salvation of individual Irish subjects to Britain's prosecution of its global military campaign against revolutionary France. While Dickson sought to inspire his auditors to resist what he described as a war of aggression against a 'great and enlightened' republic, Russell placed the emphasis of his account on the evils of the slave trade, which had a unique ability to ensnare anyone who engaged in the consumption of colonial goods in the commission of sin. In both cases, objections to Ireland's participation in the war against France were framed not through appeals to a merely Irish pride and patriotism, but to the duty of Christian subjects to resist a war of aggression, waged against the interests of mankind.

Arthur O'Connor and the 'Natural Progress of Opulence'

Dickson and Russell each framed their arguments for an Irish alliance with revolutionary France in terms of the moral aspirations of a republic that had publicly committed itself to the pursuit of peace in Europe. For Arthur

[79] Ibid., 23.   [80] Ibid., 24.

O'Connor, an aristocratic radical who enjoyed good relationships with many opposition British Whigs, there was a more pragmatic reason for Ireland to align itself with the interests of revolutionary France: the republic was overwhelmingly likely to win the war.

A champion of Catholic Emancipation who made his name in radical circles with an incendiary speech to the Irish parliament during the Fitzwilliam episode, O'Connor's primary intellectual influences were the political economy of Adam Smith and the philosophical history of the Marquis de Condorcet.[81] His writings and speeches articulated a radicalised version of Smith's political economy, arguing that the corrupted property order of Britain and Ireland, and its consequent derangement of both political representation and religious liberty, could only be corrected by a French invasion. Political economy provided a justification for revolution by demonstrating that British authority in Ireland was rooted in a broader system of 'feudal' property relations that were structurally impervious to popular demands for reform. O'Connor's position was grounded in an innovative reading of the third book of Smith's *Wealth of Nations*. This had set out a crucial distinction between a 'natural progress of opulence', to be observed in the pristine setting of colonial America, and the 'unnatural and retrograde order' of economic growth in Europe following the fall of the Roman Empire.[82] On the one hand, the 'natural progress of opulence' represented a steady development from agriculture to commerce and industry, as towns expanded in line with the growing productive capacities of the countryside, and markets expanded in line with the evolution of human needs.[83] On the other, the unnatural and retrograde order was the expansion of towns before the expansion of the country. This order was 'unnatural' because growth came from the top-down, not the bottom-up, catering to aristocracy and luxury before small farmers and subsistence.[84]

The key moment in this philosophical history was the barbarian conquest of Europe. Vast tracts of land had been appropriated by invading barbarian chieftains in the post-Roman anarchy, and these usurpations had been frozen in place by the laws of primogeniture and entailed settlements. These had been developed for political reasons: the feudal lord was a sort of petty sovereign, whose inheritance needed to be

---

[81] MacDermot, 'Arthur O'Connor'. [82] Hont, *Jealousy of Trade*, 354–89.
[83] Smith, *Wealth of Nations*, III.i.1–9. [84] Ibid., III.i.9; III.iv.1–24.

kept intact between generations if feuding and division were to be avoided. In modern states, where the sovereign guaranteed security, primogeniture and entails were 'absurd'. The engrossment of land removed it from productive circulation. Moreover, 'it seldom happens ... that a great proprietor is a great improver'.[85] Smith had laid down in Book I of the *Wealth of Nations* that productivity gains accruing from an increased division of labour permitted by large estates would be marginal. Since food production shifted with the seasons, the psychological incentives acting on the farmer were more important than the specialisation of tasks, which mattered more to artisans and manufacturers.[86] Feudal landowners pursued the status conferred by luxury and servants rather than agricultural efficiency:

> To improve land with profit, like all other commercial projects, requires an exact attention to small savings and small gains, of which a man born to a great fortune, even though naturally frugal, is very seldom capable ... Compare the present condition of those [large] estates with the possessions of the small proprietors in their neighbourhood, and you will require no other argument to convince you how unfavourable such extensive property is to improvement.[87]

Smith's history of European property and agriculture was crucial to his subsequent analysis of 'the mercantile system' and the dangers of public debt. The emergence of a rural cash economy and the breakdown of relationships of feudal dependence was a product of the luxury reintroduced into Europe by merchants trading to the Levant and beyond. City-dwellers' growing power in European states produced a counterweight to the landed interest and enabled the rise of modern sovereignty.[88] But they also encouraged politicians to violently rig markets and secure their profits through colonial warfare, allowing mercantile interests to be mistaken for national interests across the major states of Europe.

Smith was sceptical about the possibilities for instituting a radical reform of the 'unnatural and retrograde order' of economic growth in modern Europe, fearing the political consequences of the sort of exertion of absolute power that might be necessary to overturn, at a stroke, the number of interests already invested in the existing system.[89] For O'Connor, however, the French Revolution had invalidated Smith's

---

[85] Ibid., III.ii.1–7.   [86] Ibid., I.i.4.   [87] Ibid., III.ii.6–7.   [88] Ibid., III.iii.13–16; III.iv.4–15.
[89] Ibid., IV.ix.28.

assessment of the possibilities for radical reform to the 'unnatural and retrograde order' of primogeniture and luxury in Europe. Thomas Paine, who praised Smith's 'talents' over Burke's 'prejudices' in the *Rights of Man*, was a likely conduit for this judgement.[90] Opposition to primogeniture and entailed settlements became a touchstone of radicalism in England: it was central to Thomas Paine and Mary Wollstonecraft's responses to Edmund Burke's *Reflections on the Revolution in France* (1790). Where Paine and Wollstonecraft, following Smith, had condemned primogeniture and entail as engines of inequality and corruption, Burke – in line with his own predisposition against the 'gavelkind' partitive inheritance imposed on Irish Catholics under the Penal Laws – had defended them as indispensable guarantors of social hierarchy and cohesion.[91] In France, the reformation of laws of inheritance proved to be among the most durable and radical legacies of the revolution. Under both the *Code Civil* promulgated in 1794 and the *Code Napoleon* adopted in 1804, primogeniture was outlawed, and partitive inheritance was mandated for all forms of property.[92]

Arthur O'Connor's personal manifesto for the 1798 rebellion, *The State of Ireland* (1798), argued that Ireland should emulate this specific kind of French legal reform. Its author was a sharp critic of the luxury and inequality created by the uneven progress of economic development in Europe, contrasting it with the natural order of equality and subsistence described by Smith. O'Connor agreed with Paine that the large landed estates created and sustained by the laws of primogeniture and entails corrupted the *moeurs* of political society. Property, he claimed, was 'the machinery by which self-interest is worked . . . the laws which monopolize property, monopolize power also: hence the direction which the laws give to the descent of property, the freedom or restraint with which they admit its transfer or sale, influence the nature of government'.[93] An inegalitarian distribution of landed property therefore limited opportunities for democratic reform. Even a legislature reformed in line with the demands for the expansion of the franchise, O'Connor asserted, would be pointless if electors were not economically independent; a tenant's vote could always be bought, unlike that of the independent small proprietor. 'To violate the

[90] Paine, 'Rights of Man', 57–155, at 93.
[91] Goodrich, *Debating England's Aristocracy*, 59–62, 68–72.
[92] Suzanne Desan, '"War between Brothers and Sisters": Inheritance Law and Gender Politics in Revolutionary France', *French Historical Studies*, 20 (1997), 597–634.
[93] Ibid., 71. Cf. James Harrington, 'The Commonwealth of Oceana', in J. G. A. Pocock (ed.), *The Political Works of James Harrington* (Cambridge, 1977), 155–361, at 11–13, 48–68.

right of universal suffrage, is to infringe the most sacred right of Man', he conceded. 'But as long as those laws of monopoly exist, the general exercise of the right, under the appearance of Democracy, renders Aristocracy omnipotent.'[94]

'Aristocracy', however, was fighting a losing battle against the progress of European commerce and civilisation. As Smith had explained, the very predilection for luxury that great proprietors developed as a result of their over-endowment with landed property tended to its sale and alienation, and produced the weakening of the 'laws of monopoly' that O'Connor, after Smith, observed in England since the time of Henry VII.[95] Luxury multiplied the forms of available property and disrupted the total hegemony that the great lords had historically exercised over the polity through their control of the limited varieties of property available in the feudal era. Unlike Smith, however, O'Connor subscribed to a view that politics was a matter of epistemic certainty: a 'science', driven by the operation of self interest in history, the truth of which could only be obscured by ignorance or an excess of passion.[96] *The Press* (1797–8), a United Irish newspaper edited by O'Connor, made frequent references to the sensationalist philosophy of the *philosophe* Claude-Adrien Helvetius and the revolutionary mystic Constantin de Volney, who both subscribed to this view, in advancing its case against the political and religious corruption of Britain.[97] The task for the Enlightened politician, O'Connor accordingly declared, was to discern the self-interest of the mass of society and to refashion its governing institutions accordingly:

> mankind is advancing into a state far beyond any thing they had ever attained; where, as the mass have changed their dependencies, relations, and habits of thinking, their institutions must undergo a similar change . . . as self-interest, tempered by sympathy, is the acknowledged principle which regulates and governs the existence and movements of human action and human society.[98]

O'Connor's account of a collective, historical realisation of the principle of 'self-interest' bore traces of another French influence: the Marquis de Condorcet's last work, *Esquisse d'un Tableau Historique des Progrès de l'Esprit Humain* (1795), which was translated and re-published in

---

[94] Arthur O'Connor, *The State of Ireland* (Dublin 1798), 85.
[95] Ibid., 111–11; Smith, *Wealth of Nations*, III.ii.14, III.iv., 9–10.   [96] O'Connor, *Ireland*, 165.
[97] Claude Adrien Helvétius, *De L'Esprit: Or, Essays on the Mind, and its Several Faculties* (London: Dodsley, 1759), 112–13.
[98] O'Connor, *Ireland*, 70–1.

Dublin in 1796. Condorcet offered a stadial history of humanity that placed intellectual and economic progress in a reciprocal relationship, whereby the division of labour gave individuals the leisure for philosophical and technological innovation.[99] The genius of the seventeenth-century natural lawyers had been to construct a political philosophy on the foundation that man 'is a being endowed with sensation, capable of reasoning upon and understanding his interests, and of acquiring moral ideas'.[100] An Enlightened collective consciousness would have revolutionary effects: Condorcet, like O'Connor, believed that 'every thing tells us that we are approaching the era of one of the grand revolutions of the human race'.[101]

For O'Connor, Irish political corruption was the result of a disjuncture between the declining social power of the landed class and the political power afforded to them in the unreformed constitution. Unable, in this new age of commerce and Enlightenment, to overawe the people through the sheer weight of their property ownership, the laws of primogeniture and entailed settlement nevertheless allowed the Ascendancy to hang on to political power 'by generating the few with dispositions and means to influence, bribe and debauch the constituent body, and by reducing the constituent body to that state of dependence and poverty which renders it liable to influenced, bribed and debauched'.[102] Britain and Ireland were part of an identical political system, the excesses of which were merely more visible in the latter, thanks to the military occupation that was now being instituted to put down the Defenders and the United Irishmen.[103] The corruption and violence used to uphold the constitution within the British Isles was of a piece with Pitt's needlessly bellicose foreign policy:

> The Minister of the Crown, and the Lords, who make a property of the national representation, after actually destroying the constitution, are the loudest to trumpet its excellence, and to deluge the world with blood to support its subversion; and, as it fares with the feet of the women of China, they have so squeezed the representative basis in the vice of monopoly, that as the other parts have grown, the constitution is unable to stand.[104]

---

[99] Jean-Antoine-Nicolas de Caritat Condorcet, *Outlines of an Historical View of the Progress of the Human Mind* (Dublin: John Chambers, 1796), 6.
[100] Ibid., 187–8.   [101] Ibid., 15.   [102] O'Connor, *Ireland*, 117.   [103] Ibid., 130–1.
[104] Ibid., 113.

Britain's leadership of the anti-French alliance was the doomed effort of a ministerial faction to sustain the old order of aristocracy and monopoly against the irrepressible progress of commerce and Enlightenment in Europe. This social and intellectual progress had received institutional expression in the French Republic. O'Connor advanced a strikingly minimal reading of the politics of the French Revolution, which aligned with the Directory's developing efforts to suppress the radical social egalitarianism of the 1793 Jacobin Constitution and 'Gracchus' Babeuf's 'Conspiracy of Equals'.[105] Alluding to the early reforms passed by the National Assembly 1789–92, O'Connor concluded that 'the Revolution of France was nothing more than the Abolition of those Laws of Monopoly; and all the Calamity and Bloodshed with which it has been attended, were caused by those who conspired against it'.[106] In line with Smith's theory, O'Connor concluded that the liberation of French agriculture from feudal restraints placed the Republic's power on a far more sustainable foundation than Britain's tottering edifice of mercantile monopoly, aristocracy and debt. After the violent purgation of the French Revolution, the 'natural progress of opulence' was now taking hold:

> If the property of France is much more divided than that of Great Britain, and if the abolition of the laws of monopoly in the one country, whilst they are retained in the other, must make this division of property much greater in France – is it not manifest that France will be every day approaching nearer to a state of repose and security, whilst England will be every day drawing nearer and nearer to a Revolution?[107]

The core of O'Connor's case for Catholic Emancipation was similar to the case he advanced against primogeniture: there was no foundation for Catholic political exclusion bar the determination of 'a few families' to 'monopolise' the nation's political life, assuring their complicity in the British system of corruption, commercial restriction and military oppression.[108] The dangerous doctrines of 'political popery' were now as redundant as the Penal Laws: the progress of Enlightenment and commerce had transformed the terms of political competition.[109] The French Revolution had had a huge effect on the 'Irish Mind' by

---

[105] Peter M. Jones, 'The "Agrarian Law": Schemes for Land Redistribution during the French Revolution', *Past and Present*, 133 (1991), 96–133.

[106] O'Connor, *Ireland*, 121.   [107] Ibid., 122.

[108] Arthur O'Connor, *Speech of Arthur O'Connor, Esq. in the House of Commons of Ireland, Monday, May 4th, 1795, on the Catholic Bill* (Dublin: P. Byrne, 1795), 5–6.

[109] Ibid., 35.

convincing the Protestants that a Catholic people could strive for liberty as much as a Protestant one.

> Before this great epoch, an opinion had been generally accredited among the Protestants of Ireland, that Catholics were incapable of either claiming or possessing civil or political freedom ... like the slave-drivers in the West Indies, the Irish Protestants, after lashing their Catholic countrymen into a mental torpor, set up the debasement caused by their own tyranny as an eternal barrier against Catholic freedom.[110]

The liberation of Protestant opinion from this narrow view made the construction of an Irish nation possible, and with it the purification of the Irish constitution through the reform of laws of landed property. Resistance to British power was an act of patriotic reform, not of treason. He cited Locke in support of his case: first on 'the Supreme power' of the people 'to remove or alter the legislative, when they find the legislative act contrary to the trust reposed in them', and second in support of his assertion that the Pittite regime of parliamentary corruption constituted just such a violation of trust.[111] O'Connor provocatively invoked the principles of 1688 as part of a justification of the United Irishmen's embrace of French military support. Every country that had won its liberties in modern European history – Holland, England, the United States – had done so, O'Connor observed, with foreign support.[112]

The pages of *The Press*, the successor to the *Northern Star* published by O'Connor in 1797–8, had made much of the support the Directory had offered to the formation of the Helvetic Republic, the Swiss satellite established by the regime in 1798.[113] The fall of the Swiss cantons – the historic citadels of republican liberty in Europe – had been greeted in Britain as conclusive evidence of France's unprincipled plunder and usurpation.[114] By way of a rebuttal, *The Press* printed a lengthy extract from Edward Gibbon's *Lettre sur le government du Berne* (1756), recently re-published by the Earl of Sheffield, as evidence of the 'iniquitous Aristocracy' of the leading canton in the fallen confederation.[115] *The Press* stressed 'the degrading situation in which the people of the Pays de Vaud are held by the Burghers of Berne ... Fertile and populous districts

---

[110] O'Connor, *Ireland*, 131–2.   [111] Ibid., 158–63.   [112] Ibid., 163–4.

[113] On the Helvetic Republic, see Marc Lerner, 'The Helvetic Republic: An Ambivalent Reception of French Revolutionary Liberty', *French History*, 18 (2004), 50–75.

[114] Whatmore, *Against War and Empire*, 265–7.

[115] Edward Gibbon, *Miscellaneous Works of Edward Gibbon, with Memoirs of His Life and Writings, Composed by Himself* (Dublin: P. Wogan, 1796).

are held in the most degrading situation of dependence'. The analogy – right down to the Catholic religion of the Vaudois – was obvious: 'such a Confederacy may have been long much respected in Europe', noted *The Press*, 'but we, for our parts, cannot regret its dismemberment'.[116]

O'Connor's model of an Irish revolution echoed this laudatory account of the dismantling of aristocratic liberty in Switzerland, tearing down Protestant Ascendancy in favour of a rational property order that would provide the basis for a modern system of representative government. *The State of Ireland* demanded the creation of a representative 'constituent body' of the sort advocated by the first generation of French revolutionaries: Condorcet, Paine and Sieyès.[117] O'Connor's sole substantive prescription for the convention was that it must remove any existing law of primogeniture or entail that upheld the 'unnatural and retrograde' progress of commercial society. In the absence of a reform to the laws of property, O'Connor warned his fellow radicals in Ireland and Britain alike, those who benefited from a more equal franchise would still be prey to aristocratic influence. Only adoption of the republican political economy of the French Revolution could ensure that a new Ireland would not succumb to the same inequality that now made revolution inevitable.[118]

O'Connor's late arrival in the United Irish movement, his evident vanity, and his tendency to invent incidents in his own life story have all served to limit the attention paid by scholars to his ideas and revolutionary career.[119] The depth of O'Connor's engagement with Smith, Paine and Condorcet, however, marked him out as a singular intellectual force within the movement. O'Connor's *State of Ireland* converted Smith's theory of the 'natural progress of opulence' into a single-minded case for an Irish insurrection. The distribution of Irish property – distorted, like its British counterpart – by the persistence of feudal laws of primogeniture and entail lay at the root of the corruption and poverty of the Kingdom. These same laws of primogeniture and entail would ultimately doom the tottering edifice of the British fiscal state, which was already being outmatched by the modern system of representative government and partitive inheritance being implemented in France. In applying the insights of political economy to Ireland's distinctive circumstances, O'Connor connected the rising

[116] 'A Few Observations on the Government of Switzerland', *The Press*, No. 59, 13 February 1798.

[117] Michael Sonenscher, 'Introduction', in Sonenscher (ed.), *Sieyès: Political Writings* (Indianapolis, IN: Hackett, 2003), vii–lxiv.

[118] O'Connor, *Ireland*, 168–70.

[119] MacDermot, 'Arthur O'Connor', 48–69; James Livesey, 'Introduction', in J. Livesey (ed.), *Arthur O'Connor: The State of Ireland (1798)* (Dublin, 1998: Lilliput), 1–43.

of 1798 to the shifting terrain of a European debate on the fiscal and military contest between France and Britain.

Ireland and French Empire

In the years surrounding 1798, Ireland occupied a crucial role in the French propaganda war against Britain. French efforts to engage and encourage Irish rebellion paralleled contemporary efforts to encourage revolution in other neighbouring states.[120] They were part of a combined strategy of espionage and publicity, which employed emissaries to sympathetic political movements while producing pamphlet and newspaper literature. This was designed both to rally French domestic opinion and to undermine the attachment of rival populations to their monarchical and aristocratic governments. The German lands, which included principalities (notably Prussia) that were neutral in the conflict and could be turned against Britain, were a notable focus in the later 1790s. Under the new regime of the Consulate, France's war aims were no longer projected as revolutionary, but as the only ones compatible with the maintenance of a recognisable form of European order.[121] In a major manifesto for the new regime, Alexandre d'Hauterive, a senior official in Talleyrand's foreign ministry, argued that the revolution itself had been a product of a deep disequilibrium in the European order created by the rise of English commercial power since the Treaty of Westphalia (1648).[122] Blame for the war lay not with French expansion, but the British naval and colonial hegemony that had rendered it necessary.

Ireland was deployed by pro-French writers as an emblematic symbol of Britain's corrupt and aggressive commercial reason of state. This portrayal had credibility because it conformed to established pre-revolutionary images of Ireland. As the case of Montesquieu has already illustrated, the place of Ireland in the British Empire had been an object of curiosity in France since the middle of the previous century. During the American crisis, the Kingdom had begun to be used as an index of Britain's own prospects in a changing international system. One of the earliest

---

[120] Elliott, *Partners in Revolution*, xiv–xv.

[121] Murray Forsyth, 'The Old European States-System: Gentz versus Hauterive', *The Historical Journal*, 23 (1980), 521–38.

[122] Alexandre Maurice Blanc de Lanautte, Comte d'Hautive, *De l'état de la France, à la fin de l'an VIII* (Paris: Henrics, 1800), 22–44.

continental speculations on the prospects for an a British-Irish parliamentary union was a 1767 essay in the physiocratic journal *Ephemerides du citoyen*. This had set out to disprove the idea that Ireland would benefit from a closer connection to London by asserting that, once the proper, physiocratic method was applied to establish the 'net product' of British agriculture, the state's capacity to secure rising public debt was a great deal weaker than its champions suggested.[123] Ireland had burst in to German political consciousness, meanwhile, following the constitutional revolution of 1782 and the rise in Celtophilia prompted by the Ossian forgeries, which played a central role in Johann-Wolfgang Goethe's *Leiden des jungen Werthers* (1774).[124] The lengthy 1784 article on Ireland in Johann Georg Krünitz's *Oekonomische Enclycopädie,* one of the major lexika of the *Aufklärung,* marvelled at the insistence of England's influential mercantile classes on the restraint of Irish trade and the peculiar intolerance of the Irish constitution against Catholics and Dissenters.[125]

As the Thermidorian republic stabilised and Irish politics polarised, Francophile critics of Britain moved to link perfidious Albion's treatment of its Irish neighbour to broader claims about the nature and purposes of its global empire. Charles-Guillaume Théremin was the descendent of Huguenot émigrés to Prussia, who had resigned a diplomatic post with the ruling Hohenzollern dynasty in order to travel to France and serve the Directory.[126] In a major work produced in 1795 and circulated in French, Dutch and German, *De l'intérêts des puissances continentales, relativement de l'Angleterre,* Théremin advocated an alliance of the 'continental' powers, under French leadership, to defeat Britain's system of mercantile domination.[127] In claiming to discover *'le grand secret d'état de l'Angleterre'*, he offered an exemplary account of British power as a

---

[123] Anon., 'Paradoxe politique, addressé aux Irlandois', *Ephemerides du citoyen, ou bibliotheque raisonnée des sciences morales et politiques* 1(1767), 55–97.

[124] Patrick O'Neill, *Ireland and Germany: A Study in Literary Relations* (New York: P. Lang, 1985), 78–83.

[125] Johann Georg Krünitz, 'Irrland', in *Oeconomische Encyclopädie, oder allgemeines System der Staats- Stadt- Haus- und Landwirthschaft, in alphabetischer Ordnung,* vol. 30, 242 vols. (Berlin, 1784), 742–63, at 758–9.

[126] Andrew Jainchill, *Reimagining Politics after the Terror: The Republican Origins of French Liberalism* (Ithaca, NY: Cornell University Press, 2008), 115–16.

[127] Charles Theremin, *De belangen der mogendheden van het vaste land met betrekking tot Engelland* (The Hague: J.C. Leeuwestyn, 1796); Charles Théremin, *Des intérêts des puissances continentales relativement à l'Angleterre* (Paris: Louvet, 1795); Karl Theremin, *Von dem Interesse der Mächte des festen Landes in Bezug auf England* (The Hague: J.C. Leeuwestyn, 1795).

commercial iteration of princely reason of state, through which the pride and vanity of a self-serving mercantile and ministerial elite had corrupted the British constitution and despoiled Europe and India.[128] 'England' aimed 'not at universal monarchy through arms, but at a universal *influence* through commerce, only employing arms to extend the latter'.[129]

Through a forceful practice of securing the markets of competitor states in Europe and India alike for British products, the British government gained access to huge quantities of precious metals, which it used to corrupt both foreign princes and the people's representatives at home. The ministry's opposition to parliamentary reform and its defence of princely government in Europe stemmed from the same source – a desire to restrict the number of individuals it was necessary to bribe: 'she likes to treat with an absolute prince, because there is only one person to win, but she fears free peoples, because a Senate is more difficult to buy than a King; in the same manner, she resists the reform of Parliament at home'.[130] Until Britain was invaded and its credit destroyed by the capture of London, its 'artificial' concentration of resources extracted from her vast Indian Empire would retain the capacity to sow dissension among the sovereigns of Europe and to subsidise the war against republican France.[131] Théremin thereby identified Britain and its empire as the primary obstacle to the realisation of peace in Europe and the progress of European civilisation.[132]

For Théremin, it was the case of Ireland that most clearly demonstrated Britain's exclusionary and avaricious character. Where Britain practised a vengeful politics of domination and influence over states it had absorbed, the expansion of the 'continental' powers of France and Prussia had led to the successful incorporation and recognition of subjugated peoples. This process produced the integrated and advanced states necessary to create a 'ferment of ideas', the development of culture and the advancement of the arts and sciences.[133] As French armies marched in to Italy and the Netherlands, and Prussia consolidated its hold over the vast territories gained in the Second and Third Partitions of Poland, Théremin calmly observed that 'the territorial aggrandisement of a continental power must not at all seem contrary to the general civilisation of this continent'.[134] The English, by contrast, could not 'recognise the humanity of those who do

[128] Théremin, *Intérêts*, 4–8.   [129] Ibid., 21.   [130] Ibid.   [131] Ibid., 103–9.
[132] Ibid., 117–19.   [133] Ibid., 11–12.   [134] Ibid., 11.

not inhabit their territory; they remain strangers to all others and regard them as enemies'. The treatment of Ireland showed that the assimilation of conquered peoples, a central aspect of French and Prussian state-building, was impossible for the insular and seaborne empire of Britain. 'As the sea prevents the incorporation of territory that might otherwise take place, a sincere reconciliation, and a true harmony, between the conquering and the conquered, is never established.' Driving the point home, he concluded that 'the Poles will become, in ten years, better Prussians than the Irish have become good English in many centuries'.[135]

Théremin's construction of the contrasting civilisational properties of landed and seaborne empires recalled positions in French political and economic thought that long predated the Revolution. The physiocratic theory of political economy that had emerged in France in the 1750s and 1760s had insisted on the primacy of agriculture and population in the 'natural and necessary order of human societies', a claim that had always had obvious implication for the relationship between France – Europe's most populous, territorially extensive, and agriculturally productive economy – and Britain, its smaller, commercial, and maritime neighbour.[136] Like Arthur O'Connor, Théremin claimed that English power was 'artificial': 'she does not have, like the great states of the Continent, a vast territory and a numerous population'.[137] The 'artificiality' of British power was invoked in predictions of the exhaustion of Britain's heavily extended system of public credit, which allegedly lacked a secure productive base to sustain its ever-rising expenditure.

Since an invasion of Ireland had the potential to bring about a collapse in financial confidence, it played a central role in revolutionaries' predictions of the inevitable disintegration of the British war machine.[138] Andreas Riem, a radical Lutheran priest exiled from the Prussian territories for his public statements in support of France, proclaimed in 1797 that

> the imminent Revolution, or regeneration of the English state-constitution, which threatens to break out with the bankruptcy of the government, must also make Ireland completely independent [...] If the New Franks and Batavians make a successful landing in Ireland, it will not be necessary to wait for such a time, and the Irish will free themselves through the assistance of the friends of freedom.[139]

[135] Ibid., 70–1.   [136] Whatmore, *Against War and Empire*, 186.   [137] Théremin, *Intérêts*, 5.
[138] Ibid., 110–11.
[139] Andreas Riem, *Reise durch England, in verschiedener, besonders politischer Hinsicht*, 2 vols. (Leipzig: Auf kosten des Verfassers, 1798), I:476–7.

The example of Ireland united German revolutionaries like Théremin and Riem with more conservative figures like Johann Wilhelm von Archenholz, the Prussian editor of the journal *Minerva,* in harsh criticism of Britain. *Minerva* was at this point one of the most important and popular journals in the German-speaking world, enjoying a circulation of 3,000–5,000 that was further magnified by its frequent use as discussion material in hundreds of reading societies.[140] Archenholz's writings in *Minerva* in the years after the Franco-Austrian peace agreed under the Treaty of Campo Formio (1797) were harshly critical of Francophile Prussians like Théremin and Riem, whom he saw as wilfully divisive figures who lacked proper German patriotism.[141] But he also attacked Pitt and Dundas, whom he styled as corrupt sinecurists; he took Fox for his hero in English politics and showed a strong sympathy for the parliamentary opposition.[142]

During and after the Irish risings of 1796–8, Ireland rapidly became central to Archenholz's critical account of Britain's political leadership. Irish service in the British army and navy and the suppression of Irish economic activity though imperial legislation were connected to England's oriental ambitions and monopolistic trade policies:

> In order to support England's power and trade monopoly, the Irish sacrificed at every opportunity their own benefits, their own wellbeing and felicity. Although they had long suffered the restriction of their trade and the decline of their manufactures, although they had long borne the greatest part of the people to be excluded from constitutional privileges; yet still they gave up, under all these melancholy circumstances, their brave and trained sons to fight a powerful enemy in the most hideous affairs of the world, and in the most damaging climates for the human species. And what was their reward – to be oppressed, persecuted and exiled![143]

The failure of the 1798 landing precipitated a turn from Ireland in French strategy and propaganda. Napoleon pursued the conquest of

---

[140] Hans Erich Bödeker, 'Journals and Public Opinion: The Politicization of the German Enlightenment in the Second Half of the Eighteenth Century', in E. Hellmuth (ed.), *The Transformation of Political Culture: England and Germany in the Late Eighteenth Century* (Oxford: Oxford University Press, 1990), 433–4.

[141] Johann Wilhelm von Archenholz, 'Ueber die Politik unserer Zeit', *Minerva: ein Journal historischen und politischen Inhalts,* 25 (1798), 1–12, at 3–4.

[142] Johann Wilhelm von Archenholz, 'Zur Geschichte der jetzigen Machthaber in England', *Minerva: ein Journal historischen und politischen Inhalts,* 25 (1798), 186–8; Johann Wilhelm von Archenholz, 'Ueber den jetzigen Krieg der Engländer und der Staatsmann Fox', *Minerva: ein Journal historischen und politischen Inhalts,* 27 (1798), 287–302.

[143] Anon., 'Über die neuste Geschichte Irlands (Beschluss)', *Minerva,* 2 (1798), 520–46, at 539–40.

Egypt, before returning to the Europe to consolidate his control of the Italian peninsula and what remained of the Holy Roman Empire.[144] After the crushing British naval victory at Aboukir Bay in August 1798, it seemed increasingly impossible that the stalemate between French landed dominance and Britain's naval strength could be broken. In Ireland, the British administration seized the initiative by pressing forward with the prosecution of rebels and a union of the Dublin and Westminster parliaments.

Over the short period of peace ushered in by the Treaty of Amiens (1802), however, French interest in British invasion projects revived. Thomas Emmet's failed rebellion the following year encouraged the creation of an 'Irish Legion' under the leadership of O'Connor, who had overcome British imprisonment and the hostility of his colleagues to win the backing of the French regime. Upon the renewal of the war, Napoleon began preparing a huge armada for simultaneous invasions of Ireland and Britain.[145] Pamphlets advertising the invasion were produced by O'Connor alongside the Catholic doctor and scientist William James MacNeven, who had acted as a United Irish emissary to France in 1797–8.[146] O'Connor's work *The State of Great Britain* (1804) was written for a British audience and largely reiterated earlier material. MacNeven, however, sought to address the 'maritime powers of Europe' in explaining the centrality of Ireland to Britain's system of mercantile domination.

Writing in November 1803 for the official paper the *Moniteur*, MacNeven carefully homed in on the controversy over British seizures of neutral shipping, which had prompted Denmark, Sweden and Russia to form a second 'League of Armed Neutrality' against Britain in 1801–2.[147] 'Overwhelmed with debt, and with no recourse but exclusive trade to meet her expenditure', MacNeven wrote, 'she [Britain] employs her remaining vigour to crush, ere it be too late, the alarming increase of any other naval power, the rising competition of all foreign industry, and the incipient freedom of its circulation'.[148] British sea power was a greater threat to Europe than France's expansion could ever be: 'The experience of the past

[144] Schroeder, *Transformation of European Politics*, 176–80.
[145] Elliott, *Partners in Revolution*, 324–33.   [146] Woods, 'MacNeven, William James'.
[147] Schroeder, *Transformation of European Politics*, 218–21. On the debate over neutral shipping in relation to contemporary theories of international law, see Nakhimovsky, 'Ignominious Fall of the European Commonwealth', 177–90.
[148] William James MacNeven, 'Of the Interest of the Maritime Powers in the Present War', in J.-J. Lavayasse (ed.), *Letters on the Events of the Revolution in France* (New York: John Forbes, 1817), at 222.

and the present unite against the possibility of that universal monarchy of a continental sovereign of which England has so long and carefully propagated the puerile fear.'[149] Landed military dominance, MacNeven claimed, was rendered impossible by military technology and logistics, particularly 'among nations with the same arms and the same tactics'. Britain's naval prowess, by contrast, was far more effective. It could remove colonies from rivals at will and interfere with neutral shipping, with devastating effects on European populations who were now dependent on foreign luxuries:

> If she [England] turns away from men and iron, she precipitates herself on slaves and gold; and witholds, or distributes at will, those foreign commodities at present almost as necessary to Europe as the bread of the people; such is the nature and such the effect of naval dominion, so much more potent, more extensive, more dangerous, than any continental power that now exists, or that can arise in Europe. It is the only Empire that can be universal.[150]

Unlike Théremin, O'Connor and a range of other French writers, MacNeven did not insist that British naval power was ultimately dependent on its 'artificial' system of credit and commerce. As a later series of essays on Irish minerals, population and agriculture demonstrated, MacNeven's conception of the foundations for national economic power prioritised 'physical' resources over the abstract conception of 'stock' or 'capital' favoured by Smith, Paine and O'Connor.[151] While Britain's population was far smaller than that of France, MacNeven observed, the proportion that was 'maritime' – capable of active service at sea – was far greater, because many more individuals lived on Britain's and Ireland's extended coasts. 'The maritime pre-eminence of Great Britain reposes on a real physical basis, replete with the materials of naval power', MacNeven observed. 'This circumstance alone, far better than the precarious prosperity of commerce, solves the problem of her superiority'.[152]

Ireland, MacNeven asserted, was a disproportionate supplier of men, victuals and taxation for the British fleet. If Ireland were separated from Britain by a French invasion, 'I shall venture to say, not that [Britain] is undone, but most assuredly that her despotic dictates will no longer be the law of the ocean'.[153] MacNeven, therefore, believed that Britain could be

---

[149] Ibid., 224.   [150] Ibid., 225.
[151] William James MacNeven, 'Statistical Essay on the Population and Resources of Ireland', in W. J. MacNeven and T. A. Emmet (eds.), *Pieces of Irish History Illustrative of the Condition of the Catholics of Ireland, of the Origin and Progress of the Political System of the United Irishmen, and of their Transactions with the Anglo-Irish Government* (New York: Bernard Dornin, 1807), 249–54.
[152] MacNeven, 'Maritime Powers', 230.   [153] Ibid., 231.

brought to relinquish its pretensions to global dominance if it were deprived
of Ireland. 'If once herself unable to tyrannise', MacNeven suggested, 'she
would be the first to raise her voice in support of neutral commerce, and her
existence, instead of being a general nuisance, might perhaps become a
universal good'.[154] Not only Ireland's resources, but her ports and location,
rendered her strategically vital. An independent Irish Republic would be in a
position, in conjunction with France, to obstruct British naval expeditions
and deny her the ability to land prizes at Irish ports.

MacNeven fiercely rejected the suggestion that his country would
become a mere dominion of France in the event of a successful invasion.
Like O'Connor, he compared the Irish case to that of the Netherlands in the
sixteenth century or the North American colonies a generation previously.
'France did not succeed to the dominion which her rival had lost; but a new
and independent people took their rank among the nations of the earth.' He
persisted with the vision of Irish unity that had been articulated by
O'Connor and Tone, asserting that there would be no substantive opposition within the Kingdom to liberation from 'the oppressive yoke of the
modern Carthage'.[155] Since it had a population nearly half that of Britain,
MacNeven argued that 'Ireland is defensively stronger against Great Britain
than the latter is in regard of France'.[156] France's invasion would be conducted in the interest of all the trading nations of Europe, since she would
not reappropriate Ireland's 'surplus of forces' for herself.[157] 'Irish independence is important from similar motives and wants to all commercial
nations', MacNeven asserted in conclusion. 'An enlightened policy ...
exacts that they should all be eager to support the efforts of a people who
represent their common interests; that they should all act in concert with
France to put a stop to the dominion of the universal enemy.'[158]

O'Connor, too, insisted in his *State of Great Britain* that France was a
new sort of world power, one that aimed not at universal dominion but at
a pacified Europe whose political institutions were in accordance with the
progress of commerce and Enlightenment. France's embrace of partitive
inheritance – which O'Connor described as the 'policy of nature' –
ensured that she would never act the part of conqueror to Ireland.
'Champion of Europe, is at best but a suspicious and dangerous title', he
conceded,

> but the interests of France are so clearly marked out, that they cannot be
> mistaken ... France has no interest to join herself to any coterie for the

---

[154] Ibid.   [155] Ibid., 232.   [156] Ibid., 234.   [157] Ibid., 238.   [158] Ibid., 237–8.

support of the miserable remnant of feodality, that still loiters in Europe . . . In France, those great causes I have mentioned have had their effect; and the great predisposing law that establishes this free circulation of property, upon which liberty is firmly placed, is in perfect unison with the popular spirit which pervades the mind of all Europe.[159]

It was Britain, not France, that was the 'scourge' of the small states of Europe. 'We have seen them attempt to force the small states from their neutrality by the most indecent bullying and menace; and when all Europe panted for peace, we have seen these ministers redouble their subsidies to frustrate its wishes.'[160] Britain's commitment to 'feodality' and 'monopoly' continued to mark her out as the disruptive element in the modern European states system. 'While France has cleansed her soil of the Augean filth of feodality', he declaimed, 'the British ministry seek to consecrate its miserable remnants'.[161]

Rival Universalisms

In preparing the ground for a fresh French invasion of Ireland, O'Connor and MacNeven reaffirmed a long-standing United Irish attachment to the idea that France could represent a new kind of empire: one that existed not to pursue its own state interest, but to advance that of 'mankind' as a whole. Following the coronation of Napoleon as Emperor of the French in 1804, both men began to lose faith in this ideal. MacNeven left France for America, while O'Connor retreated from the Irish Legion and settled into marriage with Eliza de Condorcet, the daughter of the famous French liberal philosopher and his widow, Sophie de Grouchy.[162] Over the previous decade, however, O'Connor, MacNeven and their fellow United Irishmen had been deeply involved in the promotion not only of a general 'French' commitment to republican government, but of a specific project for French hegemony within a re-fashioned European states system.

The United Irish movement provided a platform for a diverse range on perspectives on the question of empire and political economy in the age of the French Revolution. Where Wolfe Tone saw French intervention as the means of overcoming the indignities of Irish poverty and subordination, Russell and Dickson described insurrection against the British Empire as a Christian duty demanded by the iniquities of slavery and conquest.

---

[159] Arthur O'Connor, *The Present State of Great-Britain* (Paris, 1804), 97–8.   [160] Ibid., 99.
[161] Ibid., 101.   [162] MacDermot, 'Arthur O'Connor', 6; Woods, 'MacNeven, William James'.

O'Connor and MacNeven, meanwhile, applied their respective interests in Smithian political economy and the 'physical resources' of Europe's states to make the case for the inevitability of French victory and the necessity of Irish separation from Britain. This rendered them suitable participants in the new discourse of republican empire that was taking shape among Francophile writers on the European continent during the years of the Directory and the Consulate. This rested, above all, on a case for the effectiveness of France's new system of law and government as guarantors of prosperity and military effectiveness. For Théremin, Britain's misgovernment of Ireland proved not only its unreformed mercantile rapacity, but its civilisational inferiority to the modern form of empire exercised by France over its new European conquests.

The failure of the French landing of 1796, and the crushing defeat of the 1798 rebellion by forces loyal to the Crown, destroyed the United Irishmen's vision of a non-sectarian republic. The questions raised by the rebellion, however, would dominate Irish, British and European discussions of the problem of Irish government down to the middle of the nineteenth century and beyond. The United Irishmen had advanced a politics that directly connected the condition of Ireland's rural interior to the military and ideological stakes of Franco-British imperial confrontation. They had argued that the example of revolutionary France proved the need to destroy an Irish aristocracy that was comparable – in behaviour if not in origin – to other 'feudal' elites across Europe. France thereby re-entered Irish consciousness in a radically new guise: not simply as a sympathetic Catholic neighbour, but as the representative of a different and superior kind of commercial modernity to that embodied by the British Empire and the 'English' constitution. Ireland, meanwhile, increasingly came to be seen by continental Europeans as a place where the confident moral aspirations of British commercial civilisation could be observed, tested – and found wanting.

CHAPTER 4

Enlightenment against Revolution
Commerce, Aristocracy and the Case for Union, 1798–1801

The United Irish insurgencies against British rule represented the moment of maximum danger for Britain and its empire in the course of its long war against the French Republic and Napoleon. They bookended a period marked by the suspension of cash payments at the Bank of England, the mutinies of English, Scottish and Irish sailors at Spithead and the Nore, and the grain scarcities of 1795–1801.[1] With France rampant on the continent and its internal dissensions apparently at an end, supporters of the revolutionary cause confidently predicted the imminent downfall of the British system of commerce and war finance, even in the absence of a successful invasion. 'I say', wrote Thomas Paine from Paris in 1796, 'that the English system of finance is on the verge, nay even in the gulph [sic] of bankruptcy'.[2]

Alongside the introduction of the income tax in 1799, the British–Irish Union of 1801 was the central response offered by the cabinet of Pitt the Younger to this seemingly existential crisis of empire. As we saw in Chapter 1, union had been long discussed in Britain as part of a solution to the interlocking problems of imperial government and public debt that had arisen in the aftermath of the Seven Years' War (1756–63). By the time it was passed in 1801, however, union had been reimagined as an intervention in an Irish society that was still reeling from the shock of the 1798 rebellion and its bloody repression. Union's advocates in government held that the power of the Anglo-Irish Ascendancy – already diminished through the repeal of most of the Penal Laws, but still sustained through an Anglican monopoly of representation in the Irish parliament – was the only thing that could explain the ease with which the sedition of the

---

[1] Hiroki Shin, 'Paper Money, the Nation, and the Suspension of Cash Payments in 1797', *Historical Journal*, 58 (2015), 415–42.
[2] Thomas Paine, *The Decline and Fall of the English System of Finance* (Paris: Hartley, Adlard & Son, 1796), 32.

United Irishmen and the Defenders had spread through the Irish countryside. Pitt, Dundas and their supporters in the Irish press and Irish parliament articulated a new vision of union, part-Smithian and part-Burkean, that held it to be an agent of aristocratic reform. Aristocracy needed to be tamed if property and subordination were to be saved. Denying Ascendancy its parliamentary playground in Dublin would allow Ireland's Anglican landholding class to return to their true vocation of agrarian improvement. The integration of the Irish Kingdom within the British system of government would, meanwhile, encourage British manufacturers, merchants and landowners to invest capital in Ireland, enabling the broad-based prosperity that they believed to be the mark of British commercial society. Union would thereby vindicate a moderate, commercial vision of British power against the depredations of the French Revolution.

This case for union rested on a body of late Enlightenment thinking concerning the nexus of inequality, commerce and liberty that, for thinkers such as Montesquieu, Hume and Smith, had defined the European modernity of the eighteenth century. It was articulated at a distinct moment in the history of British political thought, when different aspects of the moral, historical and economic enquiries of the Scottish Enlightenment were developed, adapted and combined with other influences into something approaching a governing ideology. There were multiple conduits for transmission of this Enlightened conception of union to the governing classes of Britain and Ireland at the close of the eighteenth century. The most important was the Scottish connection in the Pitt ministry. Since the 1770s, the most consistent advocate of union at the top of British politics had been Henry Dundas. As Secretary of War in Pitt's cabinet, and a key ally on the question of Catholic Emancipation, Dundas was a key conduit through which a counter-revolutionary interpretation of Scottish moral philosophy reached the highest levels of government.[3]

A further impetus came from younger figures in the ministry, such as the Irish Chief Secretary Robert Stewart – the future Viscount Castlereagh – and Pitt himself. Both men were vital to the implementation of union. Each had begun their political careers as reformers encouraged by Enlightened conceptions of society and government. Stewart's early education was suffused with the influence of the rational 'New

[3] Alexander Murdoch, 'Henry Dundas, Scotland and the Union with Ireland, 1792–1801', in Bob Harris (ed.), *Scotland in the Age of the French Revolution* (Edinburgh: John Donald, 2005), 125–39.

Light' Presbyterianism of his 'Ulster Scot' family, which had also inspired William Drennan and William Steel Dickson.[4] Pitt the Younger's career and self-presentation, meanwhile, was notable for its embrace of the 'sceptical' vision of politics espoused by Hume, Smith and William Robertson.[5] In the hands of the Prime Minister and his allies, these intellectual resources were mobilised to develop the new model of imperial economic and political integration applied in the Union of 1800.

The philosophical politics of Edmund Burke, who had died in 1797 as a relatively isolated advocate of a relentless war policy aimed at reversing the 'usurpation' of the French Revolution, supplied another key inspiration for union. Burke had engaged in his most sustained and passionate commentaries on Irish politics in the final years of his life, as he witnessed the Irish Kingdom's slide towards confessional polarisation and revolutionary violence.[6] With Irish property open to Catholics since the repeal of the 1704 'Act to Prevent the Further Growth of Popery' in 1778, Burke's attentions in the last years of his life focussed on the problem of Catholic representation in the Irish parliament. His *Letter to Sir Hercules Langrishe* (1792) had argued in favour of granting Irish Catholics the county franchise, both to encourage their sympathetic identification with the Irish constitution and to dissuade them from uniting with revolutionary Dissenters in threatening Church and state. A similar logic underpinned his later, more muted, arguments in favour of allowing Catholic MPs to sit in the Irish parliament itself. The message of Burke's politics for the framers of Union, however, was decidedly ambiguous. Key Irish supporters, such as the Anglo-Irish MP William Cusack Smith and the erstwhile Catholic radical Theobald McKenna, interpreted his support for Catholic Emancipation, and his famous description of the Protestant Ascendancy as a 'plebeian oligarchy', as an endorsement of the potential of Union. Former allies among the Whigs in the Westminster parliament, however, continued to support the multi-layered conception of empire elaborated by Burke during the 1780s.

The passage of the Act of Union was accompanied by a systematic attempt to win a political support from a broad, albeit bounded, public, with government-sponsored pamphlets and petitions seeking to wrest the

---

[4] John Bew, *Castlereagh: Enlightenment, War and Tyranny* (London: Quercus, 2011), 6–32.

[5] Jennifer Mori, 'The Political Theory of William Pitt the Younger', *History*, 83 (1998), 234–48.

[6] James Conniff, 'Edmund Burke's Reflections on the Coming Revolution in Ireland', *Journal of the History of Ideas*, 47 (1986), 37–59, Bourke, *Edmund Burke*, 866–86.

initiative from the rowdy and well-organised Protestant patriots of Dublin.[7] Prominent among these were speeches advocating union given in the British parliament, which were distributed in Ireland using public funds at key moments during the measure's difficult passage through the Irish Parliament.[8] The most pressing argument advanced by Pitt and his supporters was for the urgent consolidation of Britain's European dominions in the face of a French Republic that was both expanding and – crucially – directly incorporating neighbouring territories such as the Austrian Netherlands, the left bank of the Rhine, Savoy, Avignon and Geneva into metropolitan France. The geopolitical imperative of union was further explained and reinforced using arguments derived from Smith, Hume and Burke, which sought to render it plausible as a means of pacification.

It was these Enlightened critiques of the revolutionary and sectarian enthusiasm behind the bloody rising of 1798 that ultimately drove the case for the abolition of the Irish parliament. By reducing the influence of local passions on Irish political representation, union would discourage the recurrence of insurrectionary violence. It would also reform and rebalance the economies of both Britain and Ireland, bringing commercial prosperity and agricultural improvement to the Irish countryside. The flight of British commerce and manufactures to Ireland, once a threat demanding ruthless action against the parliament at Dublin, was now redescribed by Pitt as a beneficial 'diffusion of capital' to Ireland. It was actively willed by politicians who were more confident than ever before in the transformative power of British commerce and the British constitution.

The ambition and intellectual provenance of the case made for the Union of 1801 ensured that it had a broad resonance not only in Britain and Ireland, but in continental Europe. While Whig opponents asserted that it represented the translation, into a British context, of Jacobin centralism and despotism, the Prussian publicist and diplomat Friedrich Gentz concluded that the reform offered a model for a necessary consolidation of the European states-system in the wake of France's revolutionary expansion. Indeed, the Enlightened case for union described here had a better reception

---

[7] Jim Smyth, 'The Act of Union and "Public Opinion"', in J. Smyth (ed.), *Revolution, Counter-Revolution and Union: Ireland in the 1790s* (Cambridge, 2000), 146–61; James Kelly, 'Popular Politics in Ireland and the Act of Union', *Transactions of the Royal Historical Society*, 10, 6th ser. (2000), 259–87.

[8] PRONI, Castlereagh Papers, D3030/393 Letter from Sir George Hill to Castlereagh, 10 November 1798; D3030/435 Portland to Castlereagh, 31 December, 1798; D3030/452 Longueville to Castlereagh, 6 January 1799; D3030/861 J. de Joncourt to Edward Cooke, 8 July 1799; D3030/939 Douglas to Castlereagh, 26 August 1799.

abroad than it did within Ireland itself. In 1801, the Catholic Emancipation that had been privately sought (though never publicly avowed) by Pitt and his associates was obstructed by hard-line Anglican elements in both the British ministry and the Irish parliament. The distinctiveness and radicalism of the Enlightened vision of union was made plain by the angry resistance it provoked from those opposed to what the most trenchant defender of the Ascendancy and the Penal Laws, Patrick Duigenan, the Grand Master of the Orange Lodges, described as its 'spirit of Burkism'.

An Empire Divided

The Union of 1801 was grounded in an analysis of the origin of the 1798 rebellion that perceived a dangerous interplay between the unrestrained political enthusiasm of the Anglo-Irish elite and poverty of the Irish countryside. This account of the rebellion was overlaid by an additional, conspiratorial dimension, heavily indebted to Augustin de Barruel's and John Robison's presentations of the French Revolution as an *Illuminati* plot against religion and social order. This system was extended into Ireland by means of the secretive and hierarchical Society of United Irishmen, who had organised and colluded with the agrarian violence of Catholic Defenders to construct a revolutionary and democratic army.[9] A report from the Irish House of Lords outlined how through 'the licentious abuse of the press' and their rigid command structure, the United Irishmen had constructed a nationwide 'system of treason' which roused the diffuse discontents of the 'lower orders' into 'tumult and outrage, as leading to the abolition of tithes, hearth and county taxes, and the reduction of rents'.[10] There was in Ireland, Henry Dundas claimed in 1799, 'a spirit of clamour and dissention, of treachery and treason, which menaces the overthrow of the present Government'. 'Conspiracies' were 'widely extended', and 'their influence is ... deeply infused into the minds of the people of Ireland'.[11]

From the outset, the struggle against Irish sedition and agrarian violence was set in the international context of war with the French Republic. The

[9] Michael Taylor, 'British Conservatism, the Illuminati, and the Conspiracy Theory of the French Revolution, 1797–1802', *Eighteenth-Century Studies*, 47 (2014), 293–312, at 300–3.

[10] House of Lords (Ireland), *Report From the Secret Committee of the House of Lords* (Dublin: W. Sleater, 1798), 3–4.

[11] Henry Dundas, *Substance of the Speech of the Right Hon. Henry Dundas in the House of Commons, Thursday, Feb. 7, 1799, on the Subject of the Legislative Union with Ireland* (London: J. Wright, 1799), 8–9.

leading manifesto for the administration's plans, produced by the Castle official Edward Cooke in 1798, positioned Union as an unavoidably necessary rationalisation of Britain's dangerously outdated structure of multiple monarchy. Cooke argued that the recent experiences of partitioned Poland, the defeated Dutch Republic and the confederated American states proved that that *imperium in imperio* was a 'vice of constitution' and a 'radical evil'. The Union of Britain and Ireland, like that of the American Republic under the Constitution of 1787, established the 'common imperial controul [*sic*]' necessary to modern statehood.[12] The ultimate example of this unavoidable tendency towards administrative centralisation, Cooke asserted, was that of the French Republic itself, which practised its own policy of *réunion* in the course of its rapid eastward expansion into the Low Countries and the Rhineland in 1792–7.[13] The French example should now be followed in Britain, Cooke explained, the better to frustrate the Republic's ambitions to divide the Britisih nations from one another:

> France well knows the principle and the force of incorporations. Every state which she unites to herself, she makes part of her empire, *one and indivisible*, and will not suffer any mention to be made in negotiation of restitution. Whilst in her affected plans of policy for the liberties of the British Empire, she maintains the principle of separation, as essential to freedom; she considers the Union of England and Scotland as an usurpation of the former, and leaving England to her fate, would make Scotland and Ireland separate Republics. France well knows the adage, *dum singuli pugnant universi vincuntur*; and she has played that game successfully; but as we wish to check the ambition of that desperate, and unprincipled power, and if that end can only be effected by maintaining and augmenting the power of the British Empire, we should be favourable to the principle of Union, which must increase and consolidate its resources.[14]

Pitt himself rested his case for Union on similarly urgent, and military, foundations. 'If we were to ask the Ministers of our Allies', he told the British parliament, 'what measure they thought the most likely to augment the power of the British Empire, and consequently increase that strength by which they were now protected – if we were to ask the Agent of our Enemies, what measure would be the most likely to render their designs

---

[12] Edward Cooke, *Arguments for and against an Union, between Great Britain and Ireland, Considered* (London: John Stockdale, 1798), 12.
[13] Belissa, *Reprense l'ordre Européen*, 210–22.   [14] Cooke, *Arguments*, 9.

abortive – the answer would be the same in both cases, viz. the firm consolidation of every part of the Empire'.[15]

This straightforward identification of legislative uniformity with imperial strength, however, was far from evident to Irish or British critics of the union. The Clogher MP Charles Ball claimed that Cooke's list of contemporary examples of state consolidation proved the opposite of what he claimed. In particular, 'the Union of the American States is as different from the Union proposed to Ireland, as any two political arrangements that were ever found to subsist in the world'. The American system preserved the equality of its component states so that 'no one state, as would be the case in the instance under discussion, can *by a plurality of voices bear down the interests of another, or of all the rest*'. Nowhere in the American constitution, moreover, was it provided for that central authority could interfere 'in the *internal and separate economy of any individual state*'.[16] The existing system of multiple monarchy in Britain, where the Crown preserved unity in external affairs and the estates of multiple realms acted as a guarantee of their interests, was a far better approximation to the new kind of federalism that was emerging in the United States.

While Clogher's defence of the Irish parliament recalled the arguments of Charles Sheridan in the 1780s, Burke's literary executor, the lawyer and journalist French Laurence, echoed his mentor's sceptical approach to the Commercial Propositions of the 1780s, urging the need for a 'union of affection', rather than 'parchment'.[17] Like Ball, Laurence denied that centralised power was a necessary characteristic of a modern state. Gesturing to the examples of the Prussian and Habsburg monarchies – each composed of multiple realms, some with local Estates, some without – he ridiculed Pitt's suggestion that the elimination of the Irish Kingdom could seriously be desired by Britain's allies against France. Imperial patriotism was aided, not diminished, by the preservation of plural forms of government and administration among the inhabitants of a large and complex state.

More sophisticated advocates of Union than Cooke succeeded in turning these assertions of 'emulous zeal' against the defenders of the Irish parliament. According to the Scottish peer Gilbert Elliot, Lord Minto, the Irish parliament was an incubator for an assertive form of provincial

---

[15] William Pitt, *Speech of the Right Honourable William Pitt, in the House of Commons, Thursday January 31, 1799* (J. Wright, 1799), 31.
[16] Charles Ball, *Union neither Necessary or Expedient for Ireland: Being an Answer to the Author of Arguments for and against an Union* (Dublin: William Porter, 1798), 15.
[17] Cobbett, *Parliamentary History*, XXXIV:309.

patriotism that had threatened imperial stability since the 1770s. Minto, a Scottish lawyer, diplomat and future Governor General of the East India Company, drew a clear distinction between a 'federal connection', such as that which existed among the states of the Dutch Republic, the Swiss cantons or the Holy Roman Empire, and 'those connexions which consist ... in having some part or member of their governments the same, with a distinctness and separate independence in all the rest'.[18] Both suffered from a 'fundamental vice', that in 'professing to provide only for some common interests, they not only leave, but it is, in some sort, their spirit to establish, a distinctness, and even an opposition of interests on all or many other points'.[19] Whether the states were connected via a Crown, or by a constitutive treaty of permanent alliance, 'the attention of each country is still pointed towards a separate view of individual interest; and the public mind, if I may so express it, of the two nations, is kept distinct'.[20]

The United Irishmen were only the latest and most extreme manifestation of a tendency towards 'separation' that was implicit in all demands for Irish political autonomy. Under the existing structure of multiple monarchy, a conflictual dynamic was inevitable, since Britain and Ireland were 'two distinct and unequal countries' where 'the superior must be predominant and the inferior subordinate in their common concerns, and in the administration of the common parts of their Government'. Demagogues in the smaller country were rewarded with honours and popularity for converting patriotism into 'jealousy' against the more powerful nation. This was what had ultimately given rise to the United Irishmen. The inchoate and spasmodic discontents of the Irish countryside had to be given form by sections of the movement's elite political leadership, epitomised by figures such as Henry Flood, Henry Grattan and Wolfe Tone:

> Hence we shall observe a restless and never satisfied struggling with every circumstance either in the constitution of their government, or in the counsels and measures of their administration, which seems, even to the most subtle refinements of jealousy, to affect that object; hence a perpetual straining after its improvement and perfection ... as each succession of patriots, or of demagogues, seeking to enhance on the exploits of their predecessors, the improvement of independency is pushed forward until the true goal for that course comes in view – I mean separation.[21]

---

[18] Gilbert Elliot, *The Speech of Lord Minto, in the House of Peers, April 11, 1799 ... Respecting an Union between Great Britain and Ireland* (Dublin: John Exshaw, 1799), 20–1.
[19] Ibid., 17.   [20] Ibid., 21–2.   [21] Ibid., 23–5.

Tempting Ireland's fractious elite away from the popular politics of insurrection required a subtle grasp of the dynamics of aristocratic faction. Here, British politicians were able to draw on their experience of managing the crisis in the American colonies. Henry Dundas' speech in favour of the Union drew transparently on Adam Smith's analysis of the origins of the American Revolutionary War. Smith had argued that during the political crises produced by the Stamp Act and the Townshend Duties, American colonial leaders had been undermined by a centre bent on fiscal integration. They had embraced violent resistance to sovereign authority rather than allowing their sense of self-importance to be undermined. For Smith, one of the attractions of a transatlantic union was that 'a new method of acquiring importance, a new and more dazzling object of ambition would be presented to the leading men of each colony'. The metropolis could draw off and neutralise the factional political energy of the colonies:

> Instead of piddling for the little prizes which are to be found in what may be called the paltry raffle of colony faction; they might then hope, from the presumption which men naturally have in their own ability and good fortune, to draw some of the great prizes which sometimes come from the wheel of the great state lottery of British politicks.[22]

Dundas dangled a very similar prospect of advancement before Irish MPs in his speech promoting the Union. He urged Irish parliamentarians to remember 'that if their genius be ever so acute, their talents ever so transcendent, their eloquence ever so splendid, all these wonderful powers are confined to one little island'. The British parliament had 'enabled this proud country to exalt its head amidst the wreck of surrounding nations; had given it energy and vigour to resist the pernicious doctrines of the French Republic; and held us up as a monument of admiration and envy to the remotest corners of the world'. It would be 'worthy of true ambition ... a more respectable body than what had been described by a gentleman who, in talking of the limitations of the parliament of Ireland, compared it to a Grand Vestry or Parish Meeting'.[23]

Faction, Religion and Aristocracy

Channelling the vanity of the Irish political elite into the great game of Westminster would have benefits further down the social scale.

---

[22] Smith, *Wealth of Nations*, IV.vii.c.75.   [23] Dundas, *Speech on Union*, 17–18.

Proponents of union believed that the root of the Irish tendency to agrarian violence lay in confessional divisions among the population, which were aggravated by the political constitution of the Irish Kingdom. Smith's analysis of the dynamics of faction in large and small states, already discussed in Chapter 1, was frequently cited in Irish debates on the Union. It was reinforced by the reputation of Edmund Burke, who believed, like Smith, that the political exclusion of Catholics rested on the persistence of an exclusionary 'spirit of conquest' among the Anglo-Irish, derived ultimately from the historical memory of the seventeenth-century wars.[24]

Burke, however, had been ambivalent about union as a solution to this problem. A key refrain of his later political analysis was that the complexity of Irish society required a distinct form of government, capable of managing the Kingdom's 'peculiar' mixed population under the ambit of a mixed constitution and Established church modelled on that of Britain.[25] The granting of the franchise to Catholics and the opening of the Irish parliament to Catholic members were measures of conciliation rather than transformation. There was little chance, given the uneven distribution of landed property in the Irish Kingdom, that the opening of the franchise or the parliament itself to Catholic voters or MPs would bring about a rapid transformation in its composition. What mattered was that the Irish constitution ceased to set 'numbers against property' by removing its 'stigma' against Catholicism.[26] Writing to his friend William Cusack Smith following the failure of Whig proposals to admit Catholics to the Irish parliament in 1795, Burke had stressed the danger posed by refusing further political concessions to the Irish majority, who might yet turn for support to the Dissenters and Jacobins who constituted the United Irishmen.[27] 'You have now your choice for full four fifths of your people, the Catholick religion of Jacobitism', he cautioned. 'If things appear to you to stand on this alternative; I think you will not be long in making your opinion.'[28]

Cusack Smith, an Irish MP then sitting for Lanesborough, County Longford, was a leading advocate for the Catholic cause in the Irish parliament. He alluded to Burke's commitment to Emancipation as the guarantor of security against revolution in his widely circulated

---

[24] Edmund Burke, 'Letter to Sir Hercules Langrishe' (1792)', *Writings and Speeches*, IX:594–639, at 615–19.

[25] Edmund Burke, 'Letter to Richard Burke (1792)', *Writings and Speeches*, IX:640–58, at 641.

[26] Burke, 'Letter to Langrishe', 634–5.

[27] Edmund Burke, 'Letter to William Smith (1795)', *Writings and Speeches*, IX:658–65.

[28] Ibid., 663.

1799 speech to the Irish parliament proposing the Union.[29] The latter was now, however, a sad necessity, occasioned by the violence of the 1798 rebellion. Since Burke's death, Cusack Smith claimed, 'opposite parties had ... vied with each other in civil rage, and supplied, by their distractions, so many arguments for Union'. Events had brutally vindicated Adam Smith's judgement that 'without a Union with Great Britain, the inhabitants of Ireland are not likely for many ages to consider themselves as one people'.[30] Cusack Smith interpreted Adam Smith's comment in line with the Scottish philosopher's discussion of a transatlantic union in the *Wealth of Nations*. 'He recommends the measure, as calculated to deliver the [the colonies] from *rancorous and virulent factions,* and to promote American *tranquillity and happiness* ... I think that Ireland, as well as America, has *its* rancorous factions to remove; and tranquillity and happiness, yet to attain!'[31] It was now clear that only the removal of political competition to Westminster, rather than the admission of Catholics to a purely Irish political nation, would effect the dissolution of Burke's 'monster' of 'plebeian oligarchy' – the Anglican monopoly of representation that disfigured Irish politics. Cusack Smith noted with approval that Union would 'exclude many Protestants from that political importance, which the present state of things permits them to enjoy'. With a much smaller caste of absentee politicians left to agitate over the country's future in Westminster, the remainder would abandon their prized 'political distinction' and dedicate themselves to the peaceable lives of gentry improvers. His concluding remarks followed Smith's word for word: 'After Union', he projected, 'our *resident* aristocracy would be founded on those distinctions of birth and fortune, which are as attainable by those of one religion, as of the other'.[32]

In a series of pamphlets published over the course of 1799 and aimed at a Catholic audience, the reforming lawyer Theobald McKenna made a still more strident case along similar lines. In the early 1790s, McKenna had been a notable Catholic advocate for the expansion of the franchise and the admission of Catholics into the Dublin parliament, but he adopted a more cautious position in the wake of the Jacobin Terror.[33] His case for Union

[29] William Cusack Smith, *The Substance of Mr. William Smith's Speech on the Subject of a Legislative Union ... in the Irish House of Commons, Thursday, January 24th 1799* (London: J. Wright, 1800), 80–1.
[30] Ibid.; cf. Smith, *Wealth of Nations*, V.iii.90.   [31] Smith, *Speech on Legislative Union*, 64–6.
[32] Ibid., 82–3.
[33] Manuela Ceretta, 'Theobald McKenna', in J. McGuire & J. Quinn, *Dictionary of Irish Biography* (Cambridge: Cambridge University Press, 2009). McKenna himself provided an instructive account

hitched a recognisably Burkean analysis of the sectarian perversion of Irish social hierarchies to a skilful play on the anxieties of Catholics following the 1798 rebellion and the rise to prominence of the Orange Order, a militantly Protestant social club and paramilitary organisation. The Order, McKenna asserted, represented a lethal democratisation of the internal structure of the 'plebeian oligarchy' Burke had described in 1793. Dedicated to the reintroduction of the Penal Laws out of a 'spirit of vengeance' animated by a misreading of the 1798 rebellion, they ignored that Catholics 'supply almost entirely the labouring and industrious classes of the community'. By setting up its members as a 'superior order in the state, with a superior title to every kind of consideration and privilege', they threatened social order at every level. 'The Protestant Mechanic who has studied manner and politics in an Orange Lodge', would introduce a wealth of petty oppressions and insults into the life of his Catholic neighbour, driving the majority 'either into seditious turbulence, or enervated despondency'.[34]

McKenna claimed to ground his analysis of political behaviour in the theories of 'Dr. Adam Smith, an excellent judge of the springs by which men are moved'.[35] The advantage of union lay in its modification of the relationship between centre, periphery and faction that Smith had described:

> Open governments, those I mean in which political affairs are discussed without reserve, are of themselves prone to faction – where there is a difference of religion, it tends in proportion, as the parties are nearly balanced, to increase this propensity. That is a very urgent reason to render Ireland as little as possible the scene of political activity.[36]

McKenna adhered to a definition of the 'liberties of the people' that emphasised the modern civil liberty of security and 'happiness', described by prominent contemporary legal authorities including Montesquieu, Blackstone and Delolme. Trial by jury and the protection of property rights, McKenna claimed, were 'the first object of civil society. This is the

---

of his political evolution in the introduction to his collected works: Theobald McKenna, *Political Essays Relative to the Affairs of Ireland, in 1791, 1792, and 1793, with Remarks on the Present State of That Country* (London: J. Debrett, 1794), ix–lxiii.

[34] Theobald McKenna, *A Memoire on Some Questions Respecting the Projected Union of Great Britain and Ireland* (Dublin: John Rice, 1799), 16–20.

[35] Ibid., 20–2.

[36] Theobald McKenna, *Constitutional Objections to the Government of Ireland by a Separate Legislature, in a Letter to John Hamilton, Esq.* (Dublin: H. Fitzpatrick, 1799), 13.

end; Peers and Representatives are but the means'.[37] The attraction of Union for Catholics was that, coupled with the granting of the full political rights that McKenna had agitated for since the early 1790s, it had the potential to diffuse the English system of constitutional liberty into Ireland. McKenna cited with approval an observation made by one of Smith's most prominent students, the jurist John Millar, at the opening of the latter's *Historical View of the English Government* (1787). Millar believed that 'the British government is the only one in the annals of mankind that has aimed at the diffusion of liberty through a multitude of people, spread over a wide extent of territory'.[38] The small republics of Italy and Switzerland, he had observed, bestowed 'very unequal privileges upon different individuals', and the liberties of the formed United Provinces had been upheld by their confederal political order, which ensured that 'every particular province' constituted 'an independent political system'.[39]

McKenna was scornful of the notion that Ireland could ever operate as such an 'independent political system' within the British Empire. 'The definition of our political establishment is, a qualified sovereignty, vested in an assembly, which may be a wise and virtuous senate, but cannot pretend to be a popular delegation.'[40] He agreed with Burke that Irish assertions of sovereign equality were ultimately futile, given the clear predominance of Britain in the counsels of the empire. In a single sentence, he sought to puncture the illusions of those Anglo-Irish patriots who had sought to place Ireland in the same category as Hanover: an independent state joined by a merely dynastic union with the British monarchy. The formal dependence of the Irish Crown on the British was such that this point of view was unsustainable. 'The public law of Europe recognises no such state as independent Ireland', McKenna observed, 'whilst the rights and possession of our executive government, are inseparably annexed to the British Crown, it cannot recognise us otherwise than as an undiscriminated portion of that monarchy'.[41]

The claims of Anglo-Irish patriots to an autonomous Irish Kingdom therefore amounted to nothing more than 'an unprofitable and delusive imitation of British forms', attempted in the absence of Britain's natural and representative system of social distinctions.[42] Wales and Scotland, like Ireland, lacked these 'proper materials for a mixed monarchy, but both

---

[37] McKenna, *Memoire*, 3.   [38] McKenna, *Constitutional Objections*, 4; Millar, *Historical View*, 12.
[39] Millar, *Historical View*, 12.   [40] McKenna, *Constitutional Objections*, 25.   [41] Ibid., 29.
[42] Ibid., 45.

nations enjoy that advantage, *engrafted* on the capability of England. Ireland stands, at least as much as the latter, in need of this assistance'.[43] Projects of reform that simply sought to recreate the conditions for English liberty, including McKenna's previous demand for Catholic Emancipation within the Irish Kingdom alone, were doomed to failure. 'You do not act in the spirit of enlightened attachment', he observed, 'but in a ridiculous and pedantic bigotry, when you chain yourself down to the forms of British liberty. You ought to propose for your object the social happiness, that these forms confer; and you should pursue it by whatever means it is most easily attainable'. McKenna's analysis carried a sharp warning for erstwhile radical colleagues who had embraced the risks of revolution and invasion rather than contemplate the possibilities for reform on an imperial level. Reform within Ireland risked the dissolution of political society itself – a hazard that would not be presented by Union.[44]

The writings and speeches of Gilbert Elliott, Henry Dundas, William Cusack Smith and Theobald McKenna represented a distinct set of arguments for the the Union of 1801. In a series of observations on the politics of Ireland that were recognisably grounded in the scientific study of human dispositions attempted by Hume, Smith, Burke and Millar, they conceptualised union as a new art of imperial government, designed to conciliate Irish discontent through the subtle manipulation of opinion and sentiment. The conciliation of violent political enthusiasms, however, would also require a durable expansion of public prosperity in Ireland. Only a reformed political economy, one that finally secured to Ireland the fruits of commercial growth and political stability, could durably ensure its British allegiance.

Poverty and Disaffection

British and Irish elites were united in the view that the 1798 rising had deep roots in the poverty and disaffection of the Irish peasantry. In 1798, George Canning, the future Foreign Secretary and then-editor of the popular loyalist *Anti-Jacobin* newspaper, told the British House of Commons that French influence had partially succeeded in converting Ireland's long tradition of agrarian violence into an attempt at political revolution:

> Where is the country whose state of society is more adapted to receive and cherish, and mature the principles of the French revolution – principles

[43] Ibid., 49.   [44] Ibid., 50.

which go to array the physical force of the lower orders of the people, against the educated and governing parts of the community, to arm poverty against property, labour against privilege, and each class of life against its superior, than a country, like Ireland, where the inhabitants are in general poor and uncivilised, and where religious distinctions prevail to such an extent? In such a country, the seeds of the French revolution must be sown deep indeed! It is not, I am afraid, the act of a day or a year which will destroy its baneful influence. The government of France know, that wherever their principles are scattered, it will be difficult to eradicate them; they know that they have taken root in Ireland.[45]

This willingness on the part of British politicians to comment so extensively on the social condition of the Irish peasantry was almost entirely new. During the 1780s, the commercial and constitutional relationship between the Kingdoms of Great Britain and Ireland was largely considered in isolation from the simmering tensions of the Irish countryside. As we have seen, debate centred on what kind of constitutional relationship with Britain was likely to safeguard the Irish polity's potential for commercial growth under the undisputed leadership of its Anglican landed aristocracy. While the economic terms of the Union bore several resemblances to Pitt's 1785 attempt at a final settlement of Anglo-Irish relations, the political context for the negotiations had been transformed.[46] At stake now was the question of who was ultimately responsible for the condition of the Irish interior – the Anglo-Irish landholding class, or the imperial parliament at Westminster. In the Union, the Anglo-Irish culture of improvement was confronted by a rival mode of imperial government that prized the philosophical detachment of Smith's 'science of a legislator' over the local virtues of the noble agriculturalist.

The tension between the reforming visions of Anglo-Irish improvement and Enlightened union were evident from the outset of the pamphlet debate. Cooke had opened his manifesto for Union with a stark proclamation of Ireland's inferiority to Britain and the limitations of its elite. He attributed the 1798 rebellion to 'defects in civilisation and policy – that the former is not sufficiently diffused, to prevent irregularity and

---

[45] Cobbett, *Parliamentary History*, XXXIV:236.
[46] Instead of immediately folding Ireland's distinct fiscal system into a unitary British whole, the resolutions proposed the retention of a separate currency, exchequer and national debt. Irish taxation would still be levied separately, in a fixed ratio to British revenues that ministers regarded as generous. As in 1785, countervailing duties were to be retained, although this time they were to be subject to phased reductions over subsequent decades. See Terence McCavery, 'Politics, Public Finance and the British-Irish Act of Union of 1801', *Transactions of the Royal Historical Society*, 10 (2000), 353–75.

licentiousness, nor the latter strong enough to repress them'. After the Union, Cooke declared, 'Ireland will be gradually rising to the level of England; or England gradually sinking to the level of Ireland; and it is obvious which is most probable'. As such, Irish patriotism and unionist allegiance were easily reconciled. 'What can any sanguine Irish Patriot wish for his country, but that its inhabitants should attain the same habits, manners, and improvement which make England the envy of Europe?' Cooke demanded. 'And by what means can he hope to attain that end so effectually as by uniting with her Government, and binding up all her interests and concerns in the same bottom?'[47]

Cooke identified three major economic opportunities arising from the Union, each relevant to different sections of Irish society. To the 'landed gentlemen', he promised a rise in land prices and increased British investment in Irish agriculture, encouraged by 'steadiness of administration, and regular subordination'. Cooke foresaw an Irish property boom following Union and peace with France. 'Notwithstanding the enormous loans which have been borrowed by Government, the monied men are embarrassed in what manner to invest the capitals with advantage and security', he claimed. 'When a peace arrives, and loans shall cease, the difficulty of employing capital will be augmented; and there can be no doubt that if the state of this country can be rendered secure, it will be abundantly employed in Irish purchases and Irish speculation.' This was even more likely given Ireland's suitability as a breadbasket for Britain, where population and levels of urbanisation were rapidly rising. This was a major opportunity for Ireland's agricultural exporters. 'Great Britain does not produce sufficient corn for her consumption', declared Cooke. 'It must be a great object, therefore, for Irish landed gentlemen to secure a preference in the British market for ever, which an union would certainly effect.'

Unlike other proponents of union such as Thomas Brooke Clarke and Richard Watson, the Bishop of Llandaff, Cooke was careful not to describe union in exclusively agrarian terms. He made an appeal to Irish merchants and manufacturers, urging them to trust to Britain's mercantile system as a guarantor of future Irish prosperity. 'The British administration, in order to increase the wealth of the kingdom for the purposes of power, are perpetually employed in devising the means of extending the commerce of England', he claimed.

[47] Cooke, *Arguments*, 8.

> Under the wise regulations of that Government, a commerce has been established, and by the late naval victories has been secured, which is the astonishment of the world. An union then will place the Irish merchant upon an equality with the British, and he will be certain to enjoy for ever the same privileges, protection, regulations, bounties and encouragements, as are enjoyed by the greatest commercial country that ever flourished.[48]

Given continued Irish bitterness at the imposition of restrictive commercial legislation by the British parliament in the seventeenth and eighteenth centuries, it was perhaps unwise on Cooke's part to remind his readers of the ruthless self-interest that had characterised British economic policy since the time of Cromwell. Such reasoning could be extended to Union itself. One of Cooke's many Irish critics, the Dublin barrister Joshua Spencer, alluded to the fiscal case for Union put forward by Josiah Tucker. 'The curious reader will easily satisfy himself', Spencer observed, 'that all the arguments in favour of the measure, centre in the convenience and alleviation of publick burthen to England'.[49]

Still more provocative was Cooke's relaxed stance on the fraught question of absentee landlords, the source of recurrent moral panics within the brittle political culture formed by the junction of Irish agricultural improvement with popular patriotism. 'The Absentee proprietors of land might in some degree increase', Cooke admitted. 'London, as at present, would be the general resort for business, for advancement, for pleasure.' The disadvantages of increased absenteeism, Cooke claimed, would be outweighed by 'the solid advantage of a fixed unalterable Constitution'.[50] Speaking in January 1799, William Pitt himself addressed the problem of absenteeism in a similarly dismissive vein. Neatly illustrating the divergent forms of political knowledge that underpinned the British and Anglo-Irish positions, he insisted that the relatively small additional proportion of Irish landlords who would be required to attend parliament in London could not be statistically significant. Far more important was the diffusion of capital and industry to Ireland that a free and stable commercial connection with Britain would enable. 'Can industry, can civilisation increase among the whole bulk of the people', he demanded, 'without much more than counterbalancing the partial effect of the removal of the few individuals who, for the small part of the year, would follow the seat of Legislation'?[51] More provocative still was the trenchant response of

---

[48] Ibid., 21–2.
[49] Joshua Spencer, *Thoughts on an Union*, 4th ed. (Dublin: William Jones, 1798), 7–9.
[50] Cooke, *Arguments*, 11.   [51] Pitt, *Speech on Union*, 70.

Henry Dundas, which used the historical experience of Anglo-Scottish Union to ridicule Irish anxieties regarding the risks of aristocratic desertion. He took great pleasure in reading long extracts of the Scottish Earl of Belhaven's passionate oration against the Union of 1707, which had lamented how the 'Honourable Peerage of Scotland' would be placed by the loss of their parliament 'even on an equal footing with their own very vassals'. 'If the Union has had a tendency to break asunder the bands of feudal vassalage', Dundas commented, 'wise and virtuous men will not be disposed to consider this as one of the evil consequences to be lamented in the formation of a Legislative Union of the two Kingdoms'.[52]

John Foster and Thomas Brooke Clarke on Commerce and 'Feudalism'

Dundas' equation of aristocratic power with 'feudalism' demanded an urgent rebuttal from the defenders of the improving mission of Ireland's Anglican landholding class. The most determined statement of the Anglo-Irish position was made in a monumental speech by the Speaker of the Irish parliament, John Foster, delivered on 11 April 1799 and repeatedly reprinted and discussed over the following year.[53] Foster's case for a resident Anglo-Irish aristocracy was deeply rooted in his own practices of estate management and cultural patronage. 'I have ever understood', he observed,

> that the example of the upper ranks, was the most effectual means of promoting good morals and habits among the lower orders; that their attention to the education, the health, and the comforts, as well as the protection they afforded the lower ranks, all of which can only arise from residence, were the surest mode of conciliating their affections.[54]

Foster argued that the Union would exacerbate the absenteeism that had been long decried by Anglo-Irish improvers by drawing the greatest aristocratic families away to Westminster for parliamentary business. It could not change 'the actual state of the country' at all, except through the introduction of likely tax rises. Generalised theories regarding the benefits of trade between Britain and Ireland were no compensation for the loss of

---

[52] Dundas, *Speech on Union*, 22.
[53] George C. Bolton, *The Passing of the Irish Act of Union: A Study in Parliamentary Politics* (Oxford: Oxford University Press), 120–4.
[54] John Foster, *Speech of the Right Honorable John Foster, Speaker of the House of Commons of Ireland, Delivered in Committee, on Thursday the 11th Day of April, 1799* (Dublin: James Moore, 1799), 68.

a parliament and resident aristocracy: 'Mr. Pitt says, it will give to Ireland the common use of the British capital – will identify Ireland with England, and so forth; these general unsupported expressions have no meaning.'[55] In order to make a judgement about the commercial benefits of the Union, it was necessary to consider in detail the status of individual industries, rather than making vague assertions about the communication of capital and civilisation. Foster insisted on the necessity of a distinctively Irish system of economic policy, one that relied on the autonomy of the Dublin parliament and the 'local knowledge' of its representatives for its integrity. 'New laws equal in appearance and in phrase, may be very unequal in effect, to countries differently situated', he warned. The effect of free trade, Foster insisted, would be to further consolidate Ireland's existing status as a supplier of food, raw textiles and labour to Britain's surging industrial sector.[56]

Foster's speech had a wide resonance in the subsequent debate on the economic terms of the Union. Even committed political opponents, such as William James MacNeven, found much to agree with in his critique of the distant and undiscriminating character of centralised legislative authority.[57] For the anonymous author of a series of *Observations on the Commercial Principles of the Projected Union* (1800) the constant aim of Pitt's Irish policy had been to construct a 'crafty system' of 'selfish policy', of which the 'ultimate object was that of holding us fast, as we now are, a consuming province'.[58] Another writer feared that the ultimate aim of British policy was to reduce Ireland to the status of an agricultural dependency. 'I am perfectly aware, that in political economy, there are many respectable patrons of opinions unfriendly to the encouragement of manufactures', they observed. 'I have no doubt, if an Union took place, but that the depression of the manufacturing part of the Community, would leave Ireland no resource, but in the agricultural system, the provision trade, and the staple manufactures.'[59] Citing Alexander Hamilton's 'Report on Manufactures' (1791), the text concluded that 'the agricultural system has intrinsically a strong, but not an exclusive,

---

[55] Ibid., 68.   [56] Ibid., 71–6.
[57] William James MacNeven, *An Argument for Independence, in Opposition to Union, Addressed to All His Countrymen* (Dublin: J. Stockdale, 1799), 9.
[58] Anon., *Observations on the Commercial Principles of the Projected Union* (London: R. Pitkeathley, 1800), 14.
[59] Anon., *The Commercial System of Ireland Reviewed, and the Question of Union Discussed, in an Address to the Merchants, Manufacturers, and Country Gentlemen of Ireland* (Dublin: James Moore, 1799), 44–5.

claim to pre-eminence over every other kind of industry; but I contend that it is advanced by the due encouragement of manufactures'.[60]

Foster's most prolific and innovative opponent on the pro-Union side of the debate was the Church of Ireland clergyman Thomas Brooke Clarke, who at this point was a librarian to the Prince of Wales. Little is otherwise known about Clarke, but his Irish pamphlets reveal connections of friendship and patronage to both Josiah Tucker and the Earl of Shelburne.[61] Clarke edited and significantly modified Josiah Tucker's private advocacy of parliamentary union in a major contribution, *Union or Separation* (1799), and offered further commentary of his own in subsequent works designed to rebut Foster's case. Brooke Clarke's vision of Irish development rejected Foster's and MacNeven's calls for Ireland to emulate the state-led economic development of eighteenth-century Britain. It drew instead on the long tradition of critical Irish and Scottish thinking concerning the primacy accorded to foreign trade and manufacturing industry in imperial economic policy.

As for Arthur O'Connor, Adam Smith's description of a the 'natural progress of opulence', driven by mutually reinforcing trade between town and country, provided a crucial theoretical framework. Brooke Clarke, however, placed a much more pronounced emphasis on the ultimate priority of agriculture in commercial society, potentially drawn from discussions of similar issues in the works of the leading Latitudinarian moralist, William Paley, and a fellow Shelburne acolyte, the American merchant Benjamin Vaughan.[62] 'Agriculture is not only the first and great source of wealth to a State', Brooke Clarke urged. 'Agriculture and Population are like the ocean and the rivers which supply each other. Agriculture promotes Population, by invigorating the bodies of Men, and by furnishing food for an increased progeny. And Population promotes Agriculture by the consumption of the fruits of the earth.'[63] Brooke Clarke and Richard Watson, the Bishop of Llandaff and another recipient of Shelburne's patronage, each projected an agrarian vision of British power. 'Sixty millions of acres, so fertile by nature, if improved by art, will maintain much more than thirty millions of men', they argued. 'Out of

---

[60] Ibid., 52.

[61] Josiah Tucker & Thomas Brooke Clarke, *Union or Separation*, 2nd ed. (London: J. Hatchard & J. Wright, 1799), i–iii; Hont, '"Rich Country-Poor Country" Debate Revisited', 301–4.

[62] William Paley, *The Principles of Moral and Political Philosophy* (London: R. Fauldner, 1785), 611–12; Benjamin Vaughan, *New and Old Principles of Trade Compared* (London: J. Johnson, 1787), 65–79.

[63] Tucker & Clarke, *Union or Separation*, 13–14.

these thirty millions, five millions may bear arms; and out of these five millions, one million may be always in arms without prejudice to agriculture or commerce, to protect the other twenty-nine millions in peace and industry.' A regenerated empire within the British Isles would be well placed to defend itself against a Napoleonic Empire in Europe, even if it succeeded in turning the other powers of the continent against Britain:

> With such a body of united Britons, with the commerce resulting from this Union, with a navy thus supported, with riches and resources thus secured, with such strength form Nature and from Union, we may bid defiance to the world. Then we may look down in calm and supreme dignity upon the little disputes and wars of Continental Princes, wholly uninterested in their artificial balance of power. Our confederacy will be then at home – in Union: our balance of power will be then – the population, the riches, the resources of Great and United Britain.[64]

In their correspondence during the 1785 crisis, Tucker had offered Brooke Clarke a trenchant critique of the whole direction of Irish economic policy under the direction of Ascendancy notables like Foster. 'Ireland is continually complaining that her Trade is *crampt*, and her People have not Work; yet there are no People under the Sun who take so much Pains to cramp her Trade, and check her Industry, as the Irish themselves', he declared.

> They unhappily expect a Foreign Trade, without an Home Consumption; thereby grasping at the Shadow, and letting go the substance. They think it good policy to keep the Mass of their People so poor, and so destitute of the three great Necessaries of Life, Food, Raiment, and Dwelling (which, by the by, are the foundation of all commerce whatever, even the most brilliant and extensive) that their *black cattle* are almost, if not altogether, *as good Customers to the Community*, and as much promote the Trade of it, as the Peasantry.[65]

Like Arthur O'Connor, Brooke Clarke asserted that Ireland's problem was fundamentally one of luxury and corruption: the country's Protestant settler aristocracy lived in a condition of idleness akin to that of Smith's feudal barons, spending their rack-rents in the 'pleasures, amusements and diversions' of Dublin.[66] The rebellion of 1798 had been at root a social conflict, in which 'polished luxury' had been 'at war with civil misery'.[67] Union would act as a corrective to both British and Irish preoccupations with luxury and long-distance trade. Foreign markets would not

---

[64] Thomas Brooke Clarke, *The Political, Commercial, and Civil State of Ireland, Being an Appendix to 'Union or Separation'* (Dublin: J. Milliken, 1799), 3; Cobbett, *Parliamentary History*, XXXIV:737.
[65] Tucker & Clarke, *Union or Separation*, 11.   [66] Ibid., 12–13, 22.   [67] Ibid., 65.

> be so necessary for Commerce, when there is through home Industry an home Trade and good price for the Commodities ... Perhaps a better criterion of the happy effects of industry can not be had than the home consumption of Britain compared with its trade all over the Globe.[68]

Free access to the huge British market would end the Irish elite's misguided obsession with competing with Britain in long-distance and colonial trade, increasing demand for agricultural goods and consequently raising the incomes of the peasantry.

Brooke Clarke's system was by no means exclusive in its attachment to agriculture, however. He drew on the authority of David Hume, publishing correspondence between Hume, his fellow Scottish philosopher Lord Kames and Josiah Tucker, where Hume had added a theory of the spatial division of labour to his original account of the potential advantages of 'poor countries' in international trade competition. 'The finest arts will flourish best in the capital', Hume had written, 'those of next value in the more opulent provinces: the coarser in the remote countries'.[69] Just as McKenna had argued that civil liberty could only be secured in Ireland if she were 'engrafted' onto Britain's constitutional monarchy, so Brooke Clarke saw the Irish Kingdom taking its place in an extended division of labour linking the core and peripheries of a united British state. British investment in agriculture and manufacturing, designed to take advantage of Ireland's lower wage costs, would increase productivity and provide work for the starving poor. 'Incorporation' would be the 'angular stone' of 'a whole system of industry, encouragement and happiness'. Commerce would 'advance' the Catholic poor, with the resulting reduction in inequality restoring the 'polished' Protestants to 'that point of political morality, where *happiness* will secure *virtue* amongst the people, and *virtue* insure *happiness* among the great'.[70]

'Happiness' is a term that seems to have had a distinct meaning within Brooke Clarke's rhetoric; as in Paley's moral philosophy, it denoted the 'exercise of the social affections ... the exercise of our faculties ... the prudent constitution of the habits'.[71] With Ireland's political order stabilised and English skills and capital flowing in to the country, the conditions would be in place for a regulation of the dissolute and licentious

---

[68] Ibid., 11–14.

[69] Quoted by Brooke Clarke in Thomas Brooke Clarke, *A Survey of the Strength and Opulence of Great Britain, with Observations by Dean Tucker, and David Hume, in a Correspondence with Lord Kaimes* (London: T. Cadell), 23–4.

[70] Tucker & Clarke, *Union or Separation*, 70.   [71] Paley, *Principles*, 27–30.

moral behaviour of the Irish: an 'amelioration of manners' enabled by the civilising effects of commerce and luxury. It was on this that Brooke Clarke ultimately pinned his hopes for the pacification of the Irish poor and the resolution of sectarian conflict:

> Amidst the golden glory of virtuous and active commerce, men will contemplate blessings beyond the dreams of fancied power, and liberty beyond the flights of Republicanism. Imperial strength will then be found paramount to all parties in the state, – paramount to all enemies over the globe. It is under such important advantages of Incorporation, that men will become attached to the Government and to the State: they will feel that they have a country; their first idea will be, security, and imperial strength; their second, prosperity and national peace.[72]

Brooke Clarke's glowing prognostications of social progress under the Union relied on the mechanism of unintended consequences outlined in the final pages of Smith's history of European commerce, which detailed how the vanity of feudal barons had led them to disband their retinues and spend surplus income on foreign luxuries. This had freed their tenants from labour services and political violence and empowered monarchs and the rising urban bourgeoisie. Brooke Clarke summarised the moral crisply: 'Commerce brings in riches; riches produce luxury; luxury puts down the high and exalts the low.'[73]

Brooke Clarke was keen to distinguish, however, between luxury that was brought in to a state through commerce and that which was brought in by military expropriation. The former made a people 'polished' but also 'civilised' – enjoying 'political morality'. The latter exacerbated inequality and corrupted manners, as in imperial Rome and, Brooke Clarke offered as 'a prophecy', Republican France.[74] The fact that British luxury had brought commerce, industry and a relatively high degree of equality to the country was also at the heart of Brooke Clarke's subsequent case for the health of the British war economy.[75] 'In modern times', he argued, 'the French amidst their luxury were polished: the English with luxury on one side, and commerce on the other, stand between and enjoy polish and political morality: whereas the Irish are in the extremes'.[76]

Brooke Clarke's argument rested ultimately on a straightforward application of Adam Smith's history of commerce to Ireland's distinctive circumstances. Union, and its attendant commercial growth, would play

---

[72] Tucker & Clarke, *Union or Separation*, 47*. [73] Ibid., 69. [74] Ibid., 67–9.
[75] Hont, '"Rich Country-Poor Country" Debate Revisited', 303–4.
[76] Tucker & Clarke, *Union or Separation*, 70.

a vital role in moderating social distinction and religious enthusiasm, just as it had done in Scotland. Provocatively, Brooke Clarke substituted the Anglo-Irish aristocracy for the violent and unruly Scottish barons who figured heavily in Enlightened histories of the Scottish Middle Ages. He made the point clear in a particularly sharp attack on John Foster, closing by declaring,

> Let us remember, that through commerce the lordly yoke of feudal tyranny has been broken throughout Europe, KINGS *freed* from tyranny, and PEOPLE from OPPRESSION. Let us be assured that if Union be lost, the commerce of Ireland is lost: that if Union be established, the commerce of Ireland is established; and upon a firm basis for incalculable improvement. And it cannot be too often repeated and impressed upon the heart and mind of the Irish nation, that it is through *commerce*, and *only* through commerce, the *barbarous spirit* of feudal power will *finally depart* from Ireland. *Thus* will the old and *corrupt body* of *civil* defects find a SEPULCHRE in the UNION.[77]

The economic debate around the Union of 1801 represented, therefore, a contest between the visions of Irish reform described in the first two chapters of this book. Defenders of the Irish parliament articulated a conception of 'improvement' that relied on the purposeful action of individual landlords who served their country through commitment to agriculture and proto-industry on their personal estates. The Irish parliament was a collective expression of the duties of industry and charity, and a custodian of the Kingdom's sovereign right of access to European and imperial markets. Brooke Clarke's rejoinder to Foster articulated the redefinition of British Empire in Ireland as a vessel for commercial sociability that was capable of civilising and stabilising an impoverished province. In combination with his demand for a reorientation of economic activity away from long-distance trade and towards agricultural production, it pointed towards the governing ideology of the Union in the first decades of the nineteenth century.

William Drennan and the Radical Critique of Union

The distinctiveness and radicalism of the case for the Union presented by Brooke Clarke and others was recognised by those who conceptualised it in broader, European terms. Contemporaries were well aware that the

---

[77] Thomas Brooke Clarke, *Misconceptions of Facts, and Mistatements of the Public Accounts, by the Right Hon. John Foster* (London: John Hatchard, 1799), 66.

British–Irish Union was occurring at a time when the European order was being remade by French expansion. They were divided, however, as to whether it represented an effective response to the French challenge, or a degeneration into a parallel form of military despotism to that represented by Napoleon's Consulate. Whig opponents frequently equated it with the revolutionary violence it was designed to frustrate. Richard Sheridan, still, as in 1785, the leading defender of the Irish parliament in Westminster, noted the continued presence of large numbers of British troops in Ireland and directly compared the proposed union to the plebiscites on incorporation that were forced by France on its conquered peripheries in the Low Countries and Savoy. 'What would be thought of France if she bounteously proffered her assistance, sent her troops, lent her money, and when refusal was impossible, incorporated a subjected people? Would you not treat the pretence of free choice with scorn?' he asked. 'We hear French principles reprobated. Let us be careful at the same time to avoid French practices.'[78]

A more sustained and conceptually sophisticated comparison of the Union with the French Revolution was undertaken by William Drennan, a figure who was now largely absent from direct political struggle. Following an early period of United Irish commitment, Drennan had left the movement over its alliances with France and the Defenders, but remained too tainted by association to insert himself back into the mainstream of Whig patriotism.[79] His detachment was signalled by the gently satirical tone of his *Letter to William Pitt* (1799). Noting that the territorial integrity and unity of France was a constant theme of revolutionary theory and rhetoric, from Sieyès to Napoleon via Robespierre, he observed of Pitt that 'in the uniform habit of cursing and mimicking the French revolution your inverted order ends where *it* began, by decreeing the unity and indivisibility of the empire'.[80] Drennan's account of the Union reflected a far more sceptical strand of Scottish analysis of the British constitution than that presented by McKenna, William Smith or Brooke Clarke. He took as his starting point Millar's ambiguous assessment of the relationship between commerce and modern liberty in the *Origin of the Distinction of Ranks* (1771). 'So widely different are the effects of opulence and refinement', Millar had written,

[78] Cobbett, *Parliamentary History*, XXXIV:213–16.
[79] Michael Durey, 'The Dublin Society of United Irishmen and the Politics of the Carey-Drennan Dispute, 1792–1794', *The Historical Journal*, 37 (1994), 89–111.
[80] William Drennan, *A Letter to William Pitt* (Dublin: James Moore, 1799), 4.

which, at the same time that they furnish the king with a standing army, the great engine of tyranny and oppression, have also a tendency to inspire the people with notions of liberty and independence. It may thence be expected that a conflict will arise between these two opposite parties, in which a variety of accidents may contribute to cast the balance upon either side.[81]

Millar's account of the effects of 'opulence' on politics had been geared to the explanation of the English Civil War and the rise of French absolutism; in his later writings, however, he warned against the recrudescence of the conflictual dynamic of democracy and tyranny within British politics. He was heavily critical of the hysterical response of British elites to the French Revolution, asserting that absurd caricatures of the 'levelling' principles of 1789 had been converted into a powerful ideological weapon to oppose moderate parliamentary reform and promote arbitrary power at home.[82]

Drennan's portrayal of union aligned closely with Millar's analysis of the risks war posed to Britain's fragile constitutional balance. In his public letter to Pitt, they were a further instance of the British state's decline into a form of military despotism:

> France wishes to assimilate abroad. Britain hastens to consolidate at home. The strength which the one acquires by expansion, by compressing all its parts closer to a common centre, by making its own centre the centre of the whole system. This is the purpose of the Union – *not* to give speed to the plough, or add wings to the shuttle – but to concentrate the military force of the empire, and to organise the country so as best to favour the action of the military machine.[83]

The majority of Drennan's pamphlet took the form of an imagined dialogue between an Anglo-Irish 'aristocrat' (Drennan named Foster alongside the Anglo-Irish notables Barry Yelverton and John Beresford as likely candidates) and a 'democrat', who assumes the voice of Drennan himself. Drennan's 'aristocrat' ascribes to Union the 'daring deed of a revolutionary spirit, instigated by the demon of democracy'. But the 'democrat' styles Pitt 'the indirect minister of Providence', who via the Union would 'take the middle term out of the Irish constitution, and will leave nothing but king and people, the monarch seen only through the medium of a military rule'. While Pitt combined 'the fierce policy of

[81] John Millar, *The Origin of the Distinction of Ranks* (Indianapolis, IN: Liberty Fund, 1771), 240.
[82] John Millar, *Letters of Crito, on the Causes, Objects and Consequences of the Present War*, 2nd ed. (Edinburgh: Scots Chronicle, 1796), 98–109.
[83] Drennan, *Letter to Pitt*, 9.

Richelieu' with 'the serpentine guile of Mazarin' so as to 'break down those provincial kingships' and 'wheel away the obstructing rubbish of borough feudality', the unintended consequence of Pitt's desperate militarism would be the rise of liberty and equality. 'The annihilation of the aristocracy (far indeed beyond your consideration, as it was far from that of Richelieu) may turn out a providential *preparation* of the soil for the growth of a national character joining ornament with utility, and literature with liberty, without any artificial manure or any parliamentary compost.'[84]

For Drennan, the contradictions of Union held out the prospect of a rival route to the civilisation and pacification of the Irish population, in which the prudent virtues of a commercial republic would be inculcated in the school of organised resistance to Britain's military despotism. 'Under a Union', he declared, 'the nature of government will become *too plain*, which, in the guise of an independent legislature and an appendant Crown, used to play so prettily with the fancy, and preserved an influence over men's minds, nearly in proportion to its unintelligibility'. 'Democracy will then operate upon the disencumbered mind on the simple policy of sound understanding, and they whose object it has been through life to incite their despised country to a sense of its own dignity, will act with a stronger purchase.'[85]

Friedrich Gentz on Union and the Balance of Power

A more sympathetic commentary on the place of the Union in European history was offered by the Prussian publicist and diplomat Friedrich Gentz, a former student of Immanuel Kant and a leading contemporary expert on British politics and philosophy.[86] Gentz was famed as the German translator of Edmund Burke's *Reflections on the Revolution in France,* and had also encouraged his friend Christian Garve to produce the authoritative German edition of Smith's *Wealth of Nations.*[87] For Gentz, the consolidation of the Irish and British

---

[84] Ibid., 14.   [85] Ibid., 19–20.

[86] For a fuller account of Gentz's Irish essays and their contexts, see James Stafford, 'The Alternative to Perpetual Peace: Britain, Ireland and the Case for Union in Friedrich Gentz's *Historisches Journal,* 1799–1800', *Modern Intellectual History,* 13 (2016), 63–91.

[87] Jonathan Green, 'Friedrich Gentz's Translation of Burke's *Reflections*', *Historical Journal,* 57 (2014), 639–59; Friedrich Karl Wittichen (ed.), *Briefe von und an Friedrich von Gentz,* 3 vols. (Munchen, 1909), vol. 1, Gentz to Garve, 5 December 1790, 181–2.

parliaments represented something more than the elimination of constitutional complexity in the name of military efficiency. Union instead offered a model for the regeneration of Europe's established monarchies in the face of a revolutionary challenge that threatened the fragile civilisational progress made under the modern monarchies of the eighteenth century.[88] In an essay on the theme of 'political equality' in his *Historisches Journal* (1799–1800), Gentz had argued that the diffusion of commercial wealth that characterised contemporary European society made its population harder, not easier, to govern. 'The progress of culture, wealth, and education' had not created a commercial form of sociability that strengthened the ties of society and reduced the need for strong forms of sovereignty; it had merely diffused to the majority the pride and vanity that had once been the sole property of Roman and feudal aristocracies, creating 'an interminable, a more than civil war . . . in the hearts of states'.[89] The only basis for the stable development of commercial society was unified and absolute state sovereignty. His enthusiasm for Adam Smith was underpinned by a shrewd appraisal of the latter's political economy as 'a new theory . . . lying in the middle between the physiocratic and the mercantile systems'.[90] For Gentz, the British–Irish Union was a clear signal that Britain had embraced the principles of Smith's enlightened reason of state in its future conduct of foreign and domestic policy.

In a series of essays written in 1799–1800, Gentz provided extensive reports to readers of his Berlin periodical detailing this interpretation of the Union. His texts included annotated bibliographies of every publication in the Union debate, produced in Dublin or London, that he regarded as being worthy of notice.[91] The target of these essays on Ireland was the pro-French account of perpetual peace articulated by Kant, Théremin and Alexandre d'Hauterive, after the Treaty of Basel (1795) had confirmed Prussia's neutrality in the war with France.[92] Gentz was passionately opposed to this policy and used both private and public means to lobby

---

[88] Friedrich Gentz, 'Ueber den ewigen Frieden', *Historisches Journal*, 4 (1800), 711–90, at 788–90.
[89] Friedrich Gentz, 'Ueber die politische Gleichheit', *Historisches Journal*, 1 (1800), 1–51, at 38.
[90] Friedrich Gentz, 'Ueber den jetzigen Zustand der Finanz-Administration und des Nazional-Reichthums von Großbrittannien (Beschluss)', *Historisches Journal*, 3 (1799), 143–244, at 183–4.
[91] Friedrich Gentz, 'Ueber die Final-Vereinigung zwischen Großbrittannien und Irrland', *Historisches Journal*, 4 (1800), 500–614, at 603–13.
[92] For discussion of the Prussian political context, see Philip Dwyer, 'The Politics of Prussian Neutrality 1795–1805', *German History*, 12 (1994), 351–73.

for a swift re-entry into the war on the side of Britain.[93] He believed that Napoleon posed an existential threat to the European order. Instead of forming – in Kant's terms – a 'great republic' that sought perpetual peace, revolutionary France had succeeded in recreating republican Rome's fatal combination of civil dissension and foreign expansion.

Referring to Montesquieu's landmark work of philosophical history, the *Considérations sur les causes de la grandeur des Romains et de leur décadence* (1734), Gentz marvelled at how this 'great mind' had 'described the future, even as he depicted the past with masterfully true strokes'.[94] Gentz was correspondingly relaxed about the accusations levelled by Thérémin and others that the British constitution had degenerated over time from a true 'balance of powers' (*Gleichgewicht*) into a ministerial despotism.[95] Inverting half a century of British and European praise for Britain's mixed and balanced constitution, he argued that its real genius lay in its total fusion of executive with legislative power. Because government was impossible without a majority in the House of Commons, the authority of the Crown-in-Parliament was, in the end, just as absolute as that of the ruler in a 'pure' monarchy: 'so hangs the whole security and wellbeing of the state', Gentz observed, 'from the justice and wisdom of the King and his ministers'.[96]

The Union of Great Britain and Ireland was a sign of the continued vitality of this British alternative to France's corrupted republican empire. It marked the conclusion of a slow process of recovery from the botched conquest of the Middle Ages and the sectarian violence of the seventeenth century. As proof of the reformed direction of Britain's Irish policy, Gentz listed the lifting of restrictions on trade and Catholic property rights in 1778, the concession of legislative autonomy in 1782, the Commercial Propositions of 1785, the admission of Catholics to the county franchise in 1793 and the inclusion of Ireland within the Navigation Acts in the same year.[97] Older excesses, meanwhile, were ascribed not simply to 'England',

---

[93] Paul Wittichen, 'Das preussische Kabinett und Friedrich von Gentz. Eine Denkschrift aus dem Jahre 1800', *Historische Zeitschrift*, 89 (1902), 239–73.

[94] Friedrich Gentz, *Ueber den Ursprung und Charakter des Krieges gegen die Französische Revoluzion* (Berlin: Heinrich Frölich, 1801), 186–7.

[95] Friedrich Gentz, 'Darstellung und Vergleichung einiger politischen Constitutions-Systeme die von dem Grundsatze der Theilung der Macht ausgehen', *Neue Deutsche Monatsschrift*, 3 (1795), 81–157, at 151–7.

[96] Friedrich Gentz, 'Ueber die Natur and und den Werth der gemischten Staatsverfassungen', *Historisches Journal*, 1 (1799), 487–98, at 497–8.

[97] Friedrich Gentz, 'Ueber die Final-Vereinigung zwischen Großbrittannien und Irrland (Beschluss)', *Historisches Journal*, 4 (1800), 615–710, at 688–9.

but to past iterations of the religious and political enthusiasm that animated both the French Revolution and the United Irish rising.[98] Readers were reminded that Cromwell and Ireton, the cruellest persecutors of the Irish, were 'decided republicans'.[99]

The integration of Ireland into Britain's flourishing commercial economy and global commercial empire signalled its newly elevated status as the prime beneficiary, rather than the first victim, of British colonisation. 'The Union', Gentz wrote, 'is a great social contract, through which Ireland is at once incorporated in to the full community of the whole British national property and commerce, through which it conquers the British colonies, and transforms the East and West Indies in to its provinces'.[100] Only the durable consolidation of executive and legislative power in a single parliament would permit the new Union-state to function as a dependable vessel for the liberal doctrines of political economy that Gentz placed at the heart of what he termed 'true politics'. 'In the old system', Gentz observed of the constitution of 1782, 'the trade relationships between both countries were, even after accomplished agreements, still dependant on the changing maxims and whims of the separated legislatures'.[101]

One of the few progressive trends in contemporary European history arising from the French Revolution, Gentz asserted, was the consolidation of the sovereign state as an institutional form capable of incubating complex commercial societies. His description of the modern territorial state emphasised the interplay between a powerful and unified sovereignty and the diverse operations of an advanced market economy:

> The more important the matters of legislation, the greater and more diverse the concerns of government become, the more necessary it becomes, that in a great circuit of the earth, the endless divergence of private goals and the private activities of men, and the free play of their powers, are held together in the unity of a highest goal and a highest power.[102]

This was an argument with significant local resonances, given the nature of Prussia's own civilising mission in the Polish territories acquired in the partitions of 1772, 1793 and 1795. Prussian commentators frequently justified the conquest of Poland by arguing that the Prussian state was

---

[98] Gentz, 'Final-Vereinigung', 544.
[99] Friedrich Gentz, 'Plan zu einer engern Vereinigung zwischen Großbrittannien und Irrland', *Historisches Journal*, 1 (1799), 439–86, at 447–8.
[100] Gentz, 'Final-Vereinigung', 537–8.   [101] Gentz, 'Final-Vereinigung (Beschluss)', 638.
[102] Gentz, 'Ueber den ewigen Frieden', 731.

capable of guaranteeing the civil liberty of ordinary Poles, who had always been oppressed by the privileges of their noble masters.[103] Gentz had first-hand experience in the administration of the Polish territories gained by Prussia in the partition of 1793. The history of British government in Ireland, offered as background to his analysis of the Union, aligned neatly with a contemporary Prussian discourse of self-congratulation over the transmission of orderly monarchical government to the former Commonwealth.[104] 'The tendency to build great states', Gentz wrote, 'does not only arise from rulers' ambition and obsession with power. It is an unavoidable consequence, a natural and beneficial tendency arising from the higher culture of nations'.[105]

Union was the enlightened counterpart to the British state's necessarily brutal defence of legal order in Ireland in the face of the revolutionary threat posed by the United Irishmen. By consolidating the territorial sovereignty of a single Crown-in-Parliament, it guaranteed a kind of civil liberty, defined by security of property and the free operation of a market economy, for Ireland's entire population. Union re-established a workable form of sovereignty in the British Isles by advancing the fusion of executive and legislative power that Gentz regarded as the defining characteristic of Britain's modern constitution. It stripped Ireland of its threatening capacity to reach sovereign decisions that conflicted with those of Westminster, reducing Irish MPs to 'an ever-present highest counsel within the common government'.[106] Ireland's insurance against discrimination by a non-Irish majority lay in the dualistic character of British parliamentary representation. British MPs were ministers of a unitary sovereign, as well as representatives of a plural people. Gentz wrote that 'it is a principle of the British constitution, as it must be of any well-understood representative constitution, that every single representative represents the whole, not just the separate district that selected him'.[107]

Gentz's invocation of the dualistic character of British parliamentary representation did not, however, suggest that he embraced any part of the case for popular sovereignty. The structure of British representation was a matter of prudence, not of right, since civil, not political, liberty was the

---

[103] Otto Tschirch, *Geschichte der öffentlichen Meinung in Preussen: vom Baseler Frieden bis zum Zusammenbruch des Staates*, 2 vols. (Weimar: Böhlhaus, 1933), vol. 1, 155–81.

[104] Harro Zimmermann, *Friedrich Gentz: die Erfindung der Realpolitik* (Paderborn: Schöningh, 2012), 70, 157.

[105] Gentz, 'Ueber den ewigen Frieden', 732.

[106] Gentz, 'Ueber die Final-Vereinigung zwischen Großbrittannien und Irrland', 525.

[107] Ibid., 526.

purpose of the state as a legal institution. 'All the ostentatious declamations about the joys of freedom', Gentz had written in 1799, 'were only panegyrics to the means to an end, and transform themselves into vain phrases, if this freedom is unable fully to realise its true ultimate end, the unlimited domination of the laws'.[108] Gentz was correspondingly sceptical about the need to address the most glaring deficiency in Irish representation – the exclusion of Catholic electors from the borough franchise, and from membership of parliament itself. Prudence counselled against rapid reform: the alteration of the confessional character of the British state during an age of revolution was certain to be a risky endeavour. Since the reforms of 1778 and 1793, Irish Catholics were able to hold property and pursue professions on terms equal to Anglicans and Presbyterians. Gentz was content to speak of their residual political disadvantages in terms 'the relatively small evil of a political, rather than a civil, intolerance'.[109]

Gentz's ambivalence on the question of Catholic Emancipation was suggestive of his ultimate preference for lawmaking by individual monarchs over elected assemblies. 'A single man can often be a truer and more just representative of the general will ... than five hundred lawmakers', Gentz wrote in 1799.[110] The strict distinction Gentz drew between 'civil' and 'political' liberty ensured that he disagreed with Burke regarding the necessity for equal Catholic access to the parliament of the United Kingdom. The composition of the legislature was irrelevant; what mattered was that, duly educated by Enlightened public opinion, it adopted what Gentz termed 'true policy': the maintenance of a European balance of power and the adoption of Smith's approach to international trade.[111] The future of Europe lay in the development of civil, not political, liberty. 'The true independence of citizens and the nation', he wrote of Ireland, 'will be increased, not reduced, through the combination of parliaments; this true independence hangs from the progress of culture, and the freedom of trade'.[112]

Because more expansive and effective forms of state sovereignty were essential to the further development of the human species, Gentz regarded the Irish Acts of Union as a rare progressive development in the devastated landscape of post-revolutionary Europe. 'The Union', he declared, 'must in a moment, where everything in the political world points to division

[108] Friedrich Gentz, 'Beiträge zur Berichtigung einiger Ideen der allgememeinen Staatswissenschaft', *Historisches Journal*, 4 (1799), 277–312, at 308.
[109] Gentz, 'Final-Vereinigung', 596–7.   [110] Gentz, 'gemischten Staatsverfassungen', 490.
[111] Gentz, 'Ueber den ewigen Frieden', 762–3.
[112] Gentz, 'Plan zu einer engern Vereinigung', 482.

and dissolution, be the most effective and decisive of all measures salutary to the public that the British government could conceive of.[113]

The 'System of Burkism'?

Taking Drennan's, Sheridan's and Gentz's writings on the Union together with the other texts discussed thus far, it is possible to draw some conclusions regarding its ideological character and implications. Union represented the triumph of a counter-revolutionary iteration of Enlightenment: the translation of the sceptical 'science of man' developed by the Scottish philosophers into an imperial art of government in the hands of politicians and theorists attempting the reform of empire under revolutionary pressure. Union sought to uphold the rights of property and aristocracy – in Ireland, Britain and across Europe – by bringing about the reformation of an Irish landed class that Enlightenment thinkers such as Smith, Hume and Burke had long regarded as dangerously aberrant and illegitimate. It trusted to the capacity of British commerce and civilisation to diffuse its benefits across the Irish Sea, anathematising the license and religious enthusiasm that contemporaries associated with Irish politics. It prized a firm commitment to strong and centralised forms of state sovereignty as the necessary guarantor of property and civil liberty – even at the expense of the constitutional forms of ancient representative institutions like the Irish parliament.

In this context, it is notable that there was a strong connection between the personnel involved in the Irish Union and those who remade the European order as a significantly more consolidated and centralised system of states in the wake of Napoleon's defeat in 1814–15.[114] Castlereagh was followed to the Congress of Vienna by his former secretary at Dublin Castle during the passage of the Union, Edward Cooke.[115] Gentz was a key advisor to the Austrian diplomat Klemens von Metternich and the secretary to the Congress. From this perspective, we could see the Irish Union as the first of a series of efforts to make larger and more effective states – the Kingdom of Norway and Sweden, the United Kingdom of the Netherlands, the Kingdom of Savoy, the Confederation of the Rhine – in response to the revolutionary crisis.

Within Britain and Ireland, however, the long-run impact of this Enlightened vision of union was more limited. Vital currents of intellectual and political life in both countries stood in opposition to the kind of

---

[113] Gentz, 'Ueber die Final-Vereinigung zwischen Großbrittannien und Irrland (Beschluss)', 701.
[114] Schroeder, *Transformation of European Politics*, 517–83. [115] Bew, *Castlereagh*, 372–3.

political and economic thinking that informed ministerial efforts to pacify Ireland in the years following the invasions and risings of 1796-8, and it was these that shaped subsequent Irish politics. No amount of persuasion on the part of Dundas could persuade a hostile King George III to accept that his arguments for Emancipation were anything other than 'damned Scotch metaphysics'![116] The Irish judge Patrick Duigenan, soon to be named the Grand Master of the Orange Lodges, wrote an endorsement of Union that nonetheless contained a scathing attack on the 'system of Burkism' that 'has made no inconsiderable progress among the Ministers of the British Empire'.[117] An older vision of Protestant union, with roots in Anglo-Irish desires for protection in the years following the Williamite war, was presented in Duigenan's writings and the speeches of John Fitzgibbon, Earl of Clare, a staunch opponent of Catholic Emancipation and a leading figure in Anglo-Irish politics. As McKenna had feared, a coercive and intolerant approach to the problem of Irish government gained a new lease of life in the aftermath of the 1798 rebellion. 'My unaltered opinion', Clare declared to the Irish parliament during the final debates on the Union, 'is that so long as Human Nature and the Popish Religion continue to be what I know they are, a conscientious Popish ecclesiastic never will become a well attached subject to a Protestant state'.[118] Nor was resistance to the Pittite reform agenda described here confined to the Anglo-Irish elite. The terms on which Catholic Emancipation had been informally promised by Pitt and Castlereagh had specified the need for royal oversight for future appointments in the Catholic hierarchy. This compromise with the Anglican confessional state was angrily rejected by the Kingdom's Catholic community during the Veto controversy of 1809–12. By the time that Catholic Emancipation became a *cause celebre* for the Holland House Whigs of the early nine-teenth century, Pitt's original proposals had lost the support of their intended beneficiaries.[119]

---

[116] Robert James Mackintosh, *Memoirs of the Life of Sir James Mackintosh*, 2nd ed., 2 vols. (London: Edward Moxon, 1836), vol. 1, 170.

[117] Patrick Duigenan, *A Fair Representation of the Present Political State of Ireland* (Dublin: J. Milliken, 1800), 136.

[118] John Fitzgibbon, 1st Earl Clare, *The Speech of the Right Honourable John, Earl of Clare, Lord High Chancellor of Ireland, in the House of Lords of Ireland, on a Motion Made by Him, on Monday, February 10th, 1800* (Dublin: J. Milliken, 1800), 69.

[119] Cadoc Leighton, 'Gallicanism and the Veto Controversy: Church, State and Catholic Community in Early Nineteenth-Century Ireland', in R. V. Comerford, M. Cullen, J. Hill & C. Lennon (eds.), *Religion Conflict and Coexistence in Ireland: Essays Presented to Monsignor Patrick J Corish* (Dublin: Gill and Macmillan, 1990), 135–58.

The ultimate rejection of the Enlightened vision of Union described here serves only to further draw attention to its distinctiveness. The debate over the measure mobilised considerable intellectual resources, derived from the Scottish Enlightenment, from Anglican theological utilitarianism and from the thought of Edmund Burke, to vindicate the ability of the British Empire to reform Irish society. The measure was recognised by contemporaries within and beyond the British Isles as representing a variety of reform to rival that undertaken by revolutionary France. Both of these European empires now appealed to a universalist conception of European 'civilisation' in advancing their claims to global dominance. With France's adoption of a Concordat with the Papacy in 1801 and the crowning of Napoleon as 'Emperor of the French' in 1804, some of the ideological heat was taken out of a conflict that could no longer be styled as a crusade against atheism, democracy or 'Jacobinism'. As Britain and France hunkered down for another decade of war, the evaluation of Union came to hinge more than ever before on the promise of an Irish agrarian transformation, brought about through closer integration with Britain's embattled, but resilient, mercantile empire.

CHAPTER 5

The Granary of Great Britain
War, Population and Agriculture 1798–1815

The early years of the British–Irish Union unfolded in an extraordinary political conjuncture. The measure's advocates had made their case based on optimistic readings of Hume, Smith, Montesquieu, Vattel and Burke. In their different ways, these figures had all argued that empires of conquest would struggle to endure in the conditions of modern Europe. They had insisted on the need for sophisticated commercial and financial systems to sustain the professional armed forces of the major powers and had identified significant (though not immutable) tendencies towards political and economic equilibrium. The consolidation of the Napoleonic Empire following the Treaty of Amiens (1802) suggested that these understandings of contemporary politics were mistaken. Against all but the darkest predictions of the Enlightenment, a neo-Roman 'universal monarchy', based on raw military power, had become a seemingly immovable fixture of European politics. The pressures of war meanwhile exerted a powerful influence on Britain's state and society. Supplying the army and the navy was a constant strain on the Exchequer, and produced a significant expansion in taxation and public debt.[1] The suspension of cash payments at the Banks of England and Ireland, combined with extraordinary demand for food and military supplies, led to rapid inflation. After 1801, Ireland was integrated into a strained war economy, rather than the idealised commercial society projected by many of the Union's advocates.

It was against this harsh wartime backdrop that post-Smithian political economy assumed its distinctive character, and its profile in imperial politics. In Britain, the emerging orthodoxy was institutionalised in the foundation of the *Edinburgh Review* and the East India college at Haileybury, and gained notable supporters among a younger generation

---

[1] Patrick K. O'Brien, 'Public Finance in the Wars with France, 1793–1815', in H. T. Dickinson (ed.), *Britain and the French Revolution* (London: Macmillan, 1989), 165–87.

of politicians.[2] The demands of war, the transformation of rural society, the fear of revolution and the broader cultural appeal of a science of popular 'happiness' placed the welfare of the 'labouring poor' at the centre of British political economy.[3] The most dramatic intervention of the period, Robert Malthus' *Essay on the Principle of Population* (1798), had barely registered in the debate on the Union, but embodied these broader tendencies.[4] In the longer and more sophisticated form presented after the second edition of 1803, it steadily extended its influence over discussions of Ireland.

Malthus plays a central role in this chapter, but prior to 1815 his concerns about the rapid growth of Ireland's population – expressed in two lengthy essays written for the *Edinburgh Review* – remained a minority view. His interventions need to be placed in the context of a broader range of contemporary understandings of the lineaments of Irish rural society and of its place in the imperial war economy. The key conceptualisation of Ireland during this period was as the granary and the manpower store of an embattled and isolated empire. Articulated by both friends and critics of the Union and of Catholic Emancipation, this populous, agrarian image of Ireland proved to be both powerful and enduring. It was not a creation of the Victorian era or its 'colonial' political economy; nor was it initially articulated as a criticism of Irish society.[5] Instead, Ireland's rising population and agricultural production were seen as evidence of the Union's success, amid a broader agrarian turn in the empire as a whole.

War, population and agriculture were intimately connected in the political-economic discussions of the Napoleonic era. The disruption of foreign grain supplies drove British improvers, such as Arthur Young and Sir John Sinclair, to explore new techniques for achieving agricultural self-sufficiency. Sinclair and Young were instrumental in the foundation of the quasi-official Board of Agriculture, which sought to formalise and central-ise the gathering of information concerning farming and to supply

[2] Biancamaria Fontana, *Rethinking the Politics of Commercial Society: The Edinburgh Review 1802–1832* (Cambridge: Cambridge University Press, 1985); Keith Tribe, 'Professors Malthus and Jones: Political Economy at the East India College 1806–1858', *European Journal of the History of Economic Thought* 2 (2007), 327–54.

[3] Gareth Stedman Jones, *An End to Poverty? A Historical Debate* (London: Profile, 2004); Joanna Innes, *Inferior Politics: Social Problems and Social Policies in Eighteenth-Century Britain* (Oxford: Oxford University Press, 2009), 110–13.

[4] Niall O'Flaherty, 'Malthus and the End of Poverty', in R. J. Mayhew (ed.), *New Perspectives on Malthus* (Cambridge: Cambridge University Press, 2017), 74–105.

[5] Thomas Boylan & Timothy Foley, *Political Economy and Colonial Ireland: the Propagation and Ideological Function of Economic Discourse in the Nineteenth Century* (London: Routledge, 1992), 2–16.

specialist policy advice to the administration.[6] As the war progressed, the Board's enthusiasms expanded to include a national Enclosure Act, the promotion of landlord housing for farm labourers and the exploration of alternative food sources for times of shortage, including rice and potato flour.[7] In 1795, Sinclair was tasked with a parliamentary inquiry into the identification of 'waste lands' capable of making up wartime shortfalls in imports.[8] The maximisation of imperial resources was presented as the primary task for Britain's farmers and landowners.

In this context, the Union inevitably increased interest in the possibil-ities for increasing the efficiency of Irish agriculture. In parliamentary and pamphlet debates over the measure, Thomas Brooke Clarke and Bishop Watson of Llandaff had already projected that it would assist the empire in its search for self-sufficiency. Ireland, argued the Irish Chancellor of the Exchequer, Isaac Corry, at the height of the British food crisis of 1800–1, 'was capable of becoming the granary of Great Britain, and of affording it that supply for which it now depends upon the caprice of foreign powers'.[9] These aspirations were supported by growing evidence that Irish agricul-ture was already playing a major role in supplying rising British demand.[10] Since the 1770s, the expanding grain trade had driven a turn from pasture to tillage agriculture that astounded contemporaries and transformed the rural landscape.[11] Contemporaries credited the change to a system of corn bounties established by the then-Chancellor of the Irish Exchequer, John Foster, in 1784.[12] With Baltic supplies cut off and American imports in doubt, Irish food production assumed critical strategic importance. After the Union, there were repeated calls, from Ireland and Britain, for the government to secure further support for Irish agriculture through public investment in canal, road and port construction. Imperial ambitions intersected with the shifting agendas of a broader domestic community gentry and clergy 'improvers', who reacted to the disorders of 1790s by redoubling their efforts to understand and reform Ireland's rural interior.

[6] Rosalind Mitchison, 'The Old Board of Agriculture (1793–1822)', *Economic History Review*, 74 (1959), 41–59.
[7] Arthur Young, *On the Advantages Which Have Resulted from the Establishment of the Board of Agriculture* (London: Richard Philips, 1809).
[8] Jonsson, *Enlightenment's Frontier*, 224–8.   [9] Cobbett, *Parliamentary History*, XXXV:1274.
[10] Thomas Brinley, 'Feeding England during the Industrial Revolution: A View from the Celtic Fringe', *Agricultural History*, 56 (1982), 328–42.
[11] David Dickson, *Old World Colony: Cork and South Munster, 1630–1830* (Cork: Cork University Press, 2005), 283–98, 377–86.
[12] James Kelly, 'Scarcity and Poor Relief in Eighteenth-Century Ireland: The Subsistence Crisis of 1782–4', *Irish Historical Studies*, 28 (1992), 38–62, at 54–5.

A succession of overburdened and divided British administrations looked askance at these bold schemes for Irish improvement. Yet the intersecting contexts of war and Union, imperial power and domestic 'happiness', nonetheless motivated a flourishing of private efforts to understand the nature and dynamics of Ireland's demographics and rural economy. This chapter explores how these were related to questions of subsistence, military recruitment and war finance, which were debated in London, Edinburgh and across Europe. Controversies over Ireland's currency and fiscal system, alongside largely forgotten works of social inquiry from figures such as Thomas Newenham, Francis d'Ivernois and Edward Wakefield, made visible the transformation of Irish society under the conditions of Union and war. They formed part of a continuing European debate concerning the durability of a British Empire confronted by the existential threat of Napoleon. For Ireland, they raised questions about the political economy of Union, as Britain's nineteenth-century industrial hegemony began to take shape. The problems posed by the coexistence of radically divergent societies under a common parliament were thematised not only by Malthus and his associates, but by an emergent tradition of Catholic nationalism that claimed the legacy of the 1798 rising. The final decade of the Napoleonic Wars, passed over by historians of both eighteenth- and nineteenth-century Ireland, was productive of ideas and narratives that would shape the rest of the pre-Famine period.

Currency and Capital

The starting point for evaluations of the impact of Union and war on Ireland's economy and society was the 1804 parliamentary investigation into the declining value of the 'Irish Pound', the distinct currency of the former Irish Kingdom. Existing scholarship highlights the significance of the Irish currency committee's conclusions in the history of British 'monetary orthodoxy' and the origins of the nineteenth-century gold standard. Yet the controversy concerned more than monetary theory. The parliamentary investigation into the money-issuing activities of the Bank of Ireland triggered a wider debate concerning the territorial distribution of capital and economic activity in the new United Kingdom. It problematised the partial nature of the integration achieved under the Union of 1801 and marked the emergence of a critical metropolitan perspective on Ireland's local administrative and financial institutions: Dublin Castle, the Irish Exchequer and a complex system of national and regional banks.

It established a pattern of reforming investigation and activity, driven by the political interests of the younger Whig circle surrounding the *Edinburgh Review*, that would come to define British government in Ireland over the early decades of the nineteenth century.

The economic and administrative background to the debate was complex. While Union aimed to promote the eventual integration of markets in goods, fiscal and monetary institutions had been left unaltered. Down to 1817, there was a separate Irish Exchequer, which retained considerable autonomy to determine the level, structure and timing of taxation and borrowing. Chancellors of the Irish Exchequer accordingly presented their own annual budgets to the imperial parliament.[13] Ireland's separate currency, meanwhile, was preserved until 1826. This was a key difference between the Irish Union of 1801 and its Scottish counterpart, which had immediately assimilated the Scottish currency to the English. Before 1797, Ireland's monetary system had been tied to the London exchanges by the common medium of transactions paid for with gold and silver. Ireland lacked a domestic mint, so its coinage consisted of a mixture of English golden guineas and foreign silver.[14]

This form of mixed currency was common in medieval and early modern Europe, where cash of various origins and denominations was weighed against a common, abstract standard used in paper or book-keeping transactions.[15] In Ireland, this abstract standard was calculated as a proportion of the value of the British Pound. The par value of the Irish Pound had been fixed early in the eighteenth century, at twelve thir-teenths of the British.[16] Subsequently, a significant Irish banking sector had developed around this set of monetary arrangements, conducting discounting and exchange business for the benefit of Irish exporters and absentees. Exchange with continental markets was mediated through London, which also provided a ready source of credit for Irish exporters.[17]

---

[13] Trevor McCavery, 'Finance, Politics and Ireland, 1801–1817', PhD thesis, Faculty of History, The Queen's University of Belfast, Belfast (1980), 218–20.

[14] Frank Fetter, *The Irish Pound 1797–1826* (London: Allen and Unwin, 1955), 9–10; Louis M. Cullen, *Anglo-Irish Trade 1660–1800* (Manchester: Manchester University Press, 1968), 155–8.

[15] Luigi Einaudi, 'The Theory of Imaginary Money from Charlemagne to the French Revolution', in R. F. Luca Inaudi & Roberto Marchionatti (eds.), *Selected Economic Essays* (Basingstoke: Palgrave Macmillan, 2006), 153–82.

[16] Frederick G. Hall, *The Bank of Ireland, 1783–1946* (Dublin: Hodges Figgis, 1949), 72.

[17] Cullen, *Anglo-Irish Trade*, 164.

After 1797, restrictions on the use of specie in commercial transactions detached both currencies from their metal bases, creating a freely floating exchange rate between the Irish and British Pounds. The Irish Pound dramatically weakened upon the resumption of war with France in 1803, prompting the formation of an Irish currency committee that included leading figures such as Foster, Castlereagh and the monetary expert Henry Thornton.[18] The committee were aware of the political and commercial significance of the problem, identifying the currency issue as a developing threat to the Union:

> That a great country, now placed as Ireland is under the same Legislature with England, forming a constituent part of the United Empire equally as England, or any county in England does, its metropolis not so distant from London as any part of Scotland, Newcastle, Carlisle or Durham, should labour in its pecuniary intercourse with England under a constant varying Exchange which the others are free from ... are positions so strange, that Your Committee cannot believe them to be founded in the common nature of things, and must impute to their own insufficient investigation, or want of sagacity, the not having pointed out an adequate remedy, if they have failed to do so.[19]

The majority view of the Irish currency committee was that the Directors of the Bank of Ireland were to blame. Irish depreciation was a classic instance of a speculative expansion of the paper money supply in the absence of a metal anchor.[20] This judgement reflected a preference for the monetary theory of Hume and Smith, who had each condemned speculative paper-money schemes as stemming from the self-interest of financiers.[21] The committee rejected submissions from witnesses sympathetic to Irish banking interests, who had insisted that the depreciation was a result of a deterioration in Ireland's balance of payments.[22] It demanded that the Bank's ability to create paper money should be restricted by an obligation to back their issues with a stock of Bank of England notes, which could be exchanged for them at par value.[23]

This effectively meant tying the Irish Bank to the probity of its English equivalent, which was largely assumed by the committee and its supporters. The young Whig MP Peter King authored a pamphlet as part of the opposition campaign against the prolongation of the suspension of cash payments in both countries, but singled out the Irish Directors for

---

[18] Fetter, *Irish Pound*, 26–31.   [19] Ibid., 82–3.   [20] Ibid., 70.
[21] Hume, 'Of Money', 28; Smith, *Wealth of Nations*, II.ii.59–63.   [22] Fetter, *Irish Pound*, 70.
[23] Ibid., 78–90.

their deliberate corruption. In Ireland, unlike England, the real purchasing power of bank notes was acknowledged to be far below their face value; in Ulster, Irish paper was rejected altogether. The fact of depreciation 'must have been felt and experienced in the daily and ordinary transactions of commerce'. King therefore concluded that 'it is impossible ... to acquit [the Directors] of the charge of gross misconduct'.[24] The Anglo-Irish Whig MP Henry Parnell had served on the committee, and he concurred with King's judgement in a pamphlet defending its conclusions. The Directors of the Bank of Ireland had clearly mistaken corporate for public interest. The remedy was greater oversight from the centre. 'Had the slightest attention been applied, by Parliament, to their conduct', Parnell concluded, 'they never could have attempted to overload the market, as they have done with their paper'.[25]

In response to the currency committee, however, defenders of the Irish banking interest opened a larger debate about the distribution of capital and labour within the integrated polity created by the Union. The committee's opponents argued that the public debt created by Ireland's contribution to imperial war expenditure was the real driver of its currency devaluation. It was the policy of successive Irish Chancellors to borrow on the London capital markets, rather than their Dublin equivalents, in the hope of securing lower interest rates.[26] Alongside rising aristocratic absenteeism driven by the Union, opponents of the Committee argued that it was this means of funding war expenditure that was causing a drain of capital and rents from the country. One anonymous pamphleteer complained that

> Incomes derived from home, and spent abroad, exhaust [the country] of those *stamina*, without which hardly any improvements, arts, or manufactures, can succeed, and no country can flourish ... England borrows her money in England, and the country is not impoverished by the debt: but our money being borrowed in London, the interest must be regularly remitted.[27]

On the question of Ireland's public debt, members of the committee increasingly found themselves in agreement with their critics, albeit for differing reasons. In an argument that would be repeated by pro-British economists across the nineteenth century, Parnell denied that it was

[24] Peter King, 7th Baron King, *Thoughts on the Effects of the Bank Restrictions* (London: Cadell and Davies, 1804), 69–70.
[25] Henry Parnell, *The Principles of Currency and Exchange*, 4th ed. (London: J. Budd, 1805), 48–9.
[26] McCavery, 'Finance and Politics', 206–8.
[27] Anon., *A Letter from an Irish Member of Parliament, upon the Report of the Select Committee of the House of Commons* (London: John Stockdale, 1805), 32.

possible for Irish absentees to drain the country of capital by spending their rents in London. The broader social consequences of absenteeism were deplorable, but its immediate economic impact was minimal, because the consumption of Irish aristocrats resident in London generated an additional demand for Irish goods.[28] Only 'the confused notion of national wealth being proportion to the stock of money' could produce criticism of the Union on these grounds.

The Irish Exchequer's policy of borrowing on the London markets, however, was a different matter. The problem created by Irish public debt lay not in its interest, but in its principal. This interfered with the process whereby absentee remittances were supported through demand for Irish goods. The stock of Irish bonds in London was

> nothing else than a fund ... by which the remittances to absentees are paid ... for, instead of the necessity existing to export Irish produce for payment of these remittances, the drafts of the Irish treasury upon the Loan supply a readier, and more obvious means, of remittance.[29]

Irish public bonds created an alternative means for the financing of absentee remittances, denying Irish exporters the benefit of the demand of their own aristocracy. The country's rising indebtedness was a market distortion that was undermining the economic logic of the Union. Its borrowing was obstructing the economic mechanisms through which the circulation of people, goods and expenditure between Britain and Ireland could be expected to enrich the poorer country.

The persistence of the currency and debt problems thereby pointed to the limits of the Union as a guarantor of the successful integration of Britain's and Ireland's parallel fiscal states. In a time of war, contemporary observers believed that the huge divergence in the capacity of Irish and British institutions to raise and manage revenue threatened the integrity of the Union. While for Parnell, it was Ireland that lost out due to the deficiencies of its own institutions, other opponents of the ministry perceived a threat to Britain from the corruption and inefficiency of the Irish revenue. Foster himself feared the shameful eventuality that Britain would ultimately have to take on the public debt of Ireland – something that did indeed ultimately occur in 1817.[30]

In a pamphlet written in 1805, meanwhile, the Scottish Whig magnate and political economist James Maitland, 8th Earl of Lauderdale, attempted

---

[28] Parnell, *Currency and Exchange*, 82. [29] Ibid., 85.
[30] PRONI, Foster-Massereene Papers, D207/10/13, 'Financial Observations on the Union of Great Britain and Ireland', fol. 27–8.

to mobilise the Irish fiscal crisis in an attempt to reconstruct the 1780s' Foxite coalition between anti-Irish manufacturers in Scotland and the West Country. Future Irish trade competition, he warned, would not take place according on the equal terms of skill and price described by Smith and Hume. Instead, rising Irish public debt, created by Irish corruption and war expenditure, would push the depreciation of the Irish currency to a point where Irish goods would be dumped on English markets. Lauderdale noted in his work that massive British remittances to continental allies had depressed the value of sterling to a level that had itself enabled the dumping of British goods in Hamburg. Irish interest payments to British creditors would have the same impact as British war subsidies to allies, and the continuing depreciation of the Irish Pound would place British manufacturers in the same invidious position as German ones.[31]

Lauderdale's attempt to render old English fears of Irish competition in a new theoretical guise drew the immediate critical attention of his younger Whig rivals at the *Edinburgh Review*. One of the journal's founders, Francis Horner, argued that the Irish administration's policy of borrowing on the larger and better-developed London money market was entirely rational.[32] Moreover, Lauderdale was reviving the prejudices of the 'mercantile system', presenting manufacturing industry as a zero-sum game. This was particularly absurd in the context of a single, united empire. If an accident of currency valuation and capital distribution was genuinely hastening the migration of manufacturing employment to Ireland, then there was nothing to be feared.[33] Since the Union, it was a matter of perfect indifference where loans were contracted or manufactures established.

The exchange between Lauderdale and Horner demonstrated a rapid progression from a debate over the causes of Irish currency depreciation to a broader discussion of the political economy of Union. At issue was no longer the behaviour of the Directors of the Bank of Ireland, but Ireland's position within the imperial war economy that was taking shape under the pressure of the long struggle with France. The exchange also revealed the limitations of a largely abstract discussion over the nature and possibilities of Irish trade competition with Britain. As interest in the Irish interior grew following the Union, the terms of debate were transformed by a

---

[31] James Maitland, 8th Earl Lauderdale, *Hints to the Manufacturers of Great Britain, on the Consequences of the Irish Union, and the System since Pursued, of Borrowing in England, for the Service of Ireland* (Edinburgh: A. Constable, 1805), 20.

[32] [Francis Horner], Art. II 'Lord Lauderdale's *Hints to Manufacturers*', *The Edinburgh Review*, July 1805, 283–90, at 287.

[33] Ibid., 288.

proliferation of efforts to describe Ireland's human and physical geography. This growing body of Irish 'statistics' confirmed the status of tillage agriculture as the country's leading export sector and placed the rapid increase of Irish population at the centre of competing evaluations of the country's prosperity. It linked the condition of the Irish interior to the economic dynamics of the Union and, with it, to Britain's own prospects in the continuing struggle with Napoleonic France.

Grain and Emancipation

The Anglo-Irish landed interest responded to the twin humiliations of the 1798 rebellion and the Union with a fresh drive to organise and understand Ireland's territory and population. As early as 1800, the Dublin Society had published guidelines to encourage its supporters to undertake county surveys modelled on Sinclair's exhaustive *Statistical Account of Scotland* (1791–9). Twenty surveys – covering much of the agrarian south and east of the country – had been completed by 1812.[34] The Society's agenda was ambitious: surveyors were asked to obtain information on everything from the landscape, ancient buildings and mineral endowments to the size of farms, use of tools, composition of tithes, forms of tenure, knowledge of English and the 'habits of industry among the people'.[35] A Farming Society, linked to the Dublin Society and designed as an Irish analogue to the Board of Agriculture, was established by Foster in 1800 to focus the efforts of local groups and expand the distribution of premiums.[36] There was renewed pressure for the active legislative agenda of the Dublin parliament to be taken over by its successor at Westminster. The ministry prolonged the tenure of the pre-Union Board of Inland Navigation, amidst complaints that funding remained insufficient to promote the necessary expansion of Irish canal-building. In 1809, Foster tasked a public commission to identify peat bogs and marshlands suitable for draining and conversion into fields fit for hemp, flax and corn.[37]

---

[34] Edward Wakefield, *An Account of Ireland, Statistical and Political*, 2 vols. (London: Longman, 1812), I:xvi.

[35] The Society's questionnaire is listed at the outset of Sir Charles Coote, *Statistical Survey of the County of Monaghan, with Observations on the Means of Improvement* (Dublin: Graisberry & Campbell, 1801), 2–3.

[36] Allan Blackstock, *Science, Politics and Society in Early Nineteenth-Century Ireland: The Reverend William Richardson* (Manchester: Manchester University Press, 2013), 95–6.

[37] Arnold Horner, 'Napoleon's Irish Legacy: The Bogs Commissioners, 1809–14', *History Ireland* 13 (2005). www.historyireland.com/18th-19th-century-history/napoleons-irish-legacy-the-bogs-commissioners-1809-14/, accessed 16 March 2018.

The goal was to dramatically increase Ireland's potential for exporting food and naval supplies. 'Half the ground of those reclaimed Bogs', claimed Foster, 'converted to purposes of agriculture, would produce in a year more corn than had ever been imported into Great Britain in any one year'.[38]

Ireland's unrealised fertility, and its indispensability to the war effort, provided the *leitmotif* of the two major works published by the County Cork politician Thomas Newenham in 1805 and 1809, at the height of Napoleon's power in Europe. In common with the Dublin Society surveys and a range of improving writings since the 1780s, Newenham's works presented an argument for Ireland's growing proclivity for tillage agriculture, assuming that future projects for national improvement would need to operate within the confines of a heavily agrarian economy.[39] Yet they stood out within the landscape of Irish improving literature, both in the range of the findings they presented and in their desire to link empirical social inquiry explicitly to controversies over the Union and Catholic Emancipation. The unusual scope of Newenham's writings attracted the attention of both the *Edinburgh Review* and the Genevan publicist Francis d'Ivernois, placing them at the centre of a European debate over the condition of Ireland during the Napoleonic Wars.

Newenham had been a Patriot opponent of Union as a member of the final Dublin parliament. After the Union's passage, he had immediately taken up the cause of Catholic Emancipation, advancing Pitt, Dundas and Castlereagh's argument that the admission of Catholics to the united parliament was vital to Britain's national security.[40] His subsequent studies of Irish demography and agriculture should be read in line with this underlying conception of the imperial interest in Irish conciliation. Ireland's rising population was a crucial factor in lending strategic and economic weight to more abstract arguments for Catholic equality and toleration. When Charles Fox presented the first of many Catholic petitions to the Westminster parliament in 1805, he could do so with the confidence that he spoke for 'one-fourth of the whole of his majesty's

---

[38] *Hansard*, HC, vol. 34, col. 337–8, 2 May 1809.

[39] Gervaise Parker Bushe, 'An Essay towards Ascertaining the Population of Ireland. In a Letter to the Right Honourable the Earl of Charlemont, President of the Royal Irish Academy', *Transactions of the Royal Irish Academy* 3 (1789), 145–55, at 151–3; Samuel Crumpe, *An Essay on the Best Means of Providing Employment for the People* (London: J. Robinson, 1795), 238, 259–68; Robert Fraser, *Statistical Survey of the County of Wexford* (Dublin: Graisberry and Campbell, 1807), 38–64.

[40] Thomas Newenham, *An Obstacle to the Ambition of France: Or, Thoughts on the Expediency of Improving the Political Condition of His Majesty's Irish Roman Catholic Subjects* (London: C. & R. Baldwin, 1803).

subjects in Europe'.[41] In this context, Newenham's works were calibrated to focus British minds on the opportunities – and dangers – posed by rapid Irish population growth in a time of war and confessional tension.

Contemporary claims about Irish population rested on conflicted and uncertain estimates. Hearth money, a system of de facto household taxation established under the Ormrond viceroyalty in Ireland but discontinued in England after 1689, had enabled seventeenth- and eighteenth-century Irish improvers – including William Petty and Arthur Dobbs – to estimate the Kingdom's population. The most recent and influential effort, produced in 1788 by the former tax official Gervaise Parker Bushe, had suggested that Ireland's population numbered around four million, arguing that the figure was likely to be rising due to the predominance of tillage agriculture, potato cultivation and early marriages among the Irish peasantry.[42]

Newenham's *Statistical and Historical Inquiry into the Progress and Magnitude of the Population of Ireland* (1805) extended this argument in new directions, arguing for a significantly higher estimate of both Ireland's current population and its capacity for further growth. It was founded on a revision of the sources for Irish demography. The key innovation, derived from careful readings of Price, Paley and Malthus, was an attempt to calculate an average rate of population increase for Ireland in the course of the eighteenth century. This allowed a current total to be extrapolated on the basis of patchy and outdated hearth tax returns; the last usable register had been produced in 1791.[43]

Comparing and evaluating totals over the century before that date, Newenham suggested that Ireland's population doubled, on average, once every forty-six years.[44] The deficiencies of the hearth tax returns, combined with comparative evidence of more rapid population growth under less favourable circumstances in Russia and the United States, suggested to him that this was a conservative estimate. Figures for Irish revenue and imports of consumer goods were employed to confirm the impression of a 'late rapid increase of people'. On this basis, he felt confident to estimate an average rate of annual increase since the last reliable hearth tax returns of 1791, enabling him to update Bushe's estimate of 4 million to a new total of 5.4 million.[45]

---

[41] *Hansard*, HC, vol. 4, col. 834.   [42] Bushe, 'Population of Ireland', 145–55.
[43] Thomas Newenham, *A Statistical and Historical Inquiry into the Progress and Magnitude of the Population of Ireland* (London: Baldwin, 1805), 1–7, 88–137.
[44] Ibid., 106.   [45] Ibid., 223–4.

Newenham observed with satisfaction that Foster's grain bounties had ensured a significant shift away from grazing and towards more civilised, and more productive, tillage agriculture.[46] By increasing opportunities for agricultural employment, this had reduced the tide of emigration and facilitated rapid population growth.[47] Irish farming was more labour intensive than its English equivalent – a factor that Newenham identified as crucial to the promotion of population. The efficiency of the Irish staple diet of potatoes and oats ensured a relative absence of scarcity. It had been the stubborn persistence of wheat consumption among the newly settled Anglo-Irish, Newenham claimed, that had produced the famines of the early eighteenth century.[48] Ireland's modern population had attained a high level of density without succumbing to the vices of urbanisation. 'Instead of England being competent to maintain a greater proportionate population than Ireland', Newenham asserted,

> we shall find that, independently of the acknowledged superiority of the latter, with regard to natural and general fertility of soil, the nature of the food on which the great majority of its inhabitants habitually subsist ... render it competent to support an infinitely more dense population than the former.[49]

Newenham's investigations shared Malthus' and Sinclair's ambition to estimate the natural limits of a given polity's ability to sustain human life – if necessary, in the absence of all commercial exchanges with the surrounding hostile powers.[50] In contrast to their projections of English and Scottish scarcity, however, Newenham held up Ireland as a land of unrealised abundance. Drawing on a range of estimates of the nutritional requirements of a family subsisting on potatoes, and on the availability of improvable land in Ireland, he calculated that even an Ireland closed off from foreign commerce would be 'competent to support 8,413,224 people'.[51] For the moment, however, Newenham only hinted at the political implications of Ireland's extraordinary capacity for population growth in his conclusion. 'A due consideration of the various facts which have been brought into view in the foregoing pages cannot, it is presumed, fail to

[46] Ibid., 44–5. [47] Ibid., 58–60. [48] Ibid., 337–8.
[49] Ibid., 335–6. Julian Hoppitt, 'The Nation, the State and the First Industrial Revolution', *Journal of British Studies*, 50 (2011), 307–31, at 313–14, confirms Newenham's impression that Irish population *density* was equal to that of England in the early nineteenth century, in spite of a far lower rate of urbanisation.
[50] Jonsson, *Enlightenment's Frontier*, 214; Frederik Albritton Jonsson, 'Malthus in the Enlightenment', in Robert J. Mayhew (ed.) *New Perspectives on Malthus* (Cambridge: Cambridge University Press, 2016).
[51] Ibid., 351.

impress every reader with the vast and increasing importance of Ireland in the political scale of the British empire', he warned.[52] 'Irishmen may find grounds for being persuaded that the statesmen of the United Kingdom, sensible of the vast real importance of Ireland, will ever be disposed to investigate promptly, patiently, and minutely the grievances and claims of that country.'[53] For British readers confronted with a fresh round of petitioning for Emancipation, the message was clear. Irish fertility and population growth could be a blessing if wisely managed, but it could threaten imperial stability if the confessional allegiance of the Irish majority was ignored.

Newenham's *View of the Natural, Political and Commercial Circumstances of Ireland* (1809) expanded on the political implications of Irish population growth. While parts of the *View* were subsequently interpreted as part of a traditional Irish literature of complaint, it was suffused with pride and optimism regarding Ireland's potential as the breadbasket of empire.[54] Newenham's central demand was for British legislators to pay as much heed to the agricultural fertility of Ireland as they did to their far-flung Caribbean and East Asian possessions:

> If their view be disinterestedly extended to the whole aggregate of the real means of imperial energy, it will, doubtless, be acknowledged, that the supplies of the east, and those of the west, industriously augmented to the utmost, must ever fall infinitely short of those which Ireland, if wisely and solicitously governed, might become capable of yielding ... These distant dependencies may even cease to be parts of the British dominions; yet Great Britain and Ireland, firmly united, sagaciously and impartially governed, with all their various sources of wealth and strength fully disclosed, and skilfully improved, may still constitute a flourishing and unvanquishable empire.[55]

In keeping with its assertions of an Irish national power based on the weight of its population, the *View* added a comparative dimension to the earlier *Inquiry*, examining available statistics on the population and revenues of the various European powers. Newenham concluded that on this basis Ireland could be classed 'in the second class of European nations', above the United Provinces, Portugal, Denmark, Sweden, Bavaria,

[52] Newenham, *Inquiry*, 355.   [53] Ibid., 355–7.
[54] Newenham's work was a major source for Matthew Carey, *Vindiciae Hibernicae*, 3rd ed. (Philadelphia: R. P. Desilver, 1837), a founding text for the transatlantic Irish nationalist tradition.
[55] Thomas Newenham, *A View of the Natural, Political and Commercial Circumstances of Ireland* (London: T. Cadell and W. Davies, 1809), iii–iv.

Switzerland or Saxony.[56] 'In respect of population and revenue, taken together', he claimed, 'Ireland may be considered as on a par with the late dominions of the King of Prussia'.[57] If Britain was now without continental allies, she had a powerful resource in her Irish neighbour – if an anti-Catholic ministry was prepared to recognise it.

Newenham argued not only for Catholic Emancipation, but for a major programme of state-sponsored investment in Irish agriculture. The *View* acted as a prospectus for the work of Foster's committees on inland navigation and bog reclamation, highlighting the importance of Irish public works for both the resolution of the Catholic Question and the stabilisation of the United Kingdom as a flourishing, self-sufficient imperial power. Investment in Irish agriculture, Newenham argued, would address the Catholic Question by promoting the interests of respectable Catholic tenant farmers. It would defuse Protestant opposition to Emancipation by allowing the distribution of an agricultural surplus to align landed wealth with the Catholic interest.[58]

Newenham took the side of the defenders of the Bank of Ireland in blaming the Irish Exchequer for the devaluation of the Irish Pound. Irish officials were draining Ireland of capital by borrowing on the London money markets and sending Irish tax revenues to the metropole to service the resulting interest. 'The remittances to British public creditors are tantamount to a vast subsidy annually paid by Ireland to Britain', Newenham claimed, 'or they are, in effect, the same as a very considerable foreign expenditure occasioned by the prosecution of a war'. The 'additional stimulus' produced by such expenditure was minimal, because the imperial military activities it supported were unproductive.[59] The way to stabilise monetary and fiscal relations within the Union was for the Irish Exchequer to use its autonomy to invest in public works that would enable the further growth of Ireland's agricultural exports. Newenham projected that 'a judicious expenditure of much less than a million annually, for four years, in promoting agriculture, and inland navigation, would occasion a permanent addition of considerably more than three millions to the aggregate incomes of the people of Ireland'. This would have 'a twenty, or a hundred times greater ultimate effect in liquidating the debt ... than the best sinking fund that ever was devised'.[60]

Rising agricultural exports would increase consumption and thereby resolve the problem of the notoriously inefficient Irish excise, producing a return on government investment that would far outstrip the costs.

[56] Ibid., 242.   [57] Ibid., 245.   [58] Ibid., 322–3.   [59] Ibid., 293–5.   [60] Ibid., 311.

Newenham conceded that 'to permit industry to take its own course, is a rule in political economy which every Legislature ought to observe', but argued that 'its strict application, in all instances, may be imprudent'. The disruptions to trade produced by the war had imposed powerful political constraints and distortions on the free use of British capital. Irish agriculture would be 'pregnant with greater ultimate benefit' than additional investment in British manufacturing, because it could generate increased food supplies at reduced marginal cost.[61]

Newenham's case for British investment in Ireland's agricultural economy was grounded in his conviction that Ireland's 'natural' potential – suggested by its location, fertility, mineral resources and ready access to sea and river routes – had been frustrated by 'commercial and civil' circumstances imposed on it by Britain. Imperial support for agriculture could act as a form of reparation for past wrongs, restoring a pattern of growth commensurate with Ireland's natural advantages and Adam Smith's 'natural progress of opulence'. Tillage, Newenham claimed, should be considered 'an immense manufacture'; it was a civilising process that had driven Ireland's ascent from a predominantly pastoral economy in the previous century.[62]

Newenham described this process in the terms of Scottish stadial history. Like John Millar, he regarded seventeenth-century Ireland as having been in the 'shepherd state, which, next to the hunter state, disposes and qualifies a people most for war'.[63] A commercial society that rested on agricultural production, by contrast, was more likely to result in a 'well governed country', even if a manufactured sector could produce more valuable exports:

> In places where extensive manufactories are established, and those engaged in them crowded together, the morals of the people are less pure; principles hostile to the public peace are more easily propagated; and contingencies, calculated to excite popular clamour, are more to be apprehended, than is the case in those districts, where, however dense the population, the people are assiduously employed in the culture of the land. Such, for the most part, is the actual condition of the people of Ireland, and it deserves to be considered whether it would not be much more prudent to direct the attention of the Irish to agriculture, than to manufactures for export.[64]

The Anglo-Irish had long regarded manufacturing for export as a means of raising Catholic living standards and defusing social tension. The potato

---

[61] Newenham, *View of Ireland*, 307. [62] Ibid., 17, 57–8.
[63] Ibid., 306; cf. Millar, *An Historical View of the English Government, From the Settlement of the Saxons in Britain to the Revolution in 1688* (Indianapolis, IN: Liberty Fund, 2006), 673.
[64] Newenham, *View of Ireland*, 306–7.

held the key to the cultivation of grain as a 'manufacture'. As an efficient primary staple crop that could readily be consumed by subsistence farmers on small plots of land, it ensured that grain was available to export to Britain, in return for the manufactured goods and luxuries that were imported into Ireland.[65] 'As there exists, and is likely to exist', he observed, 'a great void in the British corn-market, which must be supplied from some quarter or other; it seems eminently conducive to the welfare of Britain that the tillage of Ireland be seasonably improved and extended'.[66]

The Irish peasantry's reliance on the potato ensured that while in 'other countries' grain was a 'mere necessary of life: here, it is rather an exportable manufacture, by the foreign vent whereof, those who labour in preparing it for market are enabled to purchase that article of food which they have been in the habit of using'.[67] Exports of grain could drive expansion of Ireland's population and the improvement of peasant living standards, without producing a subsistence crisis. The supply of an industrial Britain by an agricultural Ireland represented the optimal division of labour available under the conditions created by Union and war.

Ireland and the Continental System

Newenham's works offered a novel argument for Irish reform, based not on appeals to the country's poverty or insecurity but on a declaration of its growing importance to an empire in urgent need of resources. In the environment of ideological polarisation produced by war and revolution, however, triumphalist accounts of Irish prosperity were ripe for reappropriation for opponents of Catholic Emancipation and defenders of the unreformed British constitution. The Genevan publicist Francis d'Ivernois cannot be counted straightforwardly among these, although by the later 1800s he was working closely with the Tory ministries of Addington and Perceval. Exiled from Geneva since the failed *représentant* revolution of 1782, d'Ivernois had once entertained hopes that a reformed French monarchy would act as a protector to the struggling city-state. After these hopes were disappointed by the Jacobin annexation of 1794, he determined to support British efforts to oppose French hegemony, acting as one of the major defenders of the British cause in Europe.[68]

---

[65] Ibid., 59–61.   [66] Ibid., 302.   [67] Ibid., 211.

[68] Otto Karmin, *Sir Francis d'Ivernois 1757–1842: sa vie, son oeuvre et son temps* (Genève: Revue Historique de la Révolution Française et de l'Empire, 1920), 295–332; Whatmore, *Against War and Empire*, 156–9, 65–78, 260–7.

D'Ivernois also had a long association with Ireland, dating back to his time in Waterford as one of the *représentant* settlers of 1782.[69] Motivated by his surprise at the strength of the Irish revenues reported in Foster's Irish budget of 1809, d'Ivernois spotted an opportunity to rebut the French charge that Napoleon's new and expanded trade embargo, the 'Continental System' proclaimed at Berlin in 1806, was bringing Britain's trading economy to its knees.[70] His *Effets du blocus continental* (1809) was a major statement of wartime British orthodoxy, aimed at disrupting the recent alliance between Napoleon and the Russian Tsar Alexander I.

D'Ivernois was an occasional correspondent of Friedrich Gentz, and his deployment of the case of Ireland in the European propaganda war was comparable to the latter's earlier pronouncements on Union itself. For d'Ivernois, as for Gentz, Ireland could act as an analogy: it represented the benign economic future that awaited other European states if they could make their peace with Britain's justly earned commercial hegemony. The intended audience for d'Ivernois' work was in Russia and the Baltic ports, territories that had long exported grain and raw materials to Britain. It was also aimed at fortifying domestic opinion: an English edition was favourably reviewed in Tory circles and contained a new appendix attacking Newenham for the more critical arguments presented in his *View* of Ireland.[71] Although a planned translation into German, facilitated by the Prussian military reformer August von Gneisenau, faltered, a second Prussian minister, Heinrich von Stein, passed the work to Tsar Alexander I at the beginning of 1812, in the hope of encouraging Russia's growing opposition to the Continental System.[72] D'Ivernois would later act as a British emissary in brokering the crucial British alliance with Russia.[73] His interest in the Russian connection was already evident in the *Effets*. The work was addressed to 'a gentleman at Riga' – most likely the prolific political economist and translator Heinrich von Storch, a member of the Academy of St Petersburg. This obscure work consequently enjoyed a long afterlife. Sections reappeared, lightly paraphrased, in the important economic textbook published by Storch in 1815 and were

[69] Karmin, *Francis d'Ivernois*, 113–17; Richard Whatmore & Jennifer Powell McNutt, 'The Attempts to Transfer the Genevan Academy to Ireland and to America, 1782–1795', *The Historical Journal*, 56 (2013), 345–68.
[70] Karmin, *Francis d'Ivernois*, 454.
[71] Anon., 'IV. Effets du Blocus Continental', *The Quarterly Review*, 50–64.
[72] Karmin, *Francis d'Ivernois*, 459.   [73] Ibid., 482–510.

translated into German by Karl Heinrich Rau, a major figure in early nineteenth-century *Staatswissenschaft*.[74]

D'Ivernois deployed the apparent agricultural prosperity of Ireland to demonstrate how much the grain producers of Prussia, Poland and Russia stood to benefit from regaining access to the thriving British market. The message of the pamphlet was a difficult and defiant one, even for potential British allies. Writing in 1799, Gentz had described British commercial supremacy in terms derived from Emmerich de Vattel: as the product of a judicious, but largely peaceful, promotion of its sovereign commercial interests. If other countries, freed from the French yoke, successfully emulated Britain's liberty, industry and innovation, they could one day hope to rival her in trade.[75] D'Ivernois' vision of British prowess was more unforgiving. Britain's dominance was not the result of 'skill and capital' in the eighteenth-century sense; rather, its 'decided superiority' was owing to more durable environmental and technological factors, particularly the ready availability of coal and growing use of steam-powered machinery. Britain was progressing exponentially ahead of her rivals:

> By means of her insular situation, her coal-mines, and the endless variety of machinery kept constantly in motion by her steam-engines, [Britain] sends to foreign markets, the works of her various manufactories (if such they may be called, in which almost every thing is performed by mechanism) with all the advantage which a farmer using the plough, would possess in the sale of his corn, over his neighbours who had no better implement of husbandry than the spade.[76]

The Continental System had not been able to interrupt Britain's industrial progress; it had merely forced her to look more aggressively for markets elsewhere. 'From her geographical position and the indisputable superiority of her navy', d'Ivernois claimed, 'England must always have the means of opening to herself a new market, almost immediately after any old one is closed'.[77] New sources of sugar and coffee had been developed in Britain's Caribbean colonies alongside Spanish Hispaniola, while India and China

---

[74] Heinrich Friedrich von Storch, *Cours d'économie politique, ou, Exposition des principes que déterminent la prospérité des nations*, 6 vols. (St-Petersburg: A. Pluchart, 1815), VI:582–600. On von Storch and Rau, see Keith Tribe, *Governing Economy: The Reformation of German Economic Discourse, 1750–1840* (Cambridge: Cambridge University Press, 1988), 188–9.

[75] Friedrich Gentz, 'Ueber das Handels-Monopol der Engländer, die wahren Ursachen der Enstehung und die Folgen einer gewaltsamen Vernichtung derselben', *Historisches Journal*, 1 (1799), 395–439; cf. Vattel, *Law of Nations*, 208.

[76] Francis d'Ivernois, *Effects of the Continental Blockade, upon the Commerce, Finances, Credit and Prosperity of the British Islands* (London: J. Hatchard, 1810), 10.

[77] Ibid., 39.

were growing consumers of English textiles and potteries.[78] The opening of the South American colonies of Spain and Portugal to British goods had also 'presented to her a new vent for the products of her industry, precisely at the moment when those of the Continent was withdrawn'. With the Russian market blocked by Napoleon, hemp for Britain's navy was arriving from Ireland and India. D'Ivernois raised the prospect that the British market would be permanently lost to the European adherents of Napoleon, as it was driven to construct an imperial autarchy by giving bounties to colonists to encourage the production of goods Britain could no longer obtain from Europe. This would create an ongoing obligation for the British government to prefer colonial over continental goods, since 'neither justice nor policy will permit her to withdraw those encouragements, when the continent may be pleased to re-open its ports'.[79]

The prime beneficiary of Britain's isolation from the continent, d'Ivernois argued, had been Ireland. D'Ivernois recognised the same basic pattern as Newenham in the evolution of the Irish economy since the Union. Absentee remittances and debt interest produced a 'great account ... between the two countries', which was settled via 'the exchange of English manufactures, for the agricultural produce of Ireland'. The distortions created by the Continental System had intensified this dynamic to the disproportionate benefit of the poorer country in the imperial partnership. 'At the present moment', he wrote,

> Ireland is advancing in industry and opulence, with more rapid strides than England ever made; and for this accelerated progress, she is indebted chiefly to the decrees of France, the *ukases* [decrees] of St. Petersburg, and the embargo of America. The wonderful concurrence of these three strange measures, has given to Ireland the monopoly of the vast market of Great Britain. We need not therefore wonder, that the most vigorous exertions of Irish industry have been called forth to produce, from their fertile soil, the various articles of agricultural produce, which not only all Europe, but even America withholds.[80]

While the blockade had increased demand for Irish corn, it had lowered demand for British exports of manufactured and luxury goods. Ireland was benefiting from the lower prices brought about by both increasing mechanisation and restricted opportunities for export. Examining Customs House statistics, d'Ivernois argued that Irish consumption of all categories of British goods – from blankets to jewellery – had more than doubled. Union had been crucial to this beneficial outcome, because it had

---

[78] Ibid., 39–40.   [79] Ibid., 58.   [80] Ibid., 114.

created a secure and integrated market between Britain and Ireland. 'This most happy Union', d'Ivernois proclaimed, 'taught Ireland to feel that her own exertions alone were wanting, to render her the granary of England and Scotland, and called forth all her energies to meet the defiance of confederated Europe'.[81] The opportunity to turn the tables on two decades of French attacks on British rule was too great for the Genevan to resist:

> Such has been the rapid advance in the comforts and enjoyments of the Irish people; – that people of whom you speak, as a constant source of anxiety and apprehension to England; – that oppressed people, for whose sufferings, the French have felt so much compassion; – that people, whom the ministers of Buonaparte have incessantly represented as depressed, by the English government, to the lowest state of poverty and wretchedness.[82]

In keeping with this triumphalist tone, however, an undercurrent of threat was maintained by d'Ivernois in the pamphlet's closing pages. Russian participation in the Continental System, he claimed, was shown by the prosperity of Ireland and Scotland in a Union with England to be a tremendous act of self-harm. 'Which of two nations trading together; the one rich, the other poor, will be least hurt by a sudden interruption of their trade?', d'Ivernois asked his correspondent. 'I may be mistaken, but to me it appears clear, that it will be the latter; and for the same reason that a man in the vigour of life, will endure hunger and fatigue better than an infant.'[83]

While efforts to secure a sympathetic translation of d'Ivernois' work for a German audience failed, a sharply critical annotated edition was produced, and retranslated into Swedish, by one Dr Julius Schmidt in 1810–11. No information was supplied in either edition as to Schmidt's origin or profession, although repeated references to the Kingdom of Saxony – a Napoleonic creation and a key German ally of France – suggest Leipzig or Dresden as likely locations for the work's production.[84] Schmidt was evidently supportive of the Napoleonic regime, claiming not only that the limited success of the Continental System was due to smuggling (a significant factor ignored by d'Ivernois), but that Napoleon's 'genius' would one day extend the system to Spanish South America and the Levant.[85] For Russia and the German states, meanwhile, the Continental System held out the potential for a manufacturing renaissance.

---

[81] Ibid., 121.   [82] Ibid., 97.   [83] Ibid., 133–4.

[84] On the benefits Saxony received under the Napoleonic dispensation, see James J. Sheehan, *German History, 1770–1866* (Oxford: Clarendon, 1989), 273–4.

[85] Francis d'Ivernois & Julius Schmidt, *Die Sperre des festen Landes und ihr Einfluß auf den Handel, die Finanzen, den Kredit und das Wohl der Brittischen Inseln* (1810), 60–3fn. A scheme to partition the

Schmidt mocked d'Ivernois' opening assertion that British advantages were immutable. 'There is not a single quality, either in the natural condition of Russia or the bodily constitution of the Russians, that makes it impossible for industry in Russia to reach the same level of perfection as it has achieved in England', he asserted.[86] 'Without doubt', he continued, 'the Saxons do not have less of a claim to industry, as the British'.[87] The principal obstruction to the development of a Saxon woollen industry, for example, was the glutting of the German market by cheap British manufactures. 'A country can have made advances in production and industry to such an extent', he observed, 'that almost no branch remains, in which the inhabitants of other nations could survive if a free competition with this state were allowed'.[88] Protection raised prices and lowered consumption in the short term, but some immediate sacrifice of luxury was to be welcomed if employment, innovation and taxation were improved over time.[89] D'Ivernois himself had conceded in his work that protective tariffs and public investment were necessary in areas where Britain's vital interests were at stake, such as food and naval supplies.[90] The Continental System was an equally legitimate assertion of the collective 'independence and self-sufficiency' of the allied states against Britain.[91]

Schmidt inverted d'Ivernois' deployment of the case of Ireland so as to make precisely the opposite point about the benefits of trade with Britain. In a lengthy note affixed to his discussion of Ireland, he took at face value the Genevan's assertions about the country's rapid progress since the implementation of the Continental System. He transformed these, however, into an additional justification for German conformity to the Berlin decrees. By giving Ireland a monopoly of British and imperial markets, the Continental System had transformed the British–Irish Union into a mirror of itself. 'This continental blockade took for the Irish the place of a restriction of trade by the British government', Schmidt asserted, 'by means of which the Irish were given certain advantages over foreign traders in the trade of various raw materials on the British markets'.[92] Ireland's wartime prosperity was the product of Europe's fracture into separate, closed trading blocks, not of free competition with the industries of Great Britain.

Ottoman Empire between France and Russia and jointly march on British India was briefly in contemplation in 1808–9, on which Schroeder, *Transformation of European Politics*, 335–37.
[86] d'Ivernois & Schmidt, *Sperre des festen Landes*, 10fn.   [87] Ibid., 12fn.   [88] Ibid., 19fn.
[89] Ibid., 13–14fn.   [90] Ibid., 35–6fn.   [91] Ibid., 87fn.   [92] Ibid., 174–5fn.

Dependency and Empire

Newenham's, d'Ivernois' and Schmidt's accounts of Ireland's agricultural boom spoke to rival political visions, but shared a common understanding of Ireland's place in an empire at war. All articulated a harmonious model of Union, in which Ireland could prosper as a supplier of raw materials and personnel to Britain's military and manufacturing industry. In pointing to the effects of potato cultivation on Ireland's ability to sustain a large population and substantial grain exports, Newenham envisaged Union as the stable coexistence of two differing political economies, founded on contrasting diets, occupations and territorial distributions of the labouring poor.

For some contemporary observers, Ireland's divergent path represented a stable form of prosperity that contrasted favourably the disruptions wrought by enclosure and consolidation in English agriculture. Robert Fraser, a Dublin Society surveyor who had earlier undertaken comparable investigations of Devon and Cornwall, noted approvingly that the flourishing small-scale agriculture of Wexford was analogous to 'that state, in which England was in the middle of the last century': before enclosures, clearances and the growth of manufacturing towns had destroyed the country's capacity to feed itself.[93] Reviewing contemporary English debates over Poor Law reform and agricultural improvement, Sarah Lloyd notes that 'Irish comparisons supplied evidence of either extreme demoralization or hardy independence'. It was the latter impression that prevailed through the years of the Napoleonic emergency.[94]

Even at the height of the wartime vogue for agriculture and autarchy, however, older visions of a more autonomous and diversified Irish economy persisted. The remnants of Irish radicalism – scattered and divided between transatlantic exile and the domestic struggle for Catholic Emancipation – identified the agrarian Unionism of the Anglo-Irish gentry as a profound betrayal.[95] William James MacNeven had already identified Union with a return of English 'jealousy of trade', entailing the destruction of Irish aspirations to commercial and manufacturing autonomy in the service of extractive imperial interests. An assault on the revived culture of

---

[93] Fraser, *Statistical Survey of the County of Wexford*, 61.

[94] Sarah Lloyd, 'Cottage Conversations: Poverty and Manly Independence in Eighteenth-Century England', *Past & Present*, 184 (2004), 69–109.

[95] David Wilson, *United Irishmen, United States: Immigrant Radicals in the Early Republic* (Ithaca, NY: Cornell University Press, 2011); S. J. Connolly, 'The Catholic Question, 1801–12', in *New History of Ireland*, V:24–47.

improvement, alongside its sentimental valorisation of peasant poverty, was a major feature of Walter Cox's *Irish Magazine, and Museum of Neglected Biography* (1807–15). Cox, a Meath gunsmith who had agitated for rebellion in 1798 before turning informer, was long regarded by historians as a marginal and unreliable eccentric.[96] His *Magazine*, however, played a crucial role in the remodelling of Irish radicalism during the later years of the war. During the eight years of its publication, the *Irish Magazine* enjoyed the largest circulation of any contemporary Irish periodical.[97] It tied earlier rhetoric of the Volunteer and the United Irish movements to Daniel O'Connell's incipient campaign for Catholic Emancipation and acted as an important medium for the development of popular memories of the 1798 rebellion.[98] In the field of political economy, the *Magazine* revived and updated the urban, artisanal wing of Irish patriotism and radicalism. Where its key ideological rival, William Drennan's *Belfast Magazine* (1808–12), rapidly aligned with the respectable, reformist Whiggism of Newenham and Henry Parnell, the *Irish Magazine* launched a series of bitter tirades against the new culture of tillage and its complicity in the crimes of empire.[99]

Cox's magazine argued that Union had drawn Ireland back into a destructive pattern of exporting foodstuffs and importing luxuries. Older, more patriotic conceptions of Irish political economy had been betrayed by the turn to tillage. In an October 1808 discussion of George Berkeley's *Querist*, a classic of the genre of eighteenth-century improving literature that had decried Ireland's tendency to export food in return for foreign luxuries, the magazine noted that, 'though a Protestant and an English Prelate', Berkeley had clearly understood 'the kind of commerce which foreign jealousy connives at, and we may say encourages'. English commercial jealousy still lay at the root of the intermittent rural discontent and harsh government repression that characterised post-Union society:

> We feed the naval and military armies of the Empire, besides a great part of the labouring classes of the English people, and in return we import tobacco. Our people are deprived of articles of the first necessity, and are

---

[96] Brian Inglis, *The Freedom of the Press in Ireland, 1784–1841* (London: Faber & Faber, 1954), 130–1.

[97] C. J. Woods, 'Cox, Walter'. *Dictionary of Irish Biography*, ed. J. McGuire and J. Quinn (Cambridge: Cambridge University Press, 2009). http://dib.cambridge.org/viewReadPage.do?articleId=a2130, accessed 16 March 2018.

[98] Connolly, 'Catholic Question', 18–19; Bartlett, *The Fall and Rise of the Irish Nation*, 31; Guy Beiner, *Remembering the Year of the French: Irish Folk History and Social Memory* (Madison: University of Wisconsin Press, 2007), 70, 170.

[99] On the *Belfast Magazine*, see Bew, *Glory of Being Britons*, 33–49.

allowed a poisonous weed in exchange ... partial Insurrections, and dis-
gusting ferocity are the consequences; crimes of a local and lasting nature
exist by constant irritation that want any of the character of civilization, or
even the melancholy dignity of rebellion.[100]

Cox offered a fulsome condemnation of the peasantry's over-reliance on
the potato, mocking the claims of Foster and other members of the
improving elite that it was the natural preference of the Irish people.
Instead, the adoption of such a cheap staple crop indicated their degradation under British rule.[101] The cult of agriculture was a thinly veiled
accessory to exploitation. The activities of Ireland's improving societies
were 'offensive to public understanding', because 'in professing to improve
the morals, the country and the condition of the people', they looked only
to the 'the trade and ease of our British masters'.[102] Under the sway of its
gentry elite, Ireland operated a peculiar, anti-national political economy, in
which the subsistence of the English labourer was placed before the needs
of the 'wretched' Irish farmer. 'Other countries calculate the extent of their
means and the value of their commerce, by the superabundance which
they are enabled to afford to other countries after supplying the domestic
consumption', Cox observed. 'With us the order of political and commercial economy is inverted: we feed others and starve ourselves.'[103]

This critical perspective on claims to agricultural improvement was
exemplified by an 1808 article discussing government support for extension of Ireland's burgeoning canal network. Canals, Cox argued, were the
engines of Ireland's agrarian dependence on Britain. 'This is the great
communication of commercial relations, we were promised by the Union;
for it, we have given up the trade of the world', he lamented.[104] Canals
could help transport raw materials or goods for export around a developed
manufacturing economy, but in Ireland they were mere conveyor belts for
agricultural exports.[105]

The *Irish Magazine* placed this narrative of Irish exploitation in the
context of a wide-ranging critique of Britain's global empire. Atrocities in
India were a recurring theme. The *Magazine* occasionally struck a Burkean
tone, noting the inconsistency of the British embarking on a Christian
'crusade' for European monarchy while murdering Indian sovereigns and
styling the British conquerors of the Dutch East Indies as 'Jacobins'.[106]

---

[100] Ibid., 502.   [101] *Irish Magazine*, 3 (1809), 141.   [102] *Irish Magazine*, 3 (1809), 378.
[103] Ibid.   [104] *Irish Magazine, and Museum of Neglected Biography*, 2 (1808), 411.
[105] *Irish Magazine*, 2 (1808), 411–12.
[106] *Irish Magazine*, 1 (1807), 6–7; *Irish Magazine*, 7 (1813), 103–4.

Unlike the earlier polemics of the United Irishmen, however, Cox's denunciations of the British Empire were not accompanied by an enthusiastic embrace of its French rival. The *Irish Magazine* discussed European affairs from a similar perspective to United Irishmen and the more radical Patriots of the 1770s, seeking out opportunities for Irish autonomy in the context of imperial competition.

The prospects here were distinctly unpromising: the *Irish Magazine* did little to disguise its disappointment with Napoleon's government of continental Europe. An article from 1810 discussed Napoleon's annexation of Holland to metropolitan France, conceding that French levies of troops of money were exploitative, while asserting that they were nonetheless comparable to the mass of debt interest paid by Irish taxpayers to British fundholders.[107] By contrast, Cox greeted with enthusiasm the foundation of a Venezuelan Republic in 1811 as a force independent of the warring empires of France and Britain: 'While despotism treads with unrelenting pride and cruelty on the lands and waters of Europe, liberty is unfurling her standard in the *ci devant* dominions of the Spanish monarchy.'[108] Catholicism, a warm climate, liberty and agricultural fertility would make republican South America an asylum for Catholic *émigrés*. During the War of 1812, the *Magazine* briefly speculated that a transatlantic invasion from North America was 'practicable' and that Ireland could potentially form a 'federal union' with the United States.[109] Even as the war with Napoleon still raged, the aspirations of Irish radicalism had shifted from France to the Americas.

The Congress of Vienna prompted Cox to consider afresh the changed European context. Noting Britain's professed aspiration for the restoration of international order and the protection of small and medium-sized states, the *Magazine* demanded repeal of the Union as an inevitable component of the post-war 'release of nations' from imperial bondage. 'We hope Britain will be as solicitous to do us an act of justice as she is for the Dutch, the Swiss, German and other peoples', Cox declared. This would entail enabling Ireland to develop its own commerce through an independent trade policy, in the manner that it had done prior to the Union. Cox warned, however, that British commitments to the law of nations and the freedom of commerce were only ever instrumental. 'We fear she promises

[107] *Irish Magazine*, 4 (1810), 489.
[108] *Irish Magazine*, 5 (1811), 530. On the short-lived Venezuelan Republic of 1811, see Elliott, *Empires of the Atlantic World*, 380–1.
[109] *Irish Magazine*, 7 (1813), 489.

herself a monopoly of the trade of the nations she affects to free, and an uncontrolled despotism on the seas if she is able to break up the power of France, and parcel Europe into small beggarly communities', he asserted. 'We never knew England to liberate any nation, but for the purpose of weakening an enemy or disabling a competitor.'[110] The *Magazine* consequently welcomed the return of Bonaparte in 1815 and the destruction of the 'odious bargain' between the 'combined Despots at Vienna' to the benefit of 'the Genoese, the Poles, the Belgians, and Saxons', key losers from the settlement of 1814.[111] The final defeat of France prompted two further essays, published shortly before the suspension of the *Magazine* by the Castle authorities. Ireland's prospects under the coming British hegemony were dim:

> She is at the top of the wheel, she has obtained her supremacy over France and Ireland, she has restored the obsolete old fashioned government of foolish kings, courtezans and ecclesiastics in the former country, and has abolished the old constitution of Ireland, of kings, lords and commons. The resurrection and destruction of governments are equally pursued as her convenience or ambition suggests; the old régime of France secures the trade and commerce of England against the possibility of a rival, the extinction of the Irish parliament has silenced the aspiring notions of Ireland, she has given up all idea of domestic manufacture or external trade; she sits down with folded arms under the imposing barrack, and her silence is termed attachment, happiness and allegiance.[112]

The alliance between British luxury and Russian barbarism – between 'vast pecuniary resources' and the 'naked and idle savages of Russia and Tartary' – amounted to the extinction of meaningful interstate competition in Europe.[113] With it went the prospects of Ireland exploiting the European balance of power to win greater political or commercial autonomy. Accepting the closure of his magazine, Cox took a pension from the British government and left for the United States. The political strategy of the revolutionary generation of Irish Patriots and radicals had reached its endgame.

Robert Malthus, Edward Wakefield and the Politics of the Potato

While the *Irish Magazine's* insurrectionary nationalism was an increasingly marginal force in post-Union politics, its polemics against Ireland's agrarian turn found an unlikely parallel in the pages of the *Edinburgh Review*. Robert Malthus' two essays on Ireland, published in 1808 and 1809, have

---

[110] *Irish Magazine*, 9 (1815), 66–7.   [111] Ibid., 245–7.   [112] Ibid., 397–8.   [113] Ibid.

been the subject of an increasing volume of scholarship in recent years. Interpretations have centred on their importance to later Victorian characterisations of Irish poverty and excess and to Malthus' own evolving views on emigration and settler colonialism.[114] No discussion since Patricia James' authoritative biography, however, has cited the essays in the context of the works Malthus was actually assigned by the *Review's* editors: Newenham's two large books on the political economy of Union.[115] The context outlined in the preceding sections enables a new reading of Malthus' early Irish writings, as a critique of the reductive agrarianism of Ireland's Anglo-Irish improvers.

Malthus's 1808 review of Newenham's *Historical and Statistical Inquiry* was timed to coincide with a second round of Catholic petitioning to the Westminster parliament. The essay endorsed Newenham's claim that the Irish peasantry's attachment to the potato enabled the simultaneous growth of both population and grain exports.[116] Malthus was more concerned than Newenham, however, with the underlying structures of motivation and esteem that determined modes of subsistence. In the revised and expanded 1803 edition of the *Essay on Population,* he had argued that in advanced and luxurious commercial societies, the drive to reproduce was placed in tension with the need to avoid the shame of relative poverty. Civilisation entailed gradual replacement of 'positive checks' (starvation and disease) with 'moral restraint' (celibacy and delayed marriage), or failing this, 'prudential' restraint (delayed marriage, accompanied by what Malthus termed 'irregular gratifications'). This alone had the potential to stabilise the relationship between population and subsistence at a high and relatively stable level of affluence.[117] Marriages would be delayed, and excess births avoided, where self-respecting populations became accustomed to seeking a decent standard of living.[118] This required attachment to both superior foodstuffs and longer working hours: in England, the consumption of meat and wheaten bread was a matter of popular pride, which Malthus believed set an high customary floor on wages. 'The labourers of the south of England', Malthus claimed in the *Essay* of 1803, 'are so accustomed to eat fine wheaten bread, that they will

---

[114] Lloyd, 'Potato'; Alison Bashford and Joyce Chaplin, *The New Worlds of Thomas Malthus* (Princeton, NJ: Princeton University Press, 2016), 215, 221.

[115] Patricia James, *Population Malthus: His Life and Times* (London: Routledge and Kagan Paul, 1979), 149–59.

[116] Robert Malthus, 'IV: Newenham and others on the State of Ireland', *Edinburgh Review*, 12 (1808), 336–55, at 337.

[117] Robert Malthus, *An Essay on the Principle of Population*, ed. D. Winch and P. James (Cambridge: Cambridge University Press, 1992)

[118] Ibid., 43–4.

suffer themselves to be half-starved before they will submit to live like the Scotch peasants'.[119] The limits of subsistence, Malthus suggested, were intimately connected with the collective self-esteem of the labouring classes in a given state.

In Ireland, the strong 'principle of increase' was made possible by the availability of a highly efficient staple crop among a people 'long oppressed and degraded'.[120] If growth continued unchecked – and Malthus predicted it could reach twenty million by the end of the nineteenth century – Catholic Emancipation would eventually be conceded to the sheer 'physical force' of a prodigious Irish population. In its absence it was 'quite impossible that [Ireland] should remain united to Great Britain'.[121] Rising rents and falling wages would ultimately convert Ireland's cottier subtenants into 'a set of labourers earning their pecuniary wages like the peasantry of England, but still living upon potatoes as their principal food'.[122] This would mean a much lower subsistence floor on wages, and even greater immiseration for Ireland's labouring poor. In the absence of political reform, material discontents would be channelled into resentment towards British rule:

> The mere pressure of poverty alone, though it has been felt with varied weight in every part of the world, has never, we believe, in a single instance, produced a general spirit of insurrection and rebellion against Government; but when other specific and removable causes of complaint have existed at the same time, it has invariably added to them tenfold strength, and often been productive of the most tremendous effects. The distresses of the common people of Ireland will ever continue a weapon of mighty and increasing force in the hands of the political agitator, till it is wrested form him, or its point turned aside, by the complete abolition of all civil distinctions between the Protestant and Catholic subjects of the British Empire.[123]

Malthus' argument for Emancipation was not only grounded in concerns about the security of Ireland. It aligned with his broader project to encourage forms of life that would ameliorate the environmental causes of poverty. His essay argued that Catholic Emancipation could act as an 'indirect' means of weaning the Irish off their dangerous addiction to the potato. The Irish case was an instructive example of how the degradation of staple foods could result from the deprivation of political liberty. Rather than presenting (as David Lloyd has suggested) an obstacle to the 'cultural habits' of market capitalism as practised in England, Malthus saw the potato as undermining a broader range of masculine and 'civilised' *political*

---

virtues.[124] The purchasing power of labourers was linked to prevailing levels of both luxury and liberty, and it determined their entire psychological and political disposition.

Turning his attention, in a subsequent essay, to Newenham's *View*, Malthus mounted a broader critique of contemporary visions of Ireland as an agrarian dependency of industrial Britain. Ireland's proclivity for grain exports, Malthus averred, was hardly remarkable: it was typical of a society 'in an early period of civilization and improvement'. In the absence of a significant urban population to feed, food surpluses would be exported to 'rich nations in want of corn'.[125] This resolved nothing in relation to the question of peasant living standards and the future growth of Ireland's population. The improvement of Irish agriculture was certainly worthwhile, and Malthus noted with approval that the British Isles could expect to be entirely 'independent of foreign supply' by 1814.[126] He rejected, however, Newenham's conclusion that Ireland could grow wealthy as an agricultural dependency of Britain. The relative prices of food and other commodities that determined labourers' real standard of living – and the purchasing power of the Irish peasantry – were undermined by dependence on the potato:

> It is indeed one of the radical evils of the use of potatoes, as the principal food of the lower classes, that the abundance in which they are supplied, and their consequent cheapness, by no means occasions a proportional cheapness of other commodities. On the contrary, this very abundance contributes to the high rent of land, which, of course, must tend to raise the price of cattle, wood, or materials of manufactures which are raised upon it; a proof, by the by, among many others, that the price of the common food of the labouring classes cannot be considered as regulating the prices of other commodities.[127]

Newenham's investment scheme was an irrelevance in this context: like Cox, Malthus regarded contemporary Irish agrarianism as a perverse modern manifestation of 'the true mercantile spirit' that had driven earlier attempts to prevent Ireland from diversifying into manufacturing exports.[128] He called instead for measures that would raise the living standards of the labouring poor: a shift in payment of 'the partial and oppressive county rates, and the still heavier and more oppressive burden

---

[124] Lloyd, 'Potato', 316.
[125] Robert Malthus, 'XII: Newenham on the State of Ireland', *The Edinburgh Review*, 14 (1809), 151–70, at 164.
[126] Ibid., 167.   [127] Ibid., 164–5.   [128] Ibid.

of tithes, from the poor tenantry, to the rich landlords'.[129] The best hope
for the stabilisation of Irish population would be an increase in luxury and
a diversification of diet, which demanded the 'full and complete emancipation of the Catholics, as the radical cause of the present moral and
political degradation of the mass of the Irish poor'.[130] The removal of
obstructions to this diversified Irish culture of consumption and liberty
should be the goal of British policy: 'let the spirit of the Union', Malthus
concluded, 'or what ought to have been its spirit, be carried into execution
without fear or jealousy, till Ireland is in no respect to be distinguished
from any other part of the empire, but by its situation, and superior
fertility'.[131]

Malthus' essays were published at a moment of extreme pessimism in
the circle of younger Scottish Whigs surrounding the *Edinburgh Review*.
In 1808 the journal's editor, Francis Jeffrey, wrote to Horner with the
gloomy prediction that 'Bonaparte will be in Dublin in about fifteen
months; perhaps sooner'.[132] Sydney Smith, an English Catholic and
another founder of the publication, warned in an editorial that 'the time
for petitioning may soon end, as it did with America; and the time for
demanding begins ... To conciliate Ireland, scarcely any price is too
great'.[133] A rising sense of panic over the failure of successive ministries
to fulfil the promises made at the time of the Union aligned with a
growing sense of foreboding that Napoleon's dominance of European
politics would be impossible to overturn.[134] Irish conciliation and the
dominance of Napoleon were linked in Malthus' essays by the fear that
the example of Irish population growth would 'occasion the adoption of
the same system' of potato agriculture in other European states.[135]
A staple crop that enabled the rapid replenishment of fighting populations was a form of military technology, liable to be emulated by rivals.
Irish reform was necessary not only to secure the United Kingdom, but
to assert the civilisational superiority of a commercial society based on
liberty, consumption and commerce over the bare military agrarianism of
the Napoleonic Empire.[136]

---

[129] Ibid., 167–8. By 'Economists', Malthus meant the French Physiocrats.   [130] Ibid., 353.
[131] Ibid., 169.   [132] James, *Population Malthus*, 150.
[133] [Sydney Smith] 'V: Dr. Milner and Others on the Catholics of Ireland', *The Edinburgh Review*,
April 1808, 60–4, at 64.
[134] Plassart, *Scottish Enlightenment*, 206.
[135] Malthus, 'IV: Newenham and Others on the State of Ireland', 352–3.
[136] Fontana, *Edinburgh Review*, 133–4.

Placing Malthus' essays in their Irish, Scottish and European contexts does much to illustrate what was genuinely distinctive about his views. They combined the Enlightened unionists' insistence on the control of religious faction and the liberation of Irish trade with a fine-grained analysis of the dynamics of the agrarian economy, transforming the latter into a new and urgent object of imperial reform. Malthus' essays rendered the differences between Irish and British societies newly visible and pointed towards increasingly prescriptive British agendas for overcoming the limitations of Ireland's agrarian economy. The key wartime British observer of Irish society, the Quaker land agent Edward Wakefield, recommended Malthus' articles as indispensable guides to the real condition of the country and the growing risks of a renewed slide into crisis.[137] Buried among the reams of climactic, geographic and antiquarian information gathered in his *Account of Ireland, Statistical and Political* (1812) was a novel and far-reaching argument for the remodelling of Irish society – one that went far beyond Malthus' paean to the power of political liberty to transform the condition of Ireland's labouring poor.

Wakefield's *Account* offered a radically pessimistic view of the Irish agricultural boom. While English demand was producing increased output, Irish farms remained small and undercapitalised. The system of conacre tenure observed by Arthur Young, under which labourers offered a mix of cash payment and labour service to sublet small potato plots from tenant farmers, was becoming more, not less, prevalent as Ireland became more thoroughly integrated into the British economic system.[138] Worse, leading Irish improvers – Wakefield cited the examples of the Limerick physician Samuel Crumpe and the Cork land agent Horatio Townshend – seemed not to have noticed that this labour-intensive, undercapitalised form of agriculture betokened stagnation at a low level of social complexity. Their fetishisation of tillage was profoundly mistaken:

> So far from believing, that it would be beneficial to the kingdom to convert the rich grazing lands of that country into corn fields, I freely confess, that better arguments in favour of this change than I have yet heard must be adduced, before I can be convinced of its utility. When the scheme of dividing the land into small allotments, which would cramp circulation, and oblige every man to produce for himself, and to be satisfied with a bare subsistence, without any surplus, is considered in all its consequences, it

[137] Wakefield, *Account*, I:714.
[138] Michael Beames, 'Cottiers and Conacre in Pre-Famine Ireland', *Journal of Peasant Studies*, 2 (1975), 352–4.

will be found, that instead of making the state of agriculture more flourishing, it will have a quite contrary effect.[139]

Where Young had understood conacre tenure as a side effect of Irish
poverty, Wakefield regarded it as one of its central causes. His *Account*
privileged agricultural productivity over mere population, arguing that
Ireland's utility to the empire would be increased if its numerous peasant
smallholdings were converted into well-capitalised tenant farms on the
English model. Arthur Young's *Political Arithmetic* (1774), rather than his
Irish *Tour*, provided the crucial inspiration for this argument, which recalled
Young's position in the English population controversies of the 1770s. In
the fevered atmosphere of the American crisis, Young had dismissed Richard
Price's dire warnings that enclosures and estate clearances were depopulating
the countryside and destroying the military virtue of the old English
yeomanry. Efficient modern agriculture enabled capital investment and
economies of scale, which when combined with a growing manufacturing
population would ultimately render the nation more resilient in war and
more flourishing in peacetime. 'My politicks of classing national wealth
before population, needs no exception', Young declared.[140]

In far stronger terms than Malthus, Wakefield urged Ireland's assimilation to this English logic of commercial diversification and agricultural
investment. Reversing the argumentative structure of earlier paeans to Irish
population growth, he cautioned that consumption, not mere numbers,
was the key to military strength. Weak and undernourished forces were
worse than none at all. The potato, Wakefield claimed, was a food best
suited for farm animals; it had been known to produce 'desspepsia [*sic*]'
and 'fluxes' among the Scottish peasants observed in Sinclair's *Statistical
Account*.[141] The Irish lived under an inferior bodily regimen that dissipated
their physical strength.

More damaging still were the stifling psychological and civilisational
confines of subsistence agriculture. In Ireland, Wakefield claimed, the
'division of labour is scarcely known'. In this 'degraded state of society',
there was a 'want of encouragement to every species of ingenuity'. The
nature of the 'cottier system' was to

> approximate man to the state of the savage, where the insulated being is
> obliged to supply himself by his own labour ... yet, I have been told, 'these
> people are happy, they have every thing within themselves'. They may enjoy

[139] Wakefield, *Account*, I:579.
[140] Arthur Young, *Political Arithmetic* (London: W. Nicoll, 1774), 288.
[141] Wakefield, *Account*, II:716.

the bliss of insensibility, but they are many degrees removed from that exalted happiness which gives man his proper dignity, and which always prevails in a country where the arts and moral improvement, keep an equal pace...[142]

Wakefield's text repeatedly cited the Earl of Selkirk's controversial *Observations on the Present State of the Highlands of Scotland* (1805), a manifesto for the Highland Clearances and an uncompromising statement of the unviability of 'stationary' rural populations at the peripheries of Britain's commercial empire.[143] In Ireland as in the north of Scotland, the rationalisation of agriculture and the extension of modern liberty entailed the destruction of retrograde and unsustainable systems of subsistence.

Wakefield argued for a new spatial imaginary of Irish society, challenging Newenham's account of the even distribution of population across a densely populated countryside. 'One of the principal causes of the miserable state of society in Ireland', he claimed, 'arises from the manner in which the country is peopled. In the interior, there are no cities or large towns to give employment to the surplus hands'.[144] In spite of the 'great wretchedness among the poor, in crowded and manufacturing towns', English urbanisation represented a superior alternative to Irish stagnation. Food for the English towns was 'obtained by the produce of labour fairly brought to market'; if the cities were drained and their population returned to the land, 'no greater quantity of food would be created; and the whole industry of this part of the community ... would be lost in a general cessation from labour'.[145] The defensiveness of Wakefield's tone suggested the continued strength of the agrarian paradigm in both British and Irish economic discourse. Here, and not for the last time, the case of Ireland was used to throw the character of English development into starker relief, and to legitimate the urban and industrial transformation of the imperial metropole.

The Making of an Orthodoxy

R. D. C. Black's authoritative account of British political economy's engagement with Ireland begins with the assertion that early nineteenth-century thinkers were 'virtually unanimous' in asserting that 'the improvement of economic conditions in Ireland must depend on the cottier system

---

[142] Wakefield, *Account*, II:721.   [143] Jonsson, *Enlightenment's Frontier*, 248–52.
[144] Wakefield, *Account*, II: 719–20.   [145] Ibid., 720.

being supplanted by capitalist farming, on the English model'.[146] This chapter has recovered the origins of this powerful nineteenth-century orthodoxy, locating them in the fraught conditions of the Napoleonic Wars. Instead of being a programmatic extension of Smith's political economy, the nineteenth-century British reform agenda reflected its refraction and recombination through broader frameworks of agronomic and demographic thought. Arthur Young, not Adam Smith, was the most pugnacious advocate of large-scale, capital-intensive farming as the indispensable engine of England's wealth and the leading inspiration for nineteenth-century efforts to remodel Irish agriculture. Indeed, as we shall see in the next chapter, Smith's authority was more often invoked in the sense employed by Arthur O'Connor: to vindicate a rival French model of peasant freeholding agriculture against the criticism of British economists who followed Young, Malthus and Wakefield in their criticism of Irish conditions.

Wakefield's advocacy of the application of Young's system to the Irish interior was a critical response to Newenham's rival paradigm of agrarian expansion, which argued for small-scale, labour-intensive production as a guarantor of both social stability and military strength. As d'Ivernois' assertion of the durability of the British polity in the face of Napoleon's Continental System suggested, the Union could readily be envisaged as a partnership between an urban, industrial, capital-intensive Britain and an agrarian, populous Ireland. The continued relevance of this wartime vision of the political economy of Union can be demonstrated by Irish responses to the prospect of peace: the Irish landed interest, marshalled by Henry Parnell, provided the initial impetus for the Corn Laws of 1814, arguing for agrarian protection on the basis that the interests of Ireland demanded the maintenance of imperial self-sufficiency. 'Every one who knows any thing of the interior of Ireland agrees in this', Parnell told the Commons. 'So well aware is the Irish farmer of the effects of foreign importation, that his exertions in improving his land, and embarking deeper in tillage in preference to keeping his ground in grass, are entirely governed by the probability of keeping or losing the full benefit of the English market.'[147]

While the agrarian paradigm was vulnerable to the dramatic change in market conditions brought about by the termination of the war, it represented a coherent understanding of how the Union could be expected to function and spoke to the actual condition of the Irish countryside. The

---

[146] Black, *Economic Thought*, 18.   [147] Hansard, HC, vol. 36, col. 654, 15 June 1814.

same could not yet be said of Wakefield's or Malthus' critique, which demanded a thoroughgoing process of social transformation without specifying how it might be set in motion. Their writings relocated the problematic of Irish government onto the terrain identified by the United Irishmen, moving beyond Enlightenment preoccupations with trade and faction and calling for imperial legislators to consider the complex dynamics of Irish landed society. Post-war British reformers would ultimately determine that it was the duty of imperial government to attempt, where possible, to assimilate Ireland with what they took to be an English model of production based on the consolidated ownership of land. They did so against a backdrop of renewed social and political crisis, which would re-ignite European interest in the apparent inability of Britain's victorious empire to successfully govern one of its core territories.

CHAPTER 6

Democracy, Nationality and the Social Question, 1815–1848

In 1817 and 1818, the Irish writer Sydney Owenson published two volumes of politically charged commentary on the condition of post-revolutionary France. Owenson was the famous author of the Irish 'national tale', the *Wild Irish Girl* (1806), which alongside Thomas Moore's *Irish Melodies* (1808–34) enjoyed considerable popularity in Restoration France.[1] Prefaced with a quotation from the French revolutionary Condorcet, her travelogue sought to vindicate the French Revolution's transformation of rural society. 'When the allies first approached the frontiers of the French territory', she observed, 'they invaded a country whose peasantry were the best conditioned, and most prosperous of any nation in Europe'.[2] Like the United Irish revolutionaries Wolfe Tone and Arthur O'Connor, Owenson understood the primary benefit of the revolution to have been the land reforms introduced by the National Assembly in 1790–1 and consolidated by the Civil Codes of the First Republic and the Napoleonic Empire.[3] The revolutionary 'destruction of the feudal system' had 'produced a national regeneration' in France. It had created a class of independent peasant proprietors who, though poor, cultivated their land in the knowledge that 'the frugal savings of laborious industry do not go to feed the rapacity of the tythe proctor, to meet the vexatious call of rack-rents'.[4] As famine and typhus swept through Ireland, the message of Owenson's account was clear.[5] Britain might have won the war, but the power of 'French principles' was such that – at least in Ireland – she stood to lose the peace.

Owenson's intervention on behalf of the reformist spirit of the early revolution was fulsomely praised in Benjamin Constant's liberal journal

---

[1] Patrick Rafroidi, *L'Irlande et le romantisme: la littérature irlandaise-anglaise de 1789 à 1850 et sa place dans le mouvement occidental* (Paris: Éditions Universitaires, 1972), 321.
[2] Sydney Owenson & Sir Charles Morgan, *France*, 2nd ed., 2 vols. (London: Henry Colburn, 1817), 1:15.
[3] Ibid., 1:7; see Chapter 3.   [4] Ibid., 1:46.   [5] Ó'Gráda, *New Economic History*, 158–62.

the *Mercure de France*, even as it was decried in the English Tory *Quarterly Review*.[6] Its stormy reception shows how the end of the Napoleonic Wars intensified, rather than terminated, the European debate over the contrasting political economies of Britain, Ireland and France. After 1815, Britain's industrial, naval and commercial hegemony ensured that its society and government would be scrutinised in new depth. Constitutional reformers admired Britain's press, parliament and local administration, while advocates of aristocratic restoration pointed to the benefits of a powerful, politically active landed gentry.[7] The deteriorating 'state of Ireland', however, sounded a dissonant note. Famine and epidemic were followed by the recurrence of agrarian disorder and political agitation: the 'Rockite' outrages of the 1820s were suceeded by Daniel O'Connell's unprecedented mass campaigns for Catholic Emancipation, tithe reform and repeal of the Union.[8] Repeated suspensions of *Habeas Corpus* and a regime of coercion centred on the Irish Chief Secretary Robert Peel's new Irish constabulary placed British liberty in an unfavourable light.[9] In the introduction to a major Prussian work celebrating the administrative structures of English government and the political commitment of its aristocracy, the historian Barthold Georg Niebuhr made a sharp exception for Ireland, where British rule produced 'tyranny, egoism and oppression' instead of 'freedom, love for the common weal, and justice'.[10]

Confronted with this persistent, multi-layered crisis of imperial government, the emergent school of British political economists doubled down on the criticisms of Ireland's rural economy articulated by Malthus and Wakefield. Victory in the Napoleonic Wars had proved of the indispensability of a social system founded on the concentrated ownership of landed property and an efficient agricultural proletariat. For thinkers across continental Europe, however, it was an equitable system of peasant proprietorship, rather than Britain's fissile combination of capitalist agriculture

[6] A. Jay, '*La France*; par Lady Morgan, ci-devant miss Owenson', *Mercure de France*, 3 (1817), 293–330; Anon., 'Art XI—France. By Lady Morgan', *The Quarterly Review*, 17 (1817), 260–86.

[7] Jeremy Jennings, 'Conceptions of England and Its Constitution in Nineteenth-Century French Political Thought', *The Historical Journal*, 29 (1986), 65–8; Annelien de Dijn, *French Political Thought from Montesquieu to Tocqueville: Liberty in a Levelled Society?* (Cambridge: Cambridge University Press, 2008), 40–120; Gunter Heinickel, *Adelsreformideen in Preußen: Zwischen bürokratischem Absolutismus und demokratisierendem Konstitutionalismus (1806–1854)* (Berlin: De Gruyter, 2014), 156–73.

[8] Donnelly, *Captain Rock*; Hoppen, 'Riding a Tiger'.

[9] Galen Broeker, *Rural Disorder and Police Reform in Ireland, 1812–36* (London: Routledge and Kegan Paul, 1970).

[10] Bartholt Georg Niebuhr, 'Vorrede', in L. F. von Wincke, *Darstellung der innern Verwaltung Grossbritanniens* (Berlin: Realschulbuchandlung, 1817), at viii.

and urban expansion, that represented a stable form of political modernity.[11] Not only in France, but in Belgium, Italy and much of Germany, French conquest and land reform had created a new and durable landed dispensation centred on a property-owning peasantry.[12] For defenders of these legacies of France's short-lived continental empire, Ireland's growing impoverishment supplied an argument in favour of peasant proprietorship as a durable answer to Europe's 'social question'. In the 1820s and 1830s, Ireland remained a space of contestation between rival visions of commercial society, with origins dating back to the ideological struggles of the revolutionary wars.

The question of property and its organisation could not be dissociated from broader arguments concerning the nature of the union and the claims of Irish 'nationality'. The continental European critique of British political economy was pivotal to the articulation of new demands and modes of thought among the Irish national movement of the 1840s. Long regarded as 'romantic' adherents of Thomas Carlyle or German idealism, the group of scholars and journalists known as 'Young Ireland' were, in fact, champions of a francophone variant of liberal political economy, articulated by figures such as the Genevan historian and economist Jean-Charles-Léonard Simonde de Sismondi and the French politician Gustave de Beaumont. The collective's leading thinkers on the 'land question', Thomas Davis and James Fintan Lalor, claimed that the 'nation' was the sole agent capable of reforming a property order that had been irredeemably broken by Ireland's historic conquest. As the liberal philosopher and East India Company official John Stuart Mill's response to the famines of the 1840s demonstrated, however, the concept of 'nationality' could also be adapted to fit a new conception of union, and of empire, as a plural collection of 'national

---

[11] Marta Petrusewicz, 'Land-Based Modernization and the Culture of Landed Elites in the Nineteenth-Century Mezzogiorno', in R. Halpern & E. D. Lago (eds.), *The American South and the Italian Mezzogiorno: Essays in Comparative History* (London: Macmillan, 2001); Gareth Stedman Jones, 'National Bankruptcy and Social Revolution: European Observers on Britain, 1831–1844', in P. K. O'Brien & D. N. Winch (eds.), *The Political Economy of British Historical Experience, 1688–1914* (Oxford: Oxford University Press, 2002), 61–9; Jerrold Seigel, *Modernity and Bourgeois Life: Society, Politics and Culture in England, France and Germany since 1750* (Cambridge: Cambridge University Press, 2012), 186–90.

[12] See, variously, Werner Conze, 'Die Wirkungen der liberalen Agrarreformen auf die Voksordung in Mitteleuropa in 19. Jahrhundert', *Vierteljahrschrift für Sozial- und Wirtschaftgeschichte*, 38 (1949), 2–4, Markoff, *Abolition of Feudalism*; John Davis, 'The Napoleonic Era in Southern Italy: An Ambiguous Legacy?', *Proceedings of the British Academy*, 80 (1999), 133–4; Michael Rapport, 'The Napoleonic Civil Code: The Belgian Case', in M. Broers, P. Hicks & A. Guimerá (eds.), *The Napoleonic Empire and the New European Political Culture* (Basingstoke: Palgrave Macmillan, 2012), 88–99.

characters', each requiring their own systems of law and political economy. For Mill, Ireland's reform demanded the recognition that the peculiar virtues of commercial society – industry, sobriety, self-reliance – could be produced in specific times and places through very different arrangements of property and population.

The British Economists and the 'Cottage System'

Within a decade of Waterloo, 'the State of Ireland' had become one of the central preoccupations of British politics. Agrarian poverty and disorder offered a recurring theme for countless journal articles, inquiries, parliamentary debates, caricature, fiction and improving projects.[13] Daniel O'Connell's Catholic Association dominated British party competition and remade the British constitution by forcing Catholic Emancipation in the 1820s. In the 1830s, Irish MPs aligned with O'Connell held the balance of power in the Westminster parliament.[14] Westminster, however, continued to rule Ireland through a 'parallel' system of legislation.[15] Major initiatives – from the foundation of the Irish constabulary to the institution of a Board of Works, the reform of criminal justice and the creation of an Irish Poor Law – were regulated through separate statutes and a separate Irish administration.[16] This legislative framework interacted with the broader expansion of social investigation and monitoring within the nineteenth-century British polity to create a distinct institutional space within which Irish society was incessantly explored and debated. The constitutional death of the Irish Kingdom was thus succeeded by its rebirth as a social body gripped a stylised set of pathologies – poverty, violence, popular 'ignorance' – that could be analysed and remedied by Irish, British and European observers.

This intensified knowledge of Irish difference produced a renewed drive, shared between British and Irish elites, to 'make Ireland English' by restructuring its rural economy: slowing population growth, consolidating holdings, raising wages, replacing subsistence agriculture with production for the market and diversifying consumption.[17] As Malthus explained in

[13] Ó Ciosáin, *Ireland in Official Print Culture, 1800–1850: A New Reading of the Poor Inquiry* (Oxford: Oxford University Press, 2014), 4–26.
[14] A. H. Graham, 'The Lichfield House Compact, 1835', *Irish Historical Studies*, 12 (1961), 209–25.
[15] Innes, 'Legislating for Three Kingdoms', 35–6.
[16] Jupp, 'Government, Parliament and Politics', 148–9.
[17] Gray, *Famine, Land and Politics*, 9–10; Hoppen, *Governing Hibernia*, 63–73.

his *Principles of Political Economy* (1820; 2nd ed., 1836), the influx of British capital into Ireland promised by exponents of Union could only be expected – and would only prove beneficial – once 'all kinds of property were secure' and 'an improved system of agriculture' had been implemented.[18] The Irish author of a prize-winning essay for the Royal Irish Academy asserted that a dramatic increase in agricultural profitability would be necessary before any durable growth of manufacturing could be expected.[19] If opinion in Britain and Ireland was sharply divided on the choice between coercion and concession as the proper response to campaigns for Emancipation and tithe reform, it was strikingly united on the urgency of Irish agrarian change. It was not only the Whig-aligned political economists of the *Edinburgh Review* who regarded Ireland's labour-intensive, potato-fed smallholding agriculture as a recipe for stagnation. David Robinson, a leading light of 'Ultra-Tory' political economy who endorsed the Corn Laws and plantation slavery while opposing Catholic Emancipation, insisted with equal vehemence on the need 'to see the Irish agriculturalists placed under that system which prevails in Britain'.[20]

This broad-based consensus was rooted in the agronomic debates of the previous century, which had concerned the optimum distribution of property for maximum yields. In this context, the self-styled 'political economists' of the 1820s distinguished themselves by vigorously rejecting appeals for paternalism, public charity or agricultural protection as the natural complement to the concentrated ownership of landed property.[21] When Arthur Young, in his later years, tempered his advocacy of estate clearances with proposals for cottage-building on marginal land, he was the subject of repeated criticism by Robert Malthus in successive editions of the *Principles of Population*.[22] John Ramsay McCulloch and Nassau William Senior – the two Whig economists with the most consistent interests in Ireland – were equally clear that Britain's developmental path

---

[18] Thomas Robert Malthus, *Principles of Political Economy Considered with a View to Their Practical Application*, 2nd ed. (London: J. Murray, 1836), 350.

[19] R. Ryan, *An Essay upon the Following Subject of Inquiry, 'What Are the Best Means of Rendering the National Sources of Wealth Possessed by Ireland Effectual for the Employment of the Population', Proposed by the Royal Irish Academy, 1822* (London: Hatchard, 1824), 34–5.

[20] David Robinson, 'English and Irish Landletting', *Blackwoods Edinburgh Magazine*, 17 (1825), 684–701, at 68; John Ramsay McCulloch, 'Ireland', *Edinburgh Review*, 37 (1822), 60–109, at 69.

[21] For the social and cultural context, see Peter Mandler, 'The Making of the New Poor Law Redivivus', *Past & Present* (1987), 131–5; Sarah Lloyd, 'Cottage Conversations'.

[22] James, *Population Malthus*, 147–8.

inevitably entailed disruptive change. The alternative was stagnation and eventual crisis. In the paradigmatic popular statement of this hardening orthodoxy, the *Encyclopaedia Britannica's* article on the 'Cottage System' (1824), McCulloch made this case by tying Ireland and France together as examples of societies that were unable to realise the benefits of Britain's rigorous application of capital to agriculture. The Irish agrarian crisis was positioned within a triumphalist narrative that sought to explain Britain's military and commercial victory over France with reference to its underlying distribution of property and population.

McCulloch, like Malthus and Ricardo, described 'the progress of society' as a race between rising yields, rising real wages and a growing population. In an 'improving society', McCulloch argued, the pressure of population growth was partially offset by productivity improvements made possible by the expansion of the fixed capital employed in agriculture. 'Any constitution of society, or any method of dividing landed property', McCulloch consequently argued, 'which should prevent agriculture from adopting the most efficacious methods for saving labour and expence in carrying on their business, would be materially injurious'.[23] The small farmer – here McCulloch cited notorious passages in Young's *Travels in France* (1794) on the condition of the *ancien régime* French peasantry – was incapable of sustaining the capital investment necessary to maximise production and release hands for employment in manufactures or commerce. 'The produce of a small farm of five, ten, or even twenty acres', McCulloch claimed, 'may perhaps enable its occupier to preserve his family from downright starvation, but it will never enable him to accumulate stock to any extent'.[24]

Like Thomas Newenham, whose authority he cited in the article, McCulloch believed that the proliferation of small cottier plots in Ireland had been driven by the corn bounty legislation of the 1780s.[25] Rather than hailing the growth in Irish population and fertility, however, McCulloch asserted that the population explosion enabled by the turn to tillage had crippled Irish agriculture for decades to come. 'The stimulus, intended to act as an incitement to agricultural improvement, has had a much more powerful effect in causing the subdivision of farms, and in increasing the agricultural population of the country.'[26] Irish subtenants

---

[23] John Ramsay McCulloch, 'Cottage System', in D. P. O'Brien (ed.), *The Collected Works of J. R. McCulloch*, vol. 6, 8 vols. (London: Routledge, 1995), 427–35, at 428.
[24] Ibid.   [25] McCulloch, 'Cottage System', 431; cf. Newenham, *View of the State of Ireland*, 235.
[26] McCulloch, 'Cottage System', 431.

provided McCulloch's defining example of small farmers unable to mobilise a capital that was sufficient to employ animals or machinery in order to raise yields:

> An Irish cottager cannot employ either a threshing-machine or a horse. Manual labour is his only engine for extracting produce form the earth. He cannot avail himself of natural agents, nor render them subservient to the great work of production. Those improvements which, in countries where capital is accumulating in masses, are every day rendered more efficient, and tend materially to reduce the price of raw produce, and to render the necessaries of life attainable by less labour, are altogether incompatible with a minute division of landed property.[27]

Aside from its tendency to retard capital investment in agriculture, McCulloch held cottier tenancies responsible for the absence of effective demand for luxuries or manufactures among the Irish peasantry. In a society like Ireland's, 'clogged in its progress' by subdivision and excessive agricultural population, the employment of capital could not reduce the relative costs of food, and diversification of consumption could never occur. Low-level domestic manufacturing and subsistence agriculture locked subtenants out of the cash economy and prevented the process of capital accumulation that could alone ensure a rise in wages and purchasing power.[28]

The most controversial passage of McCulloch's article, however, dealt not with economic conditions in Ireland but those in France. McCulloch claimed that his argument against smallholding was securely grounded in a scientific analysis of the factors of production. It made little difference whether the smallholders in question were impoverished Irish cottiers or the proud peasant proprietors of post-Napoleonic France. The incentive provided by the psychology of property ownership – so important in Smith's account of agricultural productivity – was dismissed as irrelevant. 'It is obvious that the division of labour would be quite as inapplicable in a country divided into small properties as in one occupied by small farmers', McCulloch declared. Investment in machinery was still likely to be impossible, while the limited size of plots militated against their 'being farmed so as to yield the largest quantity of produce with the least possible expenditure of labour'.[29] McCulloch conceded that some one-off effects of the French Revolution had been beneficial to French agriculture: 'the abolition of the feudal privileges ... and of the *gabelle*, *corvée* and other grievously

[27] Ibid., 429. [28] Ibid. [29] Ibid., 432.

oppressive and partial burdens, would of itself have sufficed to make the farmers and small proprietors more respectable and comfortable'. A rapid injection of cheap land into the markets after the confiscation of church and *émigré* land had also done its part: 'by this means small properties were augmented, and fresh energy was given to the agriculturists'.[30]

In the long run, however, the 'extreme division of landed property' encouraged by the mandatory partitive inheritance laws of the *Code Civil* would cause French society to stagnate and ultimately collapse. In Ireland as in France, the ready security provided by access to the land, combined with the lack of ambition produced by 'impossibility of . . . rising in the world', provided incentives for 'indolent habits', early marriages and overpopulation. In a contemporaneous essay on the 'French Law of Succession' (1824) authored for the *Edinburgh Review*, McCulloch argued that partitive inheritance was an engine for the creation of rural poverty:

> In no country of Europe is there such a vast body of proprietors; and in no civilised European country, with the single exception of Ireland, is there so large a proportion of the population directly engaged in the cultivation, or rather, we should say, the torture of the soil. And yet the system is only in its infancy. Should it be supported in its present vigour for another half century, *la grande nation* will certainly be the greatest pauper warren in Europe; and will, along with Ireland, have the honour of furnishing hewers of wood and drawers of water for all the other countries of the world.[31]

McCulloch's comment revealed the underlying stakes of his programme for Irish reform. This rested on a vindication of the superiority of Britain's social order over that of its French rival. Assuming that the ability of land to provide for the people was bounded, the alternative to the disruptions of capital-intensive agriculture and wage-labour was generalised poverty and stagnation. The agrarian reforms of the French Revolution would ultimately be undone by the remorseless logic of population, leaving its peasant society in a condition little better than that of Ireland.

What was to become of the stubborn fact of Ireland's rural masses, if keeping them on the land was a recipe for impoverishment and eventual starvation? Malthus, in a letter to Ricardo, offers the sharpest insight into the impatient mindset of the British economists: 'a great part of this population should be swept from the soil into large manufacturing and

---

[30] Ibid.
[31] John Ramsay McCulloch, 'French Law of Succession', *The Edinburgh Review*, 40 (1824), 350–75, at 369.

commercial towns'.[32] Yet it was also clear that the towns in question should not be those of Britain.[33] In an essay for the *Edinburgh Review* written in 1826, McCulloch complained that 'nothing so deeply injurious to the character and habits of our people has ever occurred as the late extraordinary influx of Irish labourers' enabled by the rise of regular steam transport across the Irish Sea. Not only did the Irish depress the overall level of wages in Britain: 'by the contaminating influence of example' they also diluted the work ethic and consumption habits of British workers, destroying their culturally conditioned preference for higher-quality staple foods.[34] In the radical-utilitarian *Westminster Review*, an intimate of the Political Economy Club argued that 'the magnitude of the evil would almost warrant the adoption of the harsh alternative of actual exclusion'.[35]

Given the poor prospects for Irish industrial development and the rising moral panic over Irish migration to Britain, two solutions were canvassed for the problem of Ireland's transition to an 'English' mode of agricultural development. Emigration further afield, to the settler colonies of Canada and Australia, was the subject of a parliamentary inquiry in 1826 and was managed through an increasingly effective system of Passenger Acts, but legislators resiled from the expense and coercion necessary to implement a large-scale programme.[36] The community of political economists was sharply divided as to the feasibility of emigration. Malthus, in particular, was concerned at the ethical implications of peopling the earth with the surplus of Britain and Ireland.[37] In order to be truly effective, McCulloch meanwhile observed, emigration would have to be coordinated with estate clearances and further restrictions on the letting of small plots.[38] Senior added public investment in canals, roads and covered markets to the equation.[39] McCulloch argued that, given the right support for a transition

---

[32] Piero Sraffa (ed.), *The Works and Correspondence of David Ricardo* (Indianapolis, IN: Liberty Fund, 2004), VI:175–6, Malthus to Ricardo, 17th August 1817.

[33] Gray, *Making of the Irish Poor Law*, 42–3.

[34] John Ramsay McCulloch, 'Art. II – Emigration', *The Edinburgh Review*, 45 (1826), 49–89, at 54.

[35] William Eyton Tooke, 'State of Ireland', *The Westminster Review*, 7 (1827), 1–50, at 34–5.

[36] Oliver MacDonagh, *A Pattern of Government Growth, 1800–60: The Passenger Acts and Their Enforcement* (London: Macgibbon & Kee, 1961); Peter Dunkley, 'Emigration and the State, 1803–1842: The Nineteenth-Century Revolution in Government Reconsidered', *The Historical Journal*, 23 (1980), 353–80.

[37] R. N. Ghosh, 'The Colonization Controversy: R. J. Wilmot-Horton and the Classical Economists', *Economica*, 31 (1964), 385–40.

[38] John Ramsay McCulloch, 'Sadler on Ireland', *The Edinburgh Review*, 49 (1829), 300–17, at 314–16.

[39] Nassau William Senior, *A Letter to Lord Howick on a Legal Provision for the Irish Poor*, 2nd ed. (London: John Murray, 1831); Ciara Boylan & Tom Boylan, 'The Art and Science of Political Economy: Nassau Senior and Ireland in the 1830s', in Maureen O'Connor (ed.), *Back to the Future*

to a more fully capitalist agriculture, humanitarian concerns concerning the consequences of emptying the Irish countryside of its 'redundant' population would be misplaced. The science of political economy demanded that Ireland's parlous circumstances be confronted with a decisive, masculine realism: 'the surgeon who, to preserve the life of his patient, amputates a diseased limb, may be quite as intelligent, and even as humane, as the miss who whines and blubbers . . . at the mere mention of the operation'.[40]

The political economists' failure to formulate a more convincing answer to the question of a transition to an English model of capitalist agriculture led to growing interest in a second solution: the creation of an Irish variant of the English or Scottish Poor Law.[41] This was a proposal with roots in eighteenth-century Anglo-Irish improving paternalism. It was brandished by British and Irish critics of the political economists' programme for estate clearances and market agriculture. A Poor Law, they claimed, would stem the tide of migration into Britain and cement the Union by addressing the destitution of the Irish poor. Even McCulloch would eventually be convinced of the need for a minimal system of indoor relief to incentivise landlords to control subletting and cease levying rack rents. George Cornewall Lewis, a leading Whig exponent of the policy of 'justice for Ireland', argued that a Poor Law could control Irish agrarian disorder that stemmed from a desire to preserve access to the land, the sole reliable means of subsistence. Others, most notably Daniel O'Connell, were hostile to the costs it would impose on landlords and the culture of dependency it risked creating among the Irish poor. For all the heat the debate generated, however, its participants shared fundamental assumptions concerning the inviolability of the Irish property order. As the Catholic Bishop of Kildare, James Doyle, spelled out in an early pamphlet advocating the measure, a Poor Law was a system of charity designed to stabilise an existing social hierarchy, not a charter for the redistribution of property.[42]

For a generation of European thinkers shaped by the dramatic legal and agrarian transformations of the revolutionary and Napoleonic eras,

---

of Irish Studies: Festschrift for Tadhg Foley (Bern: Peter Lang, 2010), 97–110. On covered markets, see Peter Hession, 'Social Authority and the Urban Environment in Nineteenth-Century Cork', Ph. D. thesis, Faculty of History, University of Cambridge, Cambridge, Cambridge (2018), 121–63.

[40] McCulloch, 'Sadler on Ireland', 317.

[41] On the economists and clearance, see R. D. Collison Black, *Economic Thought and the Irish Question, 1817–1870* (Cambridge: Cambridge University Press, 1960), 22–4. The rest of this paragraph draws on Gray, *Making of the Irish Poor Law*, 35–53.

[42] James Warren Doyle, *Letters on the State of Ireland* (Dublin: R. Coyne, 1825), 319.

however, British and Irish debates over Poor Laws, public works and emigration seemed frustratingly limited and piecemeal. The British, complained the French journalist Prosper Duvergier de Hauranne in 1827, were only capable of dealing with Ireland through 'half-measures'.[43] Amid complex and wide-ranging debates concerning the nature of 'restoration' following the defeat of Napoleon, the case of Ireland supplied a uniquely powerful argument in favour of revolutionary land reform.

Property and the Social Question

Writing in 1829, the French historian, novelist and economist Joseph Droz claimed that there were 'two systems' of agrarian economy in post-revolutionary Europe. The *système anglaise* – as he termed it – prioritised productivity over employment: concentrating land-ownership, employing extensive capitals in irrigation, improvement and machinery, and freeing agricultural labour to work in commerce and industry. The English system maximised absolute levels of prosperity, but threatened to increase social instability to unacceptable levels, since full-time urban wage-earners were more vulnerable to recurrent commercial crises than a self-sufficient peasantry. The alternative, Droz claimed, was the *système française*. The division of estates promoted by partitive inheritance restricted the division of labour and slowed the accumulation of capital, but it gave more of the population access to their own means of subsistence. The *système française* promised lower overall levels of wealth, but created a free and self-reliant peasantry that could act as the backbone of the state.

Droz's *système française* was as much Swiss and American in inspiration as it was French. It reflected the success of republican, rather than physiocratic, economists and agronomists in shaping the land reforms of both the French Republic and French Empire, and the powerful influence exerted on revolutionary political economy by the radical readings of Adam Smith offered by Paine and Condorcet.[44] The intellectual champions of peasant proprietorship in Restoration France were individuals with heritage and connections in the French-speaking Swiss cantons: the *Lausannois* Benjamin Constant, the Genevan Simonde di Sismondi and Jean-Baptiste Say, an erstwhile protégé of

---

[43] P. Duvergier de Hauranne, *Lettres sur les élections anglaises, et sur la situation de l'Irlande* (Paris: Sautelet, 1827), 221.

[44] James Livesey, 'Agrarian Ideology and Commercial Republicanism in the French Revolution', *Past and Present*, 157 (1997), 94–121; John Shovlin, *The Political Economy of Virtue: Luxury, Patriotism and the Origins of the French Revolution* (Ithaca, NY: Cornell University Press, 2010), 182–213.

Clavière.[45] Of the three, it was Sismondi who decisively connected the question of Irish agriculture to the elaboration of this republican framework for Europe's political economy. In his *Nouveaux Principes d'économie politique* (1819) – key sections of which were translated by a young Thomas Carlyle in an article for the *Edinburgh Encyclopaedia*, a rival to the *Britannica* – Sismondi deployed Ireland as the decisive instance of the British misconception that the expansion of productive capacity was the sole measure for the progress of a commercial society.[46]

Like Adam Smith, Sismondi located the commercial societies of modern Europe within a historical trajectory stretching back to the fall of the Roman Empire. Unlike Smith, however, he had considerable affection for a feudal system under which lords were constrained by their political position to take note of their vassals' interests. Such a system was vastly superior to the exploitative large-scale agriculture that had characterised the plantation empires of Rome and the modern slaving powers. Sismondi reserved particular praise for the *metayer* sharecropping system that he had observed in Tuscany, a residue of feudalism that allowed for both the autonomy of peasant proprietors and the paternalist attentions of the landlord.[47] Where population growth and the competition for plots began to undermine the customary foundations of peasant tenure, it was right for the state to intervene and control rents rather than allow plots to be cleared of their inhabitants.[48] The alternative was the relentless process of immiseration and alienation that distinguished Britain and Ireland from their European neighbours.

The roots of this immiseration lay in the scientific and commercial rationality that had transformed English agriculture over the preceding two centuries. Sismondi historicised and relativised the model of agricultural productivity extolled by McCulloch, explaining it as a specific product of England's recent past. A new class of large tenant farmers had emerged, who 'in some degree united the habits of the merchant with those of the cultivator', employing knowledge of 'agriculture as a science' to undertake large-scale capital investment and the rapid improvement of cultivation.[49]

[45] Richard Whatmore, 'Democrats and Republicans in Restoration France', *European Journal of Political Theory*, 3 (2004), 37–55; Bela Kapossy & Pascal Bridel (eds.), *Sismondi : républicanisme moderne et libéralisme critique* (Geneva: Slatkine, 2013).

[46] Robert Dixon, 'Carlyle, Malthus and Sismondi: The Origins of Carlyle's Dismal View of Political Economy', *History of Economics Review*, 44 (2006), 32–8.

[47] Jean-Charles Léonard Simonde de Sismondi, 'Political Economy (1818)', in D. Brewster (ed.), *Brewster's Edinburgh Encyclopaedia*, vol. 16, 1st American ed., 18 vols. (Philadelphia, 1832), 39–77, at 50.

[48] Ibid., 51.   [49] Ibid., 51–2.

The concomitant of this new system of agriculture, however, was the creation of landless labouring class – 'the truly essential part of the population' – who worked for the new breed of farmer-capitalist.[50] The condition of these landless labourers, Sismondi declared, was little better than that of the slaves who had worked on the *latifundia* of the late Roman aristocracy. The contemporary British farm labourer had no opportunity to determine 'the direction of his labour': he worked instead 'under the command of a rich farmer'. Commercial tenures and labour conditions destroyed the stable social relations produced by feudalism, leaving the modern farm worker with 'nothing to hope from the fertility of the soil or the propitiousness of the season . . . He lives each week on the wages of the last'. Once this system was instituted, however, its superior productive power served to make it general: the continuous accumulation of capital and the improvement of farming techniques drove smaller and less-efficient farms out of business.[51]

It was at this point that Ireland entered Sismondi's argument. Conacre plots were not equivalent to *metayer* holdings: they did not change the fundamental reality of a system dominated by wage labour. Holders of conacre tenures were forced to work as labourers on their masters' farms in order to sustain themselves: 'in return for their allotted portion of ground, they merely engage to work by the day, at a fixed wage, on the farm where they live; but their competition with each other has forced them to be satisfied with a wage of the lowest possible kind'. The violence sweeping the Irish countryside was the predictable consequence of an agrarian political economy that constantly depressed wages while destroying secure tenancies. This level of immiseration was not yet present in Britain, but would arrive soon in the absence of legislative action to protect its surviving smallholders. 'There is no equality of strength between the day-labourer, who is starving, and the farmer, who does not even lose the revenue of his ground, by suppressing some of his habitual operations', observed Sismondi. In conditions of overpopulation, the day labourer would always have to accept work on the terms offered: 'the result of such a struggle between the two classes, is constantly a sacrifice of the class which is poorer, more numerous, and better entitled to the protection of law'.[52]

By localising and limiting market exchanges, a more egalitarian distribution of landed property would help to stabilise the relationship between population and employment. The reforms instituted by the French

[50] Ibid., 52.   [51] Ibid., 53.   [52] Ibid.

National Assembly had succeeded in creating this more stable rural order in contemporary France. Sismondi's language echoed that of Owenson: while the peasantry of England were 'hastening to destruction', he claimed, 'their condition is improving in France; 'they are gathering strength, and without abandoning manual labour, they enjoy a kind of affluence; they unfold their minds, and adopt, though slowly, the discoveries of science'.[53] Partitive inheritance was an extremely effective mechanism for controlling population growth. Peasant proprietors were well aware of how much life their property could support and moderated their reproduction accordingly:

> When peasants are proprietors, the agricultural population stops of itself, when it has brought about a division of the land, such that each family is invited to labour, and may live in comfortable circumstances. This is the case in almost all the Swiss cantons, which follow nothing but agriculture.

Day labourers, by contrast, were 'worse informed than the peasant-proprietor, and yet ... called to perform a much more complicated calculation' as to the possibilities of sustaining their children by guessing at the value of their future labour on the open market. Defeated by the complexities of wage competition, unable to make secure plans for the future, 'they depend on being happy; they marry much younger; they bring into the world many more children, precisely because they know less distinctly how those children are to be established'.[54] An equitable distribution of landed property – even at the cost of lower levels of production and accumulation – offered the best hope for the stabilisation of Europe's commercial societies.

For Ireland, Sismondi's case for peasant proprietorship created a different transition problem to that posed by McCulloch's exposition of British agricultural development. Instead of shifting incentives to enable the removal of the peasantry from the land, it demanded a revolution in property relations. In a series of essays first published in 1835, Sismondi argued that the 'duty of the sovereign' towards Irish cultivators demanded legislation converting unstable tenancies into peasant property held at a quit-rent. The size of plots was to be locally determined to secure the provision of a single family; the quit-rent should be low enough to allow them to live on a diet of bread and occasional meat.[55] If the population

[53] Ibid.   [54] Ibid., 74.
[55] J. C. L. Simonde de Sismondi, 'Des devoirs du Souverain envers les cultivateurs irlandais, et des moyens de les tirer de leur détresse', in *Études sur l'économie politique*, vol. I, 2 vols. (Paris, 1837), 331–77, at 364–9.

were further relieved through a programme of emigration aimed at establishing self-sufficient peasant colonies in the Canadian interior, then peasant proprietorship would succeed in stabilising numbers and raising the standard of living.[56]

Sismondi's vision for a reformed Ireland – a diversified diet, a stable population, a culture of bourgeois order and civility – was similar to that entertained by the British economists. Yet British political economy, according to Sismondi, was incapable of understanding the real solutions to Irish poverty. It was a descendant of Aristotle's 'chrematistics', a science of moneymaking without proprtion or ethical orientation. British writers were incapable of locating the Irish crisis within a broader historical conjuncture, or of perceiving the need for a science of distribution, aimed at the stabilisation of commercial society.[57] Ireland already operated according to their principles: it had a vast rural proletariat, which made it a site of 'universal competition … the beautiful ideal of many economists … the fatal terminus towards which the social organisation of men among nearly all the peoples of modern Europe is tending'.[58] Far from being a retrograde holdout against Britain's advancing civilisation, Ireland appeared a dark portent of Europe's unstable future under British industrial and commercial hegemony.

Sismondi was adamant that Britain's failure to reform Irish agriculture was not one of 'charity', but of 'justice'. It was the duty of the sovereign to effect the redistribution of property to eliminate the causes of poverty, rather than relying on the 'palliative' of a Poor Law.[59] The distinction between justice and charity was a vital one for liberal critics of British political economy in the decades after 1815. Advocates of the restoration of clerical and noble authority, such as the prolific legitimist economist Maurice Rubichon in France, or the followers of Adam Müller and Ludwig von Haller in Prussia, associated the iniquities of the modern market, sharply apparent in both Britain and Ireland, with the revolutionary overthrow of medieval chivalry and charity.[60] Vindicating commercial society against these self-consciously 'conservative' critiques meant clarifying its form and proving that it was capable of supporting a stable social order. Not only in France, but also in Prussia, the case of Ireland was deployed to defend and uphold the reforms of the revolutionary era and to

---

[56] Ibid., 351.   [57] Sismondi, 'Devoirs du Souverain', 241–5.   [58] Ibid., 248.
[59] Ibid., 276–7.
[60] Robert Berdahl, *The Politics of the Prussian Nobility: The Development of a Conservative Ideology, 1770–1848* (Princeton, NJ: Princeton University Press, 1988), 250–61.

make the case for a commercial society founded on an equitable distribution of landed property.

Many commentators have speculated as to the extent to which G. W. F. Hegel's theory of 'civil society' was shaped by an encounter with Sismondi's *Nouveaux principes*.[61] The Prussian philosopher's 1831 essay on the British parliamentary reforms of 1832 mounted a comparable critique of British approaches to Irish policy, drawing on the Prussian, rather than the French, experience of land reform.[62] Historiographical debate continues to rage over the long-run impact of the reform edicts of 1807 and 1811, which formally abolished serfdom, required the division of heavily indebted noble domains between landlords and hereditary tenants and provided for the conversion of temporary into permanent tenancies.[63] For Hegel, however, the specific terms of the reform were less significant than the approach it represented to the questions of legislation and property as such. The inability of the British political system to formulate comprehensive solutions for Ireland grew out of the 'positive' character of its constitution and legal order and its reluctance to interfere with property rights to serve the common good. The condition of Ireland provided decisive proof that Britain had failed to create the legal and ethical structures required to contain a market economy and render it compatible with real freedom.[64]

Hegel drew a sharp distinction between the British legal system and that of the 'civilised states of the Continent'. In Britain, 'constitutional rights [*Staatsrechte*]' retained the 'private' and 'contingent' character they had received in the Middle Ages. English law had not yet undergone the 'development and transformation' achieved by the French Revolution and the Prussian reform era, which had produced clearly distinguished systems of public and private law based on 'general principles . . . common sense and sound reasoning'. Only powerful monarchs and enlightened administrators had been capable of overcoming privilege and private

[61] Ernst Erdös, 'Hegels politische Oekonomie im Verhältnis zu Sismondi', in Heinz Kimmerle, Wolfgang Lefèvre, Rudolf M. Meyer (eds.), *Hegel-Jahrbuch 1986* (Bochum: Germinal, 1988), 75–8; Douglas Moggach, Jones, 'National Bankruptcy and Social Revolution', 80–8; Douglas Moggach, 'Introduction: Hegelianism, Republicanism and Modernity', in D. Moggach (ed.), *The New Hegelians: Politics and Philosophy in the Hegelian School* (Cambridge: Cambridge University Press, 2006), 1–23.

[62] For more wide-ranging discussions of this essay, see Shlomo Avineri, *Hegel's Theory of the Modern State* (Cambridge: Cambridge University Press, 1972), 208–20.

[63] Sean Eddie, *Freedom's Price: Serfdom, Subjection, and Reform in Prussia, 1648–1848* (Oxford: Oxford University Press, 2013), 196–243.

[64] On Hegel's conception of the market, see Lisa Herzog, *Inventing the Market: Smith, Hegel, and Political Theory* (Oxford: Oxford University Press, 2013), 47–61.

interest in the fashioning of modern states. Britain's privatised, oligarchic and traditionalist parliamentary system lacked a comparable locus of reforming will:

> England has lagged so conspicuously behind the other civilised states in institutions based on genuine right, for the simple reason that the power of government lies in the hands of those who possess so many privileges which contradict a rational constitutional law and a genuine legislation.[65]

The condition of the Irish interior supplied proof that the problem of a prescriptive, arbitrary system of law extended throughout the British body politic. Ireland represented a flawed transition from 'feudal tenure' to true 'property'. While serfdom had been abolished, the law of property had not been modernised. The precedents for such modernisation were supplied by the French Code Civil as well as the Prussian *Bauernbefreiung*:

> ...changing the rights of inheritance, introducing equal distribution of parental assets among children, allowing property to be requisitioned and sold in settlement of debts ... changing that legal status of landed property which [currently] involves indescribable formalities and costs in the event of sale.[66]

The formal absence of serfdom in Ireland meant little if agricultural labourers endured 'even greater deprivation than that of serfs', since they were not protected by customary, patrimonial guarantees of access to land for subsistence.[67] The scandal of estate clearances, which Hegel learned of through regular reading of the Whig *Morning Chronicle*, guided the philosopher's analysis.[68] Ireland's landowners, he claimed, were empowered by English law to dispossess their peasants and even burn down their cottages if they 'happened to find more advantage in a mode of agriculture which requires fewer workers'. The Irish poor – unlike their British counterparts – could not find work in the industrial towns or draw on the support offered by a Poor Law.[69] Yet the British parliament responded only with 'pious hopes that the Irish landlords might take up residence in Ireland' or 'palliatives' like the 1826 legislation controlling the subletting of estates.[70] Thoroughgoing reform, modelled on that of France and Prussia, was beyond the capacity of Westminster's parochial political culture: 'National pride', Hegel claimed, 'prevents the English from

[65] Georg Wilhelm Friedrich Hegel, 'On the English Reform Bill (1831)', in L. Dickey & H. B. Nisbet (eds.), *Political Writings* (Cambridge: Cambridge University Press, 1999), 234–70, at 239.
[66] Ibid., 248.   [67] Ibid., 246–7.
[68] M. J. Petry, 'Hegel and *The Morning Chronicle*', *Hegel Studien*, 11 (1976), 11–80.
[69] Hegel, 'English Reform Bill', 247.   [70] Ibid., 248.

studying and acquainting themselves with the advances made by other nations in developing their legal institutions'.[71]

One of strongest advocates of peasant property within the Prussian reform ministries of the Napoleonic era, the administrator and historian Friedrich von Raumer, further spelled out the Irish lesson for Prussia in his successful travelogue, *England im Jahre 1835* (1836).[72] 'Go to Ireland', von Raumer urged Prussian readers, 'to recognise with outrage the consequences of a intolerant, barbaric system of legislation, and the bless the course of advancement in Prussia'![73] The legislation of 1807–12, von Raumer claimed, had 'awakened that enthusiasm and energy which led to the overthrow of French tyranny, to intellectual freedom, and to a progress in industry and wealth, such as a narrow policy can never produce'.[74] The regeneration of the British state in Ireland demanded a similarly expansive approach to Irish grievances. Union was desirable in theory, but the shortcomings of British government offered ample justification for O'Connell's new and threatening campaign for its repeal. Support for Catholic schooling, the abolition of Church of Ireland tithes, the introduction of a Poor Law and restrictions on absenteeism would all count for nothing if they were not supported by the 'conversion of all these tenants-at-will into proprietors'. Like Hegel, von Raumer believed that such a proposition was scandalous to British elites and would be greeted with accusations of 'robbery, Jacobinism, the destruction of civil society'.[75] Yet English claims to constitutional liberty rang hollow in Ireland, where 'all the highly praised forms of the constitution' were 'paralyzed by the force of passion and prejudice'.[76] Through the concerted action of a strong monarchy and an enlightened administration, the Prussian reform ministries had produced more real freedom for their subjects in a few years then the hallowed British constitution had been able to achieve in Ireland over centuries of misrule.

Von Raumer, Hegel and Sismondi all used the case of Ireland to contest the proposition that Britain represented a stable or successful model for Europe's political economy. In spite of their contrasting backgrounds and politics, they shared an emphasis on equitable access to landed property as the keystone of political stability. Substantive justice and freedom for the majority demanded sovereign intervention to suspend the property rights

---

[71] Ibid., 251.
[72] Frederick von Raumer, *England in 1835*, trans. S. Austin, 3 vols. (London: John Murray, 1836). On von Raumer's role in drafting the 1811 reform edict, see Eddie, *Freedom's Price*, 204–13.
[73] Raumer, *England*, III:200–1.   [74] Ibid., II:142–3.   [75] Ibid., III:198.   [76] Ibid., III:201.

of Ireland's delinquent aristocracy. Ireland was thus shown to be an integral part of a British polity in which an unreflective attachment to tradition enabled the unrestrained exploitation of the poor. It exposed the limits of the vision of political economy pursued by Malthus, Ricardo and McCulloch, which was incapable of integrating its innovative science of wealth into a broader understanding of society or the state.

Gustave de Beaumont, Ireland and the Future of Democracy

What remained unclear, at least from this perspective, was the impact Ireland's persistent instability was likely to have on British politics, or the connection between the politics of Irish property and the remarkable popular mobilisation achieved by Daniel O'Connell's Catholic Association. O'Connell had become a major figure in European politics following the success of the Emancipation campaign. After 1829, his fame grew rapidly among defenders of the Rhineland Catholic interest within Prussia's sprawling, multi-confessional monarchy.[77] In the aggressively secular France produced by the 1830 revolution, meanwhile, a new generation of liberal Catholics associated with the *L'Avenir* journal romanticised the primitive, egalitarian, popular Catholicism of the Irish masses.[78] The injection of Irish political agency into longstanding European discussions of its poverty inspired fresh engagements with the polity's past and future.

Foremost among these was Gustave de Beaumont's *Irlande: Sociale, Politique, Religieuse* (1839), which remained a major reference point for British, Irish and continental European discussions down to the end of the nineteenth century.[79] A relation of the famous revolutionary the Marquis de Lafayette, Beaumont served as a member of the House of Deputies under the July Monarchy (1830–48), and as French ambassador to Britain under the Second Republic (1848–52). *Irlande* was a major contribution to the new 'political science' advanced by his closest friend and collaborator, Alexis de Tocqueville, and doubled as a multi-layered critique of

---

[77] Bernhard Schneider, 'Insel der Märtyrer oder ein Volk von Rebellen? Deutschlands Katholiken und die irische Nationalbewegung', *Historishces Jahrbuch*, 128 (2008), 225–76.

[78] Seamus Deane, 'A Church Destroyed, the Church Restored: France's Irish Catholicism', *Field Day Review*, 7 (2011), 202–49.

[79] Tom Garvin & Andreas Hess, 'Introduction', in *Ireland: Social, Political, Religious*, trans. W. C. Taylor (Cambridge, MA: Belknap, Harvard, 2006).

contemporary French thought.[80] Beaumont's analysis located Ireland at the junction of Europe's 'social' and 'national' questions. It redescribed the intellectual rivalry between French and British visions of commercial society as a clash between rival principles of 'democracy' and 'aristocracy', identifying Ireland as a bridgehead of democratic revolution within the British polity.

Tocqueville's *De la democratie en Amérique* (1835–40) had claimed to be a guide to Europe's future, an analysis of 'the gradual development of equality of conditions' as 'a providential fact' that would affect 'all the Christian universe'.[81] According to de Beaumont, however, the remarkably resilient and vigorous aristocracy of England 'offered to modern democracy a noble and dignified adversary', which sustained conservative illusions that aristocratic government had a future in Europe.[82] The case of Ireland showed that this claim was unsupportable. The dramas of Irish politics in the era of the Emancipation and Repeal campaigns proved that 'it is from Ireland that democracy blows onto England its most ardent passions; Ireland is delivering the blows most capable of shaking to its foundation the old edifice of the British constitution'.[83]

Beaumont used 'democracy' to describe a political system based not on universal suffrage, but on civil equality of conditions under the law, accompanied by the rising economic power of the bourgeoise and the institution of forms of representative government.[84] Beaumont and Tocqueville shared this conception of a new social order with the leading French politician and intellectual of the July Monarchy established by the Orléanist Revolution of 1830, François Guizot, but were sharply critical of the narrow, elitist parliamentarism that defined his '*doctrinaire*' liberal politics.[85] 'Administrative' power and local representation were the decisive components of a political constitution. Beaumont and Tocqueville were struck on their journeys to England by the powerful nexus of consolidated property and voluntary public service that conserved the

[80] Alexis de Tocqueville, *Democracy in America*, edited and translated by Harvey Mansfield & Delba Winthrop (Chicago, Ill.: University of Chicago Press, 2002), 7.

[81] Tocqueville, *Democracy in America*, 5–6.

[82] Gustave de Beaumont, *L'Irlande sociale, politique, et religieuse*, 2 vols. (Paris: Gosselin, 1839), I:iii.

[83] Ibid., I:iv.

[84] Lucien Jaume, *Tocqueville: The Aristocratic Sources of Liberty*, trans. A. Goldhammer (Princeton, NJ: Princeton University Press, 2013), 17.

[85] Melvin Richter, 'Tocqueville and Guizot on Democracy: From a Type of Society to a Political Regime', *History of European Ideas*, 30 (2004), 61–8; Jaume, *Tocqueville*, 251–81.

territorial power of the English nobility. This was central to their characterisation of the British Empire as a fundamentally 'aristocratic' regime.[86]

In this, they largely agreed with picture of the operation of the English
county given by the royalist author Charles Cottu in his influential
contribution to a wide-ranging post-Napoleonic French debate over aristocracy and centralisation, *De l'esprit du gouvernement d'angleterre*
(1820).[87] Beaumont echoed Cottu's descriptions of the functions of
quarterly assizes, justices of the peace, and juries, adding to it a strong
emphasis on the continuing autonomy of urban municipal corporations,
and the parish vestries who had long administered the distribution of poor
relief. 'One can in England recognise as a truth', de Beaumont observed,
'that as much as the power of making laws is centralised, so the care for
their administration is hardly so'.[88] Unlike in France, the British sovereign
had no direct administrative authority over its officers, either through the
payment of salaries or a chain of bureaucratic responsibility. Land and
wealth conferred the dignity of service. Parliament, a large assembly, was
unsuited to the inspection of the administrative functions of these semi-
autonomous agents of the state. In reality, it was the judicial power–
specifically the Court of the Queen's Bench – that ultimately regulated
the administration of the laws, and only then if specific cases were brought
against public officials.

The rise of democracy in Ireland was being encouraged by the reaction
of the landless and powerless Catholic majority to the domination of
analogous, Irish versions of these decentralised administrative institutions
by a 'vicious' Anglican aristocracy. Beaumont's description of the Union of
1800 was aimed at the *doctrinaire* delusion that a mere gathering of
educated representatives could bring unity and stability to fractured political communities.[89] The British political class, he argued, had made a
category error by assuming that a mere Act of Parliament could assimilate
Ireland into Britain's peculiarly resilient form of aristocratic government:

> Before the Act of Union, Ireland had its own institutions; it preserved them
> after the Union, with the single exception of its parliament . . . The English
> constitution is not a charter in a hundred articles which may be granted
> hastily to a nation in urgent want of a government . . . What, then, did

---

[86] Seymour Drescher, *Tocqueville and England* (Cambridge, MA: Harvard University Press, 1964),
39–40.

[87] De Dijn, *French Political Thought*, 44–45; Rudolf von Thadden, *La Centralisation Contestée*, trans.
H. Cusa & P. Charbonneau (Arles: Acts Sud, 1989), 159–60.

[88] Beaumont, *L'Irlande*, I:303.

[89] On Tocqueville and Guizot's disagreement over centralisation, see Jaume, *Tocqueville*, 251–81.

England do, when she proclaimed the Union with Ireland? She declared that for the future all laws necessary to the two countries should be made in a common parliament, to which each should send representatives; but whilst providing for the future, she left the past untouched.[90]

Ireland's surviving institutions were themselves flawed copies of their English equivalents, produced by a distended process of conquest and expropriation. Beaumont argued that the Anglo-Norman colonists' continuing proximity to England and their ultimate dependence upon an absent sovereign had removed from them the incentives felt by the French and English nobilities – also products of medieval conquests – to integrate and ally with their tenants and form a community of sentiment.[91] The feudal liberties that, in England, had formed the basis of the modern constitution were reserved to the privileged inhabitants of the Pale.[92] This suited English monarchs, who regarded the reconciliation of conquerors and conquered in Ireland as a threat to their authority, as well as the Anglo-Norman settlers themselves, who could enjoy arbitrary power over the Irish outside the Pale.[93] The municipal corporations, meanwhile, as merchant bodies, were already imbued with an 'exclusive tendency' and regarded it as in their interests to exclude native traders from the merchants guilds. A system of primitive commercial monopoly was thereby converted into a means of ethnic exclusion.[94]

At the point where something approaching modern sovereignty was established through the proclamation of an Irish Kingdom by Henry VIII, the Reformation intervened to alienate the majority population still further from new waves of settlers. The ensuing wars of religion and the implementation of the Penal Laws, via a further process of colonisation, had obstructed any reconciliation that might have been expected under conditions of commercial growth.[95] It was the enduring 'mixed government' of Ireland, 'semi-feudal, semi-colonial', that lay at the root of the deep divisions of the modern polity.[96]

Ireland's stacked juries, Orange judges, tiny Anglican parish vestries and Anglican-dominated municipal corporations had been left untouched by the Union and Catholic Emancipation. O'Connell's movement had grown up under their rotten carapace, as 'a government within a government, a young and robust authority, springing up within the breast of an authority aged, feeble, and decrepit: a centralised national power which grinds to

---

[90] Beaumont, *Ireland*, 115–16.   [91] Ibid., 15–18.   [92] Ibid., 25–6.   [93] Ibid., 127.
[94] Ibid., 26–7.   [95] Ibid., 97–104.   [96] Beaumont, *L'Irlande*, I:20.

powder all the scattered and petty power of an antinational aristocracy'.[97] His political party constituted an entire sovereign people within itself: an Irish analogue to the rule of all by all described in Rousseau's *Social Contract* (1761) and developed within Tocqueville's description of US-American popular sovereignty as the means through which 'society acts by itself and on itself'.[98] O'Connell was not a demagogue, but a sort of informal representative of the Irish popular sovereign; the means through which the Association allowed itself to be organised as if

> by one central power emanating from the universal will, expressed or understood; collecting within itself all the national elements; omnipotent by popular assent; absolute in every one of its actions, though constantly subjected to the control of all; levelling all above it, summoning to its bar all the aristocratic powers of the nation; thus accustoming the people to social and political equality; a power fluctuating and varying, though perpetual, incessantly changing its name, form, and agents, though always the same; that is to say, a democracy organised in a country supposed to be governed by aristocratic institutions.[99]

Beaumont's characterisation of Ireland's emergent democracy was far more ambivalent than that of his French contemporaries Felicité de Lamennais and Charles de Montalembert, or the strongly partisan readings of Irish Catholic politics advanced in the Rhineland or Bavaria. This attitude matched the pair's broader concern with democratic excess: Tocqueville had intended his work on America as a form of political education for the French partisans of both aristocracy and equality. He sought to move beyond an 'intellectual world ... divided between democracy's blind friends and its enraged detractors' and to 'teach democracy to know itself and thus to guide itself and restrain itself'.[100]

Beaumont's *Irlande* suggested that the labour of educating Ireland's democracy had scarcely begun. O'Connell's movement was dominated by the twin forces of the Catholic middle class and the popular Catholic priesthood. Beaumont approved of both, and of the strong disciplinary element within contemporary liberal Catholic politics, exemplified by the rising temperance movement.[101] Yet the process of education was far from complete. The small size and political inexperience of Ireland's middle class meant that de Beaumont doubted its capacity to manage the institutions of the state or to restrain itself from ruling tyrannically over the

---

[97] Beaumont, *Ireland*, 221–2.   [98] Tocqueville, *Democracy in America*, 55.
[99] Beaumont, *Ireland*, 223.   [100] Quoted in Jaume, *Tocqueville*, 336.
[101] Beaumont, *Ireland*, 222.

Protestant minority. Only a generation removed from the abuses of the Penal Laws, Ireland's Catholic merchants, lawyers and farmers had

> a remnant of the vices of the slave, who always desires to act the tyrant when he becomes free ... before it can govern well, [Irish democracy] must learn the science of government. It is in this respect that the labour of the national association are still of such immense importance: it is a school for government where instruction is every day afforded to the class that is destined to govern.[102]

At this point, *Irlande* revealed its underlying stakes: as a critical, but friendly, counsel to Ireland's British rulers. Unlike Lamennais and Montalembert, Tocqueville and de Beaumont had closer contacts with London politicians and intellectuals than they did with leading figures in O'Connell's movement.[103] Admiration – alongside envy and occasional irritation – characterised the pair's attitude to Europe's commercial and imperial hegemon. Both men bemoaned France's apparent inability to develop a successful settler empire on the British model and took an active part in campaigning for the French conquest of Algeria.[104] Like many in the France of the July Monarchy, they sought collaboration with Britain in a global project of informal empire: yet they also sought parity of status for France in imperial and foreign affairs.[105]

Beaumont's writing about Ireland was characteristic of this conflict between collaboration and rivalry. He advised British politicians that the task of imperial administration was to educate Irish democracy so as to reconcile it to British government. This required a dramatic process of institutional transformation, extirpating the corrupt Anglo-Irish aristocracy on the very model of the French Revolution itself. In Ireland's exceptional circumstances, a levelling, potentially despotic form of centralisation – which Tocqueville and Beaumont deplored in other contexts – was a lesser evil than permitting the continuing survival of Ascendancy.[106] A tutelary despotism, involving the abolition of all institutions of local government and the removal of the Dublin Castle administrative machine to London, was a necessary stage in Irish political development. In 'overturning an aristocracy', Beaumont claimed, it was necessary to 'concentrate

---

[102] Ibid., 251.
[103] Alexis de Tocqueville, *Journeys to England and Ireland*, trans. S. Drescher (New Haven, CO: Yale University Press, 1958), 193–6.
[104] Jennifer Pitts (ed.), *Alexis de Tocqueville: Writings on Empire and Slavery* (Baltimore, VA: Johns Hopkins University Press, 2001); Gustave de Beaumont, *État de la question d'Afrique* (Paris: Paulin, 1843).
[105] Todd, 'Transnational Projects'.   [106] Beaumont, *Ireland*, 305.

the entire public force in a single point, from which one can assault all the condemned summits and rebel superiorities'.[107]

Beaumont defined the task of this tutelary despotism with reference to the parallel histories of the English and French Revolutions. While England had restored its aristocracy alongside its monarchy after 1660, France had introduced fundamental changes to its 'civil laws', above all in those governing the inheritance of land. Faithfully absorbing the authoritative account of British political economy provided by McCulloch, de Beaumont argued that, in Britain, the great estates maintained by primogeniture and entails acted as incentive to prosperous manufacturers: they amassed great capitals and then purchased (or married) into landed property and public office. The mass of the population, meanwhile, participated in a sort of 'cult' of the soil, treating the great estates of the ancient nobility as *biens nationaux*.[108] The British nobility were capable of absorbing new money, but nonetheless rested their power on a firm foundation of entailed property.[109] France, by contrast, had become 'democratic' through the creation of widely dispersed property. Contrary to the dire prognostications of 'English economists' who 'frequently quote the example of poor Ireland, to prove the great injury of the extreme division of land in France', the further division of properties was now halting as the population stabilised.[110]

Beaumont's programme of institutional reform was thus wedded to what Droz had described as the French 'system' of agrarian economy. It pointed to the failure of Britain's aristocratic and industrial model to effect the transformation of Ireland's economic fortunes. In Ireland, the 'feudal principle' operated without the counteracting influence of industry, producing the 'perpetual growth' of luxury among the Protestant caste and 'progressive ruin' for the majority of the population.[111] Until it was forced on them by the British government under the Irish Poor Law of 1838, the Irish nobility had never even developed a system of public charity. 'On the day when the conquerors became, as Protestants, the religious enemies of the Catholics', de Beaumont wrote, 'it may be said that the sources of charity dried up in Ireland'.[112]

---

[107] Ibid., 302–3.   [108] Beaumont, *L'Irlande*, II:205–6.   [109] Beaumont, *Ireland*, 130.
[110] Ibid., 308, referring to Léon Faucher, *État et tendance de la propriété en France* (Paris: H. Fournier, 1836).
[111] Beaumont, *Ireland*, 127.   [112] Ibid., 171.

Tocqueville and Beaumont's account of a contrasting, 'democratic' political economy was heavily indebted to Jean-Baptiste Say's *Cours complêt d'économie politique* (1828–9), which the pair had heard delivered as lectures in Paris.[113] The two men followed both Say and Sismondi in arguing that poor relief was an inferior substitute for the redistribution of land and industrial capital.[114] Property ownership, whether in smallholdings, shares of industrial profits or the establishment of savings accounts, would encourage a spirit of responsibility, foresight and planning among the poor. Only in this way could the '*prévoyance*' demanded of the working classes by the 'principle of population' be ensured.[115]

Simply attempting to recreate the British economic system in Ireland, via public works programmes, emigration and estate clearances, was therefore a dead end.[116] Peasant proprietorship offered a different model of productivity and was the key to modern patriotism and the cohesion of democratic societies. 'In vain would economists prove to me that by the division of land less produce is obtained from the ground at greater expense', he declared. 'I would reply, that I know no means of covering the surface of the country with inhabitants more prosperous, more independent, more attached to their native land, and more interested in its defence.'[117]

The challenge for Irish democracy was to manage the transition to a democratic property order in a fashion that preserved concord between the rich and the poor. 'There is a bad democracy, it is that which is hostile to the fortunes created by industry', observed Beaumont, 'but there exists also a good democracy, it is that which combats the fortunes maintained by privilege alone'.[118] The French author referenced the writings of Sismondi and von Raumer in his formulation of a solution for the crisis of the Irish polity, but resiled from the implications of an overnight transformation of cottiers into freeholders. Ireland, he warned, had already witnessed more than enough violent and arbitrary transfers of landed property. To legitimise expropriation via an Act of Parliament was a recipe for civil war.

---

[113] Michael Drolet, 'Democracy and Political Economy: Tocqueville's Thoughts on J.-B. Say and T. R. Malthus', *History of European Ideas*, 29 (2003), 159–81.

[114] Richard Whatmore, *Republicanism and the French Revolution: An Intellectual History of Jean-Baptiste Say's Political Economy* (Oxford: Oxford University Press, 2000), 206.

[115] Alexis de Tocqueville, 'Second Mémoire sur le paupérisme', in F. Mélonio (ed.), *Alexis de Toqueville Oeuvres Complètes Tome XVI: Mélanges* (Paris: Gallimard, 1989), 140–59.

[116] Beaumont, *Ireland*, 263–89.   [117] Ibid., 309.   [118] Ibid., 307.

It would be better, Beaumont argued, to reach the goal of peasant proprietorship through a reform to inheritance law alone. The heavily indebted Anglo-Irish aristocracy would welcome release from entails that restricted their ability to take out fresh loans against their estates. Introducing legislation to mandate partitive inheritance in the case of intestate estates would produce a revolution in manners by undermining the assumption that eldest sons would automatically inherit. A short-term injection of land, meanwhile, would be produced by the enforced sale of the property of the Church of Ireland in small parcels. It was by developing an open market for Irish land, rather than simply transferring it to proprietors, that a free peasantry could be gradually and peacefully placed on the soil.[119]

Even as Beaumont portrayed British imperial tutelage as the handmaiden of Irish democracy, his analysis questioned the capacity of the British political system to deliver the necessary, French-inspired programme of reform. None of the English parties, Beaumont asserted, was sufficiently equipped with 'general ideas' of 'rational equality' to understand the nature of democracy in Ireland.[120] The governing Whig party were cautiously favourable to the democratic principle in 'political society' and showed a limited desire to implement what Beaumont called *demi-centralisation* in the cause of social reform, appointing Poor Law Commissioners with a direct line of responsibility to parliament.[121] But they saw no possible connection between these predilections and the reform of English land law. The English Whigs seemed to think 'that property will remain the monopoly of a small group, even after political rights have become the share of all'.[122]

Governed by the passions, habits and convention, British politics lacked the self-conscious reforming impulse that had brought France into the age of democracy. This set up a dangerous dynamic that threatened the peace of the Union. Ireland's population, fully one-half that of England and radicalised by Daniel O'Connell's powerful Repeal Association, was reviving the democratic movement in England, which had once been inspired by revolutionary France but was repressed by Pitt and Liverpool. The Whigs would become trapped in a pattern of bitter Irish agitation and concession, which could ultimately trigger a violent reaction in favour of Church and King.[123] This would be supported by the bulk of the English

---

[119] Ibid., 311–12.   [120] Ibid., 341–55.   [121] Ibid., 348–53.   [122] Ibid., 248–9.
[123] Ibid., 372–3.

population, which already supported the Conservative Party by large majorities. The Whigs, he noted, were currently kept in office by Irish and Scottish votes. 'Will not the singular desire that England feels to stop short in the road on which she is hurried onward by Ireland', he speculated, 'produce in the long-run some extreme resolution in the English people'?[124]

If the retention of Ireland in the Union threatened the destabilisation of England's peculiar social and political system, could its repeal be contemplated? Here, Beaumont was equally pessimistic. The British system of aristocracy and industry, he claimed, rested on perpetual military, as well as economic, expansion. For centuries, the English aristocracy had resisted bourgeois encroachment because

> in order to procure for that society a magnificent destiny, they opened for it the markets of the entire world, established for it flourishing colonies, founded for it colossal empires in India, rendered its vessels sovereign on every sea, and made the nations of the earth its tributaries.[125]

Conquest and empire were even more vital to the survival of English aristocracy given its current, lonely eminence in Europe. 'What is the empire that would consent to its own dismemberment'? Beaumont asked. 'Does not every power, whose territory is diminished, appear to be on the decline?'[126]

Beaumont saw, therefore, no obvious resolution to the three-sided problematic of Irish reform. Radical centralisation and land redistribution were necessary for Ireland's recovery from centuries of war and exploitation, but unacceptable to large sections of British opinion. Separation, even in the form of Repeal, could not resolve these problems; indeed, it was certain to exacerbate them, given Ireland's large population and high visibility in British political debate.[127] The epochal conflict between the principles of aristocratic and democratic government could not be contained within a single polity. 'The great difficulty', he concluded, 'is that the same political rule which is salutary to one people is pernicious to the other; and that one feels it must die of the government which is the very life of the other'.[128] The Union of 1801 had done nothing to alleviate the economic, religious and national grievances that challenged Britain's empire in Ireland. Instead, it had encased irreconcilable differences within a rigid and inescapable constitutional form.

---

[124] Ibid., 373.   [125] Ibid., 134–6.   [126] Ibid., 362.   [127] Ibid., 362–3.   [128] Ibid., 361.

Young Ireland and the Political Economy of 'Nationality'

Beaumont's analysis of the politics of Union at the close of the 1830s had ambivalent implications for his readers in Britain, Ireland and across Europe. *Irlande* saw little potential in either the Irish Catholic movement led by O'Connell, or the Whig policy of 'justice for Ireland', administered through limited doses of social and administrative reform.[129] At the same time, however, it saw repeal of the Union as a demand capable of tearing apart the British Empire and heralding its decline as a major power. As *Irlande* attracted review and comment across Europe, the gathering strength of O'Connell's popular agitation for Repeal contributed to a broader impression of Britain as a polity in crisis.

Writing in 1844, the future Prime Minister of Piedmont and Italy, Camilo di Cavour, complained that French enthusiasm for O'Connell was driven by a widespread belief that a 'day of vengeance' was at hand for Britain's victory in 1814–15. The belief that Union was 'fallible' – that the British Empire was 'mined at its base' – was being inflamed by irresponsible press reports that talked up the potential for an Irish civil war provoked by O'Connell.[130] 'Moderate' liberals like Beaumont and Tocqueville – friends whom Cavour had encountered during his own sojourns in London – admired Britain in theory, but lacked any 'instinctive sympathy' for its politics or institutions.[131] In an increasingly frenzied atmosphere of melodramatic Anglophobia, Cavour warned that the cause of Irish nationality could provide the trigger for a new and terrible war against British hegemony, 'as disastrous for the material interests of peoples as for their intellectual progress'.[132]

Cavour and Beaumont were far from alone in locating the Repeal crisis within a broader context of European flux and uncertainty. Thomas Davis, the leading intellectual within the 'Young Ireland' circle who founded the popular newspaper *The Nation*, argued in an article of 1840 that the moment had arrived for Irish MPs at Westminster to formulate 'a foreign policy for Ireland' and act in concert to inflect British policy in line with Irish preferences. Association with the successful Belgian Revolution of 1830, alongside sympathy with refugees from the failed Polish rising of 1831, had long been a mainstay of O'Connellite rhetoric. What made

---

[129] Gray, *Irish Poor Law*, 27–36.
[130] Camilo di Cavour, 'Considérations sur l'état actuel de l'Irlande et sur son avenir', *Bibliothèque Universelle de Genève*, 29 (1844), 5–47, at 5–6.
[131] Ibid., 7.   [132] Ibid., 9.

Davis' variety of cosmopolitan nationalism distinctive was the consistency with which it employed the French liberal categories of 'aristocracy' and 'democracy', in this instance as a set of guiding principles for Irish action in the imperial parliament. Ireland had a natural affinity, Davis argued, not only with other nations oppressed by imperial rule, but with those European powers, led by France, that had fought for 'national freedom'.[133]

A close reader of Tocqueville, Beaumont, Sismondi and the French liberal historian Augustin Thierry, Davis was the major conduit for the introduction of Francophone historiography and political economy into the mainstream of the Repeal movement. Davis employed his French sources to argue for a more consistent orientation in the Irish national movement. O'Connellism was famously eclectic in its politics, formed from an unlikely blend of popular Catholicism, utilitarianism, and revived patriot constitutionalism.[134] Like Beaumont, Davis saw a need for the 'education' of this rough form of 'democracy', which threatened to descend into demagoguery and violence before it succeeded in mobilising the people of Ireland behind repeal of the Union. Beaumont had proposed that British government exercise a sort of tutelary despotism over the O'Connellite movement, removing the social obstacles that threatened a violent political and sectarian conflagration. Young Ireland, by contrast, hoped that the cultivation of a common culture – literary, linguistic and historiographical – would overcome the alienation of the Irish aristocracy wrought by the distended violence of Ireland's repeated conquests.

For Davis, reckoning with the legacies of conquest in Ireland was one of the central tasks of a mature national historiography. His essay 'Udalism and Feudalism' (1842) developed Beaumont's argument that Ireland could act as a bulwark for democratic property in a British Empire defined by aristocracy and inequality. Yet it invested 'democracy' with 'nationality' at a deeper level than either Tocqueville or Beaumont had done, stating that a system of free peasant proprietorship was not only the product of the 'general ideas' of revolutionary France, but the elemental condition of all human communities that had avoided – or transcended – the ordeal of conquest. Thanks to its waspish criticisms of the agricultural improvers and their 'Anglicising' political economy, Davis' essay has been placed at the centre of modern accounts of Young Ireland's 'romantic' or 'Carlylean'

---

[133] Thomas Davis, 'The Foreign Policy of Ireland', *The Citizen, or Dublin Monthly Magazine*, II (1840), 445–63, at 460–1.
[134] Nowlan & O'Connell, *Portrait of a Radical*.

rejection of utilitarian and 'laissez-faire' political economy.[135] There is a strong case, however, for recognising it as a more constructive argument on behalf of the 'social economy' demanded by Sismondi, and routinely associated by contemporary observers with the smallholding, artisanal 'system' of post-revolutionary France.[136] While Davis' historical sensibilities were certainly formed through a close engagement with the emergent French tradition of 'national' history, embodied by the popular liberal historian Augustin Thierry, considerations of law and economy weighed as heavily as any transcendent attachment to a continuously existing Irish nation. In an 1843 commentary produced for *The Nation*, Davis would complain that Thierry had essentialised national difference in a manner that obscured the significance of 'legal and personal incidents' and thereby made it impossible to believe that mixed, post-conquest society like that of Ireland could ever develop a cohesive political consciousness or agency. True 'nationality', Davis wrote – in a thinly veiled rebuke of Daniel O'Connell's polemical *Memoir on Ireland, Native and Saxon* (1843) – was motivated by more than the unthinking 'wrath' produced by centuries of difference and oppression.[137]

'Udalism and Feudalism' explored the legal and economic conditions under which nationality could be developed and protected in the conditions of commercial, industrial Europe. It developed a distinction between integrated, homogenous human communities, in which property was held by those who worked the land; and divided, post-conquest societies, riven by distinctions that were the product of arbitrary violence and subsequently corrupted by luxury and inequality. This, in its way, was a quintessentially Enlightened narrative, one that further developed Sismondi's filtration and recombination of Smith and Rousseau. Via Sismondi, Davis recast Smith's 'natural progress of opulence' as the 'natural history of landed property'. The Irish author employed 'Udalism' as an *Urtyp* for a broad range of property regimes, ancient and modern, European and Asian. For Davis, Udalism embodied 'the law of

---

[135] David Dwan, 'Young Ireland and the Horde of Benthamy', in R. Swift and C. Kinealy (eds.), *Politics and Power in Victorian Ireland* (Dublin: Four Courts Press, 2006), 109–18; John Morrow, 'Thomas Carlyle, Young Ireland, and the "Condition of Ireland" Question', *The Historical Journal*, 51 (2008), 643–67.

[136] Thomas Davis, 'Norway and Ireland, No. 1: Udalism and Feudalism', *Dublin Monthly Magazine*, 1 (1842), 218–38, at 222, 26.

[137] Thomas Davis, 'Continental Literature – Augustine Thierry, No. 1', *The Nation*, 26 November 1842, 107. Attribution via Kevin MacGrath, 'Writers in the "Nation", 1842–5', *Irish Historical Studies*, 6(21) (1949), 189–223, at 200.

human nature . . . the universal law of mankind'.[138] It formed the basis for a political economy that was capable of preserving national cultural and literary distinction, resisting the effects of 'Anglicisation' and free trade in Ireland. Irish nationality was associated not with the historical and particular, but the rational and universal. The preservation of national difference demanded the assertion of principles of social organisation that were common to all healthy human communities, and destined to triumph over the temporary, British peculiarities of 'landlordism' and the 'factory system'.[139]

'Udalism' denoted a system of landed proprietorship created by the peaceful, customary modification of an original principle of communal or 'clan' ownership. In the earliest human civilisations, a combination of lifetime leases and periodic redistribution enabled a primitive form of landholding that combined incentives to regular production with the taming of inequality. The subsequent introduction of rights of inheritance had been a simple modification of this underlying system of managed, communal property. It had eliminated the direct interposition of the 'clan' in the process of redistribution without harming the principle that property 'still remained, and *ever does remain*, subject to the will and wants of the tribe or nation'.[140] The generational redistribution of property, instead of resting on positive political decision, was now rendered automatic by the law of 'gavelkind', or partitive inheritance.

The myriad societies – from ancient Athens and Persia to latter-day Norway, Afghanistan, France and Switzerland – who instituted systems of property on this basic model came up with contrasting answers to questions such as the alienability of family shares, the inheritance rights of women or the claims of family members who were not the children of the deceased. Yet the principle that 'land, where parted with by the tribe, was given as a strict inheritance of the support of a family in *all* generations, not the enjoyment of *one*', remained consistent. 'Gavelkind' was the 'national rule of inheritance', employed by all clans and tribes that had succeeded in preserving their elemental unity and social peace.[141]

'Feudalism', by contrast, denoted a system in which the chiefs among conquering peoples had taken advantage of the exceptional circumstances created by war to arrogate vast holdings to themselves. They had then consolidated their position through the ill-founded and contingent legal instruments of primogeniture and entail: 'in conquests, as in other great

---

[138] Thomas Davis, 'Norway and Ireland, No. 2', *Dublin Monthly Magazine*, 1 (1842), 314.
[139] Davis, 'Norway and Ireland, No. 1', 223, 31.   [140] Ibid., 219.   [141] Ibid., 220–1.

bursts of mind, the law of present impulse is the prevailing law'.[142] These replaced the gentle oscillations of industry and redistribution under 'udal' regimes with a rigid and intractable inequality that placed the majority in a condition of slavery. Crucially, and in contrast to Thierry, Davis did not reduce feudal law to the rule of one race over another. Instead, it represented a usurpation *within* conquering nations, or the creation of new inequalities through fresh waves of conquest. The Norman conquest of England provided the paradigmatic instance of the latter phenomenon. It was the 'struggles of the Saxons and Danes with these Normans', not the first wave of post-Roman invasions, that had resulted in the 'confiscation of the greater part of England'.[143]

Davis' account of the downfall of English feudalism echoed that offered by Sismondi and Carlyle.[144] England, in common with France and Germany, had seen a gradual amelioration in conditions as the 'socman grew into a freeholder, the villein into a copyholder'. This 'modified feudality' was a 'noble state', capable of supporting successful wars against France, Scotland and Spain; yet it had been fatally undermined by the turn away from militia troops to finance and mercenaries and the corruption of luxury and 'gold-worship'. Far from the liberation of serf labour, the commercialisation of agriculture – what Davis called 'landlordism' – had been a process of re-enslavement and depopulation. The agricultural population was now artificially depressed, and the urban engorged, through the conversion of farms into 'huge manufactories of grain and capital, for the benefit of the landlord'.[145]

The long wars for control of Ireland had been waged not merely between Catholic and Protestant, but between the rival legal orders of Udalism and feudalism. The first invasion of the twelfth century had occurred at the height of the Anglo-Norman feudal regime; while the 'extension of the modern English laws' – first beyond the Pale in the wars of the sixteenth and seventeenth centuries, and then to Catholics through the abolition of the Penal Laws – had coincided with the English turn to 'landlordism'. Quoting Sismondi's essays of 1835, Davis concluded that the 'social order' produced by this imposition of English landlordism on Ireland was 'essentially bad, and must be changed from top to bottom'.[146] Like Sismondi and Beaumont, Davis argued that any attempt to address

---

[142] Ibid., 221.   [143] Ibid., 222.
[144] On Carlyle's debt to Sismondi, see John Morrow, *Thomas Carlyle* (London: Hambledon Continuum, 2006), 84–6.
[145] Davis, 'Norway and Ireland, No. 1', 223–4.   [146] Ibid., 226.

Irish poverty that did not touch on the 'master-grievance' of an alienated aristocracy was doomed to failure. Clearing estates and consolidating farms could only be achieved by means of emigration or extermination. 'How do you establish large farms'? asked Davis mockingly. 'Emigrate, say the quacks. Exterminate, say the squires. To the latter our reply is short: *try it.*' The best that English, Tory opponents of the doctrines of the *Edinburgh Review* could offer was 'pious feudalism': an appeal to noble paternalism and charity that would never develop in a divided, post-conquest society. 'How can that thorough sympathy arise, without which a good aristocracy is impossible?'[147]

The French Revolution offered a vastly superior model for reform, one that addressed the needs of the poor through a reassertion of the immutable laws of national property. It had been a paradoxical feat of destruction and restoration, returning landed property to its original, udal condition even as it swept away centuries of precedent and privilege:

> France ... retained the worst ills of feudalism till the revolution came, with its tremendous legislation, to repeal the deeds of all the conquerors of France, Keltic, Roman, and Teutonic; came with torch and sword, to enlighten and destroy, to smite and save; came with confiscation to the noble, and udalism to the peasant. Strange unconscious antiquarians were Mirabeau and Danton, who treated primogeniture and landlordism as vulgar novelties, and restored the land to the people.[148]

Britain, meanwhile, was hastening towards the final collapse predicted by Sismondi. The strength of the campaign for repeal of the Corn Laws demonstrated the weakness of England's aristocracy, which was no longer capable of resisting challenges to their interests within the polity. Yet England's middle-class radicals were fundamentally mistaken in their attachment to free trade and industrial expansion. While cheaper food and lower wages would 'enable England to force her goods farther than ever', this would constitute the 'last reserve' of an overextended, artificial social system: 'the people will fall back on the land, their native property and ultimate resource'.[149]

In a rebuke to the O'Connellite campaign for native manufactures, Davis cautioned that Ireland's response to British industrial hegemony could not be founded on a simple attempt to develop its own 'manufacturing system' on the basis of a system of protective tariffs.[150] He admired the

---

[147] Ibid.   [148] Ibid., 223.   [149] Ibid., 227.
[150] Paul Pickering, '"Irish First": Daniel O'Connell, the Native Manufacture Campaign, and Economic Nationalism, 1840–4', *Albion*, 32 (2000), 598–616.

German customs union (*Zollverein*) as an initiative founded in 'national government'. But an Irish drive for manufacturing growth was hardly conducive to 'the equal distribution of comfort, education, and happiness ... the only true wealth of nations'.[151] Rather than the rigid and degrading division of labour imposed by the industrial exports, Davis demanded that Irish nationalists understand 'Home manufactures' as 'manufactures made at home':

> That frieze, spun in the farm house, of winter nights, and wove by the country weaver ... is precious in our eyes. This cloth from the mill tells of man and woman, and tender child, all day long, from year's end to year's end, in a factory room, with nothing to ennoble, purify, or comfort them, and liable by the slightest change in the most changeable of things, trade, to unsolved pauperism.[152]

The sentimentality of Davis' imagery obscured the seriousness of his argument: grounded, as he explained, in the ample evidence that other European societies – France, Switzerland, Norway, Belgium – were capable of combining smallholding agriculture and domestic manufacturing with high levels of productivity. Davis quoted approvingly from the radical journalist Samuel Laing's *Journal of a Residence in Norway* (1836): 'the happy condition and wellbeing of a people seem to depend ... on the wide distribution of employment over the face of a country, by small but numerous masses of capital'.[153] A rejection of the merciless logic of 'chrematistics' did not imply a rejection of political economy understood in its older, eighteenth-century meaning: a systematic investigation of the economic foundations for political life.

James Fintan Lalor and John Stuart Mill on Famine and Revolution

Davis wrote his universal history of property in expectation of something like an Irish revolution – albeit a bloodless one. Popular unity and resolve, under the careful management of an aristocracy educated in the work of 'nationality', was the avowed project of Young Ireland and the *Nation* newspaper. An Irish political economy founded on the principle of 'udal' property was, Davis claimed, the compliment, not the alternative, to repeal of the Union: a merely 'political change' that would be a 'good means to

---

[151] Davis, 'Norway and Ireland, No. 1', 230.   [152] Ibid., 231.
[153] Thomas Davis, 'Norway and Ireland, No. 2', 30; Samuel Laing, *Journal of a Residence in Norway, during the Years 1834, 1835, and 1836: Made with a View to Enquire into the Moral and Political Economy of that Country, and the Condition of Its Inhabitants* (London: Longman, 1836), 299.

that social end'.[154] The Young Ireland collective took up the campaign in the pages of the *Nation* newspaper, urging the broader Repeal movement to make the land question a central plank of its agitation. 'We say revolutionise by law, for this was done in France successfully, and in Prussia successfully', it demanded in 1843.[155]

Yet what Ireland experienced in the 1840s was not revolution or even Repeal, but famine on an unimaginable scale. Writing for *The Nation* in 1847, James Fintan Lalor, Young Ireland's most ardent and unorthodox advocate for a new popular agitation behind the land question, drew a bitter parallel between famine and revolution as constitutive moments in the histories of Ireland and France:

> The failure of the potato, and consequent famine, is one of those events which come now and then to do the work of ages in a day, and change the very nature of an entire nation at once. It has even already produced a deeper social disorganisation than did the French revolution: greater waste of life, wider loss of property, more of the horrors, with none of the hopes. For its direction still seems dragging downwards, while her revolution took France to the sun – gave her wealth, and victory, and renown – a free people and a firm peasantry, lords of their own land.[156]

The blight that struck the potatoes consumed by the bulk of Ireland's cottier peasantry pitilessly exposed the vulnerability of the system of agrarian economy that had once been championed by Irish landlords and British parliamentarians alike. Famine dramatically intensified British and Irish debates over land reform; not only – or even primarily – because of the visible effects of mass starvation, but because the escalating costs of famine relief and the bankruptcy of many Irish landlords seemed to render a radical solution to Irish poverty unavoidable.[157]

A fringe figure in Young Ireland circles until the desperate later years of the 1840s, Lalor had disdained the O'Connellite tactic of organising the Irish masses to petition the British parliament in the pursuit of their rights. Davis, too, had operated within this paradigm, differing only with the O'Connellite leadership on the question of how far it was necessary to make the land question a second focus of the Repeal campaign. Lalor, by contrast, had always maintained that Irish proprietors, rather than the

[154] Davis, 'Norway and Ireland, No. 2: Udalism and Feudalism', 315.
[155] 'The Land Question', *The Nation*, 23 December 1843, 168.
[156] James Fintan Lalor, 'A New Nation: Proposal for an Agricultural Association between the Landowners and Occupiers (April 19, 1847)', in L. Fogarty (ed.), *James Fintan Lalor: Patriot & Political Essayist (1807–1849)* (Dublin: The Talbot Press, 1919), 7–26, at 8–9.
[157] Gray, *Famine, Land and Politics*, 3.

British Crown, should take the lead in the reformation of Ireland's property order. Now, famine had rendered the familiar parade of Irish demand and British concession still more irrelevant. It had already effected the total collapse of the laws of 'landlord property'. After the downfall of Ireland's 'social constitution', 'a clear original right returns and reverts to the people: the right of establishing, and entering into a new social arrangement'.[158] As such, Lalor's comparison between Ireland's famine and the French Revolution was more than rhetorical. The potato blight had created a constitutive moment, in which the Irish nation was called upon to convene itself and to reimagine its laws of landed property.

In a series of public and private letters to the *Nation* and its editors, Lalor argued that Ireland's 'social constitution' could now be refounded on the principle of national property in land. His proposal involved a series of subtle modifications to Davis' conception of 'Udalism', accentuating the subversive potential of Davis' argument while offering the Anglo-Irish aristocracy an escape route from the dangers of expropriation. In a flourish typical of Young Ireland's inventive conflations of Irish antiquarianism and French revolutionary precedent, Lalor invoked the process of 'surrender and regrant' instituted by the Tudor conquerors of Ireland. Existing landholders would voluntarily swear an oath of fealty to the nation that recognised its people's ultimate, 'allodial' property in the entire national territory. They would then be regranted the holdings they had hitherto possessed, as vassals of the nation he styled 'this island-queen'.[159]

The principle of national property would permit, in turn, a substantial modification to the terms under which Irish farmers enjoyed access to the land: the generalisation of the custom of Ulster 'tenant-right', which enabled holdings to be traded and rents to be co-determined by committees of landlords and tenants.[160] If landlords refused to comply with this national imperative, they rendered themselves vulnerable to rent strikes and expropriation. 'I hold and maintain that the entire soil of a country belongs of right to the people of that country', Lalor wrote, 'and is the rightful property not of any one class, but of the nation at large, in full effective possession, to let to whom they will on whatever tenures, terms, rents, services, and conditions they will'.[161] Davis had presented 'udal' property as a historical fact that had been recreated in revolutionary France by the actions of its National Assembly. Lalor, by contrast, believed in it as

---

[158] Lalor, 'A New Nation', 13–14.
[159] Lalor, 'Letter to James Mitchell', in Fogarty (ed.), *Lalor*, 44.   [160] Lalor, 'Tenant Right'.
[161] Ibid., 61.

a present Irish reality, one that had long been obscured by 'the laws of landlord property', but which was now revealed by the catastrophe of the famine.

Lalor's demand that the landlords and tenants of Ireland associate to regenerate its 'social constitution' reflected a growing fear within the Irish national movement that the British parliament was about to impose its own solutions on the crisis of Irish property. In Westminster, the dominant proposals for a post-famine land settlement envisaged a renewed process of internal colonisation. British proponents of schemes for the settlement of 'waste land' and for the auctioning of indebted Irish estates to new, British owners, sought to use the opportunity offered by famine to re-fashion Ireland's property order.[162] The moment for the 'intervention of the legislator', demanded by Hegel, Sismondi, von Raumer and de Beaumont, seemed finally to have arrived.

In a series of leader articles written for *The Morning Chronicle* in the winter of 1846–7, the liberal philosopher and political economist John Stuart Mill made the case for a limited adoption of the principles of land reform advocated by Thomas Davis and *The Nation*, as well as by continental authorities on the Irish rural economy. Mill sought, however, to detach the economic case for peasant proprietorship from the revolutionary demand for the abolition of established property rights that Sismondi, Hegel, von Raumer and de Beaumont had all regarded as essential to any reform of Irish land. Forcing Irish landlords to effectively gift large portions of their holdings to their tenants, Mill warned, would amount to 'a social revolution', one requiring the suspension of 'the fixed habits of thought, and artificial feelings stronger than nature itself' that predisposed an 'English legislature' to respect the rights of property.[163] Thankfully, however, the physical geography of Ireland supplied a ready-made solution to the problem of revolution in the form of the same tracts of 'waste land' – bogs, marshes and mountains – that had entranced the Bog Commissioners of the 1810s.

Mill claimed that marshland in Ireland had already been spontaneously settled and drained by cottiers seeking to escape the rack-rents levied by their landlords. Contrary to the dominant English impression of the Irish as lazy and improvident, he asserted, these 'squatters' were willing to 'make

---

[162] Gray, *Famine, Land and Politics*, 153–212.
[163] John Stuart Mill, '311. The Condition of Ireland [5], *The Morning Chronicle*, 14 Oct 1846', in A. P. Robson & J. P. Robson (eds.), *Newspaper Writings by John Stuart Mill, Part III, January 1835–June 1847*, Collected Works of John Stuart Mill (Toronto: University of Toronto Press, 1986), 895–8, at 897.

the land worth taking, before the landlord steps in and takes it'.[164] Parliament could legislate to compel the sale of unimproved land at its (low) real value and offer it to Irish subtenants who showed proof of their willingness and ability to make it their own. The Exchequer could demand a low quit rent so as to recoup its initial investment in the land. In many cases, Mill claimed, 'labour' alone would be sufficient to the task of improving the territory thus gained for cultivation; where extensive capital was required to drain large areas of marshland, the state, rather than Irish landlords, would undertake the work directly.[165]

It was not necessary, Mill argued, for every cottier to be made a proprietor for the benefits of peasant proprietorship to spread throughout the country.[166] Indeed, the reclamation of 'waste land' could instead function as a vital complement to the rationalisation of holdings on the majority of Ireland's existing estates. 'Waste land' supplied the safety valve that had been missing from earlier British analyses of the need to relieve Irish territory of its surplus labouring population. 'English capital and English farming might *then* be introduced with advantage to all', Mill claimed, 'because the cottier population would no longer exceed the numbers who could, with benefit to the farmer, be retained on the land as labourers'.[167]

The colonisation of waste lands, Mill argued, was a superior alternative to the policy of 'extensive emigration' counselled by a generation of commentators on the Irish land problem. 'Why offer them [the Irish cottiers] landed property at the other side of the globe, when there is landed property vacant at their very door'? he asked. Enabling 'systematic emigration' was certainly a task for 'the state': it constituted 'a branch of the general arrangements for maintaining a good economical condition'. Yet it was

> a serious question whether, in laying the foundation of new nations beyond the sea, it be right that the Irish branch of the human family should be the predominant ingredient [. . .] Ireland must be an altered country at home before we can wish to create an Ireland in every quarter of the globe, and it is not well to select as missionaries of civilisation a people who, in so great a degree, yet remain to be civilised.[168]

---

[164] John Stuart Mill, '312. The Condition of Ireland [6], *The Morning Chronicle*, 15 Oct 1846', in *Newspaper Writings*, 898–901, at 899.
[165] Ibid., 900.   [166] Mill, 'Condition of Ireland [5]', 898.
[167] Mill, 'Condition of Ireland [6]', 901.   [168] Mill, 'Condition of Ireland [11]', 915.

The task of imperial reform, Mill urged, was not simply to turn the Irish into 'hired labourers' on 'Scotch or English' farms in Britain's expanding settler empire. It should seek instead to 'regenerate their character', using the institution of peasant proprietorship to 'to make their slack labour vigorous, to convert their listlessness into activity, their careless self-indulgence into forethought and prudence'. Malthus had described an Irish laziness that was the product of the political depression of the Penal Laws. For Mill, however, a disinclination to 'labour for hire from infancy to old age' was a part of the 'national character' of all peoples bar the English, where 'work itself might almost seem to be the motive' for industrious labour. Instead of seeking to 'make them Englishmen', British policy had to be inclined towards inducing the Irish to work on their own terms. 'To make them work, they must have what makes their Celtic brethren, the French peasantry, work', Mill concluded. 'They must work, not for employers, but for themselves. Their labour must not be for wages only, it must be a labour of love – the love which the peasant feels for the spot of land from which no man's pleasure can expel him.'[169] Only the tutelary power of British government, suitably informed by an accurate understanding of the political economy of post-revolutionary France, would be capable of educating the Irish peasantry to a level that would fit them to join their 'Saxon' brethren in the settlement of the distant wastes of 'Upper Canada or New Zealand'.[170]

The Young Ireland radicals who split from the Repeal Association in 1846 enthusiastically welcomed the French Revolution of 1848, speculating that the Second French Republic, which had listed Ireland among the 'struggling nationalities' of Europe, might follow its illustrious predecessor in sending military aid for the foundation of an Irish Republic.[171] Mill's admiring application of the French model of peasant proprietorship to the challenges of Irish government, however, suggests that a different 'French affinity' was equally relevant to the shifting patterns of imperial thought in the crisis decade of the 1840s.[172] Mill's developing theory of nationality and civilisation mapped a plural appreciation for the varied characters of nations onto a hierarchical, stadial account of overall human development.[173] As his writings on famine in Ireland show, by the later 1840s

---

[169] Ibid., 916.   [170] Ibid., 914–15.

[171] Petler, D. N., 'Ireland and France in 1848', *Irish Historical Studies*, 24 (1985), 493–505.

[172] Matthew Kelly, 'Languages of Radicalism, Race and Religion in Irish Nationalism: The French Affinity, 1848–1871', *Journal of British Studies*, 49 (2010), 801–25.

[173] Georgios Varouxakis, 'National Character in John Stuart Mill's Thought', *History of European Ideas*, 24 (1998), 375–91.

he had come to the view that the civilisation of Ireland required that Britain adopt and modify the institutions of France, a peer nation to Britain that had followed its own path towards the summits of human achievement. The internal colonisation of Ireland's waste land supplied, for Mill, a miraculous exit from the dilemma posed by Gustave de Beaumont, whom he had met during the latter's tours in England and Ireland.[174] It was the reclamation of waste land, rather than the exercise of British sovereignty to overturn the remnants of Protestant Ascendancy, that would enable Ireland's burning need for peasant property to be reconciled with Britain's counter-revolutionary prejudice in favour of great estates and primogeniture. Inter-imperial emulation and exchange, as much as nationalist solidarity with the oppressed peoples of Europe, continued to structure the three-sided relationship between Britain, Ireland, and France, and to frame the politics of reform.

The Legacies of Revolution

The catastrophic famines of the 1840s destroyed the Irish agrarian system that had rendered it such a potent source for European discussions of the possible trajectories of Britain's empire of commerce in the early nineteenth century. Despite the popularity of *The Nation* and other, more radical papers like the *Irish Felon*, there would be no Irish revolution to match those of the European continent in 1848. The 'confederate' rising organised by the Young Irelanders in July 1848 was a source of fleeting concern for the Irish administration, but it would ultimately be put down using the ordinary tools of the Irish Constabulary and the suspension of *habeas corpus*.[175]

In the political struggle to shape the future of Ireland's devastated rural society, the case for peasant proprietorship was ultimately suborned to a renewed emphasis on the Anglicisation of Irish agriculture. The Encumbered Estates Acts of 1848 and 1849, and the new Encumbered Estates Court established to settle the debts and sell off the lands of bankrupt Irish proprietors, sought yet again to render the promise of Union, the diffusion of British capital into Irish agriculture, a reality.[176] For the key advocate of the court, Sir Robert Peel, famine had created an opportunity for an alliance of British and Irish mercantile capital to re-

---

[174] Hugh Brogan, *Alexis de Tocqueville: A Biography* (London: Profile, 2006), 303–8.
[175] Christine Kinealy, *Repeal and Revolution: 1848 in Ireland* (Manchester: Manchester University Press, 2009).
[176] Pádraig Lane, 'The Encumbered Estates Court, Ireland, 1848–1849', *The Economic and Social Review*, 3 (1972), 413–53.

enact – on peaceful and tolerant terms – the civilising mission of the Jacobean plantation of Ulster amidst the devastation of post-famine Connacht. 'The west of Ireland affords opportunities for improvement which no other part of the world appears to give', the former Prime Minister declared to the House of Commons in March 1849. Like the Irish Patriots of the 1780s, Peel was enthralled by Ireland's potential to act as a gateway to North America. 'I see a great world growing up on the other side of the Atlantic', he rhapsodised. 'I see the facilities of communication by railways and by steam.'[177]

The greatest beneficiaries of the scheme, however, ultimately proved to be the more solvent among Ireland's existing landholders, who availed themselves of the opportunities offered to clear their existing debts and buy up cheap holdings from their distressed peers.[178] Death and emigration advanced the work of 'clearing' Irish estates, far beyond the earlier hopes of Malthus, McCulloch and Senior. Farms which had once been occupied by conacre plots were converted back to the grassland that had dominated the rural economy of Ireland for much the eighteenth century. A new alliance of landlords and graziers assumed a leading position in the Irish landed society of the 1850s and 1860s.[179] Despite their defeat in the political struggle to reorder Irish property in the wake of famine, however, British and Irish representatives of the 'French system' of political economy had staked out a series of powerful positions in the ever-evolving debate on what a young Benjamin Disraeli had recently christened 'the Irish question'.[180]

Discussions of the problems of Irish agriculture and population in the 1840s touched on issues in European political economy that had been agitated since the French Revolutionary Wars. The division of landed property through partitive inheritance was understood by French thinkers to be the basis for a society governed by the Third Estate and the principle of democratic equality. It was rejected in Britain by economists who attributed their empire's victory against France to the productivity enabled by large-scale agriculture and the economic incentives created by the consolidation of landed property in the hands of a strong aristocracy. Gustave de Beaumont's crucial insight was that this British political economy could not be successfully imposed onto Ireland's radically differing historical circumstances. In the hands of Thomas Davis,

---

[177] Hansard, HC, vol. 103, col. 192, 5 March 1849.
[178] Peter Gray, 'Famine and Land, 1845–80', in A. Jackson (ed.), *Oxford Handbook of Modern Irish History* (Oxford: Oxford University Press, 2013), 545–58, at 554–5.
[179] Whelan, 'The Modern Landscape', 97–9.
[180] Hansard, HC, vol. 72, col. 1016–17, 16 February 1844.

James Fintan Lalor and John Stuart Mill, this argument became the backbone of a new and more radical conception of landed property that was capable of serving an Irish 'nation'. This centred on the alternative model of commercial society represented by the smallholding agriculture and artisanal manufacturing of the European continent. As such, the central concerns of nineteenth-century Irish politics – property, the nation and the manner in which both were entwined and reproduced through law and custom – must be counted among the complex legacies of the French Revolution's transformation of European political economy.

Conclusion
Ireland between Empires

Reviewing the situation of Ireland a generation after the famine, John Stuart Mill made a striking observation about its history since the close of the eighteenth century. Ireland would have been better governed, he speculated, if the United Irishmen had in fact succeeded in separating Ireland from Britain in 1796–8. French invasion had offered the only real prospect for Irish reform: a redistribution of landed property out of the hands of the Anglo-Irish Ascendancy.

> At that moment it was on the cards whether Ireland should not belong to France, or at least be organised as an independent country under French protection. Had this happened, does any one believe that the Irish peasant would not have become even as the French peasant? When the great landowners had fled, as they would have fled, to England, every farm on their estates would have become the property of the occupant, subject to some fixed payment to the State. Ireland would then have been in the condition in which small farming, and tenancy by manual labourers, are consistent with good agriculture and public prosperity.[1]

Mill's remarkable counterfactual was prompted by the first outbreaks of Fenian violence in 1867, a profound shock to British liberals who had hoped that Catholic Emancipation, the Irish Poor Law and the famines of the 1840s had cured the overpopulation and religious strife that they held to have animated Irish grievance since the Union of 1801. Yet it also evokes something that is fundamental to the argument of this book: the manner in which the complex, triangular relationship between Ireland, Britain and France structured eighteenth- and nineteenth-century debates over the vicissitudes of empire in Ireland. The significance of this relationship, I have suggested, was not reducible to the military threat France occasionally posed to British rule. It lay instead in the influence Franco-British rivalry and emulation exerted over the political economy of empire,

---

[1] John Stuart Mill, *England and Ireland* (London: Longman and Green, 1868), 20.

and in the manner this was interpreted by contemporaries in Ireland, Britain and Europe. The threat, and the example, of France inspired British efforts to reform and consolidate empire, alongside Irish attempts to escape from it.

Rivalry and emulation between Britain and France had shaped the contestation and regeneration of empire in Ireland since the middle of the eighteenth century. From William Molyneux onwards, leading members of Ireland's Anglican aristocracy had complained that British restraints on Irish trade – themselves a by-product of the wars against Louis XIV – were limiting the Irish Kingdom's ability to contribute to the wealth and revenue of the empire. This argument was only taken seriously by British thinkers such as Hume, Tucker, Smith and Young, however, once the fiscal crisis threatened by repeated wars with France exposed the limits of a system of mercantile regulation so exclusionary that it denied to Britain's closest dependency the fruits of its own commerce. In turning their attention to the condition of the eighteenth-century Irish Kingdom, Smith and Young also understood the broad ramifications, both imperial and European, of the nascent critique of Anglo-Irish 'Ascendancy' that had been launched by Charles O'Conor, Edmund Burke and other representatives of Ireland's majority Catholic communion. There could be no route to a durable Irish prosperity that did not run through the reform of the Kingdom's sectarian settlement of property and constitution. For Smith, this could only be achieved by means of a union that would equate that of Scotland, using the authority of Westminster to break the power of an aristocracy founded on religious 'faction'. By the final quarter of the eighteenth century, a distinctively Scottish and Enlightened vision of a British–Irish parliamentary union, informed by novel understandings of the sentimental underpinnings of social order in an age of commerce, could already be discerned in outline.

Its further articulation, however, was dramatically derailed by French intervention in the imperial civil war that followed the American Declaration of Independence. The success of the Volunteers' campaigns for Irish 'Free Trade' and 'legislative independence' signified a shift in the balance of imperial power produced by the loss of the North American colonies to a French-supported insurgency. It proved impossible, however, to establish a stable configuration of imperial government in Ireland once Westminster's legislative supremacy had been rejected by the Volunteer movement and its parliamentary supporters. Peace with France and the opening of transatlantic trade – not only to the new United States but also to the British Caribbean – inspired a flurry of speculation concerning

Ireland's potential as a bridge between the Old and New Worlds. This set the stage for an inconclusive, three-way confrontation between British slaving and manufacturing interests, an increasingly fractured coalition of Irish Patriots and Volunteers, and a British ministry set upon 'submitting the frenzy of political, to the wisdom of commercial regulation'.[2] The failure of Pitt's proposals demonstrated that the cause of Irish liberty could not be reconciled with continuing participation in Britain's mercantile empire.

The French Revolution, and the generation of European warfare that followed from it, shattered the uneasy equilibrium of Irish government in the later 1780s. It did so by making possible new visions of Irish independence within a Europe transformed by the military power of revolutionary France. From differing standpoints – the trenchant Irish patriotism of Wolfe Tone and William James MacNeven, the pacific and abolitionist radicalism of Thomas Russell and William Steel Dickson, the Smithian political economy of Arthur O'Connor – leading United Irish propagandists and emissaries to France each saw an Irish revolution as a necessary step towards the liberation of Europe from the mercantile power and aristocratic corruption of Britain. This view was shared by those European thinkers, Charles-Guillaume Théremin foremost among them, who used the case of Ireland to demonstrate the brittle and exploitative nature of the British Empire and the progressive and durable character of the French alternative. It led some among the United Irishmen, most notably MacNeven and O'Connor, to themselves become propagandists for French power following the failure of the 1798 rebellion.

The threat posed by this Franco-Irish alliance against the British Empire was significant enough to produce a major response, both from the British ministry and by the defenders of British power in the European public sphere. Confronted with a United Irish insurgency that threatened the foundations of property in Britain's closest and most strategically vital dependency, British and Irish politicians such as Pitt, Castlereagh and Dundas re-fashioned Adam Smith's case for a British–Irish union for the changed conditions of the 1790s. In the heated pamphlet and parliamentary debates that accompanied the tortured passage of the 1801 Act of Union through the Irish and British parliaments, its proponents claimed that it could bring about a transformation of Ireland's social and political circumstances. Union would cool the factional passions that had inspired

---

[2] Thomas Orde, *The Commercial Regulations with Ireland, Explained and Considered, in the Speech of the Right Hon. Mr. Orde* (London: Debrett, 1785), 13.

the 1798 rising and encourage the best improving instincts of the Anglo-Irish aristocracy by enabling the diffusion of British capital into Irish land and manufactures. This vision of Union was upheld, not only by Pitt, Edward Cooke and Thomas Brooke Clarke, but also by the leading Prussian proponent of the counter-revolutionary cause, Friedrich Gentz, as indisputable evidence of the expansive reforming potential of British power. For Gentz, as for McKenna and Brooke Clarke, Union was proof of Britain's ability to act as the guarantor of a modern form of liberty suited to life in large commercial states. This was contrasted favourably with both the ineffectual Whig posturing of what remained of Anglo-Irish Patriotism after 1798, and the violent republican zeal of the United Irishmen and revolutionary France, which had promised peace and freedom, but delivered only war and tyranny.

For Tone and O'Connor, French intervention in Irish politics had presented an opportunity to dismantle the Irish Kingdom's sectarian property order and replace it with the peasant proprietorship being spread by French arms in the Low Countries, the Rhineland and northern Italy. This vision of Irish agrarian reform was lost for two decades following the defeat of the 1798 rising, but it returned in new forms as Ireland's rural economy collapsed into crisis at the end of the Napoleonic Wars. The scandal of Irish poverty and agrarian disorder would cast a long shadow over Britain's victory in the Napoleonic Wars. It would supply crucial evidence for those thinkers who upheld the legacies of revolution for the social order of the continent and questioned Britain's suitability as either a model or a custodian for European commercial civilisation.

These doubts were far from the minds of British or Irish thinkers in the early years of the nineteenth century as Napoleon's Continental System threatened to close off European grain markets and Irish exports to Britain rapidly grew. The extraordinary conditions of the war produced an optimistic reading of the political economy of the freshly concluded Union, one that joined old Anglo-Irish dreams of 'improvement' to a newly urgent British concern with population and subsistence in an isolated empire. Wounded by the loss of their parliament, the landowners and agents who took part in the Dublin Society's post-Union surveys of the Irish interior nonetheless argued for Ireland's new importance as a provider of food and manpower to the British war effort. For Francis d'Ivernois, Ireland's agrarian boom proved that Britain's mercantile empire was not only durable, but indispensable to the commercial well-being of the entire continent. Prussia and Russia, both sworn to uphold the Continental

System, were missing a vital opportunity to join Ireland in supplying the wants of Britain's rapidly growing industrial cities.

When a new generation of British political economists, led by Robert Malthus, turned to consider the internal dynamics of Ireland's potato-driven rural economy, however, they were horrified by what they saw. For Malthus as for Edward Wakefield, the apparently exponential growth of an underclass of potato-farming subtenants was a social and political disaster in the making. The grounds for their judgement lay in a commitment, itself drawn from the agronomic theories of Arthur Young, to the principle of large-scale, capital-intensive farming as the root cause of Britain's domestic stability and international resilience. The Irish famines and agrarian outrages of the later 1810s and the 1820s served only to confirm this view. British figures such as John Ramsay McCulloch responded with a new demand for the British legislator to enforce a brutal rationalisation of Irish tenancy arrangements, through a system of estate clearances and Poor Laws modelled on their English and Scottish analogues. Drawing on a reading of Adam Smith that was arguably more faithful than that of his British counterparts, Sismondi used the case of Ireland to argue the opposite. Smallholding agriculture offered a more durable form of security against the dangers of 'underconsumption', while also encouraging industry and republican virtue amongst a class of free property owners. Prussian reformers, including Friedrich von Raumer and Hegel, similarly argued that the case of Ireland proved the inability of unreformed Britain to formulate convincing answers to the 'social question' that was posed by the parlous condition of both the British working classes and the Irish peasantry.

It was Gustave de Beaumont, however, who decisively expanded these arguments into a thoroughgoing critique of the political economy of Union, one which would ultimately inspire the accounts of 'nationality' and 'national character' that underpinned Thomas Davis' and John Stuart Mill's campaigns for the reformation of Irish political economy along lines of peasant proprietorship. For de Beaumont, Ireland was the place where the dynamics of social change unleashed across Europe by the French Revolution would ultimately catch up with Britain's anomalous, 'aristocratic' political and social system. If the Union was to be preserved in the face of the shadow Irish polity represented by O'Connell's popular movement, Westminster would have to take it upon itself to act as the French revolutionaries had done, using sovereign authority to crush the stubborn remnants of aristocratic power in Ireland. In the 1840s, as in the 1790s, the question of Irish land stood at a junction between rival visions of Europe's future.

The government of Ireland was not, therefore, a narrowly Irish problem. Indeed, in the eyes of many contemporaries – and particularly continental observers – its primary significance lay in its illumination of the underlying character of *Britain's* empire, constitution and society. The nature and prospects of British government in Ireland were central to contemporary European debates over the impact of its mercantile empire on international politics. Montesquieu deployed the case of Ireland to illustrate the revealed preferences of England's fractious party politics. A more lurid version of this argument was used by propagandists for French Empire, and resisted in Gentz's account of Union. This highlighted the capacity of the British political elite to respond to the spirit of the age and the interests of the governed, which lay in the consolidation of unitary states that commanded loyalty on the basis of the commercial wealth guaranteed by effective sovereignty. For Francis d'Ivernois, meanwhile, the case of Ireland was conclusive proof that British commercial hegemony could be reconciled with the broader interests of the peoples of Europe in the age of Napoleon.

Gentz's and d'Ivernois' writings were rare, however, in holding out Britain's government of Ireland as a model for European emulation. More common was the argument that connection with Ireland might have the inadvertent effect of reforming (or destroying) Britain's shaky political and economic system. Britain, as much as Ireland, could be perceived as a troubling anomaly in contemporary Europe: initially as an aggressive commercial empire, latterly as a strikingly unequal industrial society. Montesquieu and Théremin utilised the case of Ireland to draw something like the first conclusion; Sismondi, von Raumer, Hegel and de Beaumont the second. The case of Ireland showed that Britain's fabled regime of commerce and constitutional liberty was potentially more flawed and vulnerable than its political class yet realised.

As Britain's primary European dependency, Ireland was meanwhile subject to particularly intense influence from French ideas and French politics across this period – both directly, through the material assistance and intellectual inspiration France provided to successive groups of Irish patriots, radicals and nationalists; and indirectly, through the geopolitical and ideological pressure that so often prompted British initiatives towards Irish reform, even after the fall of Napoleon Bonaparte. The Union of 1801 was the most significant and long-lasting consequence of Britain's long confrontation with revolutionary France. The latter's conquest of much of the European continent increased the plausibility of a powerful set of new ideas concerning the merits of smallholding farming and peasant proprietorship – ideas that would return again and again in Irish debates over land reform in the nineteenth century and help to define an Irish 'nationality' that British politics would ultimately have to reckon with. By examining the British–Irish relationship in this European context, then, we can see it as one of many areas in which the supposedly hegemonic Britain of the early nineteenth century was as much acted upon as it was acting. Ireland was a place where its power and self-confidence would be challenged and disrupted – not because it was a recalcitrant, atavistic periphery, but because it was open to the alternative modernities suggested by the social and political systems of Britain's continental neighbours.

If our image of imperial Britain is changed by this awareness of Ireland's centrality to a complex inter-imperial field of political-economic debate, so too should our impressions of the different Irish movements that changed the country's politics from the late eighteenth through the mid-nineteenth centuries. As we have seen, these were not just confronted by the challenges – formidable as these were – of establishing cross-confessional coalitions of support for different visions of Irish autonomy and independence, or of establishing how far violence could be legitimately employed in the pursuit of these political goals. They were also faced with profound and difficult choices concerning the kinds of political economy they wished to realise in Ireland, and the nature of the foreign alliances they were prepared to make. For better or for worse, the options canvassed by different Irish thinkers and politicians during the period considered here have continued to shape the twentieth- and twenty-first-century Free State and Republic. Since the 1960s, the vision of an agrarian, smallholding republic, so attractive to both the United Irishmen and Young Ireland, has given way to the breakneck globalisation – and subsequent shipwreck – of the 'Celtic Tiger' economy, one whose own heritage can be traced back to Etienne Clavière's early speculations about the Irish Kingdom's potential to act as a low-tax entrepôt for transatlantic commerce.

Ireland's historical trajectory, then, might usefully be understood alongside that of other political communities – both within and beyond Europe – who have been shut out from the main centres of power and accumulation in the hierarchical orders of global capitalism. Indeed, in the increasingly multi-polar world of the twenty-first century, small and middle powers are once again grappling with the same problems that confronted eighteenth and early nineteenth-century Ireland, caught, as it was, in the middle of an epochal rivalry between France and Britain. Is it possible to find a niche that exploits the gaps between larger and more powerful jurisdictions? Is it more beneficial to simply seek to reap the rewards of integration with the nearest and most benevolent-seeming large power? Do the costs of economic isolation outweigh the benefits of political autonomy? Are these even commensurable goods, or does the surrender of autonomy always ultimately lead to poverty and exploitation? These questions are as urgent now as they were in the eighteenth and nineteenth centuries, because we still live in a world in which economic interdependence and political coercion are uncomfortably entangled. These entanglements are often most legible, for contemporaries as for historians, in those places which, like eighteenth- and nineteenth-century Ireland, test the limits of what is possible under the prevailing global dispensation of wealth and power.

The global capitalism of the twenty-first century, and the complex political orders through which it is sustained and reproduced, have little in common with the archaic mercantile empires that have been the subject of this book. The forms of political understanding that we can best employ to comprehend it, however, are lineal descendants of those that have been considered here. We can still analyse the rivalry of modern commercial empires in terms of 'political economy', linking domestic political regimes and interests to the pursuit of prestige and influence abroad. Our political judgement on the dominant powers of today's capitalism can still be formed by the manner in which they treat their most vulnerable citizens and most fragile dependencies. We can still remain open to the idea that – as Montesquieu, Sismondi and Davis, among others, clearly knew – there is no one set of political or institutional arrangements, represented by one or more dominant states, that constitute the definitive form of 'modernity', towards which all development must inevitably tend. The case of Ireland can deepen our understanding of all of these things. This was why it mattered to the political thought of eighteenth- and nineteenth-century Europe. It is also why it should matter to us today.

Bibliography

Manuscript Sources

Autograph Collection. National Library of Ireland, Dublin.
Bolton Papers. National Library of Ireland, Dublin.
Castlereagh Papers. Public Record Office of Northern Ireland, Belfast.
Foster/Massereene Papers. Public Record Office of Northern Ireland, Belfast.
Melville Papers. National Library of Ireland, Dublin.
Union Papers. National Library of Dublin, Ireland.

Printed Sources

Alexandre Maurice Blanc de Lanautte, comte d'Hauterive, *De l'état de la France, à la fin de l'an VIII* (Paris: Henrics, 1800).
Annesley, Frances, *Some Thoughts on the Bill, Depending before the Right Honourable the House of Lords, for Prohibiting the Exportation of the Woollen Manufactures of Ireland to Foreign Parts* (London: J. Darby, 1698).
Anon., 'Paradoxe politique, addressé aux Irlandois', *Ephemerides du citoyen, ou bibliotheque raisonnée des sciences morales et politiques*, 1 (1767), 55–97.
A Defence of the Conduct of the Court of Portugal, with a Full Refutation of the Several Charges Alleged against That Kingdom, with Respect to Ireland (London: J. Stockdale, 1783).
An Address to the King and People of Ireland, upon the System of Final Adjustment, Contained in the Twenty Propositions, Which Have Passed the British House of Commons, and Are Now before the British House of Lords (Dublin: R. Marchbank, 1785).
'Über die neuste Geschichte Irrlands (Beschluss)', *Minerva*, 2 (1798), 520–46.
The Commercial System of Ireland Reviewed, and the Question of Union Discussed, in an Address to the Merchants, Manufacturers, and Country Gentlemen of Ireland (Dublin: James Moore, 1799).
Observations on the Commercial Principles of the Projected Union (London: R. Pitkeathley, 1800).
'Art XI – France. By Lady Morgan', *The Quarterly Review*, 17 (1817), 260–86.

The Annual Biography and Dictionary, for the Year 1823 (London: Longman, Hurst, Rees, Orme and Brown, 1823).

Arbuckle, David (ed.), *A Collection of Letters and Essays on Several Subjects*, Lately Publish'd in *The Dublin Journal*.

Archenholz, Johann Wilhelm von, 'Ueber den jetzigen Krieg der Engländer und der Staatsmann Fox', *Minerva: ein Journal historischen und politischen Inhalts*, 27 (1798), 287–302.

'Ueber die Politik unserer Zeit', *Minerva: ein Journal historischen und politischen Inhalts*, 25 (1798), 1–12.

'Zur Geschichte der jetzigen Machthaber in England', *Minerva: ein Journal historischen und politischen Inhalts*, 25 (1798), 186–8.

Ball, Charles, *Union Neither Necessary or Expedient for Ireland: Being an Answer to the Author of Arguments for and Against an Union* (Dublin: William Porter, 1798).

Beaumont, Gustave de, *L'Irlande sociale, politique, et religieuse*, 2 vols. (Paris: Gosselin, 1839).

État de la question d'Afrique (Paris: Paulin, 1843).

Ireland: Social, Political, Religious, trans. W. C. Taylor (Cambridge, MA: Belknap, Harvard, 2006).

Blackstone, William, *Commentaries on the Laws of England*, 12th ed., 4 vols. (London: T. Cadell, 1793).

Briefe von und an Friedrich von Gentz, ed. F. K. Wittichen (München: R. Oldenbourg, 1909).

Britain, Privy Council of Great, *Report of the Lords of the Committee of Council, Appointed for the Consideration of Matters Relating to Trade and Foreign Plantations* (London: John Stockdale, 1785).

Burke, Edmund, *The Writings and Speeches of Edmund Burke*, ed. R. B. McDowell et al. 10 vols. (Oxford: Clarendon Press, 1981–2016).

Bushe, Gervaise Parker, 'An Essay towards Ascertaining the Population of Ireland. In a Letter to the Right Honourable the Earl of Charlemont, President of the Royal Irish Academy', *Transactions of the Royal Irish Academy*, 3 (1789), 145–55.

Cary, John, *An Essay on the State of England: In Relation to Its Trade, Its Poor, and Its Taxes, for Carrying on the Present War against France* (Bristol: W. Bonny, 1695).

Cavour, Camilo di, 'Considérations sur l'état actuel de l'Irlande et sur son avenir', *Bibliothèque Universelle de Genève*, 29 (1844), 5–47.

Chalmers, George, *An Answer to the Reply to the Supposed Treasury Pamphlet* (London: John Stockdale, 1785).

The Arrangements with Ireland Considered (London: John Stockdale, 1785).

Clarke, Thomas Brooke, *Misconceptions of Facts, and Mistatements of the Public Accounts, by the Right Hon. John Foster* (London: John Hatchard, 1799).

The Political, Commercial, and Civil State of Ireland, Being an Appendix to "Union or Separation" (Dublin: J. Milliken, 1799).

A Survey of the Strength and Opulence of Great Britain, with observations by Dean Tucker, and David Hume, in a Correspondence with Lord Kaimes (London: T. Cadell, 1802).

Cobbett, William, *The Parliamentary History of England from the Earliest Period to the Year 1803*, 36 vols. (London: T. C. Hansard, 1806–20).

Commons, House of, *Minutes of the Evidence Taken before a Committee of the House of Commons* (Dublin: P. Byrne, 1785).

Condorcet, Jean-Antoine-Nicolas de Caritat, *Outlines of an Historical View of the Progress of the Human Mind* (Dublin: John Chambers, 1796).

Cooke, Edward, *Arguments for and against an Union, between Great Britain and Ireland, Considered* (London: John Stockdale, 1798).

Coote, Sir Charles, *Statistical Survey of the County of Monaghan, with Observations on the Means of Improvement* (Dublin: Graisberry & Campbell, 1801).

Cox, Walter (ed.), *The Irish Magazine, and Museum of Neglected Biography* (Dublin, 1807–15).

Crumpe, Samuel, *An Essay on the Best Means of Providing Employment for the People* (London: J. Robinson, 1795).

Davies, John , '*A Discovery of the True Causes why Ireland was never brought under Obedience of the Crown of England, until his late Majesty's Happy Reign*', in Historical Tracts by Sir John Davies, (London: John Stockdale, 1786), pp. 1–227.

Davis, Thomas, 'Continental Literature – Augustine Thierry, No. 1', *The Nation*, 26 November 1842, 107.

'The Foreign Policy of Ireland', *The Citizen, or Dublin Monthly Magazine*, II (1840), 445–63.

'Norway and Ireland, No. 1: Udalism and Feudalism', *Dublin Monthly Magazine*, 1 (1842), 218–38.

'Norway and Ireland, No. 2: Udalism and Feudalism', *Dublin Monthly Magazine*, 1 (1842), 293–316.

Debrett, John, *The Parliamentary Register*, 54 vols. (London: John Debrett, 1785).

Dickson, William Steel, *Three Sermons on the Subject of Scripture Politics* (Belfast, 1793).

D'Ivernois, Francis, *Effects of the Continental Blockade, Upon the Commerce, Finances, Credit and Prosperity of the British Islands* (London: J. Hatchard, 1810).

D'Ivernois, Francis with Julius Schmidt, *Die Sperre des festen Landes und ihr Einfluss auf den Handel, die FInanzen,d en Kredit und das Wohl der Brittischen Inseln* (1810).

Dobbs, Arthur, *An Essay on the Trade and Improvement of Ireland*, 2 vols. (Dublin: J. Smith & W. Bruce, 1729).

Doyle, James Warren, *Letters on the State of Ireland* (Dublin: R. Coyne, 1825).

Drennan, William, *A Letter to William Pitt* (Dublin: James Moore, 1799).

A Letter to Edmund Burke, Esq.; by Birth an Irishman, by Adoption an Englishman, Containing Some Reflections on Patriotism, Party-Spirit, and the Union of Free Nations (Dublin: William Hallhead, 1780).

Duigenan, Patrick, *A Fair Representation of the Present Political State of Ireland* (Dublin: J. Milliken, 1800).

Dundas, Henry, *Substance of the Speech of the Right Hon. Henry Dundas in the House of Commons, Thursday, Feb. 7, 1799, on the Subject of the Legislative Union with Ireland* (London: J. Wright, 1799).

Duvergier de Hauranne, P., *Lettres sur les élections anglaises, et sur la situation de l'Irlande* (Paris: Sautelet, 1827).

Dwan, David, 'Young Ireland and the Horde of Benthamy', in R. Swift and C. Kinealy (eds.), *Politics and Power in Victorian Ireland* (Dublin: Four Courts Press, 2006), 109–18; John Morrow, 'Thomas Carlyle, Young Ireland, and the "Condition of Ireland" Question', *The Historical Journal*, 51 (2008), 643–67.

Elliot, Gilbert, *The Speech of Lord Minto, in the House of Peers, April 11, 1799 ... Respecting an Union between Great Britain and Ireland* (Dublin: John Exshaw, 1799).

Emmett, Thomas Addis, Arthur O'Connor & William J. MacNeven, *Memoire; or, Detailed Statement of the Origin and Progress of the Irish Union* (1800).

Faucher, Léon, *État et tendance de la propriété en France* (Paris: H. Fournier, 1836).

Ferguson, Adam, *An Essay on the History of Civil Society* (Edinburgh: Edinburgh University Press, 1978).

Fitzgibbon John, 1st Earl Clare, *The Speech of the RightHonourable John, Earl of Clare, Lord High Chancellor of Ireland, in the House of Lords of Ireland, on a Motion Made by Him, on Monday, February 10th, 1800* (Dublin: J. Milliken, 1800).

Foster, John, *Speech of the Right Honorable John Foster, Speaker of the House of Commons of Ireland, Delivered in Committee, on Thursday the 11th Day of April, 1799* (Dublin: James Moore, 1799).

Fraser, Robert, *Statistical Survey of the County of Wexford* (Dublin: Graisberry and Campbell, 1807).

Gentz, Friedrich, 'Darstellung und Vergleichung einiger politischen Constitutions-Systeme die von dem Grundsatze der Theilung der Macht ausgehen', *Neue Deutsche Monatsschrift*, 3 (1795), 81–157.

'Beiträge zur Berichtigung einiger Ideen der allgememeinen Staatswissenschaft', *Historisches Journal*, 4 (1799), 277–312.

'Plan zu einer engern Vereinigung zwischen Großbrittannien und Irrland', *Historisches Journal*, 1 (1799), 439–86.

'Ueber den jetzigen Zustand der Finanz-Administration und des Nazional-Reichthums von Großbrittannien (Beschluss)', *Historisches Journal*, 3 (1799), 143–244.

'Ueber die Natur and und den Werth der gemischten Staatsverfassungen', *Historisches Journal*, 1 (1799), 487–98.

'Ueber den ewigen Frieden', *Historisches Journal*, 4 (1800), 711–90.

'Ueber die Final-Vereinigung zwischen Großbrittannien und Irrland', *Historisches Journal*, 4 (1800), 500–614.

'Ueber die Final-Vereinigung zwischen Großbrittannien und Irrland (Beschluss)', *Historisches Journal*, 4 (1800), 615–710.

'Ueber die politische Gleichheit', *Historisches Journal*, 1 (1800), 1–51.

Ueber den Ursprung und Charakter des Krieges gegen die Französische Revoluzion (Berlin: Heinrich Frölich, 1801).

On the State of Europe before and after the French Revolution, trans. J. C. Herries (London: J. Hatchard, 1802).

Gentz, Friedrich & Paul Wittichen, 'Das preussiche Kabinett und Friedrich von Gentz. Eine Denkschrift as dem Jahre 1800', *Historische Zeitschrift* 89 (1902), 239–73.

Gibbon, Edward, *Miscellaneous Works of Edward Gibbon, with Memoirs of His Life and Writings, Composed by Himself* (Dublin: P. Wogan, 1796).

Griffith, Richard, *Thoughts on Protecting Duties* (Dublin: Luke White, 1784).

Grotius, Hugo, *The Rights of War and Peace*, ed. Richard Tuck (Indianapolis, IN: Liberty Fund, 2012).

Harrington, James, 'The Commonwealth of Oceana', in J. G. A. Pocock (ed.), *The Political Works of James Harrington* (Cambridge, 1977), 155–361.

Hegel, Georg Wilhelm Friedrich , 'On the English Reform Bill (1831)', in Laurence Dickey & H. B. Nisbet (eds.), *Political Writings* (Cambridge: Cambridge University Press, 1999), 234–70.

Helvétius, Claude Adrien, *De L'Esprit: Or, Essays on the Mind, and Its Several Faculties* (London: Dodsley, 1759).

Hely-Hutchinson, John, *The Commercial Restraints of Ireland Considered* (London: T. Longman, 1780).

A Letter from the Secretary of State to the Mayor of Cork on the Subject of the Bill Presented by Mr. Orde (Dublin: P. Byrne, 1785).

Holroyd, John, Lord Sheffield, *Observations on the Commerce of the American States*, 6th ed. (London: J. Debrett, 1784).

Holroyd, John, *Observations on the Manufactures, Trade, and Present State of Ireland*, 3rd ed. (London: Debrett, 1785).

Horner, Francis Art. II 'Lord Lauderdale's *Hints to Manufacturers*', *The Edinburgh Review*, July 1805, 283–90.

Hume, David, *A Treatise of Human Nature* (Oxford: Oxford University Press, 1978). *Essays Moral, Political and Literary*, ed. Eugene F. Miller (Indianapolis, IN: Liberty Fund, 1985).

Ireland, House of Lords, *Report from the Secret Committee of the House of Lords* (Dublin: W. Sleater, 1798).

Jay, A., '*La France*; par Lady Morgan, ci-devant miss Owenson', *Mercure de France*, 3 (1817), 293–307.

Jebb, Frederick, *The Letters of Guatimozin, on the Affairs of Ireland* (Dublin: R. Marchbank, 1779).

Johnson, Robert, *Considerations on the Effects of Protecting Duties, in a Letter to a Newly-Elected Member of Parliament* (Dublin: W. Wilson, 1783).

King, Peter, 7th Baron King, *Thoughts on the Effects of the Bank Restrictions* (London: Cadell and Davies, 1804).

Krünitz, Johann Georg, 'Irrland', in *Oekonomische Encyclopädie, oder allgemeines System der Staats- Stadt- Haus- und Landwirthschaft, in alphabetischer Ordnung*, 242 vols. (Berlin: Joachim Pauli, 1784), vol. 30, 742–63.

Küttner, Karl Gottlob, *Briefe über Irland, an seinen Freund, den Herausgeber* (Leipzig: Johann Phillip Haugs Wittwe, 1785).

Laing, Samuel, *Journal of a Residence in Norway, During the Years 1834, 1835, and 1836: Made with a View to Inquire into the Moral and Political Economy of that Country, and the Condition of its Inhabitants* (London: Longman, 1836).

Lalor, James Fintan, *Patriot & Political Essayist (1807–1849)*, ed. Lilian Fogarty (Dublin: The Talbot Press, 1919).

Lewis, George Cornewall, *On Local Disturbances in Ireland, and on the Irish Church Question* (London: B. Fellowes, 1836).

Lolme, Jean-Louis de, *A History of the British Empire in Europe* (Dublin: P. Byrne, 1787).

Mackintosh, Robert James, *Memoirs of the Life of Sir James Mackintosh*, 2nd ed. ed., 2 vols. (London: Edward Moxon, 1836), vol. 1.

MacNeven, William James, *An Argument for Independence, in Opposition to Union, Addressed to All His Countrymen* (Dublin: J. Stockdale, 1799).

'Statistical Essay on the Population and Resources of Ireland', in William J. MacNeven & Thomas A. Emmet (eds.), *Pieces of Irish History Illustrative of the Condition of the Catholics of Ireland, of the Origin and Progress of the Political System of the United Irishmen, and of Their Transactions with the Anglo-Irish Government* (New York: Bernard Dornin, 1807), 249–54.

'Of the Interest of the Maritime Powers in the Present War', in J.-J. Lavayasse (ed.), *Letters on the Events of the Revolution in France* (New York: John Forbes, 1817).

Malthus, Thomas Robert, 'IV: Newenham and Others on the State of Ireland', *Edinburgh Review*, 12 (1808), 336–55.

'XII: Newenham on the State of Ireland', *The Edinburgh Review*, 14 (1809), 151–70.

Principles of Political Economy Considered with a View to Their Practical Application, 2nd ed. (London: J. Murray, 1836).

Manners John, 7th Duke of Rutland (ed.), *Correspondence between the Right Honourable William Pitt, and Charles Duke of Rutland, Lord Lieutenant of Ireland, 1781–1787* (London: William Blackwood and Sons, 1890).

Maxwell, Henry, *An Essay Upon an Union of Ireland with England* (Dublin: Eliphal Dobson, 1704).

McCulloch, John Ramsay, 'Ireland', *Edinburgh Review*, 37 (1822), 60–109.

'French Law of Succession', *The Edinburgh Review*, 40 (1824), 350–75.

'Art. II – Emigration', *The Edinburgh Review*, 45 (1826), 49–89.

'Sadler on Ireland', *The Edinburgh Review*, 49 (1829), 300–17.

'Cottage System', in D. P. O'Brien (ed.), *The Collected Works of J. R. McCulloch*, 8 vols. (London: Routledge, 1995), vol. 6, 427–35.

McKenna, Theobald, *Constitutional Objections to the Government of Ireland by a Separate Legislature, in a Letter to John Hamilton, Esq.* (Dublin: H. Fitzpatrick, 1799).

A Memoire on Some Questions Respecting the Projected Union of Great Britain and Ireland (Dublin: John Rice, 1799).

Political Essays Relative to the Affairs of Ireland, in 1791, 1792, and 1793, with Remarks on the Present State of That Country. (London: J. Debrett, 1794).

Mill, John Stuart, *Newspaper Writings Part III, January 1835–June 1847*, ed. Ann P. Robson and John P. Robson, Collected Works of John Stuart Mill (Toronto: University of Toronto Press, 1986).

Millar, John, *The Origin of the Distinction of Ranks* (Indianapolis, IN: Liberty Fund, 1771).

Letters of Crito, on the Causes, Objects and Consequences of the Present War, 2nd ed. (Edinburgh: Scots Chronicle, 1796).

An Historical View of the English Government, From the Settlement of the Saxons in Britain to the Revolution in 1688 (Indianapolis, IN: Liberty Fund, 2006).

Molesworth, Robert, *Some Considerations for the Promoting of Agriculture, and Employing the Poor* (Dublin, George Grierson, 1723).

Molyneux, William, *The Case of Ireland's Being Bound by Acts of Parliament in England Stated*, 2nd ed. (Dublin: Anon., 1706).

The Case of Ireland's Being Bound by Acts of Parliament in England Stated (Dublin: J. Milliken, 1773).

Montesquieu, Charles de Secondat, *The Spirit of the Laws*, trans. Anne M. Cohler, Basia Carolyn Miller & Harold Samuel Stone (Cambridge: Cambridge University Press, 1989).

Newenham, Thomas, *An Obstacle to the Ambition of France: Or, Thoughts on the Expediency of Improving the Political Condition of His Majesty's Irish Roman Catholic Subjects* (London: C. & R. Baldwin, 1803).

A Statistical and Historical Inquiry into the Progress and Magnitude of the Population of Ireland (London: Baldwin, 1805)

A View of the Natural, Political and Commercial Circumstances of Ireland (London: T. Cadell and W. Davies, 1809).

Niebuhr, Bartholt Georg, 'Vorrede', in L. F. von Wincke, *Darstellung der innern Verwaltung Grossbritanniens* (Berlin: Realschulbuchandlung, 1817).

O'Beirne, Thomas Lewis, *A Letter from an Irish Gentleman in London, to His Friend in Dublin, on the Proposed System of Commerce* (London: J. Debrett, 1785).

A Reply to the Treasury Pamphlet, Entitled the Proposed System of Trade with Ireland Explained (London: J. Debrett, 1785).

O'Connor, Arthur, *Speech of Arthur O'Connor, Esq. in the House of Commons of Ireland, Monday, May 4th, 1795, on the Catholic bill* (Dublin: P. Byrne, 1795).

The State of Ireland (Dublin, 1798).

The Present State of Great-Britain (Paris, 1804).

O'Conor, Charles, *The Case of the Roman-Catholics of Ireland, Wherein the Principles and Conduct of That Party Are Fully Explained and Vindicated*, 3rd ed. (Dublin: P. Lord, 1756).

Orde, Thomas, *The Commercial Regulations with Ireland Explained and Considered, in the Speech of the Right Hon. Mr. Orde* (London: J. Debrett, 1785).

Paine, Thomas, *The Decline and Fall of the English System of Finance* (Paris: Hartley, Adlard & Son, 1796).

'Rights of Man, Part 1', in Bruce Kuklick (ed.), *Political Writings*, (Cambridge: Cambridge University Press, 1989), 57–155.

Paley, William, *The Principles of Moral and Political Philosophy* (London: R. Fauldner, 1785).

Parnell, Henry, *The Principles of Currency and Exchange*, 4th ed. (London: J. Budd, 1805).

Pitt, William, *Speech of the Right Honourable William Pitt, in the House of Commons, Thursday January 31, 1799* (London: J. Wright, 1799).

Pollock, Joseph, *The Letters of Owen Roe O'Nial* (Dublin: W. Jackson, 1779).

Price, Richard, *Observations on the Nature of Civil Liberty, the Principles of Government, and the Justice and Policy of the War with America*, 8th ed. (Dublin: W. Kidd, 1776).

Prior, Thomas, *A List of the Absentees of Ireland, and the Yearly Value of Their Estates and Incomes Spent Abroad; with Observations on the Present Trade and Condition of that Kingdom*, 2nd ed. (Dublin: R. Gunne, 1729).

Raumer, Frederick von, *England in 1835*, trans. Sarah Austin, 3 vols. (London: John Murray, 1836).

Ricardo, David, *The Works and Correspondence of David Ricardo*, ed. Piero Sraffa (Indianapolis, IN: Liberty Fund, 2004).

Riem, Andreas, *Reise durch England, in verschiedener, besonders politischer Hinsicht*, 2 vols. (Leipzig: Auf kosten des Verfassers, 1798).

Robinson, David, 'English and Irish Landletting', *Blackwoods Edinburgh Magazine*, 17 (1825), 684–701.

Rose, George, *The Proposed System of Trade Explained* (London, 1785).

Rousseau, Jean-Jacques, 'Abstract and Judgement of Saint-Pierre's Project for Perpetual Peace' [1756], in Stanley Hoffman and David Fidler (eds.), *Rousseau on International Relations* (Oxford: Clarendon Press, 1991), 53–101.

'The Social Contract', in Victor Gourevitch (ed.), *The Social Contract and Other Later Political Writings* (Cambridge: Cambridge University Press, 1997), 39–153.

Rubichon, Maurice, *De L'Angleterre*, 2 vols. (Paris: Le Normant, 1815–19).

Russell, Thomas, *A Letter to the People of Ireland, on the Present Situation of the Country* (Belfast: Northern Star, 1796).

Ryan, R., *An Essay upon the Following Subject of Inquiry, "What are the best means of rendering the National Sources of Wealth possessed by Ireland Effectual for the Employment of the Population", Proposed by the Royal Irish Academy, 1822* (London: Hatchard, 1824).

Senior, Nassau William, *A Letter to Lord Howick on a Legal Provision for the Irish Poor*, 2nd ed. (London: John Murray, 1831).

Sheridan, Charles, *Observations on the Doctrine Laid Down by Sir William Blackstone, Respecting the Extent of the Power of the British Parliament, Particularly with Relation to Ireland* (London: J. Almon, 1779).

A Review of the Three Great National Questions, Relative to a Declaration of Right, Poynings' Law, and the Mutiny Bill (Dublin: M. Mills, 1782).

Free Thoughts Upon the Present Crisis, in Which Are Stated the Fundamental Principles, Upon Which Alone Ireland Can, or Ought to Agree to Any Final Settlement With Great Britain (1785).

Sheridan, Richard Brinsley, *The Legislative Independence of Ireland Vindicated, in a Speech of Mr. Sheridan, on the Irish Propositions in the British House of Commons* (Dublin: P. Cooney, 1785).

Sismondi, J. C. L. Simonde de, 'De la condition des cultivateurs irlandais et des causes de leur détresse', in *Études sur l'économie politique*, 2 vols. (Paris: Treuttel et Würtz, 1837), vol. 1, 239–78.

'Des devoirs du Souverain envers les cultivateurs irlandais, et des moyens de les tirer de leur détresse', in *Études sur l'économie politique*, 2 vols. (Paris: Treuttel et Würtz, 1837), vol. 1, 331–77.

'Political Economy (1818)', in D. Brewster (ed.), *Brewster's Edinburgh Encyclopaedia*, 1st American ed., 18 vols. (Philadelphia: Joseph and Edward Parker, 1832), vol. 16, 39–77.

Smith, Adam, *An Inquiry into the Nature and Causes of the Wealth of Nations*, 2 vols. (Oxford: Clarendon Press, 1976).

The Theory of Moral Sentiments (Indianapolis, IN: Liberty Fund, 1976).

The Correspondence of Adam Smith (Oxford: Oxford University Press, 1977).

Smith, William, *The Substance of Mr. William Smith's Speech on the Subject of a Legislative Union . . . in the Irish House of Commons, Thursday, January 24th 1799* (London: J. Wright, 1800).

[Smith, Sydney]. Art. V 'Dr Milner and others on the Catholics of Ireland', *The Edinburgh Review*, April 1808, 60–4, at 64.

Spencer, Joshua, *Thoughts on an Union*, 4th ed. (Dublin: William Jones, 1798).

Sydney, Owenson, Lady Morgan & Sir Charles Morgan, *France*, 2nd ed., 2 vols. (London: Henry Colburn, 1817).

Temple, William, 'An Essay Upon the Advancement of Trade in Ireland', in Thomas Courtney (ed.), *The Works of Sir William Temple*, 4 vols. (London: Rivington, 1814), III:1–28.

Théremin, Charles, *Des intérêts des puissances continentales relativement à l'Angleterre* (Paris: Louvet, 1795).

Von dem Interesse der Mächte des festen Landes in Bezug auf England (The Hague: J.C. Leeuwestyn, 1795).

De belangen der mogendheden van het vaste land met betrekking tot Engelland (The Hague: J.C. Leeuwestyn, 1796).

Tocqueville, Alexis de, *Journeys to England and Ireland* (New Haven, Conn.: Yale University Press, 1958).

'Second Mémoire sur le paupérisme', in F. Mélonio (ed.), *Alexis de Toqueville Oeuvres Complètes Tome XVI: Mélanges* (Paris: Gallimard, 1989), 140–59.

Alexis de Tocqueville: Writings on Empire and Slavery, ed. J. Pitts (Baltimore, VA: Johns Hopkins University Press, 2001).

Democracy in America, ed. and trans. Harvey Mansfield & Delba Winthrop (Chicago: University of Chicago Press, 2002).

Tone, Theobald Wolfe, *Spanish War! An Enquiry How Far Ireland Is Bound, of Right, to Embark in the Impending Contest on the Side of Great-Britain?* (Dublin: P. Byrne, 1790).

An Argument on Behalf of the Catholics of Ireland (Dublin: P. Byrne, 1791).

The Writings of Theobald Wolfe Tone, 1763–1798, 3 vols. Eds. T.W. Moody, R. B. McDowell & C. J. Woods. (Oxford: Clarendon Press, 1998–2007).

Tooke, William Eyton, 'State of Ireland', *The Westminster Review*, 7 (1827), 1–50.

Tucker, Josiah, *A Brief Essay on the Advantages and Disadvantages Which Respectively Attend France and Great Britain, with Regard to Trade, with Some Proposals for Removing the Principal Disadvantages of Great Britain*, 3rd ed. (London: T. Trye, 1753).

Reflections on the Present Matters in Dispute between Great Britain and Ireland: And on the Means of Converting These Articles into Mutual Benefits to Both Kingdoms (London: T. Cadell, 1785).

Tucker, Josiah & Thomas Brooke Clarke, *Union or Separation*, 2nd ed. (London: J. Hatchard & J. Wright, 1799).

Vattel, Emmerich de, *The Law of Nations, or, Principles of the Law of Nature, Applied to the Conduct and Affairs of Nations and Sovereigns* (Indianapolis, IN: Liberty Fund, 2008).

Vaughan, Benjamin, *New and Old Principles of Trade Compared* (London: J. Johnson, 1787).

Wakefield, Edward, *An Account of Ireland, Statistical and Political*, 2 vols. (London: Longman, 1812).

Wittichen, Friedrich Karl (ed.), *Briefe von und an Friedrich von Gentz*, 3 vols. (Munchen: R. Oldenbourg, 1909).

Wittichen, Paul, 'Das preussische Kabinett und Friedrich von Gentz. Eine Denkschrift aus dem Jahre 1800', *Historische Zeitschrift*, 89 (1902), 239–73.

Young, Arthur, *Political Arithmetic* (London: W. Nicoll, 1774).

A Tour in Ireland, with General Observations on the Present State of That Kingdom, Made in the Years 1776, 1777 and 1778, and Brought Down to the End of 1779, 2nd ed., 2 vols. (London: T. Cadell and J. Dodsley, 1780).

'Observations on the Commercial Arrangement with Ireland', *Annals of Agriculture*, III (1785), 257–91.

On the Advantages Which Have Resulted from the Establishment of the Board of Agriculture (London: Richard Philips, 1809).

Secondary Literature

Armitage, David, 'The Political Economy of Britain and Ireland after the Glorious Revolution', in Jane H. Ohlmeyer (ed.), *Political Thought in Seventeenth Century Ireland: Kingdom or Colony?* (Cambridge: Cambridge University Press, 2000), 221–43.

Armitage, David & Sanjay Subrahmanyam (eds.), *The Age of Revolutions in Global Context, c. 1760–1840* (Basingstoke: Palgrave Macmillan, 2009).

Aspinall, Arthur, 'The Reporting and Publishing of House of Commons Debates, 1771–1834', in Alan J. P. Taylor & Richard Pares (eds.), *Essays Presented to Sir Lewis Namier* (London: Macmillan, 1956), 227–58.

Avineri, Shlomo. *Hegel's Theory of the Modern State* (Cambridge: Cambridge University Press, 1972).

Bairoch, Paul and Susan Burke, 'European Trade Policy, 1815–1914', in Peter Mathias and Sidney Pollard (eds.), *The Cambridge Economic History of Europe since the Decline of the Roman Empire, Volume 8: The Industrial Economies: The Development of Economic and Social Policies* (Cambridge: Cambridge University Press, 1989), 23–51.

Barnard, Toby C., *Irish Protestant Ascents and Descents, 1641–1779* (Dublin: Four Courts, 2004).

  Improving Ireland? Projectors, Prophets and Profiteers, 1641–1786 (Dublin: Four Courts, 2008).

  'The Dublin Society and Other Improving Societies, 1731–85', in James Kelly & Martyn J. Powell (eds.), *Clubs and Societies in Eighteenth-Century Ireland* (Dublin: Four Courts Press, 2010), 53–88.

Bartlett, Thomas, 'An End to Moral Economy: The Irish Militia Disturbances of 1793', *Past and Present*, 99 (1983), 41–64.

  The Fall and Rise of the Irish Nation: The Catholic Question, 1690–1830 (Dublin: Gill and MacMillan, 1992).

  'From Irish State to British Empire: Reflections on State-Building in Ireland 1690–1830', *Études irlandaises*, 20 (1995), 23–37.

Bashford, Alison & Joyce E. Chaplin, *The New Worlds of Thomas Robert Malthus: Rereading the Principle of Population* (Princeton, NJ: Princeton University Press, 2016).

Bayly, Christopher A., *Imperial Meridian: The British Empire and the World, 1780–1830* (London: Longman, 1989).

  The Birth of the Modern World, 1780–1914: Global Connections and Comparisons (Oxford: Blackwell, 2004).

Belissa, Marc, *Repenser l'ordre européen 1795–1802: de la sociètè des rois aux droits des nations* (Paris: Editions Kimé, 2006).

Benton, Lauren & Lisa Ford, *Rage for Order: The British Empire and the Origins of International Law, 1800–1850* (Cambridge, MA: Harvard University Press, 2016).

Berdahl, Robert, *The Politics of the Prussian Nobility: The Development of a Conservative Ideology, 1770–1848* (Princeton, NJ: Princeton University Press, 1988).

Beiner, Guy *Remembering the Year of the French: Irish Folk History and Social Memory* (Madison: University of Wisconsin Press, 2007).

Bew, John, *The Glory of Being Britons: Civic Unionism in Nineteenth-Century Belfast* (Dublin: Irish Academic Press, 2009).

Castlereagh: Enlightenment, War and Tyranny (London: Quercus, 2011).

Black, R. D. Collison, 'Theory and Policy in Anglo-Irish Trade Relations, 1775–1800', *Journal of the Statistical and Social Inquiry Society of Ireland*, 28(3) (1950), 312–26.

Economic Thought and the Irish Question, 1817–1870 (Cambridge: Cambridge University Press, 1960).

Blackburn, Robin, 'Haiti, Slavery, and the Age of the Democratic Revolution', *The William and Mary Quarterly*, 63 (2006), 643–74.

Blackstock, Allan, *Science, Politics and Society in Early Nineteenth-Century Ireland: The Reverend William Richardson* (Manchester: Manchester University Press, 2013).

Bödeker, Hans Erich, 'Journals and Public Opinion: The Politicization of the German Enlightenment in the Second Half of the Eighteenth Century', in E. Hellmuth (ed.), *The Transformation of Political Culture: England and Germany in the Late Eighteenth Century* (Oxford: Oxford University Press, 1990), 423–45.

Bolton, G. C., *The Passing of the Irish Act of Union: A Study in Parliamentary Politics* (Oxford: Oxford University Press, 1966).

Bourke, Richard, 'Party, Parliament, and Conquest in Newly Ascribed Burke Manuscripts', *Historical Journal*, 55 (2012), 619–52.

Empire and Revolution: The Political Life of Edmund Burke (Princeton, NJ: Princeton University Press, 2016).

Bowen, Huw V., *The Business of Empire: The East India Company and Imperial Britain, 1756–1833* (Cambridge: Cambridge University Press, 2006).

Boylan, Ciara & Tom Boylan, 'The Art and Science of Political Economy: Nassau Senior and Ireland in the 1830s', in Maureen O'Connor (ed.), *Back to the Future of Irish Studies: Festschrift for Tadhg Foley* (Bern: Peter Lang, 2010), 97–110.

Boylan, Thomas & Timothy Foley, *Political Economy and Colonial Ireland: The Propagation and Ideological Function of Economic Discourse in the Nineteenth Century* (London: Routledge, 1992).

Bradshaw, Brendan, *The Irish Constitutional Revolution of the Sixteenth Century* (Cambridge: Cambridge University Press, 1979).

Brinley, Thomas 'Feeding England during the Industrial Revolution: A View from the Celtic Fringe', *Agricultural History*, 56 (1982), 328–42.

Brogan, Hugh, *Alexis de Tocqueville: A Biography* (London: Profile, 2006).

Broeker, Galen, *Rural Disorder and Police Reform in Ireland, 1812–36* (London: Routledge and Kegan Paul, 1970).

Brown, Christopher Leslie, *Moral Capital: Foundations of British Abolitionism* (Chapel Hill: University of North Carolina Press, 2006).

Brown, Michael, *The Irish Enlightenment* (Cambridge, MA: Harvard University Press, 2016).

Burns, Arthur & Joanna Innes, 'Introduction', in *Rethinking the Age of Reform: Britain 1780–1850, Past and Present Publications* (Cambridge: Cambridge University Press, 2003), 1–77.

Burrow, John Wyon, *Whigs and Liberals: Continuity and Change in English Political Thought* (Oxford: Clarendon Press, 1988).

Butterwick-Pawlikowski, Richard, Simon Davies & Gabriel Sánchez Espinosa (eds.), *Peripheries of the Enlightenment* (Oxford: Voltaire Foundation, 2008).

Canny, Nicholas, *Making Ireland British, 1580–1650* (Oxford: Oxford University Press, 2001).

Carter, Nick (ed.), *Britain, Ireland and the Italian Risorgimento* (Basingstoke: Palgrave Macmillan, 2015).

Case, Holly 'The "Social Question," 1820–1920', *Modern Intellectual History*, 13 (2016), 747–75.

Ceretta, Manuela, 'Theobald McKenna', in James McGuire & James Quinn, *Dictionary of Irish Biography* (Cambridge: Cambridge University Press, 2009).

'L'Irlande entre histoire et politique française', *The Tocqueville Review/La Revue Tocqueville*, 31 (2010), 139–57.

Il Momento Irlandese. L'Irlanda nella cultura politica francese tra Restaurazione e Secondo Impero (Edizioni di Storia e Letteratura, 2013).

Collini, Stefan, Donald Winch & John W. Burrow, *That Noble Science of Politics: A Study in Nineteenth-Century Intellectual History* (Cambridge: Cambridge University Press, 1983).

Conniff, James, 'Edmund Burke's Reflections on the Coming Revolution in Ireland', *Journal of the History of Ideas*, 47 (1986), 37–59.

Connolly, Sean J., 'The Catholic Question, 1801–12', in W. E. Vaughan (ed.), *A New History of Ireland, Volume V: Ireland under the Union, 1801–1870* (Oxford: Oxford University Press, 1989), 24–47.

Religion, Law and Power: The Making of Protestant Ireland, 1660–1760 (Oxford: Oxford University Press, 1992).

Conze, Werner, 'Die Wirkungen der liberalen Agrarreformen auf die Voksordung in Mitteleuropa in 19. Jahrhundert', *Vierteljahrschrift für Sozial- und Wirtschaftgeschichte*, 38 (1949), 2–43.

Crawford, William H., 'The Evolution of the Linen Trade in Ulster before Industrialization', *Irish Economic and Social History*, 15 (1988), 32–53.

Crowley, John E., 'Neo-Mercantilism and the Wealth of Nations: British Commercial Policy after the American Revolution', *The Historical Journal*, 33 (1990), 339–60.

Cullen, Louis M., 'The Value of Contemporary Printed Sources for Irish Economic History in the Eighteenth Century', *Irish Historical Studies*, 14 (1964), 142–55.

Anglo-Irish Trade 1660–1800 (Manchester: Manchester University Press, 1968).

'Economic Development, 1691–1750', in T. W. Moody & W. E. Vaughan (eds.), *A New History of Ireland IV: Eighteenth-Century Ireland 1691–1800* (Oxford: Oxford University Press, 1986), 130–59.

'Economic Development, 1750–1800', in T. W. Moody & W. E. Vaughan (eds.), *A New History of Ireland IV: Eighteenth-Century Ireland 1691–1800* (Oxford: Oxford University Press, 1986), 159–95.

Cunningham, John, *Conquest and Land in Ireland: The Transplantation to Connacht, 1649–1680* (London: Royal Historical Society, 2011).

'"Tis Hard to Argue Starvation into Quiet": Protest and Resistance, 1846–7', in Enda Delaney and Breandán Mac Suibhne (eds.), *Ireland's Great Famine and Popular Politics* (London: Routledge, 2016), 10–34.

Curtin, Nancy J., 'The Transformation of the Society of United Irishmen into a Mass-Based Revolutionary Organisation, 1794–6', *Irish Historical Studies*, 24 (1985), 463–92.

The United Irishmen: Popular Politics in Ulster and Dublin, 1791–1798 (Oxford: Clarendon Press, 1994).

D'Aprile, Iwan-Michelangelo, *Die Erfindung der Zeitgeschichte: Geschichtsschreibung und Journalismus zwischen Aufklärung und Vormärz* (Berlin: Akademie Verlag, 2013).

Darcy, Eamon, *The Irish Rebellion of 1641 and the Wars of the Three Kingdoms* (London: Royal Historical Society, 2013).

Davis, John, 'The Napoleonic Era in Southern Italy: An Ambiguous Legacy?', *Proceedings of the British Academy*, 80 (1999), 133–48.

De Dijn, Annelien, *French Political Thought from Montesquieu to Tocqueville: Liberty in a Levelled Society?* (Cambridge: Cambridge University Press, 2008).

Deane, Seamus, 'A Church Destroyed, the Church Restored: France's Irish Catholicism', *Field Day Review*, 7 (2011), 202–49.

Desan, Suzanne, '"War between Brothers and Sisters": Inheritance Law and Gender Politics in Revolutionary France', *French Historical Studies*, 20 (1997), 597–634.

Dewey, Clive J., 'Celtic Agrarian Legislation and the Celtic Revival: Historicist Implications of Gladstone's Irish and Scottish Land Acts 1870–1886', *Past & Present*, 64 (1974), 30–70.

Dickson, David, *Old World Colony: Cork and South Munster, 1630–1830* (Cork: Cork University Press, 2005).

'Town and City', in Eugenio F. Biagini & Mary Daly (eds.) (Cambridge: Cambridge University Press, 2017), 112–28.

Dixon, Robert, 'Carlyle, Malthus and Sismondi: The Origins of Carlyle's Dismal View of Political Economy', *History of Economics Review*, 44 (2006), 32–8.

Donnelly, James S., *Captain Rock: The Irish Agrarian Rebellion of 1821–1824* (Cork: Collins Press, 2009).

Donovan, Robert, 'The Military Origins of the Roman Catholic Relief Programme of 1778', *The Historical Journal*, 28 (1985), 79–102.

Doyle, William, 'The Union in a European Context', *Transactions of the Royal Historical Society*, 10 (2000), 167–80.

Drescher, Seymour, *Tocqueville and England* (Cambridge, MA: Harvard University Press, 1964).

Drolet, Michael, 'Democracy and Political Economy: Tocqueville's Thoughts on J.-B. Say and T. R. Malthus', *History of European Ideas*, 29 (2003), 159–81.

Dunkley, Peter, 'Emigration and the State, 1803–1842: The Nineteenth-Century Revolution in Government Reconsidered', *The Historical Journal*, 23 (1980), 353–80.

Durey, Michael, 'The Dublin Society of United Irishmen and the Politics of the Carey-Drennan Dispute, 1792–1794', *The Historical Journal*, 37 (1994), 89–111.

Dwan, David, *The Great Community: Culture and Nationalism in Ireland* (Dublin: Field Day, 2008).

Dwyer, Philip, 'The Politics of Prussian Neutrality 1795–1805', *German History*, 12 (1994), 351–73.

Eastwood, David, '"Amplifying the Province of the Legislature': The Flow of Information and the English State in the Early Nineteenth Century', *Historical Research*, 62 (1989), 276–94.

Eddie, Sean, *Freedom's Price: Serfdom, Subjection, and Reform in Prussia, 1648–1848* (Oxford: Oxford University Press, 2013).

Edie, Carolyn A., 'The Irish Cattle Bills: A Study in Restoration Politics', *Transactions of the American Philosophical Society*, 60 (1970), 1–66.

Ehrman, John, *The British Government and Commercial Negotiations with Europe, 1783–1793* (Cambridge: Cambridge University Press, 1962).

Einaudi, Luigi, 'The Theory of Imaginary Money from Charlemagne to the French Revolution', in R. F. Luca Inaudi & Roberto Marchionatti (eds.), *Selected Economic Essays* (Basingstoke: Palgrave Macmillan, 2006), 153–82.

Elliott, John H., *Empires of the Atlantic World: Britain and Spain in America, 1492–1830* (New Haven, CT: Yale University Press, 2006).

Elliott, Marianne, *Partners in Revolution: The United Irishmen and France* (New Haven, CA: Yale University Press, 1982).

Wolfe Tone: Prophet of Irish Independence, 2nd ed. (Liverpool: Liverpool University Press, 2012).

Erdös, Ernst, 'Hegels politische Oekonomie im Verhältnis zu Sismondi', in Heinz Kimmerle, Wolfgang Lefèvre & Rudolf M. Meyer (eds.), *Hegel-Jahrbuch 1986* (Bochum: Germinal, 1988), 75–86.

Flaherty, Martin, 'The Empire Strikes Back: Annesley v. Sherlock and the Triumph of Imperial Parliamentary Supremacy', *Columbia Law Review*, 87 (3) (1987), 593–622.

Fontana, Biancamaria, *Rethinking the Politics of Commercial Society: The Edinburgh Review 1802–1832* (Cambridge: Cambridge University Press, 1985).

'The Thermidorian Republic and Its Principles', in B. Fontana (ed.), *The Invention of the Modern Republic* (Cambridge: Cambridge University Press, 1994), 118–38.

Forsyth, Murray, 'The Old European States-System: Gentz versus Hauterive', *The Historical Journal*, 23 (1980), 521–38.

Frost, Alan, 'Nootka Sound and the Beginnings of Britain's Imperialism of Free Trade', in Robin Fisher & Hugh Johnson (eds.), *From Maps to Metaphors: The Pacific World of George Vancouver* (Vancouver: University of British Columbia Press, 1993), 104–27.

Garnett, Jane, 'Religious and Intellectual Life', in Colin Matthew (ed.), *The Nineteenth Century* (Oxford: Oxford University Press, 2000), 195–229.

Garvin, Tom, 'Defenders, Ribbonmen and Others: Underground Political Networks in Prefamine Ireland', in Charles H. E. Philpin (ed.), *Nationalism and Popular Protest in Ireland* (Cambridge: Cambridge University Press, 1987), 219–44.

Garvin, Tom & Andreas Hess, 'Introduction', in *Ireland: Social, Political, Religious*, trans. W. C. Taylor (Cambridge, MA: Belknap, Harvard, 2006).

Geoghegan, Patrick M., *The Irish Act of Union: A Study in High Politics, 1798–1801* (Dublin: Gill and Macmillan, 1999).

Ghosh, R. N., 'The Colonization Controversy: R. J. Wilmot-Horton and the Classical Economists', *Economica*, 31 (1964), 385–400.

Gibney, John, *The Shadow of a Year: The 1641 Rebellion in Irish History and Memory* (Madison: University of Wisconsin Press, 2013).

Gill, Conrad, *Rise of the Irish Linen Industry* (Oxford: Oxford University Press, 1925).

Gillen, Ultán, 'Monarchy, Republic and Empire: Irish Public Opinion and France, c.1787–1804', DPhil thesis, Faculty of History, Oxford University, Oxford (2005).

'Le directoire et le républicanisme Irlandais', in Pierre Serna (ed.), *Républiques soeurs: Le directoire et la révolution atlantique* (Rennes: Presses Universitaires de Rennes, 2009).

'Constructing Democratic Thought in Ireland in the Age of Revolution, 1775–1800', in Mark Philp & Joanna Innes (eds.), *Re-imagining Democracy in the Age of Revolutions: America, France, Britain, Ireland, 1750–1850* (Oxford: Oxford University Press, 2013).

Godechot, Jacques, *La Grande Nation* (Paris: Aubier Montaigne, 1983).

Goodrich, Amanda, *Debating England's Aristocracy in the 1790s: Pamphlets, Polemics, and Political Ideas* (Woodbridge: Boydell Press, 2005).

Gough, Hugh & David Dickson (eds.), *Ireland and the French Revolution* (Dublin: Irish Academic Press, 1990).

Graham, A. H., 'The Lichfield House Compact, 1835', *Irish Historical Studies*, 12 (1961), 209–25.

Gray, Peter, *Famine, Land and Politics: British Government and Irish Society, 1843–50* (Dublin: Irish Academic Press, 1999).

'The Peculiarities of Irish Land Tenure, 1800–1914: From Agent of Impoverishment to Agent of Pacification', in Donald Winch & Patrick K. O'Brien (eds.), *The Political Economy of British Historical Experience, 1688–1914* (Oxford: Oxford University Press, 2002).

The Making of the Irish Poor Law, 1815–43 (Manchester: Manchester University Press, 2009).

'Famine and Land, 1845–80', in Alvin Jackson (ed.), *Oxford Handbook of Modern Irish History* (Oxford: Oxford University Press, 2013), 545–58.

Green, Jonathan, 'Friedrich Gentz's Translation of Burke's *Reflections*', *Historical Journal*, 57 (2014), 639–59.

Greene, Jack P., *The Constitutional Origins of the American Revolution* (Cambridge: Cambridge University Press, 2011).

Hall, Frederick George, *The Bank of Ireland, 1783–1946* (Dublin: Hodges Figgis, 1949).

Harling, Philip & Peter Mandler, 'From "Fiscal-Military" State to Laissez-Faire State, 1760–1850', *Journal of British Studies*, 32 (2014), 44–70.

Harlow, Vincent T., *The Founding of the Second British Empire, 1763–1793*, 2 vols. (London: Longman, 1952).

Harris, Bob, *Politics and the Nation: Britain in the Mid-Eighteenth Century* (Oxford: Oxford University Press, 2002).

Hayton, David, 'The Beginnings of the "Undertaker System"', in *Penal Era and Golden Age: Essays in Irish History, 1690–1800* (Belfast: Ulster Historical Foundation, 1979), 32–55.

'The Stanhope/Sunderland Ministry and the Repudiation of Irish Parliamentary Independence', *The English Historical Review*, 113 (1998), 610–36.

'Ideas of Union in Anglo-Irish Political Discourse, 1692–1720: Meaning and Use', in D. George Boyce, Robert Eccleshall & Vincent Geoghegan (eds.), *Political Discourse in Seventeenth and Eighteenth-Century Ireland* (Basingstoke: Palgrave, 2001), 142–69.

Ruling Ireland, 1685–1742: Politics, Politicians and Parties (Woodbridge: Boydell Press, 2004).

'"Commonwealthman," Unionist and King's Servant: Henry Maxwell and the Whig Imperative', in *The Anglo-Irish Experience, 1680–1730: Religion, Identity and Patriotism* (Woodbridge: Boydell, 2012), 104–23.

'Creating Industrious Protestants: Charity Schools and the Enterprise of Religious and Social Reformation', in D. Hayton (ed.), *The Anglo-Irish Experience, 1680–1730: Religion, Identity and Patriotism* (Woodbridge: Boydell, 2012), 149–74.

Healy, Róisín, *Poland in the Irish Nationalist Imagination, 1772–1922: Anti-Colonialism within Europe* (Basingstoke: Palgrave Macmillan, 2017).

Hechter, Micheal, *Internal Colonialism: The Celtic Fringe in British National Development* (London: Routledge & Kegan Paul, 1975).

Heinickel, Gunter, *Adelsreformideen in Preußen: Zwischen bürokratischem Absolutismus und demokratisierendem Konstitutionalismus (1806–1854)* (Berlin: De Gruyter, 2014).

Herman, Neil, 'Henry Grattan, the Regency Crisis and the Emergence of a Whig Party in Ireland, 1788–9', *Irish Historical Studies*, 32 (2001), 478–97.

Hernán, Enrique García, *Ireland and Spain in the Reign of Philip II*, trans. Liam Liddy (Dublin: Four Courts Press, 2009).

Herzog, Lisa, *Inventing the Market: Smith, Hegel, and Political Theory* (Oxford: Oxford University Press, 2013).

Hession, Peter, 'Social Authority and the Urban Environment in Nineteenth-Century Cork', Faculty of History, Cambridge University, Cambridge (2018).

Higgins, Padhraig, *A Nation of Politicians: Gender, Patriotism, and Political Culture in Late Eighteenth-Century Ireland* (Madison: University of Wisconsin Press, 2010).

Hill, Jacqueline, 'Ireland without Union: Molyneux and His Legacy', in J. Robertson (ed.), *A Union for Empire: Political Thought and the British Union of 1707* (Cambridge: Cambridge University Press, 1995).

Hilton, Boyd, *A Mad, Bad, and Dangerous People? England 1783–1846* (Oxford: Clarendon Press, 2006).

Hont, István, *Jealousy of Trade: International Competition and the Nation-State in Historical Perspective* (Cambridge, MA: Harvard University Press, 2005).

'The "Rich Country-Poor Country" Debate Revisited: The Irish Origins and French Reception of the Hume Paradox', in Carl Wennerlind & Margaret Schabas (eds.), *David Hume's Political Economy* (London: Routledge, 2008), 243–323.

Politics in Commercial Society: Jean-Jacques Rousseau and Adam Smith (Cambridge, MA: Harvard University Press, 2015).

Hoppen, K. Theodore, 'Landlords, Society and Electoral Politics in Mid-Nineteenth-Century Ireland', *Past & Present*, 75 (1977), 62–93.

'Riding a Tiger: Daniel O'Connell, Reform, and Popular Politics in Ireland, 1800–1847', *Proceedings of the British Academy*, 100 (1999), 121–43.

Governing Hibernia: British Politicians and Ireland 1800–1921 (Oxford: Oxford University Press, 2016).

Hoppit, Julian, 'The Contexts and Contours of British Economic Literature, 1660–1760', *The Historical Journal*, 49 (2006), 79–110.

'The Nation, the State and the First Industrial Revolution', *Journal of British Studies*, 50 (2011), 307–31.

Britain's Political Economies: Parliament and Economic Life, 1660–1800 (Cambridge: Cambridge University Press, 2017).

Horner, Arnold, 'Napoleon's Irish legacy: The Bogs Commissioners, 1809–14', *History Ireland*, 13 (2005). www.historyireland.com/18th-19th-century-history/napoleons-irish-legacy-the-bogs-commissioners-1809-14/. Accessed 16 March 2018.

Houston, Robert A., 'People, Space and Law in Late Medieval and Early Modern Britain and Ireland', *Past & Present* (2016), 47–89.

Howe, Anthony, 'Free Trade and Global Order: The Rise and Fall of a Victorian Vision', in Duncan Bell (ed.), *Victorian Visions of Global Order* (Cambridge: Cambridge University Press, 2007), 26–46.

Inglis, Brian, *The Freedom of the Press in Ireland, 1784–1841* (London: Faber and Faber, 1954).

Innes, Joanna, 'Legislating for Three Kingdoms: How the Westminster Parliament Legislated for England, Scotland and Ireland, 1707–1830', in

Julian Hoppit (ed.), *Parliaments, Nations and Identities in Britain and Ireland, 1660–1850* (Manchester: Manchester University Press, 2003), 15–48.

Inferior Politics: Social Problems and Social Policies in Eighteenth-Century Britain (Oxford: Oxford University Press, 2009).

Isenmann, Moritz, 'Égalité, réciprocité, souveraineté: The Role of Commercial Treaties in Colbert's Economic Policy', in Antonella Alimento & Koen Stapelbroek (eds.), *The Politics of Commercial Treaties in the Eighteenth Century: Balance of Power, Balance of Trade* (Basingstoke: Palgrave Macmillan, 2017), 77–103.

Jainchill, Andrew, *Reimagining Politics after the Terror: The Republican Origins of French Liberalism* (Ithaca, NY: Cornell University Press, 2008).

James, Patricia, *Population Malthus: His Life and Times* (London: Routledge & Kegan Paul, 1979).

Jasanoff, Maya, *Liberty's Exiles: The Loss of America and the Remaking of the British Empire* (London: Harper Press, 2011).

Jaume, Lucien, *Tocqueville: The Aristocratic Sources of Liberty*, trans. A. Goldhammer (Princeton, NJ: Princeton University Press, 2013).

Jennings, Jeremy, 'Conceptions of England and Its Constitution in Nineteenth-Century French Political Thought', *The Historical Journal*, 29 (1986), 65–85.

Jones, Gareth Stedman, 'National Bankruptcy and Social Revolution: European Observers on Britain, 1831–1844', in Patrick K. O'Brien & Donald N. Winch (eds.), *The Political Economy of British Historical Experience, 1688–1914* (Oxford: Oxford University Press, 2002), 61–92.

An End to Poverty? A Historical Debate (London: Profile, 2004).

Jones, Peter M., 'The "Agrarian Law": Schemes for Land Redistribution during the French Revolution', *Past and Present*, 133 (1991), 96–133.

Agricultural Enlightenment: Knowledge, Technology and Nature, 1750–1840 (Oxford: Oxford University Press, 2016).

Jonsson, Frederik Albritton, *Enlightenment's Frontier: The Scottish Highlands and the Origins of Environmentalism* (New Haven, CT: Yale University Press, 2013).

'Malthus in the Enlightenment', in Robert J. Mayhew (ed.) *New Perspectives on Malthus* (Cambridge: Cambridge University Press, 2016).

Jupp, Peter, 'Government, Parliament and Politics in Ireland, 1801–41', in Julian Hoppit (ed.), *Parliaments, Nations and Identities in Britain and Ireland, 1660–1850* (Manchester: Manchester University Press, 2003), 146–64.

Kanter, Douglas, *The Making of British Unionism, 1740–1848: Politics, Government, and the Anglo-Irish Constitutional Relationship* (Dublin: Four Courts Press, 2009).

Kapossy, Bela & Pascal Bridel (eds.), *Sismondi: républicanisme moderne et libéralisme critique* (Geneva: Slatkine, 2013).

Kearney, Hugh, 'The Political Background to English Mercantilism, 1695–1700', *The Economic History Review*, 11 (1959), 484–96.

Strafford in Ireland, 1633–41: A Study in Absolutism (Manchester: Manchester University Press, 1959).

Kelly, James, 'Inter-Denominational Relations and Religious Toleration in Late Eighteenth-Century Ireland: The "Paper War" 1786–88', *Eighteenth-Century Ireland : Iris an dá chultúr*, 3 (1988), 39–67.

'The Anglo-French Commercial Treaty of 1786: The Irish Dimension', *Eighteenth-Century Ireland : Iris an dá chultúr*, 4 (1989), 93–111.

'The Irish Trade Dispute with Portugal, 1780–1787', *Studia Hibernica*, 25 (1989).

Prelude to Union: Anglo-Irish Politics in the 1780s (Cork: Cork University Press, 1992).

'Scarcity and Poor Relief in Eighteenth-Century Ireland: The Subsistence Crisis of 1782–4', *Irish Historical Studies*, 28 (1992), 38–62.

Henry Flood: Patriots and Politics in Eighteenth-Century Ireland (Dublin: Four Courts, 1998).

'Popular Politics in Ireland and the Act of Union', *Transactions of the Royal Historical Society*, 10, 6th ser. (2000), 259–87.

'The Historiography of the Act of Union', in M. Brown, P. Geoghegan & James Kelly (eds.), *The Irish Act of Union, 1800: Bicentennial Essays* (Dublin: Irish Academic Press, 2003).

Poyning's Law and the Making of Law in Ireland, 1660–1800 (Dublin: Four Courts, 2007).

'"Disappointing the Boundless Ambition of France": Irish Protestants and the Fear of Invasion, 1661–1815', *Studia Hibernica*, 37 (2011), 27–105.

'Introduction: Interpreting Late Early Modern Ireland', in James Kelly (ed.), *The Cambridge History of Ireland: Volume III, 1730–1880* (Cambridge: Cambridge University Press, 2018), 1–20.

'The Politics of Protestant Ascendancy, 1730–1790', in James Kelly (ed.), *The Cambridge History of Ireland: Volume III, 1730–1880*, 5 vols. (Cambridge: Cambridge University Press, 2018), vol. 3, 48–73.

Kelly, James & Martyn J. Powell (eds.), *Clubs and Societies in Eighteenth-Century Ireland* (Dublin: Four Courts Press, 2010).

Kelly, Matthew, 'Languages of Radicalism, Race, and Religion in Irish Nationalism: The French Affinity, 1848–1871', *Journal of British Studies*, 49 (2010), 801–25.

Kelly, Patrick, 'The Irish Woollen Export Prohibition Act of 1699: Kearney Revisited', *Irish Economic and Social History*, 7 (1980), 22–44.

'William Molyneux and the Spirit of Liberty in Eighteenth-Century Ireland', *Eighteenth-Century Ireland : Iris an dá chultúr*, 3 (1988).

'The Politics of Political Economy in Mid-Eighteenth-Century Ireland', in S. J. Connolly (ed.), *Political Ideas in Eighteenth-Century Ireland* (Dublin: Four Courts Press, 2000).

'Recasting a Tradition: William Molyneux and the Sources of *The Case of Ireland ... Stated* (1698)', in Jane H. Ohlmeyer (ed.), *Political thought in*

Seventeenth-Century Ireland: Kingdom or Colony? (Cambridge: Cambridge University Press, 2000), 83–107.

'Molyneux (Molyneaux), William', in James McGuire and James Quinn (eds.), *Dictionary of Irish Biography* (Cambridge: Cambridge University Press, 2009), http://dib.cambridge.org/viewReadPage.do?articleId=a5878. Accessed 21 January 2020.

Kelly, Paul, 'British and Irish Politics in 1785', *The English Historical Review*, 90 (1975), 536–63.

Kindleberger, Charles P., 'The Rise of Free Trade in Western Europe, 1820–1875', *The Journal of Economic History*, 35 (1975), 20–55.

Kinealy, Christine, *Repeal and Revolution: 1848 in Ireland* (Manchester: Manchester University Press, 2009).

Kleinman, Sylvie, 'Initiating Insurgencies Abroad: French Plans to "chouannise" Britain and Ireland, 1793–1798', *Small Wars & Insurgencies*, 25 (2014), 784–99.

Koselleck, Reinhart & Michaela Richter, 'Introduction and Prefaces to the *Geschichtliche Grundbegriffe*', *Contributions to the History of Concepts*, 6 (2011), 1–37.

Lähme, Jorg, *William Drennan und der Kampf um die irische Unabhängigkeit: Eine politische Biographie* (Göttingen: Wallstein Verlag, 2012).

Lane, Pádraig G., 'The Encumbered Estates Court, Ireland, 1848–1849', *The Economic and Social Review*, 3 (1972), 413–53.

Larkin, Emmet, 'The Devotional Revolution in Ireland, 1850–75', *The American Historical Review*, 77 (1972), 625–52.

Leersen, Joep, 'Anglo-Irish Patriotism and Its European Context: Notes towards a Reassessment', *Eighteenth-Century Ireland/Iris an dá chultúr*, 3 (1988), 7–24.

Leighton, Cadoc, 'Gallicanism and the Veto Controversy: Church, State and Catholic Community in Early Nineteenth-Century Ireland', in R. V. Comerford, M. Cullen, J. Hill & C. Lennon (eds.), *Religion, Conflict and Coexistence in Ireland: Essays Presented to Monsignor Patrick J Corish* (Dublin: Gill and Macmillan, 1990), 135–58.

Catholicism in a Protestant Kingdom: A Study of the Irish Ancien Régime (London, Macmillan, 2000).

Lerner, Marc, 'The Helvetic Republic: An Ambivalent Reception of French Revolutionary Liberty', *French History*, 18 (2004), 50–75.

Lieberman, David, 'The Mixed Constitution and the Common Law', in Mark Goldie & Robert Wokler (eds.), *The Cambridge History of Eighteenth Century Political Thought* (Cambridge: Cambridge University Press, 2006), 317–46.

Lindsay, Deirdre, 'The Fitzwilliam Episode Revisited', in David Dickson, Dáire Keogh & Kevin Whelan (eds.), *The United Irishmen: Republicanism, Radicalism and Rebellion* (Dublin: Lilliput Press, 1993), 197–209.

Livesey, James, 'Agrarian Ideology and Commercial Republicanism in the French Revolution', *Past and Present*, 157 (1997), 94–121.

'Introduction', in J. Livesey (ed.), *Arthur O'Connor: The State of Ireland (1798)* (Dublin: Lilliput, 1998), 1–43.

'Acts of Union and Disunion: The Union in Atlantic and European Context', in Kevin Whelan & Dáire Keogh (eds.), *Acts of Union: The Causes, Contexts and Consequences of the Act of Union* (Dublin: Four Courts Press, 2001), 95–105.

'The Dublin Society in Eighteenth-Century Irish Political Thought', *The Historical Journal*, 47 (2004), 615–40.

'Free Trade and Empire in the Anglo-Irish Commercial Propositions of 1785', *Journal of British Studies*, 52 (2013), 103–27.

Lloyd, David, 'The Political Economy of the Potato', *Nineteenth Century Contexts*, 29 (2007), 311–35.

'Nomadic Figures: The "Rhetorical Excess" of Irishness in Political Economy', in Maureen O'Connor (ed.), *Back to the Future of Irish Studies: Festschrift for Tadhg Foley* (Bern: Peter Lang, 2010), 41–65.

Lloyd, Sarah, 'Cottage Conversations: Poverty and Manly Independence in Eighteenth-Century England', *Past & Present* (2004), 69–109.

Macaulay, Ambrose, *The Catholic Church and the Campaign for Emancipation in Ireland and England* (Dublin: Four Courts, 2018).

MacDermot, Frank, 'Arthur O'Connor', *Irish Historical Studies*, 57 (1966), 48–69.

MacDonagh, Oliver, *A Pattern of Government Growth, 1800–60: The Passenger Acts and Their Enforcement* (London: MacGibbon & Kee, 1961).

Magennis, Eoin, 'Dobbs, Arthur', in James McGuire & James Quinn, *Dictionary of Irish Biography* (Cambridge: Cambridge University Press, 2013).

'The Irish Parliament and the Regulatory Impulse, 1692–1800: The Case of the Coal Trade', *Parliamentary History*, 33 (2014), 54–72.

Malcomson, A. P. W. (ed.), *An Anglo-Irish Dialogue: A Calendar of the Correspondence between John Foster and Lord Sheffield, 1774–1821* (Belfast: Public Record Office, 1976).

John Foster (1740–1828): The Politics of Improvement and Prosperity (Dublin: Four Courts Press, 2011).

Malthus, Robert, *An Essay on the Principle of Population*, ed. D. Winch and P. James (Cambridge: Cambridge University Press, 1992).

Mandler, Peter, 'The Making of the New Poor Law Redivivus', *Past & Present* (1987), 131–57.

Markoff, John, *The Abolition of Feudalism: Peasants, Lords, and Legislators in the French Revolution* (University Park: Pennsylvania State University Press, 1996).

Marshall, Peter J., *Remaking the British Atlantic: The United States and the British Empire after American Independence* (Oxford: Oxford University Press, 2012).

MacGrath, Kevin, 'Writers in the "Nation", 1842–5', Irish Historical Studies, 6 (21) (1949), 189–223, at 200.

McBride, Ian, 'The School of Virtue: Francis Hutchson, Irish Presbyterians and the Scottish Enlightenment', in D. G. Boyce, R. Ecceshall & V. Geoghegan (eds.), *Political Thought in Ireland Since the Seventeenth Century* (London: Routledge, 1993), 7–35.

'"When Ulster joined Ireland": Anti-popery, Presbyterian Radicalism and Irish Republicanism in the 1790s', *Past & Present*, 157 (1997), 63–93.

Scripture Politics: Ulster Presbyterians and Irish Radicalism in the Late Eighteenth Century (Oxford: Clarendon Press, 1998).

'Reclaiming the Rebellion: 1798 in 1998', *Irish Historical Studies*, 31 (1999), 395–410.

Eighteenth Century Ireland: The Isle of Slaves (Dublin: Gill and Macmillan, 2009).

'Dickson, William Steel', in James McGuire & James Quinn, *Dictionary of Irish Biography* (Cambridge: Cambridge University Press, 2009).

'*The Case of Ireland* (1698) in Context: William Molyneux and His Critics', *Proceedings of the Royal Irish Academy: Archaeology, Culture, History, Literature*, 118C (2018), 201–30, at 206.

'The Politics of *A Modest Proposal*: Swift and the Irish Crisis of the Late 1720s', *Past & Present*, 244/1 (2019), 89–122.

McCavery, Trevor, 'Finance, Politics and Ireland, 1801–1817', PhD thesis, Faculty of History, The Queen's University of Belfast, Belfast (1980), 218–20.

'Politics, Public Finance and the British-Irish Act of Union of 1801', *Transactions of the Royal Historical Society*, 10 (2000), 353–75.

McGrath, Charles Ivar, *The Making of the Eighteenth-Century Irish Constitution: Government, Parliament and the Revenue, 1692–1714* (Dublin: Four Courts Press, 2000).

McPhee, Peter, 'The French Revolution, Peasants, and Capitalism', *American Historical Review*, 94 (1989), 1265–80.

Mitchison, Rosalind, 'The Old Board of Agriculture (1793–1822)', *Economic History Review*, 74 (1959), 41–59.

Moggach, Douglas, 'Introduction: Hegelianism, Republicanism and Modernity', in D. Moggach (ed.), *The New Hegelians: Politics and Philosophy in the Hegelian School* (Cambridge: Cambridge University Press, 2006), 1–23.

Morrow, John, *Thomas Carlyle* (London: Hambledon Continuum, 2006).

Mori, Jennifer, 'The Political Theory of William Pitt the Younger', *History*, 83 (1998), 234–48.

Morley, Vincent, *Irish Opinion and the American Revolution, 1760–1783* (Cambridge: Cambridge University Press, 2002).

Murdoch, Alexander, 'Henry Dundas, Scotland and the Union with Ireland, 1792–1801', in B. Harris (ed.), *Scotland in the Age of the French Revolution* (Edinburgh: John Donald, 2005), 125–39.

Nakhimovsky, Isaac, *The Closed Commercial State: Perpetual Peace and Commercial Society from Rousseau to Fichte* (Princeton, NJ: Princeton University Press, 2011).

'The "Ignominious Fall of the European Commonwealth": Gentz, Hauterive, and the Armed Neutrality of 1800', in K. Stapelbroek (ed.), *Trade and War:*

The Neutrality of Commerce in the Interstate System (Helsinki: Helsinki Collegium for Advanced Studies, 2011), 177–90.

Nally, David P., *Human Encumbrances: Political Violence and the Great Irish Famine* (Notre Dame, IN: University of Notre Dame Press, 2011).

Nelson, Eric, 'Patriot Royalism: The Stuart Monarchy in American Political Thought, 1769–75', *The William and Mary Quarterly*, 68(4) (2011), 533–72.

Ó Ciosáin, Niall, *Ireland in Official Print Culture, 1800–1850: A New Reading of the Poor Inquiry* (Oxford: Oxford University Press, 2014).

O'Brien, Denis Patrick, *J. R. McCulloch: A Study in Classical Economics* (London: Allen & Unwin, 1970).

O'Brien, Patrick K., 'Public Finance in the Wars with France, 1793–1815', in H. T. Dickinson (ed.), *Britain and the French Revolution* (London: Macmillan, 1989), 165–87.

O'Flaherty, Niall, 'Malthus and the End of Poverty', in R. J. Mayhew (ed.), *New Perspectives on Malthus* (Cambridge: Cambridge University Press, 2017), 74–105.

Ó'Gráda, Cormac, 'Poverty, Population and Agriculture, 1801–45', in W. E. Vaughan (ed.), *A New History of Ireland, Volume V: Ireland under the Union, 1801–1870* (Oxford: Oxford University Press, 1989), 108–37.

Ireland: A New Economic History, 1780–1939 (Oxford: Clarendon Press, 1994).

O'Neill, Patrick, *Ireland and Germany: A Study in Literary Relations* (New York: P. Lang, 1985).

Ohlmeyer, Jane, *Making Ireland English: The Irish Aristocracy in the Seventeenth Century* (New Haven, CT: Yale University Press, 2012).

'Conquest, Civilization, Colonization: Ireland, 1540–1660', in Ian McBride & Richard Bourke (eds.), *The Princeton History of Modern Ireland* (Princeton, NJ: Princeton University Press, 2016), 21–47.

Osborough, W. N., 'Catholics, Land and the Popery Acts of Anne', in T. P. Power & Kevin Whelan (eds.), *Endurance and Emergence: Catholics in Ireland in the Eighteenth Century* (Dublin: Irish Academic Press, 1990), 21–56.

Osterhammel, Jürgen, *The Transformation of the World: A Global History of the Nineteenth Century*, trans. Patrick Camiller (Princeton, NJ: Princeton University Press, 2014).

Parry, Jonathan, *The Rise and Fall of Liberal Government in Victorian Britain* (New Haven, CT: Yale University Press, 1993)

Petler, D. N., 'Ireland and France in 1848', *Irish Historical Studies*, 24 (1985), 493–505.

Petrusewicz, Marta, 'Land-Based Modernization and the Culture of Landed Elites in the Nineteenth-Century Mezzogiorno', in R. Halpern & E. D. Lago (eds.), *The American South and the Italian Mezzogiorno: Essays in Comparative History* (London: Macmillan, 2001).

Petry, M. J., 'Hegel and *The Morning Chronicle*', *Hegel Studien*, 11 (1976), 11–80.

Pickering, Paul, '"Irish First": Daniel O'Connell, the Native Manufacture Campaign, and Economic Nationalism, 1840–44', *Albion*, 32 (2000), 598–616.

Pincus, Steven, 'The English Debate over Universal Monarchy', in *A Union for Empire: Political Thought and the Union of 1707* (Cambridge: Cambridge University Press, 1995), 37–62.

Protestantism and Patriotism: Ideologies and the Making of English Foreign Policy, 1650–1668 (Cambridge: Cambridge University Press, 1996).

1688: The First Modern Revolution (New Haven, CT: Yale University Press, 2009).

Pitts, Jennifer, *A Turn to Empire: The Rise of Imperial Liberalism in Britain and France* (Princeton, NJ: Princeton University Press, 2005).

Plassart, Anna, *The Scottish Enlightenment and the French Revolution* (Cambridge: Cambridge University Press, 2015).

Pocock, J. G. A., 'Josiah Tucker on Burke, Locke and Price: A Study in the Varieties of Eighteenth-Century Conservatism', in J. G. A. Pocock (ed.), *Virtue, Commerce and History: Essays on Political Thought and History, Chiefly in the Eighteenth Century* (Cambridge: Cambridge University Press, 1985).

'The Union in British History', *Transactions of the Royal Historical Society, Sixth Series*, 10 (2000), 181–96.

Powell, Martyn, *Britain and Ireland in the Eighteenth-Century Crisis of Empire* (Basingstoke: Palgrave Macmillan, 2003).

Quinn, James, 'The United Irishmen and Social Reform', *Irish Historical Studies*, 31 (1998), 188–201.

Soul on Fire: A Life of Thomas Russell (Dublin: Irish Academic Press, 2002).

Rafroidi, Patrick, *L'Irlande et le romantisme: la littérature irlandaise-anglaise de 1789 à 1850 et sa place dans le mouvement occidental* (Paris: Éditions Universitaires, 1972).

Rapport, Michael, 'The Napoleonic Civil Code: The Belgian Case', in M. Broers, P. Hicks & A. Guimerá (eds.), *The Napoleonic Empire and the New European Political Culture* (Basingstoke: Palgrave Macmillan, 2012), 88–99.

Reinert, Sophus, *Translating Empire: Emulation and the Origins of Political Economy* (Cambridge, MA: Harvard University Press, 2011).

Richter, Melvin, 'Tocqueville and Guizot on Democracy: From a Type of Society to a Political Regime', *History of European Ideas*, 30 (2004), 61–82.

Ritcheson, Charles R., 'The Earl of Shelburne and Peace with America, 1782–1783: Vision and Reality', *The International History Review*, 5 (1983), 322–45.

Robbins, Caroline, *The Eighteenth-Century Commonwealthman* (Cambridge, MA: Harvard University Press, 1959).

Robertson, John, *The Case for the Enlightenment: Scotland and Naples, 1680–1760* (Cambridge: Cambridge University Press, 2005).

Rodgers, Nini, 'Two Quakers and a Utilitarian: The Reaction of Three Irish Women Writers to the Problem of Slavery, 1789–1807', *Proceedings of the Royal Irish Academy, Section C*, 100C (2000), 137–57.

Sanderson, Mary L., 'Limited Liberties: Catholics and the Policies of the Pitt Ministry in an Early Modern Context', *Journal of British Studies*, 59 (2020), 737–63.

Schneider, Bernhard, 'Insel der Märtyrer oder ein Volk von Rebellen? Deutschlands Katholiken und die irische Nationalbewegung', *Historishces Jahrbuch*, 128 (2008), 225–76.

Schroeder, Paul W., *The Transformation of European Politics, 1763–1848* (Oxford: Clarendon Press, 1994).

Seigel, Jerrold, *Modernity and Bourgeois Life: Society, Politics and Culture in England, France and Germany since 1750* (Cambridge: Cambridge University Press, 2012).

Semmel, Bernard, 'The Hume Tucker Debate and Pitt's Trade Proposals', *Economic Journal*, 75 (1955), 759–70.

The Rise of Free Trade Imperialism: Classical Political Economy, the Empire of Free Trade and Imperialism 1750–1850 (Cambridge: Cambridge University Press, 1970).

Shin, Hiroki, 'Paper Money, the Nation, and the Suspension of Cash Payments in 1797', *Historical Journal*, 58 (2015), 415–42.

Shovlin, John, *The Political Economy of Virtue: Luxury, Patriotism and the Origins of the French Revolution* (Ithaca, NY: Cornell University Press, 2010).

'The Society of Brittany and the Irish Economic Model: International Competition and the Politics of Provincial Development', in Koen Stapelbroek & Jani Marjanen (eds.), *The Rise of Economic Societies in the Eighteenth Century: Patriotic Reform in Europe and North America* (Basingstoke: Palgrave Macmillan, 2012), 73–96.

Simms, John Gerald, *The Williamite Confiscation in Ireland, 1690–1703* (London: Faber and Faber, 1956).

Small, Stephen, *Political Thought in Ireland, 1776–1798: Republicanism, Patriotism, and Radicalism* (Oxford: Oxford University Press, 2002).

Smyth, Jim, *The Men of No Property: Irish Radicals and Popular Politics in the Late Eighteenth Century* (Basingstoke: Macmillan, 1992).

'Anti-Catholicism, Conservatism, and Conspiracy: Sir Richard Musgrave's Memoirs of the Different Rebellions in Ireland', *Eighteenth-Century Life*, 22 (1998).

'The Act of Union and "Public Opinion"', in J. Smyth (ed.), *Revolution, Counter-Revolution and Union: Ireland in the 1790s* (Cambridge: Cambridge University Press, 2000), 146–61.

Sonenscher, Michael, 'Introduction', in Michael Sonenscher (ed.), *Sieyès: Political Writings* (Indianapolis, IN: Hackett, 2003), vii–lxiv.

Stafford, James, 'The Alternative to Perpetual Peace: Britain, Ireland and the Case for Union in Friedrich Gentz's *Historisches Journal*, 1799–1800', *Modern Intellectual History*, 13 (2016), 63–91.

Stråth, Bo, *Europe's Utopias of Peace: 1815, 1919, 1951* (London: Bloomsbury, 2016).

Taylor, Michael, 'British Conservatism, the Illuminati, and the Conspiracy Theory of the French Revolution, 1797–1802', *Eighteenth Century Studies*, 47 (2014), 293–312.

Thadden, Rudolf von, *La Centralisation Contestée*, trans. H. Cusa & P. Charbonneau (Arles: Actes Sud, 1989).

Todd, David, 'John Bowring and the Global Dissemination of Free Trade', *The Historical Journal*, 51 (2008), 373–97.

'Transnational Projects of Empire in France, c.1815–c.1870', *Modern Intellectual History*, 12 (2015), 265–93.

Tribe, Keith, *Governing Economy: The Reformation of German Economic Discourse, 1750–1840* (Cambridge: Cambridge University Press, 1988).

'Professors Malthus and Jones: Political Economy at the East India College 1806–1858', *European Journal of the History of Economic Thought*, 2 (2007), 327–54.

Tschirch, Otto, *Geschichte der offentlichen Meinung in Preussen: vom Baseler Frieden bis zum Zusammenbruch des Staates*, 2 vols. (Weimar: Böhlhaus, 1933).

Varouxakis, Georgios, 'National Character in John Stuart Mill's Thought', *History of European Ideas*, 24 (1998), 375–91.

'1848 and British Political Thought on "The Principle of Nationality"', in Douglas Moggach & Gareth Stedman Jones (eds.), *The 1848 Revolutions and European Political Thought* (Cambridge: Cambridge University Press, 2018), 140–61.

Walsh, Patrick, *The Making of Irish Protestant Ascendancy: The Life of William Conolly, 1662–1729* (Woodbridge: Boydell & Brewer, 2010).

'The Fiscal State in Ireland, 1691–1769', *The Historical Journal*, 56 (2013), 629–56.

Wennerlind, Carl, *Casualties of Credit: The English Financial Revolution 1620–1720* (Cambridge, MA: Harvard University Press).

Whatmore, Richard, *Republicanism and the French Revolution: An Intellectual History of Jean-Baptiste Say's Political Economy* (Oxford: Oxford University Press, 2000).

'Adam Smith's Role in the French Revolution', *Past & Present*, 175 (2002), 65–89.

'Democrats and Republicans in Restoration France', *European Journal of Political Theory*, 3 (2004), 37–51.

'"Neither Masters nor Slaves": Small States and Empire in the Long Eighteenth Century', in Duncan Kelly (ed.), *Lineages of Empire: The Historical Roots of British Imperial Thought* (Oxford: Oxford University Press, 2009), 53–81.

Against War and Empire: Geneva, Britain, and France in the Eighteenth Century (New Haven, CT: Yale University Press, 2012).

'Liberty, War and Empire: Overcoming the Rich State-Poor State Problem, 1789–1815', in B. Kapossy, I. Nakhimovsky & R. Whatmore (eds.), *Commerce and Peace in the Enlightenment* (Cambridge: Cambridge University Press, 2017), 216–43.

Whelan, Irene, *The Bible War in Ireland: The "Second Reformation" and the Polarization of Protestant-Catholic Relations, 1800–1840* (Dublin: Lilliput Press, 2005).

Whelan, Kevin, 'An Underground Gentry? Catholic Middlemen in Eighteenth-Century Ireland', *Eighteenth-Century Ireland : Iris an dá chultúr*, 10 (1995), 7–68.

'Introduction to "The Poor Man's Catechism" (1798)', *Labour History*, 75 (1998), 22–32.

'The Modern Landscape', in F. H. A. Aalen, Matthew Stout & Kevin Whelan (eds.), *Atlas of the Irish Rural Landscape*, 2nd ed. (Cork: Cork University Press, 2011), 73–114.

Wilson, David, *United Irishmen, Untied States: Immigrant Radicals in the Early Republic* (Ithaca, NY: Cornell University Press, 1998).

Withington, Phil, 'Plantation and Civil Society', in É. Ó. Ciardha & M. Ó. Siochrú (eds.), *The Plantation of Ulster: Ideology and Practice* (Manchester: Manchester University Press, 2012), 55–75.

Woods, C. J., 'MacNeven, William James', in James McGuire and James Quinn (eds.), *Dictionary of Irish Biography* (Cambridge: Cambridge University Press, 2009).

'Cox, Walter', in James McGuire & James Quinn, *Dictionary of Irish Biography* (Cambridge: Cambridge University Press, 2009).

Zimmermann, Harro, *Friedrich Gentz: die Erfindung der Realpolitik* (Paderborn: Schöningh, 2012).

Index

CPSIA information can be obtained
at www.ICGtesting.com
Printed in the USA
LVHW081258270322
714516LV00003B/254